What Has Happened to the Quality of Life in the Advanced Industrialized Nations?

Levy Economics Institute of Bard College

Founded in 1986, the Levy Economics Institute of Bard College in New York is an autonomous, independently endowed research organization. It is nonpartisan, open to the examination of diverse points of view and dedicated to public service.

The Institute believes in the potential for economic study to improve the human condition. Its purpose is to generate viable, effective public policy responses to important economic problems. It is concerned with issues that profoundly affect the quality of life in the United States, in other highly industrialized nations and in countries with developing economies.

The Institute's present research programs include such issues as financial instability, economic growth and employment, international trade, problems associated with the distribution of income and wealth, the measurement of economic well-being and the relationship between public and private investment and their effects on productivity and competitiveness.

The opinions expressed in this volume are those of the authors. This volume is part of the Institute's research on 'Measuring Well-being', but does not necessarily reflect the views of individual members of the Board of Governors.

What Has Happened to the Quality of Life in the Advanced Industrialized Nations?

Edited by

Edward N. Wolff

New York University and Levy Economics Institute

IN ASSOCIATION WITH THE LEVY ECONOMICS INSTITUTE

Edward Elgar
Cheltenham, UK • Northampton, MA, USA

Published by
Edward Elgar Publishing Limited
Glensanda House
Montpellier Parade
Cheltenham
Glos GL50 1UA
UK

Edward Elgar Publishing, Inc.
136 West Street
Suite 202
Northampton
Massachusetts 01060
USA

A catalogue record for this book
is available from the British Library

What has happened to the quality of life in the advanced industrialized nations? /
    edited by Edward N. Wolff
        p.   cm.
    "In association with the Levy Economics Institute."
    "This volume is part of the Institute's research on 'Measuring well-being',"—P.
    Includes bibliographical references.
    1. Quality of life–Measurement. 2. Economic indicators. 3. Income
distribution. 4. Cost and standard of living. 5. Employee rights. 6. Quality of
life—Developed countries. 7. Quality of life—United States. I. Wolff, Edward N.
II. Jerome Levy Economics Institute.
HN25.W53   2004
306'.0973—dc22

ISBN 1 84376 193 9   2003049488

Printed and bound in Great Britain by MPG Books Ltd, Bodmin, Cornwall

Contents

PART III WEALTH AND LIVING STANDARDS

PART IV OTHER DIMENSIONS IN MEASURING WELL-BEING

Figures

Tables

Contributors

Dean Baker Co-Director, Center for Economic and Policy Research, Washington, DC, USA.

Robert Buchele Professor of Economics, Smith College, Northampton, MA, USA.

Jens Christiansen Professor of Economics, Mount Holyoke College, South Hadley, MA, USA.

William J. Collins Assistant Professor of Economics, Vanderbilt University, Nashville, TN, and Faculty Research Fellow, National Bureau of Economic Research, Cambridge, MA, USA.

Maria S. Floro Associate Professor, American University, Washington, DC, and Research Associate, Levy Economics Institute, Bard College, Annandale-on-Hudson, NY, USA.

Daphne T. Greenwood Professor of Economics, University of Colorado, Colorado Springs, CO, USA.

Thomas L. Hungerford Senior Scholar, Levy Economics Institute, Bard College, Annandale-on-Hudson, NY, USA.

Christopher Jencks Malcolm Wiener Professor of Social Policy, John F. Kennedy School of Government, Harvard University, Cambridge, MA, USA.

David S. Johnson Chief, Division of Price and Index Number Research, Bureau of Labor Statistics, US Department of Labor, Washington, DC, USA.

Robert A. Margo Professor of Economics and History, Vanderbilt University, Nashville, TN and Research Associate, National Bureau of Economic Research, Cambridge, MA, USA.

Susan E. Mayer Dean and Associate Professor, Irving B. Harris Graduate School of Public Policy Studies, University of Chicago, Chicago, IL, USA.

Lars Osberg McCulloch Professor of Economics, Dalhousie University, Halifax, Nova Scotia, Canada.

Dimitri B. Papadimitriou President, Levy Economics Institute, Bard College, Annandale-on-Hudson, NY, USA.

Lee Rainwater Research Director, Luxembourg Income Study, Syracuse University, Syracuse, NY, and Harvard University, Cambridge, MA, USA.

Andrew Sharpe Executive Director, Center for the Study of Living Standards, Ottawa, Ontario, Canada.

Timothy M. Smeeding Director, Center for Policy Research, Syracuse University, and Overall Director, Luxembourg Income Study, Syracuse University, Syracuse, NY, USA.

Seymour Spilerman Director, Center for the Study of Wealth and Inequality, and Julian C. Levi Professor of Sociology, Columbia University, New York, NY, USA.

Richard H. Steckel Professor of Economics and Anthropology, Ohio State University, Columbus, OH, USA.

Joseph Swingle Visiting Assistant Professor of Sociology and Laboratory Instructor, Wellesley College, Wellesley, MA, USA.

Florencia Torche Post-doctoral Fellow, Center for the Study of Wealth and Inequality, Columbia University, New York, NY, USA.

Edward N. Wolff Professor of Economics, New York University, New York, NY, and Senior Scholar, Levy Economics Institute, Bard College, Annandale-on-Hudson, NY, USA.

Ajit Zacharias Research Scholar, Levy Economics Institute, Bard College, Annandale-on-Hudson, NY, USA.

Abbreviations

AHS	American Housing Survey
BLS	Bureau of Labor Statistics
CCA	capital consumption allowance
CES	Consumer Expenditure Survey
CPI	consumer price index
CPI-U	consumer price index, all urban consumers
CPS	Current Population Survey
EI	equivalent income
EITC	Earned Income Tax Credit
EPC	strictness protection against collective dismissals
EPR	individual regular (permanent) workers
EPT	individual temporary workers
FHA	Federal Housing Administration
FTEE	full-time equivalent employee
GDP	gross domestic product
GPI	Genuine Progress Index
HOLC	Home Owner's Loan Corporation
IDA	individual development account
IPUMS	Integrated Public Use Microdata Series
IRA	individual retirement account
ISEI	International Socioeconomic Index
LIS	Luxembourg Income Study
NCVS	National Crime Victimization Survey
NFCS	National Food Consumption Survey
NHIS	National Health Interview Survey
NIPA	National Income and Product Accounts
NRC	National Research Council
OECD	Organization for Economic Cooperation and Development
OLS	ordinary least squares
PCE	personal consumption expenditure (price deflator)
PPP	purchasing power parity
PSID	Panel Study of Income Dynamics
R&D	research and development
SCF	Survey of Consumer Finances

SFC	Senate Finance Committee
SNA	System of National Accounts (Canada)
SOL	standard of living
TUS	Time Use Survey (Australia)
UI	unemployment insurance
UNICEF	United Nations Children's Fund (formerly United Nations International Children's Emergency Fund)
USA	universal savings account
USDA	US Department of Agriculture
VA	Veterans Administration

Preface

Dimitri B. Papadimitriou

The publication of this collection of essays is the product of a project undertaken by the Levy Economics Institute, to better understand the many economic aspects of well-being that help define the term 'quality of life'. During the 1990s, the gap between the United States and other advanced industrial countries increased significantly in terms of per capita income, as conventionally measured. However, as is well known, conventional measures often mask conditions of higher importance. In this respect, one may question whether the level of well-being in the United States has grown in concert with per capita income, or to put it differently, whether American citizens are now better off than their counterparts in other advanced nations. Determining this requires a means by which to measure 'well-being'.

The chapters in this volume assess the already established measures of well-being, propose new ones, and analyze and compare possible alternates. Conceptual or empirical studies that identify key issues related to measurement and evaluation of standard of living are also included, as are empirical estimates and their significance. It would be inappropriate to say more and risk preempting what the authors have written about these topics. While one may not agree with every argument and proposal made or embrace every conclusion drawn, the essays in this collection are thoughtful and perhaps some of them provocative. They need to be read and discussed, and their implications considered.

I would like to thank our senior scholar Edward N. Wolff who along with our resident scholar Ajit Zacharias head the Institute's research on 'Well-being', and who organized the conference from which these chapters are drawn. I am grateful to the contributors for their cooperation in carrying out revisions and to Frances Spring and Deborah Treadway for copyediting large parts of the volume, managing the final details of collating the changes by the authors, and overseeing all tasks of proofreading. Finally, my heartfelt thanks to the Leon Levy Foundation at Bard College for supporting the Institute's programs.

Introduction

Ajit Zacharias

The term 'quality of life' is used in a variety of disciplines, including economics.[1] Within a single discipline it is hard to find a generally accepted definition of the term. Further, the definition of quality of life as it pertains to a single aspect of life (such as health or education) varies significantly across disciplines.[2] Yet, it is striking how the assessment of the quality of a particular aspect of life necessarily involves looking at other aspects of life. Quality of life is a multifaceted phenomenon that, by its very nature, includes a high degree of interdependence among the different facets.

The assessment of individual health may elucidate the nature and extent of problems involved in the definition and conceptualization of the quality of life. 'Quantity', as distinct from quality of life, has a direct meaning in the assessment of health because the former can, in principle, be measured by how long an individual life typically lasts, that is, life-expectancy rates. Admittedly, however, although the expected length of life is a key aspect or indicator, it alone is not sufficient for an assessment of health status.[3] Living a life free from serious illness or impairment is evidently important for an individual and society, as is the ability to lead a decent life even with illness or impairment. Problems emerge as soon as an attempt is made to render substantive content to this proposition: what is a 'serious' illness or impairment? What is meant by a 'decent life'? Reflection on these questions would show that answers are dependent on the perspective and purpose of the researcher. It would also appear that as far as the second question is concerned, the answer depends on the illness or impairment in question. If one were to adopt a definition of health-related quality of life that is general enough to be applicable across concerns, perspectives and contexts, the following would be an appropriate candidate:

> Perhaps the measurement of quality of life can be approached from the point of view that the quality of life is high when the individual functions at a high level: when he is free of morbidity, impairment, or disability and when his vitality is high; when he fulfills his major social role obligations satisfactorily according to his own values and those of his group; when he has a high moral self-evaluation and evaluation of his group; finally, when he is emotionally healthy. (Lerner 1973, p. 5)

Indeed, this definition can be considered as an elaboration of the definition of health – put forward long ago in the World Health Organization's constitution[4] – as a state of complete physical, mental, and social well-being (not merely the absence of disease or infirmity), provided that social well-being is understood in a broad sense.

It is interesting to observe that Lerner's notion of health-related quality of life is similar to the much more developed and elaborate notion of quality of life put forward by Amartya Sen. At the risk of seriously over-simplifying Sen's rich conceptions, we may summarize the essentials of his view in the following manner. The basic concept in his approach is that of functioning, defined as a vector describing the state of a person; that is, a combination of that person's 'beings and doings'. In turn, the set of feasible functioning vectors, from which the person can choose, constitute the capabilities of that person. Each person is assumed to have a (scalar-valued) valuation function that allows the transformation of feasible functioning vectors into a set containing indices of personal well-being. The actual well-being of the person can then be assessed on the basis of the value of the chosen functioning vector.[5] Similarities between the two approaches lie in the focus on functioning and the broad view of what is to be included in it, as well as in the emphasis that the valuation of functioning is fundamentally a personal act.

An important feature of Sen's approach is that the traditional indicators of well-being – income and wealth – are not directly important. These are relevant only insofar as they shape functioning. And this they do, because capability is constrained by personal characteristics and resources ('entitlements') available to a person. In his formal approach to well-being, Sen treats resources as given quantities.[6] However, most theoretical inquiries into income and wealth distribution seek to shed light on the processes by which individuals get to have certain entitlements. Most of the chapters in this book can be characterized as directly addressing, in a quantitative fashion, the question of resources available to individuals and households, although, as noted below, portions of certain chapters and the whole of Part IV discuss other aspects of well-being.

Traditionally, economists have measured resources by real personal income or command over potential consumption bundles. Often, assessments made on the basis of such measurements went with the caveat that there was something more to life than attaining continual increases in real income or consumption. The above discussion has sought to place that caveat, and the relationship between resources and quality of life, in context. The remainder of the Introduction provides an overview of the major parts and individual chapters.

PART I   LIVING STANDARDS IN THE UNITED STATES

Given that economic growth in the United States in the recent past, especially during the 1990s, has often been portrayed as a model for the rest of the world to follow, trends in living standards in this country is of special interest. The chapters in Part I present quantitative evidence on living standards, poverty and inequality on the basis of trends in income, consumption and material indicators. There are well-known problems in the measurement of living standards, even using conventional yardsticks, stemming from methodological considerations and data quality. The chapters in this part also offer discussions on a range of such topics, from equivalence scales to the construction of price indices.

In Chapter 1, Edward N. Wolff presents a variety of indicators that showed stagnation or sluggish growth in American living standards since 1973, as compared to the 1947–73 period. Median family income, and, to a lesser extent, per capita disposable income have grown more slowly since 1973. The mean income of those at the bottom quintile of the distribution and the share of that quintile in total income have fallen, indicating a worsening of living standards for those at the bottom in both absolute and relative terms. According to Wolff, the main reason for stagnant median family income is the slowdown in labor earnings since 1973, as supported by a variety of estimates of labor income. Income inequality has also worsened, as indicated by the significant rise in the Gini coefficient, the share of income received by the richest 5 per cent of families and the ratio of their average income to that of the poorest 20 per cent.

Wolff argues that the standard human capital explanations are inconsistent with the behavior of labor earnings and education trends since 1973. Although average years of schooling and the share of highly educated people in the adult population have risen, average labor earnings have stagnated; inequality in earnings has widened even though inequality in educational attainment (as measured by years of completed schooling) has fallen. Yet another anomaly is the behavior of real wages and labor productivity: while both tended to grow at the same rate until 1973, there has been a sharp divergence since then, with real wages growing at a significantly lower rate than labor productivity. This has contributed to a rise in profitability and an increase in the share of profits in national income. Evidence presented by Wolff shows a shift in wealth distribution favoring the wealthiest, stagnation in median household wealth and homeownership rates for those with an average amount of wealth, and a growing burden of household debt. He concludes that the last 25 years or so has seen a stagnation of earnings, income, wealth, and consumption expenditures for the average American, as well as rising poverty and inequality.

Some economists have argued that consumption expenditures are a better measure of living standards than income (Brown 1994; Slesnick 2001). In Chapter 2, David S. Johnson examines how different the assessment of living standards would be if the yardstick used is consumption expenditures rather than income. Additionally, he points out that choices made regarding other important measurement options also complicate the assessment of intertemporal and interpersonal changes in the standard of living: interpersonal comparisons have to take into account differences in family size and composition, while intertemporal comparisons must adjust family income or consumption expenditures for inflation. There are no generally accepted principles regarding how these adjustments are to be made and, as a result, assessments of the level and distribution of living standards can vary substantially. Johnson presents a variety of estimates of living standards illustrating his arguments. For example, inequality in family income has shown a sharp increase in the 1990s while inequality in consumption expenditures appears to have remained stagnant or even declined.

In Chapter 3, Christopher Jencks, Susan E. Meyer and Joseph Swingle further explore the issue of the sensitivity to the yardstick of living standards by discussing how incorporation of additional information – in their case, material indicators of living standards – can serve to resolve inconsistencies. They focus on a particularly vulnerable segment of the population – children. The authors begin by looking at the change in real household income (weighted by the number of children in the household) from 1969 to 1999 for children at the 10th, 50th and 90th percentiles of distribution. Using the official definition of money income reveals a rather dismal picture: while high-income children experienced significant improvement during this period, middle-income children saw only modest gains and those at the bottom actually experienced a decline. However, if household income is replaced with per capita income (to adjust for the declining household size during the period) and if adjustment for cost of living is made using a purportedly better price index, the picture appears to be different, especially for those in the middle and at the bottom. The improvement in middle-income children's income is far greater and, instead of growing poorer, those at the bottom make some gains. Jencks, Meyer and Swingle argue that difficulties in the measurement of income and consumption such as biased price indices, omission of noncash government transfers, and appropriate equivalence scales makes it hard to accept one or the other. In order to adjudicate between the two, they examine evidence on changes in housing conditions, incidence of crime, ownership rates of automobiles, and access to telephones and medical care. The overall evidence suggests that children on the bottom rung of the income distribution are now living in households whose material conditions have improved over time.

In Chapter 4, Dean Baker examines in depth an issue that was raised in the previous two chapters – the efficacy of official price indices in accurately reflecting changes in cost of living. In his assessment, the work done by the Boskin Commission was politically motivated by a desire to cut the budget deficit and its main conclusion, that the consumer price index (CPI) overstates inflation by 1.1 percentage points annually, was not based on sound economic research. However, the debate around the commission's work raised several important issues whose implications go well beyond its specific recommendations. Baker argues that the commission's basic assumption that the CPI can serve as a cost-of-living index is flawed because it does not take into account changes in the physical and social infrastructure, or the provision of public goods and services (such as changed availability of clean drinking water, increased costs of commuting and pollution, and exposure to new diseases). Nor does it take into account relative consumption, that is, the changes in consumption standards brought about by changing notions of social status. These considerations suggest that the CPI can, at best, serve the narrow purpose of measuring price changes of consumption goods and services. Two main concerns raised by the Boskin Commission in this regard were substitution bias and quality change. According to Baker, the first problem could be important during times when prices of a narrowly defined group of goods change rapidly. With respect to quality change, the commission argued that the CPI was systematically recording quality improvements as price increases. Baker contends that several alleged quality improvements were not based on systematic empirical research and that the results of empirical research on quality change are, at best, mixed. Consequently, there is no strong evidence pointing to an inflationary bias in the CPI.

PART II INTERNATIONAL COMPARISONS OF LIVING STANDARDS

Just as in the assessment of several key social phenomena, international comparisons are vital also in the assessment of living standards. Yet, such comparisons are particularly hard given the limitations of data. The chapters in Part II address this important and difficult task.

In Chapter 5, Lars Osberg and Andrew Sharpe offer a comparison between the trends in the United States and Canada during 1971–99 using a new measure of economic well-being.[7] Conventional indicators, such as per capita GDP, have shown significant improvement in recent years; however, they exclude factors important to economic well-being such as costs of environmental degradation and income inequality. In order to overcome these limitations, Osberg and Sharpe have developed an index of economic well-being that is a weighted sum of current consumption, total wealth accumulation (all tangible and intangible assets, including natural resources), distribution of income, and economic security. Apart from what is usually counted as such in the national accounts, current consumption is defined broadly to include gains due to increased life expectancy and government final consumption expenditures. Decreases in family size and nonworking time, and, increases in commuting costs, crime, house pollution abatement, and auto accidents are considered as losses to current consumption. The definition of wealth accumulation is also broader than in the national accounts: increases in research and development (R&D) capital and human capital are added, and, the deterioration in the value of natural resources (as proxied by the costs of carbon dioxide emissions) and increase in net foreign debt are subtracted. Osberg and Sharpe extend their concept of economic well-being beyond the realm of monetary magnitudes, by including a measure of inequality (a combined index of income inequality and poverty rate) and of security (a combined index of income risks from unemployment, illness, old age and 'widowhood' (or being a single-female parent)).

Value judgments are inevitable in the determination of weights by which these four components are combined to form the overall index – for example, the standard use of current consumption alone as an indicator of well-being involves assigning weights equal to zero for the other three components. Thus, if current consumption is given a relatively dominant weight (0.7), then the index leads to roughly the same conclusions as would be obtained by a comparison of real per capita GDP. However, when the four components are equally weighted, the patterns are different. Worsening distribution of income and increasing economic insecurity made the index rise much more slowly than the per capita GDP in both countries.

Proponents of the American model of capitalism have often argued that a high degree of income inequality is socially acceptable, because those in the middle and at the bottom of the income distribution here are generally better off than their counterparts elsewhere. In Chapter 6, Timothy M. Smeeding and Lee Rainwater examine the validity of this proposition using data from the Luxembourg Income Study, perhaps the best existing source of data for household-level comparisons, and find almost no reason to hold on to this view. They provide estimates of distribution of disposable real personal income in 21 OECD countries, with income expressed in a common currency

– purchasing power parity adjusted dollars. The estimates show that the gap between the richest and the poorest 10 per cent of the population is the largest in the United States and the lowest in Sweden. Further, the poorest 10 per cent of US residents have a lower average income than their counterparts in all but two countries, while the richest 10 per cent in the United States have a higher average income than their counterparts elsewhere.

An additional aspect of this chapter is that it also considers the real incomes of children (computed using an equivalence scale), because it sheds light on how opportunities differ for children in low-income groups as compared to those in middle- and high-income groups. Only in the United Kingdom, the estimates showed, was the gap in real income greater than that in the United States. More importantly, it emerged that the poorest 10 per cent of US children are poorer in absolute terms than their counterparts in all but two countries. While there are limitations to the income data used (for example, omission of most noncash government transfers), these findings suggest that while the United States has a higher level of average income than other countries in the group, low-income adults and low-income children are worse off in the United States than in most other countries.

PART III   WEALTH AND LIVING STANDARDS

A strong case can be made for taking wealth into account for the assessment of living standards on the grounds that wealth has an independent effect on well-being. The ownership of real assets, such as homes, can free up resources that would have been spent on obtaining the services of such assets. Financial asset ownership can provide a degree of economic security in normal times and, in times of hardship such as that imposed by unexpected sickness, help households in maintaining their standard of living. Additionally, quantity and quality of local public goods available, access to credit, and a number of other noneconomic benefits are also strongly dependent on wealth ownership. In spite of its importance, it is fair to say that empirical studies on living standards have, by and large, concentrated on income or consumption. The two chapters in Part III offer interesting insights into the question of wealth in two different contexts.

Houses are by far the most valuable kind of asset that most families have in the United States. In Chapter 7, William J. Collins and Robert A. Margo present evidence, drawn from the decennial censuses, on black–white gaps in homeownership rates and home values. A striking piece of evidence presented by the authors is that the ownership rate among blacks in 1990 (49.3 per cent) is lower than it was among whites in 1900. Estimates show that the ratio of black to white ownership rates rose from about 45 per cent in

1900 to 67 per cent in 1980 (with most of the increases occurring after 1940), and then declined slightly to 65 per cent in 1990, indicating a large and persistent ownership gap between races. The slow decline in the racial gap in ownership prior to the 1940s was due to the virtual unavailability of conventional mortgage financing to blacks. The civil rights movement and associated legislation help explain, at least in part, why there was a relative quickening in the closing of the gap in the 1960s and 1970s. Several analysts have suggested that growing up in owner-occupied housing confers some positive effects on children. The proportion of children under age 10 living in owner-occupied housing has increased for both races over time, but much more slowly for blacks; as a result, the racial gap in the likelihood of children living in owner-occupied housing has widened over the last century. In an arithmetical sense, the growing gap stems from a combination of lower ownership rates for female-headed households and the increasing proportion of black children living in such households.

The questions of wealth inequality and its impact on living standards is explored in Chapter 8 by Seymour Spilerman and Florencia Torche in the Chilean context by utilizing the Survey of Social Mobility conducted in that country during 2001. The chapter analyzes the role of wealth holdings in shaping living standards and notes the differences in that role in the United States and Chile. The empirical part of the chapter attempts to tease out the connection between parental resources on the one hand and household income and wealth of the offspring on the other. The authors find that earnings and household income are influenced strongly by educational attainment and parental resources. The latter also has an independent effect on educational attainment; however, the schooling system in Chile does not seem to unduly favor the wealthy. But, human capital variables account for only a small portion of variation in household wealth while parental wealth has a large effect. Spilerman and Torche suggest that this may be due to the fact that average income in Chile is not sufficient enough to accumulate savings, and hence accumulation of human capital cannot offset the initial disparity in wealth determined by inheritance. These disparities, similar to those noted by Collins and Margo in the case of black–white gaps in home ownership in the United States, may be ameliorated only through conscious government policy aimed at asset accumulation by the disadvantaged.

PART IV   OTHER DIMENSIONS IN MEASURING WELL-BEING

While income and wealth shape the access of individuals and households to the means available for maintaining and enhancing their quality of life, nonmarket spheres of human activity and nonmarket institutions must be an integral part of an overall assessment of the quality of life. This belief, shared by a large number of social scientists, is grounded on the recognition that nonmarket activities and institutions are often of interest in themselves for individual lives. It is also widely recognized that they have a profound impact on market activities and that powerful feedback effects exist between the two. The chapters in Part IV address these issues in detail.

In Chapter 9, Richard H. Steckel argues that the study of physical stature ' can shed light on well-being (understood in terms of functioning as discussed at the beginning of this chapter) and inequality. It can also be used in contexts for these purposes where adequate information on usual yardsticks of well-being, such as income, does not exist (for example, eighteenth-century Norway), or where such yardsticks are not applicable (for example, slaves in the United States). Biological reasoning and international comparisons show that the relationship between height and income is highly nonlinear. Average heights between two groups of people with the same average income can differ because the proportion of people with the ability to lead a healthy life is different among them even after controlling for other relevant characteristics. Therefore, insofar as greater equality in the ability to lead a healthy life is positively related to greater equality in income, societies with greater income inequality may be jeopardizing the health of their economically disadvantaged members. Steckel presents long-run, comparative data on stature in the United States. While he discusses the complex social and historical factors driving trends in stature, it is worthwhile emphasizing, in light of the other chapters in this volume, that the relationship just noted between stature and inequality is an important factor in almost all historical periods discussed.

A well-known limitation of the conventional measures of well-being is that they ignore nonmarket activities performed by individuals. Time-use surveys have been utilized by researchers in order to arrive at estimates of time spent on such activities and impute monetary value to the output produced by them. However, a serious limitation of several available surveys is that they do not adequately take into account the simultaneous performance of multiple activities (such as mending clothes while waiting for the pot roast to cook). Ignoring this dimension poses methodological problems in models of time allocation and creates a systematic bias in the reporting of unpaid work. In Chapter 10, Maria S. Floro and Thomas L. Hungerford address these issues by analyzing time-use data from Australia for 1992, which records time spent on multiple activities by respondents. They classify data on overlapping activities into adverse (for example, cooking and cleaning at the same time) and beneficial (such as listening to music and reading) types. They also examined the extent and duration of such overlapping activities, and the incidence of such activities among individuals according to their gender, income and family type (for example, single versus married). Results show that the incidence and duration of adverse overlapping activities were greatest for women, particularly those who were relatively poor, had children and did not have full-time work.

Several analysts have pointed to the importance of worker rights and labor strength for the well-being of workers and macroeconomic performance. In Chapter 11, Robert Buchele and Jens Christiansen present an index of relative worker strength for advanced capitalist economies using indicators that can broadly be grouped into three categories reflecting key aspects of labor strength: employment protection (such as ease of dismissing workers), representational strength (such as union density) and social protection (such as unemployment benefits). Factor analysis was used to combine the different indicators into a single index. Comparison of the value of the index across countries shows that the United States ranks at the bottom and Sweden at the top in labor strength. Buchele and Christiansen also consider the relationship between their index of labor strength and other economic and social indicators, using correlation analysis. They find a positive but insignificant relation with per capita GDP growth (a result of the index being correlated positively with labor productivity growth and negatively with employment growth), a strong positive relation with real wages and mandated vacation time, and a strong negative correlation with income inequality.

Over 100 communities in the United States today compile quality-of-life indicators. Such indicators encompass a variety of aspects relevant for human well-being, including those that are specific to a particular community. Economists have generally not subjected these indicators to careful analysis, a lacuna that Daphne Greenwood attempts to fill in Chapter 12. She discusses reasons behind the emergence of these indicators and offers a detailed, comparative analysis of indicators developed in three communities. Greenwood argues that local-level indicators (as distinct from individual-level indicators) are useful because the quality of environment and neighborhoods, as well as access to cultural and natural resources, may be uniform across the locality. In addition, some policy changes that affect the overall quality of life (such as school board or zoning decisions) are made locally; good scores on such indicators can help in attracting residents and businesses to the area. The efforts to develop quality-of-life indicators are driven by increasing costs of economic growth and a growing awareness that well-being requires more than just sufficient income. However, she notes, there are also problems associated with local-level indicators, such as their incomparability over time and across localities. In spite of such difficulties, it is remarkable that some of the changes in local quality-of-life indicators mirror similar changes occurring at the national level.

NOTES

1. Economists have paid increasing attention to issues related to quality of life in the last decade. An indication of this trend is that a standard search on *Econlit* for the phrase 'quality of life' produced 1535 citations, of which 1416 were written since 1990 (search conducted with publication types restricted to book, collective volume article, journal article, and dissertation. Date: 21 October 2002).
2. Consider for example, the quality of schooling. While an economist measures quality by average term length, relative teacher pay and pupil/teacher ratio (Card and Krueger 1992), for an educationalist the relevant factors are curriculum content, effectiveness in learning and subjective evaluations of the learning experience by both teachers and students (Brown 1957).
3. It is still crucially important for large segments of the world's population, given the striking international disparities in life expectancy and the dramatic declines that have occurred in certain countries. According to the World Health Organization, healthy life expectancy at birth for total population ranged, in 2001, from a mere 33 years in Afghanistan to 50 years in Iraq and 67 years in the United States (Annex 4, available at: http://www.who.int/whr/2002/annex/en/).
4. Preamble to the Constitution of the World Health Organization as adopted by the International Health Conference, New York, 19–22 June 1946; signed on 22 July 1946 by the representatives of 61 states (Official Records of the World Health Organization, no.2, p. 100) and entered into force on 7 April 1948. Online at: http://www.who.int/about/definition/en/.
5. Strictly speaking, actual well-being as defined here corresponds to what Sen calls 'well-being achievement' (Sen [1993] 1995, p. 35).
6. See Sen ([1985] 1999, p. 9, equation 2.5). I am not suggesting that Sen ignores this question of access to resources altogether.
7. Comparisons of the level of well-being are eschewed because of data limitations.

REFERENCES

Brown, Clair (1994), *American Standards of Living*, Cambridge, MA and Oxford: Basil Blackwell.

Brown, Spencer (1957), 'Quality in education', *Journal of Educational Sociology*, **30** (8), 361–3.

Card, David and Alan B. Krueger (1992), 'Does school quality matter? Returns to education and the characteristics of public schools in the United States', *Journal of Political Economy*, **100** (1), 1–40.

Lerner, Monroe (1973), 'Conceptualization of health and social well-being', in Robert L. Berg (ed.), *Health Status Indexes*, Chicago: Hospital Research and Educational Trust.

Sen, Amartya K. ([1985] 1999), *Commodities and Capabilities*, New Delhi: Oxford University Press.

Sen, Amartya K. ([1993] 1995), 'Capability and well-being', in Martha C.

Nussbaum and Amartya K. Sen (eds), *The Quality of Life*, New York and Oxford: Oxford University Press.

Slesnick, Daniel T. (2001), *Consumption and Social Welfare*, Cambridge and New York: Cambridge University Press.

PART I

Living Standards in the United States

1. Recent trends in living standards in the United States

Edward N. Wolff

INTRODUCTION

The media have been aglow with reports of the booming economy and rising prosperity in the United States since the early 1990s. Indeed, the run-up in stock prices between 1995 and 2000 created the impression that all families were doing well in terms of income and wealth.[1] This, however, was certainly not the case. As I shall demonstrate, most American families have seen their level of well-being stagnate over the last quarter-century.

Despite this recent boom, the last quarter of the twentieth century witnessed some disturbing changes in the standard of living and inequality in the United States. Perhaps the grimmest news is that the real wage (average hourly wages and salaries of production and nonsupervisory workers in the total private sector, adjusted for inflation) has been falling since 1973. Between 1973 and 1993, the real wage declined by 14 per cent, though it has since risen by 7 per cent from 1993 to 2000, for a net change of −8 per cent.[2] Changes in living standards have followed a somewhat different course. Median family income, after increasing by 13 per cent in real terms between 1973 and 1989, fell back to its 1979 level in 1993, though it has since grown by 17 per cent between 1993 and 2000 (US Bureau of the Census 2002a). Despite falling real wages, living standards were maintained for a while by the growing labor force participation of wives, which increased from 41 per cent in 1970 to 57 per cent in 1988 (US Bureau of the Census 2002b). However, since 1989, married women have entered the labor force more slowly and by 2000 their labor force participation rate had increased to only 61.3 per cent, and with it, occurred a slowdown in the growth of real living standards.

Another troubling change was the turnaround in inequality witnessed in the United States over the last quarter of the twentieth century. Inequality in the distribution of family income, which had remained virtually unchanged since the end of World War II until the late 1960s, has increased sharply since then. What makes the rise in inequality particularly worrying is that not only has the relative share of income fallen among the bottom half of the income distribution but so has their absolute income as well. The poverty rate, which had fallen by half from a postwar peak in 1959 (the first year the poverty rate was computed) to 1973, has since risen.

The main source of the rising inequality of family income stems from changes in the structure of the labor market. Among male workers alone, wage disparities widened between the high-paid workers and the low-paid ones. Another indication of the dramatic changes taking place in the labor market is the sharp rise in the returns to education – particularly a college degree – that occurred during the 1980s and 1990s.

Current policy discussions in the United States and other advanced industrial countries have emphasized the need for better education of the labor force and the importance of the school-to-work transition. The underlying theme is that more education, more training, apprenticeship programs, and, in general, more skill creation will lead to a more productive labor force and hence higher wages and faster economic growth. Moreover, presumably, a more equal distribution of income will ensue from a more equal distribution of human capital.

There has now accumulated abundant evidence that individual workers benefit in the job market when they receive additional training and education. But it is much less clear that living standards will increase and economic inequality decline if the government enhances opportunities for Americans to improve their job skills. Indeed, this chapter will explore the reasons for this by investigating two other underlying paradoxes: (i) even as educational attainment has increased in recent decades, real wages have still fallen; (ii) As educational opportunities have improved for a broader swathe of the US population, economic inequality has not fallen but rather has increased.

The chapter will attempt to weigh whether government investment in education and training would be more or less effective at alleviating economic inequality and strengthening the US economy than direct subsidies to workers who are falling behind. Improved educational and training opportunities are essential for society for several reasons: (i) education provides benefits that transcend the job market, particularly a more knowledgeable citizenry for a democratic society (this was the original rationale for public education in the United States); (ii) more schooling and higher skills lead to more satisfying work opportunities; and (iii) investment in training made by firms lowers worker turnover.

However, the evidence the chapter will explore seems to show that such initiatives will not substantially alleviate inequality or bolster income. Confronting the inequality challenge may require direct subsidies to those at the bottom and tax relief for those workers in the middle who also have

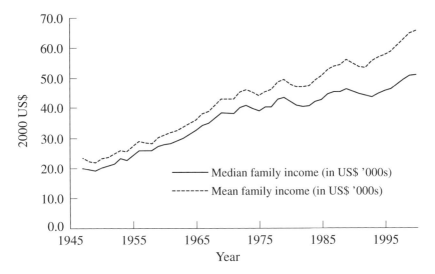

Figure 1.1 Median and average family income, 1947–2000

been falling behind. Labor law reform aimed at promoting unionization may also prove necessary to improve living standards for most workers.

RECENT TRENDS IN INCOME, POVERTY, AND EARNINGS

As shown in Figure 1.1, median family income (the income of the average family, found in the middle of the distribution when families are ranked from lowest to highest in terms of income) grew by 25 per cent in real terms between 1973 and 2000 (US Bureau of the Census 2002a).[3] In contrast, between 1947 and 1973, median family income more than doubled. Mean family income likewise doubled between 1947 and 1973, but then increased by 43 per cent in the succeeding 27 years. This is less than the increase over the preceding quarter-century but greater than the rise in median family income. The disparity between the two series is due to differences in time trends between the mean and median. While mean and median income rose at about the same pace before 1973, mean income grew at a much faster rate than median income after 1973. The discrepancy stems from rising inequality since the early 1970s (see below).

Another issue concerns the use of the new CPS deflator, the so-called CPI-U-RS price index. As noted in note 2, the CPI-U-RS deflator incorporates quality and other adjustments. However, the adjustments are made only for

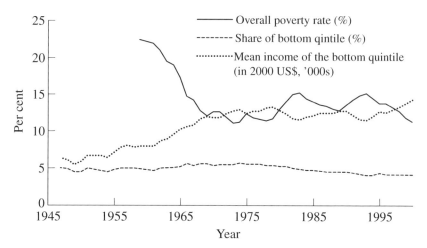

Figure 1.2   Poverty rate and share and mean income of the bottom quintile,
*   1947–2000*

1978 to the present. The CPI-U index is used for years prior to 1978. As a
result, the CPI-U-RS shows a much slower rate of inflation after 1973 than
the CPI-U: 288 versus 238 per cent. If we use the CPI-U deflator, then
median family income grew by 9 per cent between 1973 and 2000, in comparison to the 25 per cent growth rate on the basis of the CPI-U-RS deflator.

Another troubling change is with regard to poverty. Between 1959 and
1973, there was great success in reducing poverty in America, with the
overall poverty rate declining by more than half, from 22.4 to 11.1 per cent
(see Figure 1.2). After that, the poverty rate generally trended upward,
climbing to 15.1 per cent in 1993, but it has since fallen back to 11.3 per
cent in 1998, still above its low point in 1973.[4] Another indicator of the
well-being of lower-income families is the share of total income received by
the bottom quintile (20 per cent) of families. At first, their share fell, from
5.0 per cent in 1947 to 4.7 per cent in 1961, but then rose rather steadily over
time, reaching 5.7 per cent in 1974. Since then it has fallen off rather
sharply, to 4.3 per cent in 2000.

A related statistic is the mean income of the poorest 20 per cent of families (in 2000 dollars), which shows the absolute level of well-being of this
group (the share of income shows the relative level of well-being). Their
average income more than doubled between 1947 and 1974, from $6300 to
$12 700 (both in 2000 dollars), but then rose only by 12 per cent, to $14 200
in 2000. The difference in post-1974 trends between this series and the share
of income of the bottom quintile, which fell sharply, is that mean income
was rising in the general population after 1974.

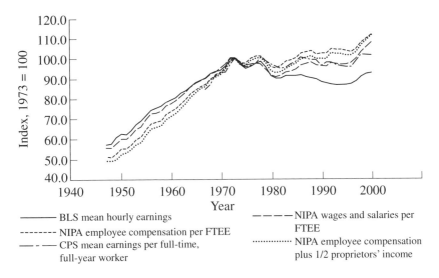

Figure 1.3   Labor earnings indices, 1947–2000 (1973 = 100)

The main reason for this turnaround is that the real hourly wage (average wages and salaries of production and nonsupervisory workers in the total private sector adjusted for inflation) has been falling since 1973. Between 1973 and 2000, the BLS real hourly wages fell by 8 per cent (see Figure 1.3). This contrasts with the preceding years, 1947 to 1973, when real wages grew by 75 per cent. Indeed, in 2000, the hourly wage was $14.08 per hour, about the same level as in 1968 (in real terms).[5]

Other measures of worker pay are shown in Figure 1.3. The results are quite consistent among these alternative series. Average wages and salaries per FTEE grew by 2.3 per cent per year from 1947 to 1973 and then 0.3 per cent per year from 1973 through 2000. Average employee compensation per FTEE increased by 2.6 per cent per year during the first of these two periods, and 0.4 per cent per year in the second, and the sum of employee compensation and half of proprietors' income had an annual gain of 2.7 per cent in the first and 0.4 per cent in the second.[6] CPS mean earnings for year-round, full-time workers grew at an annual rate of 2.7 per cent from 1960 to 1973, and by 0.0 per cent from 1973 through 2000.

The United States has also witnessed a disagreeable turnaround in inequality over the last quarter-century. Figure 1.4 shows different indices measuring economic inequality in America. The first series is the Gini coefficient for family income. The Gini coefficient ranges from a value of zero to one, with a low value indicating less inequality and a high value more. Between 1947 and 1968 it generally trended downward, reaching its

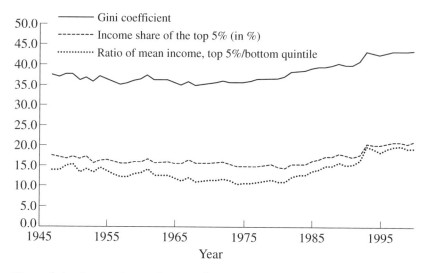

Figure 1.4   Income inequality trends, 1947–2000

lowest value in 1968, at 0.348. Since then, it has experienced an upward ascent, gradually at first and then more steeply in the 1980s and 1990s, culminating at its peak value of 0.430 in 2000.[7]

The second index, the share of total income received by the top 5 per cent of families, has a similar time trend. It fell gradually, from 17.5 per cent in 1947 to 14.8 per cent in 1974 and then rose after this point, especially in the 1990s, reaching its highest value in 2000, 20.8 per cent. The third index is the ratio of the average income of the richest 5 per cent of families to that of the poorest 20 per cent. It measures the spread in income between these two groups. This index generally declined between 1947 and 1974, from 14.0 to 10.4, then trended steadily upward, reaching 19.7 in 1998, and then declined slightly to 19.1 in 2000.[8]

Figure 1.5 shows another cut on family income inequality, based on 'equivalent income'. Equivalent income is based on the official US poverty line, which, in turn, adjusts family income for family size and composition (the number of individuals age 65 and over, the number of adults, and the number of children in the family unit). A figure of 3.0, for example, indicates that the income of a family is three times the poverty line that would apply to their family size and composition. The series begins in 1967.[9]

It is first of interest to compare the trend in the equivalent income index of the middle quintile with that of median family income. The former rose by 18.0 per cent from 1967 to 1973 and by 16.8 per cent from 1973 to 2000. In comparison, median family income increased by 16.7 per cent in the first

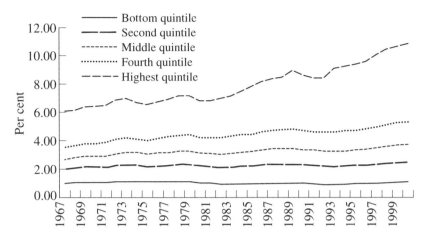

Figure 1.5   Trends in equivalent income by income quintile, 1967–2000

period and by 25.0 per cent in the second. The difference in growth rates after 1973 reflects the difference in price indices. Whereas the calculation of equivalent income is based on the CPI-U deflator (as is the computation of the poverty rate), CPS median family income is indexed by the CPI-U-RS deflator (see above). Indeed, as indicated above, median family income grew by only 9 per cent in real terms between 1973 and 2000 if the CPI-U deflator is used. The faster increase in equivalent income than median family income deflated by the CPI-U price index over the 1973–2000 period is consistent with the fact that average family size fell over the period. It is also of note that the annual growth of equivalent income slowed down for each of the five income quintiles between the two periods. In the case of the middle quintile, the annual growth rate was 1.20 per cent in the 1967–73 period and 0.25 per cent in the 1973–2000 period.

From the standpoint of inequality, the most telling result is that between 1973 and 2000, equivalent income grew faster the higher the income level. The differences are quite marked. Equivalent income increased by 54 per cent among families in the highest quintile, 26 per cent in the fourth quintile, 17 per cent in the middle quintile, 8 per cent in the second quintile, and a negative 0.9 per cent in the bottom quintile.

I also show trends in marginal tax rates of the personal income tax, since this also affects the well-being of families (see Figure 1.6). The first series is the top marginal tax rate (the marginal tax rate faced by the richest tax filers). Back in 1944, the top marginal tax rate was 94 per cent! After the end of World War II, the top rate was reduced to 86.5 per cent (in 1946), but during the Korean War it was soon back to 92 per cent (in 1953). Even

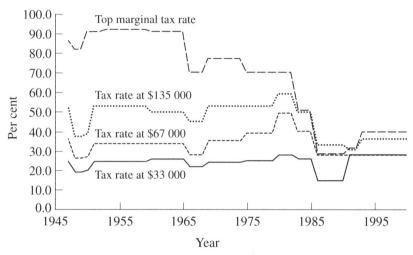

Figure 1.6   Marginal tax rates, selected income levels, 1946–2000 (in 2000 US$)

in 1960, it was still at 91 per cent. This generally declined over time, as tax legislation was implemented by Congress. It was first lowered to 70 per cent in 1966, then raised to 77 per cent in 1969 to finance the war in Vietnam, then lowered again to 70 per cent in 1975, then to 50 per cent in 1983 (Ronald Reagan's first major tax act), and then again to 28 per cent in 1986 (through the famous Tax Reform Act of 1986). Since then, it has trended upward, to 31 per cent in 1991 (under President George Bush) and then to 39.6 per cent in 1993 (under President Bill Clinton).

The second series shows the marginal tax rate faced by filers with an income of $135 000 in 2000 dollars. This income level typically includes families at the 95th percentile (the top 5 per cent). This series generally has the same trajectory as the first, declining in 1966, rising in 1975, falling in 1983 and 1986, and then increasing in 1991 and again in 1993.

The last two series show the marginal tax rates at $67 000 and $33 000, respectively, both in 2000 dollars. The time patterns are quite a bit different for these than the first two. The marginal tax rate at $67 000 (about the 60th percentile) was relatively low in 1946, at 36 per cent, generally trended upward, reaching 49 per cent in 1980, before declining to 28 per cent in 1986, where it has remained ever since. The marginal tax rate at $33 000 (about the 30th percentile) was also relatively low in 1946, at 25 per cent, but it actually increased somewhat over time, reaching 28 per cent in 1991 and since remaining at this level.

All in all, tax cuts over the postwar period have been much more gen-

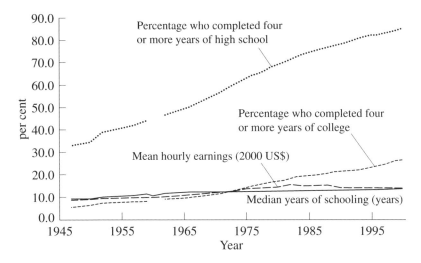

Figure 1.7   Years of schooling completed by people aged 25 years and older, 1947–2000

erous for the rich, particularly the super-rich. Since 1946, the top marginal tax rate has fallen by more than half (54 per cent), the marginal rate at $135 000 by 32 per cent, and the marginal rate at $67 000 by 35 per cent, while the rate at $33 000 actually increased by 13 per cent.

TRENDS IN SCHOOLING AND EARNINGS

One of the great success stories of the postwar era is the tremendous growth in schooling attainment in the US population. This is documented in Figure 1.7.[10] Median years of schooling among all people 25 years old and over grew from 9.0 years in 1947 to 13.6 in 2000. Most of the gain occurred before 1973. Between 1947 and 1973, median education increased by 3.3 years, and from 1973 to 2000 by only another 1.3 years.

Trends are even more dramatic for the percentage of adults (age 25 and over) who completed high school and college. The former grew from 33 per cent of all adults in 1947 to 84 per cent in 2000. Progress in high-school completion rates was almost as strong after 1973 as before – from 33 per cent in 1947 to 60 per cent in 1973 and from 60 per cent in 1973 to 84 per cent in 2000. The percentage of college graduates in the adult population soared from 5.4 per cent in 1947 to 26.2 per cent in 2000. In this dimension, progress was actually greater after 1973 than before. Between 1947 and 1973, the percentage of adults who had graduated from college rose by 7.2

Figure 1.8   Ratio of mean annual earnings between college and high-school graduates by gender, 1975–2000 (includes all workers age 18 and over with earnings)

percentage points, while between 1973 and 2000, it grew by 13.6 percentage points.

Figure 1.7 also shows the trend in real hourly wages between 1947 and 2000. As noted above, it rose by 75 per cent between 1947 and 1973 and then declined by 8 per cent in the ensuing 27 years. Yet, educational attainment continued to rise after 1973 and, indeed, in terms of college graduation rates even accelerated. This is the first paradox noted above, the growing discordance between wages and skills.

The main source of the rising inequality of family income stems from changes in the structure of the labor market. One indication of the dramatic changes taking place in the labor market is the sharp rise in the returns to education, particularly a college degree, that occurred during and after the 1980s. This trend is documented in Figure 1.8.[11] Among males, the ratio in annual earnings between a college and a high-school graduate increased slightly between 1975 and 1980, from 1.50 to 1.56, and then surged to 1.95 in 2000. For females, the ratio actually dipped slightly between 1975 and 1980, from 1.45 to 1.43, before climbing to 1.81 in 2000.

Among men, the increase in the return to a college degree relative to a high-school degree was due, in part, to the stagnating earnings of high-school graduates (see Figure 1.9). Between 1975 and 2000, their annual earnings (in 2000 dollars) gained only 4 per cent, while the earnings of men

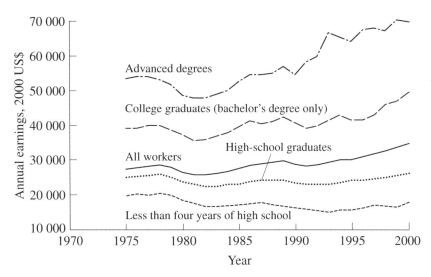

Figure 1.9   Mean annual earnings by educational attainment level,
1975–2000 (in 2000 US$)

with a bachelor's degree (but not further schooling) increased by 26 per cent. The biggest increase in earnings occurred among males with an advanced degree (master's or higher), who saw their annual incomes grow by 30 per cent. Among males who did not graduate from high school, earnings plummeted by 9 per cent.

Another indicator of the country's success in education is the dramatic decline in the inequality of schooling in this country. According to the human capital model, there is a direct and proportional relationship between earnings inequality and the variance of schooling. From the standard human capital earnings function,

$$\text{Log } E_i = b_0 + b_1 S_i$$

where E_i is the earnings of individual i, Log is the natural logarithm, S_i is i's level of schooling, and b_0 and b_1 are coefficients (see, for example, Mincer 1974). This equation states that labor earnings should rise with years of schooling. It then follows that:

$$\text{Var(Log } E) = b_1^2 \text{ Var}(S),$$

where Var is the variance. The variance of the logarithm of earnings is a standard inequality index used in the economics literature, and this

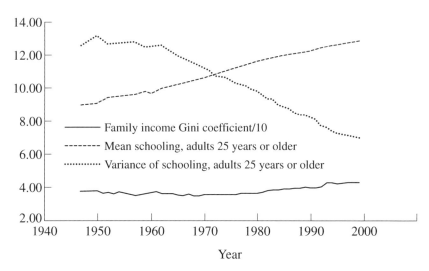

Figure 1.10   Family income inequality and educational trends, 1947–2000

equation indicates that earnings inequality rises at the same rate as that of the variance (or dispersion) of schooling levels among workers.

Yet, as shown in Figure 1.10, while income inequality has risen since the late 1960s, the variance of schooling (of adults 25 years of age or older, computed from CPS data), has trended sharply downward since 1950. In fact, the variance of schooling fell by 48 per cent over the period from 1950 to 2000 (from 12.5 to 6.9). The simple correlation between the two series is, in fact, −0.78. This finding leads to the second paradox of the chapter – namely, the growing discord between the inequality of income and the inequality of human capital.

TRENDS IN PRODUCTIVITY AND PROFITABILITY

Another anomaly arises when we consider the relation between productivity and earnings. In particular, the historical connection between labor productivity growth and real wage growth also appears to have broken down after 1973. In the case of an economy characterized by competitive input markets and constant returns to scale, it follows that wages and labor productivity should grow at exactly the same rate:

$$w = \partial X/\partial L = \alpha X/L$$

where X is total output, L is total employment, and α is the output elasticity of labor, which equals the wage share in this special case.

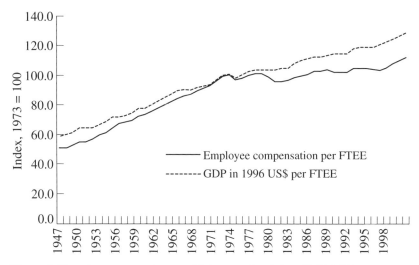

Figure 1.11   Average earnings and labor productivity, 1947–2000

From 1947 to 1973, real wages grew almost in tandem with the overall labor productivity growth (see Figure 1.11).[12] Indeed, the correlation coefficient between GDP per FTEE and employee compensation per FTEE is 1.00 for this period.

Labor productivity growth plummeted after 1973. Between 1947 and 1973, it averaged 2.0 per cent per year, while from 1973 to 2000 it averaged about 0.9 per cent per year. The period from 1973 to 1979, in particular, witnessed the slowest growth in labor productivity since World War II, 0.5 per cent per year, and the growth in real employee compensation per FTEE actually turned negative during this period. Since 1979, the US economy has experienced a modest reversal in labor productivity growth, which averaged 1.0 per cent per year by both measures from 1979 to 1997, while real wage growth was 0.6 per cent per year. Consequently, for the 1973–2000 period, the correlation coefficient between labor productivity and real earnings is lower than in the early postwar period – a value of 0.88.

If productivity rose faster than earnings after 1973, where did the excess go? The answer is increased profitability in the United States. The basic data are from the US Bureau of Economic Analysis' National Income and Product Accounts (NIPA), as well as its series on net capital stock. For the definition of net profits, I use the total gross property-type income, including corporate profits, interest, rent, and half of proprietors' income. The definition excludes the capital consumption allowance (CCA). The net rate of profit is defined as the ratio of total net property income to total private

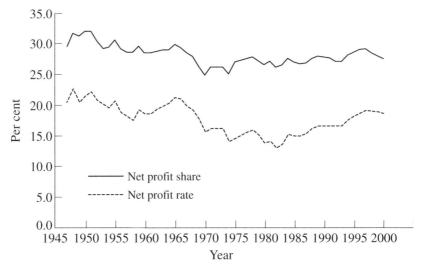

*Figure 1.12   Trends in the net rate of profit and the net profit share,
            1947–2000*

net fixed capital. The net profit rate declined by 7.5 percentage points
between 1947 and its nadir, 13.1 per cent in 1982 (see Figure 1.12). It then
climbed by 6.0 percentage points from 1982 to 1997, though it fell off by 0.5
percentage points between 1997 and 2000. However, even by 2000, it
reached 18.6 per cent, well above its low point in 1982.

Figure 1.12 also shows trends in the net profit share in national income.
It rose by 2.4 percentage points between 1947 and its peak value of 32.0 per
cent in 1950 and then fell by 7.2 percentage points between 1950 and its low
point of 24.8 per cent in 1970. It then generally drifted upward, rising by
4.2 percentage points between 1970 and its next high point of 29.1 per cent
in 1997. Since then, it has fallen by 1.7 percentage points between 1997 and
2000, though the net profit share was still above its nadir in 1970. The
results clearly show that the stagnation of earnings in the United States
since the early 1970s has translated into rising profits in the economy.

HOUSEHOLD WEALTH

As noted in the introduction to the chapter, the media has promoted the
idea of people's capitalism – that all families are benefiting from the stock
market boom of recent years. In this section, I look at recent trends in
household wealth. I use marketable wealth (or net worth), defined as the

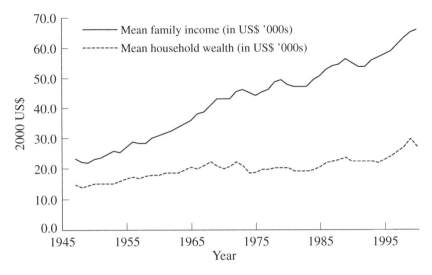

Figure 1.13   Average income and wealth, 1947–2000

current value of all marketable or fungible assets less the current value of debts. Net worth is thus the difference in value between total assets and total liabilities or debt. Total assets are defined as the sum of: (i) the gross value of owner-occupied housing; (ii) other real estate owned by the household; (iii) cash and demand deposits; (iv) time and savings deposits, certificates of deposit, and money market accounts; (v) government bonds, corporate bonds, foreign bonds, and other financial securities; (vi) the cash surrender value of life insurance plans; (vii) the cash surrender value of pension plans, including individual retirement accounts (IRAs), Keogh, and 401(k) plans; (viii) corporate stock and mutual funds; (ix) net equity in unincorporated businesses; and (x) equity in trust funds. Total liabilities are the sum of: (i) mortgage debt, (ii) consumer debt, including auto loans, and (iii) other debt.

I first look at long-term trends in average wealth on the basis of the Federal Reserve Board's Flow of Funds data (Board of Governors of the Federal Reserve 2002). Average household wealth, after surging by 42 per cent over the 1947–73 period, gained only another 10 per cent between 1973 and 1995, though it added an additional 28 per cent from 1995 to 2000, mainly because of the stock market boom of the late 1990s (Figure 1.13). The total gain from 1973 to 1998 was 30 per cent. This compares to a 43 per cent increase in mean family income over the same period.

Trends in wealth inequality, as measured by the share of total personal wealth owned by the richest one per cent of households, are displayed in

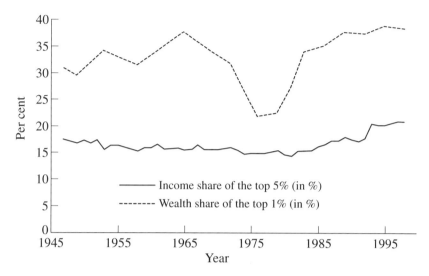

Figure 1.14   Income and wealth inequality trends, 1947–1998

Figure 1.14.[13] The share of the top percentile generally trended downward from 31.1 per cent in 1947 to 21.8 per cent in 1976 and then rose steeply thereafter, reaching 38.1 per cent in 1998 (the last date available). In contrast, the share of total income received by the top 5 per cent of families fell moderately from 17.5 per cent in 1947 to its low point of 14.8 per cent in 1974 and then climbed to 20.7 per cent in 1998. Changes in wealth inequality have thus been more marked than those in income disparities.

I next focus on the period from 1983 to 1998. The data sources used for this part of the study are the 1983, 1989, 1992, 1995, and 1998 Survey of Consumer Finances (SCF) conducted by the Federal Reserve Board of Washington. Each survey consists of a core representative sample combined with a high-income supplement, which is drawn from the Internal Revenue Service's Statistics of Income data file. The survey questionnaire consists of hundreds of questions on different components of family wealth holdings. Though there are other data sources available for analyzing household wealth in the United States, the SCF is the best one for capturing both the wealth at the top of the distribution and the complete wealth portfolio of households in the middle.[14]

Perhaps the most striking result from Table 1.1 is that median wealth (the wealth of the household in the middle of the distribution) was only 11 per cent greater in 1998 than in 1983. After rising by 7 per cent between 1983 and 1989, median wealth fell by 17 per cent from 1989 to 1995 and then rose by 24 per cent from 1995 to 1998. Overall, it grew by only 3.8 per cent

Table 1.1   Mean and median wealth and income, 1983 1998 (thousands of 1998 dollars)

	1983	1989	1992	1995	1998	Per cent change 1983–1998
A. Net worth						
1. Median	54.6	58.4	49.9	48.8	60.7	11.1
2. Mean	212.6	243.6	236.8	218.8	270.3	27.1
3. Net worth (%)						
a. zero or negative	15.5	17.9	18.0	18.5	18.0	
b. less than $5000[a]	25.4	27.6	27.2	27.8	27.2	
c. less than $10000[a]	29.7	31.8	31.2	31.9	30.3	
B. Income[b]						
1. Median	34.2	38.0	35.6	36.4	38.9	13.8
2. Mean	41.6	48.0	45.1	48.1	51.9	24.7

Notes:
a.   Constant 1998 dollars.
b.   Income data from the Current Population Survey.

Sources: Author's computations from the 1983, 1989, 1992, 1995, and 1998 Surveys of Consumer Finances; Current Population Survey.

between 1989 and 1998. One reason for the slow growth in median wealth is evident from the third row of Table 1.1, which shows that the percentage of households with zero or negative net worth increased from 15.5 per cent in 1983 to 18.0 per cent in 1998. The share of households with net worth less than $5000 and less than $10000 (both in 1998 dollars) also rose over the period.

Mean wealth is much higher than the median – $270000 versus $61000 in 1998. This implies that the vast bulk of household wealth is concentrated in the richest families. Mean wealth also showed a sharp increase from 1983 to 1989 followed by a rather precipitous decline from 1989 to 1995, and then, largely by rising stock prices, another surge in 1998. Overall it was 27 per cent higher in 1998 than in 1983, and 11 per cent larger than in 1989.[15]

A comparison with income trends is also provided. Median household income, based on the Current Population Survey, increased by 11.2 per cent from 1983 to 1989 and then by only 2.3 per cent from 1989 to 1998.[16] The pattern is similar to that of median wealth, whose growth also slowed down substantially before and after 1989. Mean household income gained 25 per cent between 1983 and 1998, in comparison to a 27 per cent growth in mean household wealth. As with wealth, income grew faster in the 1983–89 period than in the 1989–98 period.

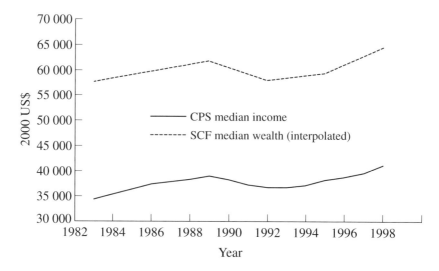

Figure 1.15   Median household income and wealth, 1983–1998 (in 2000 US$)

Figure 1.15 provides further details on the 1983–98 period for time trends in CPS median household income and SCF median household wealth. Both show similar dips in the early 1990s. Median household income in 2000 dollars rose briskly between 1983 and 1989, by 13 per cent but then dropped rather precipitously over the next four years, by 6 per cent. It then climbed upward between 1993 and 1998, just exceeding its 1989 peak by 5 per cent. Median household wealth, also in 2000 dollars, first rose by 7 per cent between 1983 and 1989, declined by 6 per cent from 1989 and its low point in 1992, and then surged by 10 per cent from 1992 to 1998.

In Table 1.2, I provide some other indicators of the fortunes of the middle class, as defined by the middle quintile of the income distribution. The first of these is home ownership. Here, there has been some progress. In 1983, 60 per cent of middle-class households owned their own home. This figure rose to 63 per cent in 1989, fell over the subsequent two periods and then climbed to 68 per cent in 1998. The second is with regard to the debt position of the middle class. The debt-to-asset ratio fell slightly from 24 per cent in 1983 to 23 per cent in 1989 and then grew to 26 per cent in 1992 (a result of the 1991–92 recession). By 1998, it had tumbled to back to 23 per cent. In contrast, the debt-to-income ratio of the middle class increased almost monotonically over the 1983–98 period, from 0.54 to 1.00.

The third indicator is stock ownership. There have been widespread reports in the media that stock ownership has substantially widened in the

Table 1.2   Wealth holdings of the middle quintile of the income distribution, 1983–1998

Wealth component	1983	1989	1992	1995	1998
A. Households owning homes (%)	60.3	63.3	60.6	62.4	68.0
B. Household indebtedness					
1. Debt/assets	0.24	0.23	0.26	0.24	0.23
2. Debt/income	0.54	0.71	0.86	0.94	1.00
C. Households owning stock directly or indirectly[a] (%)					
1. Any stock holdings	17.2	29.9	35.2	44.3	49.9
2. Stock worth $5000 or more[b]	9.2	18.5	18.7	28.4	34.8
3. stock worth $10000 or more[b]	5.9	1.4	13.5	21.0	27.7

Notes:
a.   Includes direct ownership of stock shares and indirect ownership through mutual funds, trusts, and IRAs, Keogh plans, 401(k) plans, and other retirement accounts. In 1983, ownership of stocks and mutual funds only.
b.   1998 dollars.

Source: Author's computations from the 1983, 1989, 1992, 1995, and 1998 Surveys of Consumer Finances.

United States, particularly during the 1990s. There is some truth to these reports. The proportion of middle-class households who own some stock either outright or indirectly through mutual funds, trusts, or various pension accounts increased from 17 per cent in 1983 to 50 per cent in 1998. Much of the increase was fueled by the growth in pension accounts such as IRAs, Keogh plans, and 401(k) plans. Indeed, between 1983 and 1989, direct stock ownership declined somewhat, from 14 to 13 per cent – probably as a result of the 1987 stock market plunge. However, the share of households with pension accounts nearly doubled over this period, from 11 to 23 per cent, accounting for the overall increase in stock ownership. Between 1989 and 1998, direct ownership of stocks grew rather modestly, by 6 percentage points, while the share of households with a pension account again doubled, accounting for the bulk of the overall increase in stock ownership (these figures which separate out direct from indirect stock ownership are computed by the author but are not shown in Table 1.2).

Despite the overall gains in stock ownership, only about half of middle-class households had any stake in the stock market by 1998. Moreover, many of these families had only a minor stake. In 1998, while 50 per cent of households owned some stock, only 35 per cent had total stock holdings worth $5000 or more and only 28 per cent owned $10000 or more of stock.

CONCLUSION

The last quarter of the twentieth century or so saw slow-growing earnings, income, and wealth for the middle class, as well as a stagnating poverty rate and rising inequality. In contrast, the early postwar period witnessed rapid gains in wages, family income, and wealth for the middle class, in addition to a sharp decline in poverty, and a moderate fall in inequality. Personal tax rates have generally fallen over time but by much more for the rich than for the middle class. In sum, the middle class has been squeezed in terms of income, earnings, and wealth since the early 1970s.

The 'booming 1990s' has not brought much relief to the middle class. Median household income grew by only 8 per cent between 1989 and 1998 (6 per cent with the CPI-U deflator), while median wealth gained 3.8 per cent from 1989 to 1998. The homeownership rate among the middle-income quintile did expand from 63 to 68 per cent. Household debt as a fraction of assets in this group remained steady at 0.23 but the debt-to-income ratio soared from 0.71 to 1.00. Stock ownership among the middle class grew from 30 to 50 per cent and the share of households with stocks worth $10000 or more climbed from 1 to 28 per cent. All in all, the standard of living among the middle class, as measured by these economic indicators, did not show much progress in comparison to the early postwar period and even compared to the 1980s. Part of the poor performance is attributable to the sharp drop in income, wealth, and consumption experienced during the 1991–92 recession. Income and wealth recovered after 1993 but not enough to get much ahead of 1989.

The stagnation of living standards among the middle class over the last 30 years is attributable to the slow growth in labor earnings over this period. While average earnings (employee compensation per FTEE) almost doubled between 1947 and 1973, they advanced by only 11 per cent from 1973 to 2000. From 1989 to 2000, they grew by 9 per cent. This occurred in spite of substantial progress in educational attainment made since the early 1970s. Moreover, despite incredible success in reducing disparities of schooling within the American population, the inequality of income has not only failed to decline but has actually risen sharply over the last three decades. These results suggest a growing disconnection between earnings and schooling.

The main reason for the stagnation of labor earnings derives from a clear shift in national income away from labor and towards capital, particularly since the early 1980s. Over this period, both overall and corporate profitability had risen rather substantially, almost back to postwar highs. The stock market has, in part, been fueled by rising profitability. While the capitalist class has gained from rising profits, workers have not experienced much progress in terms of wages. On the surface, at least, there appears to be a tradeoff between the advances in income and wealth made by the rich and the stagnation of income and wealth among the working class.

What can be done about the stagnating fortunes of the average (working) American? Current policy discussions in Washington have emphasized better education of the labor force and improved training. Education and training are seen to be the key remedies for two major problems that ail the economy: first, they will lead to higher skills and thus high-paying jobs and increase the real wage, and second, they will lead to a more equitable distribution of skills in the labor force and thus reduce wage inequality. The results of the chapter seem to cast doubts on the efficacy of this solution.

What should Washington do? I believe that the most effective way to reverse the decline of the real wage and to reduce income disparities is through incomes policy. Among the remedies that I propose are the following:

1. *Restore the minimum wage to its 1968 level* The minimum wage in 2000 was down about a third in real terms, from its peak level in 1968 (when the unemployment rate was only 3.6 per cent!). Raising the minimum wage will help increase the wages of the low-wage earners. A more powerful idea is to extend the coverage of 'Living Wage' ordinances, which mandate a minimum wage, usually around $10.00 per hour, for city workers and those employed under city contracts. These programs are now in effect in a few dozen municipalities around the country but could be vastly extended.
2. *Extend the Earned Income Tax Credit (EITC)* The EITC provides supplemental pay to low-wage workers in the form of a tax credit on their federal income tax return. In fiscal year 1999, the EITC provided $29 billion in supplemental aid. An expansion of this credit will further raise the (post-tax) income of low-income families.
3. *Make tax and transfer policy more redistributional* A more potent weapon to meet these objectives is to redesign our tax and income support systems so that they transfer more income from the rich to the poor. Tax policy over the last two decades, as shown above, has clearly benefited the rich over the poor (and capital over labor). Comparisons between the United States and other advanced industrial countries (including Canada), which face similar labor market conditions, indicate that tax and transfer policies can be effective in reducing inequality and increasing post-tax income (see, for example, Atkinson et al. 1995).
4. *Re-empower labor* The findings presented here and the cross-national evidence compiled elsewhere suggest that one of the principal reasons

for the greater level of inequality in this country and its relatively rapid rise in recent years in comparison to other advanced economies is the low level of unionization in this country (see, for example, Blau and Kahn 1996). This is also a principal factor in explaining declining real wages in the United States. Steps should be taken to help promote unionization in the workplace and expand the power of labor generally. This can start with reform of existing labor law. Other work has documented how existing labor law is biased against the establishment of new unions and how notoriously difficult is the certification process (see, for example, Gordon 1996).

NOTES

1. Over that time period, the S&P 500 composite index increased by a factor of 2.5.
2. These figures are based on the Bureau of Labor Statistics (BLS) hourly wage series (Council of Economic Advisers 1981, 2002). The BLS wage figures are converted to constant dollars on the basis of the consumer price index (CPI-U). The CPI has recently been criticized for overstating the rate of inflation. While this may be true, it is not clear that the degree of bias in the CPI has risen in recent years. As a result, it is likely that the sharp break in the wage series before and after 1973 would still remain even if the bias in the CPI were corrected. The Current Population Survey (CPS) data are deflated to constant dollars using the new CPI-U-RS price index. The CPI-U-RS series makes quality adjustments for housing units and consumer durables such as automobiles and personal computers and employs a geometric mean formula to account for consumer substitution within CPI item categories. As a result, the CPI-U-RS deflator is not subject to the same criticisms as the CPI-U series.
3. Figures are in 2000 dollars unless otherwise indicated. It would actually be preferable to use household income rather than family income. Unfortunately, official US Bureau of the Census series on household income begins only in 1967, whereas family income data are available from 1947 onward.
4. The data source for this section is US Bureau of the Census (2002b).
5. The first series is based on the BLS hourly wage series and refer to the wages and salaries of production and nonsupervisory workers in the total private sector. The next three wage series are the National Income and Product Accounts (NIPA) wages and salaries per full-time equivalent employee (FTEE), employee compensation (the sum of wages and salaries and employee benefits) per FTEE, and employee compensation plus half of proprietors' income per person engaged in production (PEP). The fifth series comes from the Current Population Survey (CPS). The first four series are deflated to constant dollars using the CPI-U price index. The fifth uses the CPI-U-RS deflator (see note 2).
6. The reason for including only a portion of proprietors' income is that part of the income of self-employed workers is a return on the capital invested in unincorporated businesses. Alternative calculations show that the resulting time series is quite insensitive to the fraction used in the calculation.
7. The data source for the first three series in Figure 1.3 is US Bureau of the Census (2002a). These figures are based on unadjusted data.
8. It would have been preferable to compare the average income of the top 5 per cent with that of the bottom 5 per cent but figures for the latter are not available.
9. The data are from US Bureau of the Census (2002a). The average income-to-poverty ratios are computed by dividing the mean income of families in each quintile (as ranked by family income) by the mean poverty threshold of the families in that quintile. It would

have been preferable to compute equivalent income for each family in the sample and then re-rank the sample by equivalent income to obtain new 'equivalent income' quintiles but the underlying data are not available.

10. The data are from US Bureau of the Census (2002b). Adults refer to persons of age 25 years and older in the noninstitutional population (excluding members of the Armed Forces living in barracks).

11. The figures are for annual earnings, which are not adjusted for hours worked or the experience level of the workers. The source for the data in Figures 1.6–1.9 is US Bureau of the Census (2002b).

12. Results are shown for employee compensation per FTEE. Results are almost identical for employee compensation plus half of proprietors' income per PEP.

13. The source for the wealth series is: Wolff (1996), extended to 1998 using data from the Federal Reserve Board's *1998 Survey of Consumer Finances* (Board of Governors of the Federal Reserve 1998).

14. Full technical details on data sources and methods can be found in Wolff (2001).

15. The time trend is similar when the value of vehicles is also included in net worth, as some researchers are wont to do. Instead of rising by 11 per cent between 1983 and 1998, median net worth increases by 15 per cent, and the mean rises by 28 per cent instead of by 27 per cent.

16. The statistics here differ from those portrayed in Figure 1.1, which are based on family income.

REFERENCES

Atkinson, A.B., L. Rainwater and T. Smeeding (1995), *Income Distribution in Advanced Economies: The Evidence from the Luxembourg Income Study (LIS)*, Paris: Organization for Economic Cooperation and Development.

Blau, F D., and L.M. Kahn (1996), 'International differences in male wage inequality: institutions versus market forces', *Journal of Political Economy*, **104** (4), August, 791–836.

Board of Governors of the Federal Reserve (1998), *1998 Survey of Consumer Finances*, available at: http://www.federalreserve.gov/pubs/oss/oss 2/98/scf98home.html.

Board of Governors of the Federal Reserve (2002), 'Historical data', *Flow of Funds Accounts of the United States*, available at: http://www.federalreserve.gov/releases/z1/Current/data.htm.

Boskin, M., E. Dulberger, R. Gordon, Z. Griliches and D. Jorgenson (1996), *Final Report of the Advisory Commission to Study the Consumer Price Index*, Washington, DC: US Government Printing Office.

Buhmann, B., L. Rainwater, G. Schmauss and T. Smeeding (1988), 'Equivalence scales, well-being, inequality, and poverty: sensitivity estimates across ten countries using the Luxembourg Income Study database', *Review of Income and Wealth*, **34**, 115–42.

Council of Economic Advisers (1981), *Economic Report to the President, 1981*, Washington, DC: Government Printing Office.

Council of Economic Advisers (2002), *Economic Report of the President*, Washington, DC: US Government Printing Office.

Gordon, D.M. (1996), *Fat and Mean: The Corporate Squeeze of Working Americans and the Myth of Managerial 'Downsizing'*, New York: Free Press.

Gordon, R. (1990), *The Measurement of Durable Goods Prices*, Chicago: University of Chicago Press.

Mincer, J. (1974), *Schooling, Experience, and Earnings*, New York: National Bureau of Economic Research.

US Bureau of the Census (2002a), 'Detailed historical income and poverty tables from the March Current Population Survey 1947–1998', accessed at: http://www.census.gov.hhes/income/histinc/.

US Bureau of the Census (2002b), *Statistical Abstract of the United States, 2002*, Washington, DC: United States Government Printing Office.

US Department of Labor, Bureau of Labor Statistics (1968), 'Revised equivalence scale for estimating equivalent incomes or budget costs by family type', Bulletin No. 1570-2, Washington, DC: US Government Printing Office.

US Department of Labor, Bureau of Labor Statistics (1999), *Consumer Expenditure Survey: 1980–99*, Internal files.

Wolff, E.N. (1996), *TOP HEAVY: A Study of Increasing Inequality of Wealth in America*, updated and expanded edition, New York: The New Press.

Wolff, E.N. (2001), 'Recent trends in wealth ownership, 1983–1998', in Thomas M. Shapiro and Edward N. Wolff (eds), *Assets of the Poor: The Benefits of Spreading Asset Ownership*, New York: Russell Sage Foundation, pp. 34–73.

2. Using expenditures to measure the standard of living in the United States: does it make a difference?

David S. Johnson[1]

INTRODUCTION

The question 'Are you better off than you were four years ago?' and pressures such as 'keeping up with the Joneses' reflect concerns with the standard of living or economic well-being. People are concerned about the change in their own level of well-being and the level of their well-being relative to that of others. Addressing these concerns requires dealing with fundamental issues in measuring the standard of living – making intertemporal and interpersonal comparisons of well-being. In addition, addressing these concerns requires choosing the method used to measure the standard of living.

The most widely used measures of the standard of living or economic well-being are derived by the Bureau of the Census using before-tax cash income for families, and include the poverty rate, the median income and the Gini coefficient. These statistics show a U-turn in the standard of living beginning in the early 1970s as shown in Figure 2.1; between 1959 and 1973 poverty fell (and real median income rose), and after 1973 poverty began to increase (and real median income remained fairly flat). These statistics, however, also suggest that there has been a recent improvement in the standard of living.

Currently, there is a debate in the literature about which economic resource (for example, income, consumption, or wealth) should be used to measure economic well-being (see Jorgenson 1998; Triest 1998). In his recent book, Slesnick (2001, p. 3) claims that 'consumption-based estimates of the standard of living show substantial growth, rather than stagnation, since 1970', and that using income to measure the standard of living yields a misleading picture of the standard of living. Using the consumption poverty rate as a measure of the standard of living, he shows that the U-turn, discussed in the previous paragraph, disappears, as shown in Figure 2.2.

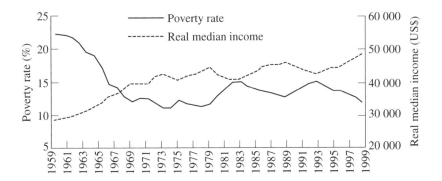

*Figure 2.1   Standard of living: real median family income and the poverty
rate, 1959–1999*

The dispute over whether income or consumption should be used to measure economic well-being is discussed in a recent National Research Council (NRC) committee report on poverty measurement (Citro and Michael 1995). The NRC report states:

> Conceptually, an income definition is more appropriate to the view that what matters is a family's ability to attain a living standard above the poverty level by means of its own resources. . . . In contrast to an income definition, an expenditure (or consumption) definition is more appropriate to the view that what matters is someone's actual standard of living, regardless of how it is attained. (Citro and Michael 1995, p. 36)

While the NRC report applied this distinction between income and expenditure to evaluate the poverty measure of the standard of living, it can also be applied to general measures of the standard of living and its distribution (for example, inequality measurement).[2] The choice of resource measure can affect both the level of and trend in the standard of living, and the relative well-being of different types of families.

In addition to the choice of resource measure, the level of and trend in the standard of living will depend on the adjustments made regarding the intertemporal and interpersonal or demographic changes that occurred during the period. Intertemporal changes are reflected in real median income, shown in Figure 2.1, by using cost-of-living adjustments to convert nominal income to real income. The family income presented in Figure 2.1, however, does not account for interpersonal or demographic changes, such as the decrease in average family size that occurred during this period. Using a measure that accounts for differences in family size increases the change in the relative standard of living given by median family income.

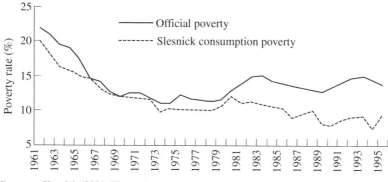

Source: Slesnick (2001, Figure 7.1).

Figure 2.2 Income and consumption poverty: official versus Slesnick, 1961–1995

Intertemporal changes are incorporated into Figure 2.1 by using the consumer price index (CPI). Recently, researchers have suggested that the CPI is biased upward, perhaps by one per cent per year (see Boskin et al. 1998; Costa 2000). Using an index with a lower inflation rate during the 1959–99 period decreases the real value of income in 1959 and, hence, increases the change in the standard of living reflected by the median income.

While the poverty rate adjusts for changes in family size, the trend in median family income does not. Equivalence scales capture the differences in family types (the interpersonal or demographic changes). The choice of the scale will affect the results in terms of the levels of and trends in the standard of living and its distribution. By examining the difference between income and consumption poverty, as shown in Figure 2.2, I show that much of the difference results from the assumptions regarding the chosen equivalence scale and not by the difference between income and consumption.

The measure of the standard of living requires the use of a summary statistic. Sen (1988) suggests that the standard of living can be viewed as the personal pleasure or utility one obtains, and Foster (1998) suggests that it is simply a point on the relative income distribution. Sen (1988) further suggests that the standard of living is 'in the living', illustrating its subjective and personal nature. This relative nature of the definition of the standard of living is also apparent in its measurement. Given Foster's definition of the standard of living as a point on the relative distribution, it is important to examine not only the level of the standard of living, but also its distribution.

In this chapter, I examine the level of and trend in the standard of living (using the median of the distribution), and the distribution of the standard of living (using the Gini coefficient). I use expenditure data from the

Consumer Expenditure (CE) survey (US Department of Labor, Bureau of Labor Statistics 1999) to update the results presented in Johnson and Shipp (1999), and Johnson and Smeeding (1998a,b). I show that the choice of resource measure (income or consumption expenditures), equivalence scale, cost-of-living adjustment and summary statistic all affect the standard-of-living and, hence, influence the responses to the two standard of living concerns posed at the beginning of this chapter. While the choice of resource measure is important, the choice of equivalence scale and price index are equally important in examining the intertemporal and interpersonal changes in the standard of living.

THE WHAT, WHO, WHEN, WHERE, WHY AND HOW OF THE STANDARD OF LIVING

To determine which standard of living to use, we need to decide whose standard of living we are measuring and how we are going to measure it and update it over time. The following questions must be answered:

- *What*   Which resource measure is going to be used?
- *Who*   Whose standard of living is being measured?
- *When*   What time period is used?
- *Where* Do the measures differ by geographic location?
- *Why*   What is the purpose of these measures?
- *How*   Which summary statistic is going to be used?

Although the where and why questions are important, this chapter focuses on the what, who, when and how questions.[3] I focus on the economic measurement of the standard of living using a variety of economic resource measures. The data and methodology I use do not account for leisure, home production, distribution within the household and changes in other quality-of-life measures.

What: The Choice of Resource Measure

Most studies of inequality are based on annual income data (for example, Karoly 1993; Gottschalk and Smeeding 1997). Slesnick (1994) and Jorgenson (1998) argue that consumption is a more appropriate indicator of well-being because utility is derived from the consumption of goods and services. In addition, consumption may be a more appropriate indicator of permanent income (see Slesnick 1993, 1994; Cutler and Katz 1991; Sabelhaus and Schneider 1997; and Johnson and Shipp 1997). In a recent address, Alan Greenspan (1998) stated: 'In the United States, we observe a noticeable difference between trends in the dispersion of holdings of *claims* to goods and services – that is, income and wealth – and trends in the dispersion of actual consumption, the bottom-line determinant of material well-being.'

While Slesnick (1994) and Powers (1995) argue that consumption and income inequality (and poverty) trends are different, Cutler and Katz (1991), Johnson and Shipp (1997), and Johnson and Smeeding (1998a) demonstrate that changes in the distribution of consumption are similar to changes in the distribution of income. Krueger and Perri (2002) show that there has been a recent divergence between the Gini coefficient for income and expenditures, and present theoretical results that suggest that this divergence is due to the 'change in the sophistication of financial markets, allowing individual households to better insure against idiosyncratic income fluctuations' (Krueger and Perri 2002, p. 3).

As stated in the NRC report, data-quality issues may affect the choice between income and consumption. Whether income or consumption should be used to measure permanent income can depend on the quality and availability of the survey data. Specifically, if income is traditionally underreported in surveys, then consumption data may be a better measure of permanent income. Alternatively, if consumption is difficult to measure or many components of consumption are missing from the survey (or the reporting period is too short to obtain an accurate measure), income may be the preferred measure. As with any measurement issue, accuracy depends on the relative importance of the measurement errors and on the availability of data for either measure.[4]

The choice of the resource measure will affect the level of and trend in the standard of living. As shown in Johnson et al. (2001), the increase in the standard of living since 1947 differs depending on which measure is used. Between 1947 and 1998, real, per capita GDP and real median family income increased by 3.0 and 2.7 times, respectively, while real family budgets (an expenditure measure) increased by only two times. Much of the difference occurred between 1966 and 1984; since 1984, the rates of growth in median income and family budgets were similar.

The measurement of expenditures (or consumption) can affect the standard of living. Although consumption may be the preferred measure for estimating permanent income, measuring consumption is difficult. Most surveys include only measures of expenditures and converting expenditures into consumption requires making assumptions regarding the value of owner-occupied housing and home production and determining which categories of expenditures should be included in the measure (for example, nondurables, necessities).

Who: Whose Standard of Living

Most measures of the standard of living use family (or household) resources and adjust these by an equivalence scale to obtain equivalent family resources. A measure of well-being for individuals is obtained by using the family size (multiplied by the household's sample weight) as a weight. Adjusting resources in this manner yields equivalent resources per person. This method assumes that all members of the household have the same level of resources.[5] Earlier research has shown that the choice of equivalence scale can have dramatic effects on both the level of and trend in the standard of living (see Coulter et al. 1992; US Department of Labor 1995; Johnson et al. 1998).

This literature has focused on the effect that equivalence scales have on inequality and poverty measures. As suggested by Deaton (1999), there are three approaches to choosing the equivalence scale:

- The analysis of behavior – using the consumption patterns of families to estimate the scale economies.
- Arbitrary but transparent formulas – using the square root of family size.
- Asking people – using subjective responses related by family size.

As discussed in Johnson (1996), standard methods for using expenditure data to estimate various types of equivalence scales yield many different scales depending on the assumptions made about the measure of well-being, the estimation method, the types of households and the data used in the analyses. An example of one of these estimated scales is presented in Slesnick (1993, 1994) and has been criticized in Triest (1998).

Because of the variability in the estimates of equivalence scales, the NRC panel recommended an arbitrary, but transparent formula. The panel recommended that the thresholds for household types, other than the reference type, be determined by using an equivalence scale that adjusts for the number of adults and children in the household. This two-parameter scale is given by $(A + PK)^F$, where A represents the number of adults and K represents the number of children. The panel recommended that the scale economy factor, F, be set at either 0.65 or 0.75 and that the parameter P be set at 0.7. The NRC panel's choice of a two-parameter scale was an attempt to be consistent with the cost-of-children literature and to smooth out the increases for larger families that were present in the poverty scale.

The NRC's choice of the two-parameter scale focused on the scale economies in families with children, and may not reflect the appropriate scale

Table 2.1   Alternative equivalence scales

Family type	Official poverty scales	Constant elasticity (0.5)	Two parameters (F=0.65; P=0.7)	Three parameters	Slesnick (mean by type)
Single adults	0.513*	0.500	0.451	0.463	0.226
Two adults	0.660*	0.707	0.708	0.653	0.529
Two adults, one child	0.794	0.866	0.861	0.880	0.742
Two adults, two children	1.000	1.000	1.000	1.000	1.000
Two adults, three children	1.177	1.118	1.129	1.114	1.104
One adult, one child	0.680	0.707	0.637	0.699	0.378
One adult, two children	0.794	0.866	0.797	0.830	0.452

Notes: *Uses non–elderly scale.

economies in childless families. The three-parameter scale (Betson 1996; Short et al. 1999) provides more economies of scale between singles and childless couples, which are more similar to those in the poverty scale. The three-parameter scale also provides more similarity between the scales for single-parent families with two children and the scales for two-parent families with one child. In addition, the three-parameter scale is consistent with the cost-of-children literature.

Some scales adjust for more than just the number of adults and children in the family. For instance, the scales implicit in the poverty thresholds adjust for the age of the household head.[6] Slesnick (1993, 1994) presents scales that depend on family size, the age, race and gender of the household head, and regional location and the farm/nonfarm status of the household. Table 2.1 presents five alternative scales; each scale is normalized so that a two-adult, two-child family has a scale of 1.0. The table shows the scales implicit in the official poverty thresholds, a scale with a constant elasticity ((family size)$^{0.5}$), the two-parameter scale, the three-parameter scale and the scales presented in Slesnick (1993, 1994). The Slesnick scales are the weighted averages of the scales for each family type for all of the other characteristics.[7]

As the table suggests, the choice of scale has a dramatic effect on the relative standard of living of different families. A lower equivalence scale implies that the family's resources will be adjusted upward, and hence, increasing their equivalent resources. For example, single adults will have a higher standard of living relative to the reference group under the three-parameter scales (compared to the poverty scales). In addition, the Slesnick scales produce a higher standard of living for single parents than any of the other alternatives. In fact, the Slesnick scales imply that there are economies of scale through divorce. As shown in Table 2.1, the scale for the reference married couple with two children is 1.00. If this couple divorces and the woman retains custody of the children, the scale for this subfamily is 0.471 and the scale for the single man is 0.32. This yields a total scale of only 0.791, which implies that these two divorced families jointly require less than the original intact family. We shall see below that these differences will also affect the trends in the standard of living.

When: Adjusting the Standard of Living Over Time

Any measure of the standard of living must be adjusted by the changes in the cost of living that occur during the time period. In discussing poverty measures, Foster claims that 'the key distinction between absolute and relative thresholds is not seen in the specific values at a given date, but in how the values change as the distribution changes' (Foster 1998, p. 337). Cost-of-living adjustments are frequently constructed using a price index such as the CPI; research shows that the CPI may be overly adjusting the cost of living, that is, the real changes in the standard of living may be larger than those found using the CPI (Boskin et al. 1998; Costa 2000; Bils and Klenow 2001). Other research shows that the poverty rates and changes in median resources are also affected by the price index used (Jencks and Mayer 1998; Johnson et al. 1998; Slesnick 2001). The Canberra Group (2001) report demonstrates that the choice of time periods can affect the changes in the distribution of income.

As discussed above, different price indices (or cost-of-living adjustments) lead to a variety of changes in living standards. Using the CPI-U and the CPI-U-X1 to adjust median family income yields a real increase in the standard of living between 1959 and 1999 of 58 and 71 per cent, respectively. Using a price index that lowers the CPI by one per cent per year produces an increase in real median income of 113 per cent. Regardless of the method used, the standard-of-living measure is sensitive to the method of converting nominal values to real values. While these aggregate price indices affect the level of the standard of living, they do not affect the trend in inequality. Slesnick (2001), however, shows that using household-specific price indices can have a small effect on the trend in inequality.

To illustrate the differences in price indices, Figure 2.3 shows three different indices using the CPI from 1959 to 1999 – the CPI-U, CPI-U-X1 and CPI-Exp (which is described in Johnson et al. 2001[8]). This figure shows that, during this 40-year period, prices increased 5.7 times using the CPI-U, yet increased only 5.3 times and 4.9 times using the CPI-U-X1 and CPI-Exp, respectively.

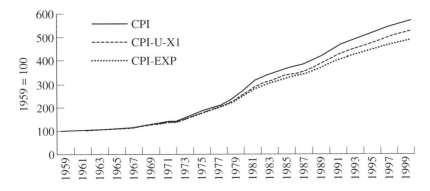

Figure 2.3 Alternative price indices, 1959–1999: CPI, CPI-U-X1, CPI-Exp

How: Which Summary Statistic

Research on the standard of living discusses both the level of the measure and its distribution. Many measures of the standard of living use the median income (or consumption) for a particular family or the median equivalent resources (adjusted by an equivalence scale). Other measures examine the distribution of this resource to obtain another picture of the standard of living. These measures include inequality measures (for example, the Gini coefficient) and poverty measures (for example, percentage with income below 50 per cent of the median).

DEFINING EXPENDITURES

I use the only data set in the United States that contains both income and consumption-expenditure information – the CES interview data – to compute various measures of consumption expenditures. Prior to 1980, CES data were collected at approximately 10-year intervals beginning in 1901. Data used in this chapter are from the 1960–61 and 1972–73 surveys, and the continuous surveys from 1980 to 1999. Although comparisons across time periods are possible, the differences in the methodology used before 1980 may affect the results. The 1960–61 and 1972–73 data are presented annually whereas the 1980–95 continuing CES data are presented quarterly.[9]

The surveys conducted since 1980 are similar to the 1972–73 survey, except that a rotating sample design is used. Data are collected from consumer units[10] five times over a 13-month period. The second through fifth interviews are used to collect expenditures for the previous three months. Because the continuing surveys use a rotating panel design, a consumer unit may be in the sample from one to five times over any particular period depending on the quarter in which their first interview is held and/or depending on whether the consumer unit continues to participate. To obtain annual expenditures for these consumer units, families are selected if they participated in the survey for all of the last four interviews. The demographic data used represent responses from the last quarter when the consumer unit was interviewed even if the response changed throughout the year.

Consumption expenditures are defined as the expenditures that a family makes for current consumption, that is, what the family actually spends for their own consumption. Consumption expenditures include expenditures for food, housing, transportation, apparel, medical care, entertainment, and miscellaneous items for the consumer unit.[11] Excluded are expenditures for life insurance, pensions (including Social Security), principal payments on mortgages, and gifts for people outside the consumer unit. Consumption expenditures are not a complete measure of consumption because the flow of services provided by durable goods is not included in consumption expenditures.

An issue that arises in constructing a measure of expenditures is determining the goods that increase the family's standard of living. For example, increased health-care expenditures might simply indicate that the family had to adjust for a health-related shock. Alternatively, the fact that a family did not purchase a television during the sample period may not indicate a lower standard of living if the family already owns four televisions. Another common measure of expenditures that is frequently used is the expenditures on nondurable goods (Krueger and Perri 2002).

The CES records what families spend for consumption, not what they actually consume. To produce a measure of consumption, the service flows from durable goods must be calculated. Johnson and Smeeding (1998a) produce a measure of consumption by subtracting the purchase price of vehicles and major appliances and the costs of home ownership from consumption expenditures, and then adding the rental equivalence of owned home and the service flows from cars, trucks and appliances. In this chapter, I use the consumption-expenditures measure and discuss the results on consumption from Johnson and Smeeding (1998a).

Using the median as a measure of the standard of living, the different distributions of income or consumption expenditures will affect the level of the median and the distribution of the standard of living as measured with an inequality index. Johnson and Smeeding (1998a) present the cumulative distributions for income, disposable income, consumption expenditures and consumption. Consumption in the lower percentiles is higher than disposable income, which suggests that households are smoothing their consumption. As expected, Johnson and Smeeding show that the Gini coefficient for consumption is less than the Gini coefficient for disposable income, which is less than the Gini coefficient for income.

SOME COMPARISONS

As discussed above, the level of the standard of living is affected by the resource measure used. This section examines the intertemporal and interpersonal or demographic changes in the relative well-being of families by comparing the trends in the median consumption expenditures and the trends in inequality and poverty measures.

Median Consumption Expenditures

Johnson et al. (2001) show that the increase in real median income is greater than the increase in expenditures, both of which are smaller than the increase in per capita GDP. Figure 2.4 illustrates the growth in the real median equivalent income and consumption expenditures between 1980 and 1999. Real consumption expenditures increased 11 per cent during this period, while real disposable income (after-tax and transfer income) increased 19 per cent. The changes in income are similar to those calculated by the Bureau of the Census. Real family income increased 20 per cent

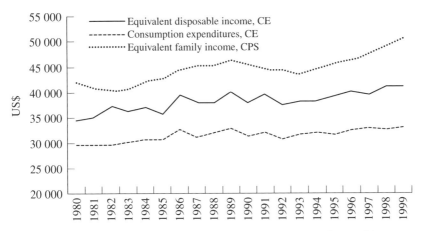

Figure 2.4   Comparison of real median resource: income, disposable income, consumption expenditures, 1980–1999

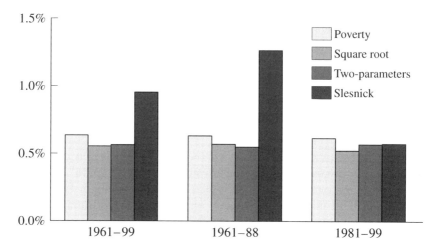

Figure 2.5   Average annual change in real median expenditure by equivalence scale

during this period. These results are similar to Wolff (2004) who shows that the trends in median income and median consumption expenditures have been similar between 1984 and 1998.[12]

These trends in the median level of resources can differ depending on the measure of expenditures used. For instance, the trend in the median consumption may be affected by the assumptions made regarding the valuation of owner-occupied housing. Using the outlay approach to measuring expenditures (which includes the principal paid on owner-occupied housing, vehicles and other major durable goods), the change between 1980 and 1999 is closer to the change in disposable income. Real median outlays increased 17 per cent during this period. Similarly, consumption also increases more during this period. These differences are mainly due to the increased value of owner-occupied housing.

As discussed above, the trend in real median income may understate the increase in the standard of living because of the decrease in family size that has occurred during the last 40 years. In addition, the trend in the median equivalent consumption expenditures may be affected by changes in demographics and the relative expenditures of different family types. Using equivalence scales to adjust for different family sizes will yield different trends, which will depend on the economies of scale implicit in the equivalence scale.

Figure 2.5 shows that the choice of equivalence scale can affect the changes in median expenditures. Using equivalent consumption expenditures weighted by people, the figure shows that the average annual increase in real consumption expenditures between 1981 and 1999 are similar for the four scales presented. The Slesnick scale, however, produces a much larger increase between 1961 and 1981. This period experienced a large increase in the percentage of female-headed families and his scale yields a larger value relative to the other family types.[13]

Inequality

Greenspan (1998), Johnson and Smeeding (1998a), and Johnson and Shipp (1999) show that even though the level of expenditure inequality is lower than that of income inequality, the trends are similar between 1980 and 1989. Slesnick (2001) claims that the trends between 1961 and 1995 are different for consumption and income. Krueger and Perri (2002) show that the trends in the inequality in income and consumption are similar until about 1986, at which point they start diverging.

Figure 2.6 compares the Gini coefficient for equivalent consumption expenditures (using the poverty scale) to the Gini coefficient for families produced by the Bureau of the Census between 1961 and 1999. As the figure shows, the trends are similar until the early 1990s. The lack of continuous expenditure data before 1980 does not allow us to determine whether there was a slight U-shape in the Gini coefficient as is apparent in the trend in income inequality. Both Gini coefficients increase during the 1980s and level off during the early 1990s, and appear to diverge in 1993. After 1994, however, the trends in income and consumption-expenditure inequality appear to be relatively flat. It could be that the

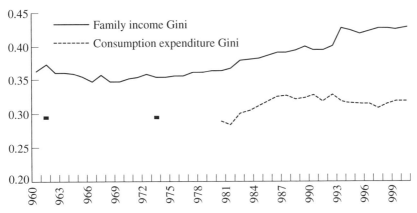

Figure 2.6   Income and consumption expenditure inequality, 1961–2000

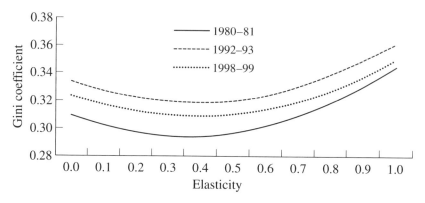

Figure 2.7   Gini coefficient and the choice of scale elasticity

changes in method of calculating the inequality measures produced by the Bureau of the Census account for some of the divergence (Ryscavage 1995).[14]

As shown in Coulter et al. (1992), the choice of equivalence scale affects the level of inequality. Using a constant elasticity scale (that is, the scale = (family size)^e), Coulter et al. show that various inequality measures have a U-shaped relationship with the parameter e, that is, inequality is highest for scales with a value of zero and one, and lowest for values between zero and one, such as 0.5. For the consumption expenditure data, Figure 2.7 shows a U-shaped relationship between the elasticity and the level of the Gini coefficient for 1980–81, 1994–95 and 1998–99. The change in inequality between years is sensitive to the choice of equivalence scale. Figure 2.8 shows the percentage change in the Gini coefficient between 1980–81 and 1998–99 for various values of the elasticity, e. As the figure shows, higher levels of e yield smaller increases in inequality.

The sensitivity of the trend in inequality to the choice of equivalence scale is shown in Johnson and Smeeding (1998a). They show that the inequality of consumption increased between 1981 and 1989 using the poverty scales, two-parameter scales and constant elasticity scales, but that the increase in inequality was much smaller using the scales in Slesnick (1994). Figure 2.9 shows the Gini coefficient for consumption expenditures between 1981 and 1999 using the poverty scales and the Slesnick scales. Similar to Johnson and Smeeding (1998a), the Slesnick scales yield a higher level of inequality than that obtained using the poverty scales mainly because of the smaller economies of scale that are implied in his scales. Both scales show a leveling off in inequality in the 1990s.[15]

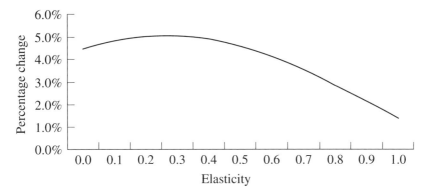

Figure 2.8   Change in the Gini coefficient (between 1980–81 and 1998–99) and the choice of scale elasticity

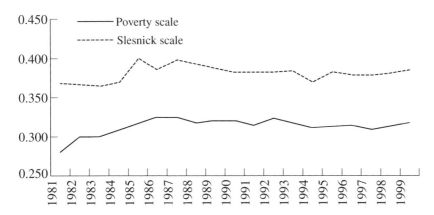

Figure 2.9   Gini coefficient for consumption and the choice of equivalence scale, 1981–1999

Poverty

To further examine the effects that different equivalence scales have on measures of the standard of living, we reconsider Figure 2.2, which compares the poverty rate using income and consumption. Many studies examine the poverty rate to gain insight into the changes in the standard of living. As shown in Figure 2.2, the U-turn in the poverty rate is not apparent in the results presented by Slesnick (2001), who shows that the trend in poverty depends on the method used to calculate poverty and that the apparent U-turn in poverty between 1973 and

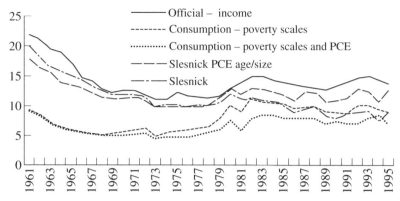

Surce: Slesnick (2001, Figures 7.3, 7.8, 7.9).

*Figure 2.10   Differences between the official poverty rate and Slesnick
            consumption poverty, 1961–1995*

1995 disappears using his consumption poverty measure. Figure 2.10
shows that the official poverty rate increased from 11.1 to 13.8 per cent,
while Slesnick's measure of consumption poverty remained almost
unchanged (going from 9.9 to 9.5 per cent). This figure shows the sensitivity of the poverty rate to the choice of resource measure (income or
consumption), cost-of-living adjustment (CPI) and equivalence scale
(poverty or Slesnick).[16]

Replacing income with consumption in the Bureau of the Census
poverty measure (and using the same equivalence scales and CPI adjustments) changes the poverty rates to 5.0 per cent in 1973 and 9.1 per cent
in 1995. This suggests that using consumption instead of income lowers
the level of poverty, as expected, but does not change the trend in poverty.
Changing the price adjustment mechanism to one using the personal consumption expenditure (PCE) price deflator decreases the poverty rates to
4.3 and 7.0 per cent, for 1973 and 1995, respectively. Using Slesnick's preferred equivalence scale and cost-of-living adjustment yields the results of
9.9 and 9.5 per cent.[17] Slesnick (2001) illustrates the importance of the
equivalence scales by using an alternative scale that only adjusts for the
age of the household head and household size (and using the PCE deflator). Figure 2.10 shows that poverty rates using this alternative scale
(PCE-age/size) are 10.0 and 13.1 per cent for 1973 and 1995, respectively.
The figure shows that these adjustments yield a poverty rate trend that
pivots around the original Slesnick poverty rates in 1973. This shows that
the disappearance of the U-turn in the poverty rates is mainly due to the
particular equivalence scale and cost-of-living adjustments used.

Family Well-being

A final issue that needs to be addressed in analyzing the two concerns posed at the beginning of the chapter is to compare the relative standard of living between different types of families. As shown in Johnson and Smeeding (1998a), the use of income or consumption changes the relative well-being of various family groups. The well-being of the elderly is most affected by the choice of the resource measure, with the elderly being better-off using consumption (rather than income).[18] Single-parent families are relatively worse off under both measures. The trends in well-being are similar for both measures, with the elderly being better off and single-parent families being worse off in later periods under both measures.

According to Johnson and Smeeding (1998b) there has been a substantial change in intergenerational equity in the United States. They show that using either income or consumption, the well-being of the elderly has improved since 1960, while the well-being of children has worsened, and also that among the elderly, older single women are markedly worse off than their married counterparts. In addition, the well-being of older married couples has improved since 1960–61, and older single women have experienced a dramatic increase in well-being since 1980–81, especially using the consumption measure, although they still lag behind their married counterparts. Among children, those living with single mothers are much worse off.

CONCLUSION

In this chapter, I present a sensitivity analysis of the measure of the standard of living and show that the level of and trend in the standard of living depend on whether income or consumption is used as the resource measure. I show that the choice of resource measure is not the only important variable in measuring the standard of living, and that the choice of price index and equivalence scale can have equally substantial effects on measuring the standard of living. Whether families are better off today than they were four years ago depends on the measure of the standard of living and the type of family. As Johnson and Smeeding (1998a) argue, both income and consumption may be complementary in the measurement of inequality. To fully examine the trends in the standard of living, various measures of the standard of living should be considered.

NOTES

1. All views expressed in this chapter are those of the author and do not reflect the views or policies of the Bureau of Labor Statistics or the views of other BLS staff members.
2. Borooah and McGregor (1992) suggest that consumption should be used as a measure of the standard of living and that income should be used as a measure of the level of resources.
3. See Johnson et al. (2001) and Burtless (1999) for a discussion of the geographic adjustments. See the Canberra Group (2001) for a discussion of the purpose of the measures.
4. Sabelhaus and Groen (2000) and Johnson and Smeeding (1998a) also discuss the issue of data quality in choosing between income and consumption.
5. Johnson (1998) discusses the impact of changing this assumption.
6. See also the scales presented in van der Gaag and Smolensky (1982) and US Department of Labor, Bureau of Labor Statistics (1968).
7. The scales were calculated for each household in the sample (discussed later), and then averages for each household type were calculated using over 1300 different household types (Johnson 1996).
8. The CPI-Exp is constructed using the CPI-U-RS (see Stewart and Reed 1999) for 1978–98, and the CPI-U-X1 for 1959–77. The trend in the CPI-Exp is similar to the trend in the PCE deflator; the PCE deflator increased 4.8 times during this 40-year period.
9. The 1960–61 survey collected expenditures using annual recall, that is, an interviewer visited a consumer unit and reconstructed the relevant year's expenditures. The 1972–73 survey collected data on a quarterly basis and the data were aggregated to obtain annual values only for consumer units who completed all four interviews or for whom expenditures could be reconstructed for a missed period.
10. A consumer unit comprises members of a household who are related or share at least two out of three major expenditures – housing, food, and other living expenses. A person living alone is a single consumer unit. Although the terms 'consumer unit' and 'households' are used interchangeably in this chapter, there are households consisting of more than one consumer unit; there are approximately 3 per cent more consumer units than households.
11. Housing includes expenses associated with owning or renting a home or apartment, including rental payments, mortgage interest and charges, property taxes, maintenance, repairs, insurance, and utilities. Expenditures for other lodging and household operations are in the miscellaneous items category. Expenditures for principal payments for mortgages are excluded. Transportation includes expenditures for the net purchase price of vehicle, finance charges, maintenance and repairs, insurance, rental, leases, licenses, gasoline and motor oil, and public transportation. Public transportation includes fares for mass transit, buses, airlines, taxis, school buses and boats. Medical-care expenditures are for out-of-pocket expenses including payments for medical-care insurance. Entertainment expenditures are for fees and admissions, televisions, radios, sound equipment, pets, toys, playground equipment, and other entertainment supplies, equipment and services. Miscellaneous expenditures are for personal-care services, reading, education, tobacco products and smoking supplies, alcoholic beverages, other lodging, and house furnishings and equipment.
12. Wolff (2004), however, adjusts the CE data to reflect the underreporting of income.
13. The Slesnick scales for a single mother with two children are 0.62 per cent of those of a similarly male-headed family.
14. These results agree with Krueger and Perri (2002) in that there has been a recent divergence in the inequality of consumption expenditures and income.
15. Johnson and Shipp (1999) show that these inequality results hold for other generalized entropy measures of inequality.
16. Triest (1998) also finds that the Slesnick scales dramatically change the trend in poverty rates.
17. Using Slesnick's scale and the PCE deflator yields poverty rates of 9.9 and 10.6 per cent.

18. Danziger et al. (1982), and Sabelhaus and Schneider (1997) show that the choice of income or consumption affects the results for measuring the well-being of the elderly.

REFERENCES

Betson, D. (1996), 'Is everything relative? The role of equivalence scales in poverty measurement', mimeo, University of Notres Dame, March.

Bils, M. and P. Klenow (forthcoming), 'Quantifying quality growth', *American Economic Review*, **91** (4), 1006–30.

Borooah, V.K., and P. McGregor (1992), 'Is low spending or low income a better indicator of whether or not a household is poor? Some results from the 1985 Family Expenditure Survey', *Journal of Social Policy*, **21** (1), 53–69.

Boskin, M., E. Dulberger, R. Gordon, Z. Griliches and D. Jorgenson (1998), 'Consumer prices, the consumer price index, and the cost of living', *Journal of Economic Perspectives*, **12** (1), pp. 2–26.

Bryan, M., and S. Cecchetti (1993), 'The CPI as a measure of inflation', *Economic Review*, **29** (4), The Federal Reserve Bank of Cleveland, pp. 15–24.

Buhmann, B., L. Rainwater, G. Schmauss and T. Smeeding (1988), 'Equivalence scales, well-being, inequality, and poverty: sensitivity estimates across ten countries using the Luxembourg Income Study Database', *Review of Income and Wealth*, **34**, 115–42.

Bureau of Labor Statistics (1966), *The Consumer Price Index: History and Techniques*, Bulletin 1517, Washington, DC: Bureau of Labor Statistics.

Burtless, G. (1999), 'Political consequence of an improved poverty measure', Paper presented at the Conference on 'Poverty: improving the definition after thirty years', Institute for Research on Poverty, University of Wisconsin, April.

The Canberra Group (2001), *Expert Group on Household Income Statistics, Final Report and Recommendations*, Ottawa: United Nations.

Citro, C.F., and R.T. Michael (1995), *Measuring Poverty: A New Approach*, Washington, DC: National Academy Press.

Costa, D. (2000), 'American living standards, 1988–1994: evidence from consumer expenditures', Working Paper no. 7650, Cambridge, MA: National Bureau of Economic Research, April.

Coulter, F.A.E., F.A. Cowell and S.P. Jenkins (1992), 'Equivalence scale relativities and the extent of inequality and poverty', *Economic Journal*, **102**, 1067–82.

Cutler, D., and L. Katz (1991), 'Macroeconomic performance and the disadvantaged', *Brookings Papers on Economic Activity*, 2.

Danziger, S., J. van der Gaag, E. Smolensky and M. Taussig (1982), 'Income transfers and the economic status of the elderly', Institute for Research on Poverty discussion paper no. 695–82, University of Wisconsin.

Deaton, A. (1999), 'Frontiers of poverty measurement in economics', talk given at the MacArthur Foundation NetworkWorkshop on Inequality in South Africa, Johannesburg, January.

Foster, J. (1998), 'Absolute versus relative poverty', *American Economic Review*, **88** (2), pp. 335–41.

Gottschalk, P., and T. Smeeding (1997), 'Cross-national comparisons of earnings and income inequality', *Journal of Economic Literature*, **35** (2), 433–87.

Greenspan, A. (1998), 'Income inequality: issues and policy options', remarks at a symposium sponsored by the Federal Reserve Bank of Kansas City, Jackson Hole, Wyoming, August.

Jencks, C., and S.E. Mayer (1998), 'Do official poverty rates provide useful information about trends in children's economic welfare?', manuscript, Northwestern University.

Johnson, D. (1996), 'The two-parameter equivalence scale and inequality between and within households', paper presented at the 24th General Conference of the International Association for the Review of Income and Wealth, Lillehammer, Norway. August.

Johnson, D. (1998), 'Equivalence scales and the distribution of well-being across and within households', in S. Jenkins, A. Kapteyn and B. van Praag (eds), *The Distribution of Welfare and Household Production: International Perspectives (Aldi Hagenaars Memorial Volume)*, Cambridge: Cambridge University Press pp. 381–97.

Johnson, D., J. Rogers and L. Tan (2001), 'A century of family budgets in the U.S.', *Monthly Labor Review*, 2 (May), 28–45.

Johnson, D., and S. Shipp (1997), 'Trends in inequality in the United States using consumption expenditures: the U.S. from 1960–1993', *Review of Income and Wealth*, **43** (2), 133–52.

Johnson, D., and S. Shipp (1999), 'Inequality and the business cycle: a consumption viewpoint', *Empirical Economics*, pp. 173–80.

Johnson, D., K. Short and T. Garner (1998), 'Poverty measurement research at the Bureau of the Census and the Bureau of Labor Statistics', Paper presented at the Annual Research Conference of the Association for Policy Analysis and Management, New York, October.

Johnson, D., and T. Smeeding (1998a), 'Measuring the trends in inequality of individuals and families: income and consumption', manuscript, Bureau of Labor Statistics, Washington, DC.

Johnson, D., and T. Smeeding (1998b), 'Intergenerational equity in the United States: the changing well-being of the old and the young, 1960–1995,' Paper presented at the 25th General Conference of the International Association for Research in Income and Wealth, Cambridge, UK, August.

Jorgenson, D. (1998), 'Did we lose the war on poverty?', *Journal of Economic Perspectives*, **12** (1), 79–96.

Karoly, L. (1993), 'The trend in inequality among families, individuals, and workers in the United States: a twenty five year perspective', in Sheldon Danziger and Peter Gottschalk (eds), *Uneven Tides Rising Inequality in America*, New York: Russell Sage Foundation, pp. 19–97.

Krueger, D., and F. Perri (2002), 'Does income inequality lead to consumption inequality? Empirical findings and a theoretical explanation', manuscript, Stanford University, Stanford, CA, June.

Krugman, P. (1996), 'The CPI and the rat race', http://www.slate.com/dismal/96-12-21/dismal.asp.

Powers, E. (1995), 'Inflation, unemployment and poverty revisited', *Economic Review*, **31** (3), 2–13.

Ryscavage, P. (1995), 'A surge in growing income inequality?', *Monthly Labor Review*, **118**, (8) (August), 51–61.

Sabelhaus, J., and J. Groen (2000), 'Can permanent income theory explain cross-section consumption patterns?', *Review of Economics and Statistics*, **82** (3), 431–8.

Sabelhaus, J., and U. Schneider (1997), 'Measuring the distribution of well-being:

why income and consumption give different answers?', *Applied Economics Quarterly* (Konjunkturpolitik), **2**, 153–76.

Sen, A. (1988), *The Standard of Living*, Cambridge: Cambridge University Press.

Short, K., T. Garner, D. Johnson and P. Doyle (1999), *Experimental Poverty Measures, 1990–1997*, US Bureau of the Census, P60-205, Washington, DC: US Government Printing Office.

Slesnick, D. (1993), 'Gaining ground: poverty in the postwar United States', *Journal of Political Economy*, **101** (1), 1–38.

Slesnick, D. (1994), 'Consumption, needs and inequality', *International Economic Review*, **35** (3), 677–703.

Slesnick, D. (2001), *Consumption and Social Welfare*, Cambridge: Cambridge University Press.

Stewart, K., and S. Reed (1999), 'CPI research series using current methods, 1978–98', *Monthly Labor Review*, June, 29–38.

Triest, R. (1998), 'Has poverty gotten worse?', *Journal of Economic Perspectives*, **12** (1), 97–114.

US Bureau of the Census (2000), *Poverty in the United States 1999*, series P-60, Washington, DC: US Government Printing Office.

US Department of Labor, Bureau of Labor Statistics (1968), 'Revised equivalence scale for estimating equivalent incomes or budget costs by family type', Bulletin No. 1570-2, Washington, DC: US Government Printing Office.

US Department of Labor (1995), 'Trends in the well-being of families', ch. 2 in *Report on the American Workforce*, Washington, DC: US Government Printing Office.

US Department of Labor, Bureau of Labor Statistics (1999), *Consumer Expenditure Survey: 1980–99*, Internal files.

van der Gaag, J., and E. Smolensky (1982), 'True household equivalence scales and characteristics of the poor in the United States', *Review of Income and Wealth*, **28**, 17–28.

Wolff, E.N. (2004), 'Recent trends in living standards', ch. 1 in this volume.

3. Who has benefited from economic growth in the United States since 1969? The case of children*

Christopher Jencks, Susan E. Mayer and Joseph Swingle

INTRODUCTION

Affluent Americans remember the 1990s as a period of remarkable prosperity, during which the stock market soared and real GDP rose 35 per cent.[1] GDP grew partly because the working-age population grew, but real GDP per worker rose 18 per cent. Although this cheery picture is widely accepted, household surveys tell a less encouraging story. According to the Census Bureau's Current Population Survey (CPS), households' mean pretax money income rose only 11 per cent between 1989 and 1999, and the bulk of this increase went to the affluent. The Census Bureau's report on its March 1999 income survey suggested that the median household's real money income had risen only 5.1 per cent since 1989 (US Bureau of the Census 2000a, Table B-2). Discrepancies of this kind have led to a long-running war of words between optimists who see America's economic system as a model for the rest of the world and pessimists who see the American system as proof that *laissez-faire* capitalism benefits the few at the expense of the many.

Those who want to demonstrate the harmful effects of slow growth and rising inequality tend to concentrate on trends among children. Figure 3.1 displays what we shall call the pessimistic picture of income trends among American children over the past generation. The data come from the CPS and show the percentage change in real household income for children at the 10th, 50th, and 90th percentiles of the distribution.[2] We concentrate on 1969, 1979, 1989, and 1999. These years have the advantage of falling at or near business cycle peaks. Using them also allows us to write about trends in successive decades, keeping our prose a little simpler than it otherwise would be.

Figure 3.1 tells a grim story, especially for the 1970s and 1980s. Although

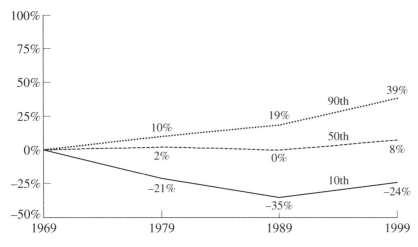

Source: Author's tabulations

Figure 3.1   *Percentage change since 1969 in the pretax income of children at the 10th, 50th, and 90th percentiles of total household income using the CPI-U*

high-income children experienced significant gains between 1969 and 1989, middle-income children gained nothing during these years and low-income children lost more than high-income children gained, at least in percentage terms. Furthermore, while real income rose throughout the distribution during the 1990s, low-income children were still much worse off in 1999 than they had been in 1969. Indeed, even middle-income children were only 8 per cent better off in 1999 than in 1969. Figure 3.1 suggests that American capitalism has not been distributing the benefits of economic growth very widely.

Figure 3.2 is based on the same CPS data as Figure 3.1, but it changes the measure of children's economic status in two ways. First, it takes account of the fact that households got smaller between 1969 and 1999. To do this we replace total household income with per capita household income. Second, it replaces the consumer price index for urban consumers (CPI-U), which the Census Bureau has traditionally used to adjust incomes for inflation, with a revised index known as the CPI-U-RS, which corrects a number of well-documented problems in the way the Bureau of Labor Statistics (BLS) used to calculate CPI-U. These problems had all been corrected by 1999. But because government benefits, tax brackets, and even private pay scales are often tied to the CPI-U, the BLS never changes it retroactively. The CPI-U-RS seeks to approximate what the CPI-U would have done if the BLS had adopted its current methods earlier.

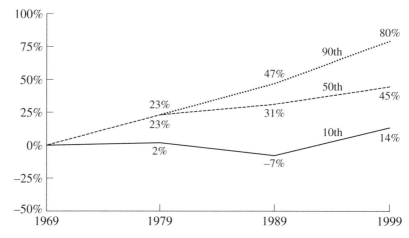

Source: Author's tabulations

*Figure 3.2   Percentage change since 1969 in the pretax income of children
            at the 10th, 50th, and 90th percentiles of per capita household
            income using the CPI-U-RS*

In one crucial respect Figures 3.1 and 3.2 tell a consistent story. High-income children always gain the most, and inequality always rises. In other respects, however, Figure 3.2 dramatically alters our picture of children's economic progress since 1969. Instead of being 24 per cent poorer in 1999 than in 1969, low-income children are now 14 per cent richer. Middle-income children's real household income now rises by 45 rather than 8 per cent. In Figure 3.1 growing inequality means that the rich grew richer while the poor grew poorer. In Figure 3.2 growing inequality means that everyone grew richer but that the rich gained more than the poor. Confronted with Figure 3.1, many Americans would probably say that 'this is unfair' or perhaps even that 'something should be done'. Confronted with Figure 3.2, these skeptics might become more cautious, saying that 'if growing inequality is the price we have to pay for making everyone better off, so be it'. But it is far from clear that Figure 3.2 tells a more accurate picture than Figure 3.1. First, no price index is perfect. The CPI-U-RS may be better than the CPI-U, but not everyone who studies such matters agrees that this is the case. Second, although household size changed and everyone agrees that smaller families need less money than large families, there is no agreement about how much less money smaller families need. In addition households' noncash income changed dramatically from 1969 to 1999, and Figure 3.2 ignores this change.

This chapter tries to adjudicate between Figures 3.1 and 3.2. The next section looks more carefully at the data on income, household size, and prices. We end up preferring Figure 3.2 to Figure 3.1, but we also conclude that theoretical arguments alone cannot resolve the controversy. Choosing between these two pictures ultimately requires us to look at direct measures of changes in children's material well-being. The subsequent section therefore examines trends in children's housing conditions, access to automobiles, telephone service, physician visits, and food consumption. Most of these measures show trends more like those in Figure 3.2 than Figure 3.1.

MEASURING CHANGES IN HOUSEHOLD INCOME AND CONSUMPTION

Most people are interested in the way family income has changed over time because they expect income statistics to tell them something about changes in the material standard of living. When 'real' income goes up, we expect living conditions to improve. When real income goes down, we expect living standards to deteriorate. Figure 3.1 is alarming because it implies that low-income children experienced substantially more material hardship in 1999 than in 1969. But anyone who uses changes in household income as a guide to changes in material well-being must solve at least four problems: how to adjust for price changes, how to adjust for changes in noncash income, how to adjust for changes in household size, and how to adjust for changes in the ratio of consumption to income.

Price changes

When inflation began to accelerate in the 1970s, economists began to pay more attention to the way in which the BLS calculated the CPI-U. As time went on, a growing number concluded that the CPI-U overstated the 'true' rate of price change.[3] In response to these criticisms – some of which came from its own economists – the BLS made numerous changes in the way it calculated the CPI-U.

The single most important change involved owner-occupied housing. A home is both a place to live and an investment. The CPI-U is supposed to track changes in the price of shelter, not changes in the value of people's real estate investments. But until 1983, the BLS estimated the cost of owner-occupied housing by tracking sale prices and mortgage interest rates. Both sale prices and interest rates soar when investors think that inflation is likely to continue. But for those who already own a home, increases in sale prices represent windfall profits, and increases in interest rates on new mortgages are irrelevant. If one wants to track the current cost of shelter, sale prices and interest rates are likely to be quite misleading. What

Table 3.1   Percentage increase in three widely used government price indices, 1969–1999

Price index (and source)	Year				Average annual percentage increase	
	1969	1979	1989	1999	1969–99	1989–99
Overall						
1. CPI-U (BLS)	100	198	338	454	5.17	3.00
2. CPI-U-RS (BLS)	100	187	308	401	4.74	2.69
3. PCE chain-price index (NIPA)	100	186	306	392	4.66	2.51
Excluding medical care						
4. CPI-U (BLS)	100	197	331	438	5.05	2.84
5. CPI-U-RS[a]	100	187	301	387	4.61	2.54
6. PCE chain price index[b]	NA	NA	306	381	NA	2.22

Notes: All three indices have been standardized to make the 1969 value 100.
a.   Authors' approximation using (Line4/Line1)*Line 2.
b.   Based on comparing NIPA estimates of real and nominal growth in the value of personal consumption after excluding medical care.

Sources: The CPI-U and PCE chain-price data are from the *Economic Report of the President, 2001* (Council of Economic Advisers 2002). The CPI-U-RS data are from US Bureau of the Census (2000a).

one needs are data on the cost of renting different kinds of residences. In 1983, the BLS began using current rents to estimate the cost of all housing, including units occupied by their owner. The BLS also produced a price index, known as the CPI-U-X1, which estimated how much the CPI-U would have changed if the BLS had begun using rent levels in 1967.

In more recent years, the BLS has made a number of other changes in the way it calculates the CPI-U. Most of these changes have lowered the estimated rate of inflation. The CPI-U-RS estimates what would have happened to the CPI-U if all these changes had been introduced in 1977.[4] The Census Bureau has extended the CPI-U-RS back to 1967 by splicing it to the CPI-U-X1. Table 3.1 shows that this version of the CPI-U-RS, which is also the one we use, rises considerably less rapidly than the CPI-U. The disparity averages about 0.43 percentage points a year. Between 1969 and 1999 the CPI-U rose 13 percentage points more than the CPI-U-RS. As a result, incomes adjusted for inflation with the CPI-U-RS rose 13 percentage points more than incomes adjusted with the CPI-U.

Unfortunately, even the CPI-U-RS is likely to overstate inflation since 1969. To begin with, the CPI-U-RS does not tell us how the CPI-U would have changed between 1969 and 1977 if the BLS had been using today's procedures. Since these changes reduced the estimated rate of inflation between 1977 and 1999, they probably would have done the same thing between 1969 and 1977. In addition, the BLS has traditionally estimated price changes by tracking the cost of a market basket that remains fixed for roughly a decade. Because consumers shift their purchasing patterns in response to changes in relative prices, using an outdated market baskct tends to exaggerate the amount of income consumers need to buy a market basket they regard as equivalent to the one they used to buy. The Commerce Department's Bureau of Economic Research, which produces the NIPA, deals with this problem by constructing a 'chain-price' index, in which the market basket for what it calls personal consumption expenditure (PCE) changes every year.

If the PCE market basket included only goods and services that consumers paid for out of their own pockets, we might want to adopt it for estimating changes in real household income. But the PCE market basket also includes some goods and services that consumers do not pay for out of their own income, the most important of which is the portion of medical care financed by Medicare, Medicaid, and employers' share of their workers' health insurance. One way to make the CPI-U-RS and the PCE chain-price index more comparable is to exclude medical services from both indices.[5] The bottom panel of Table 3.1 shows that when we do this for the 1990s, the annual increase in the chain-price index for nonmedical consumption is about 0.6 points less than that in the non-medical CPI-U and 0.3 points less than that in the non-medical CPI-U-RS.

Technical innovation may also cause all these price indices to rise faster than they should. In 1984, for example, the cost of treating a heart attack averaged $11 175 (in 1991 dollars). By 1991 the average cost had risen to $14 772. The BLS treats this change as a price increase. But heart attack victims who were still alive when they reached the hospital lived an average of 70 months in 1991, compared to 62 months in 1984 (Cutler et al. 1998). Most experts attribute this increase to technical progress. Each extra month of life expectancy thus cost about ($14 772 – 11 175)/8 = $450. Most patients and their families would presumably have thought this an acceptable price. If so, the increased cost of treatment was not a true price increase. Instead, it was analogous to the increased cost of 'motor vehicles' that occurs when people start buying tinted windows or switch from Toyotas to BMWs.

We have no way of knowing whether Cutler et al.'s (1998) findings would recur if we studied a random sample of medical price changes. The key point is that *some* part of the increase in the CPI-U-RS is probably attributable to improvements in the quality of goods and services. In other cases, of course, quality has deteriorated. Computerized menus for answering telephone calls are an obvious and irritating example. Declines in quality are probably less common than improvements, but it is hard to be sure.

Noncash Benefits

Means-tested noncash government benefits increased rapidly between 1965 and 1980, but the Census Bureau did not begin collecting data on such benefits until 1979. Since 1979 the March CPS has included questions about noncash income (including owner-occupied housing), and the Census Bureau has tried to estimate their cash value to recipients. The Bureau assigns food stamps their face value. It values housing subsidies by estimating the difference between a subsidized unit's market value and what tenants actually pay. It values Medicare and Medicaid by estimating how much they reduce beneficiaries' out-of-pocket medical spending. The Bureau's approach to medical benefits is especially controversial. It approximates the increase in recipients' nonmedical standard of living, but it assigns no value to the extra medical services that beneficiaries consume when they are covered.[6]

Table 3.2 compares trends in after-tax money and nonmoney income to trends in pretax money income. Taxes and noncash benefits make the distribution of resources per capita look far more equal. One simple measure of inequality is the ratio of mean income in the top quintile to mean income in the bottom quintile. Shifting from pretax money income to after-tax money and nonmoney income lowered this ratio by more than a third in 1999. But taking account of taxes and noncash benefits has a quite modest effect on post-1979 trends. After-tax money and nonmoney incomes rose a little faster (or fell a little less) than pretax money income for all groups. This was especially true for low-income children, whose income after-tax money and nonmoney income rose about 6 per cent more than their pretax money income.[7]

We have no data on after-tax money and nonmoney income in 1969, but we know that the number of families receiving noncash benefits grew faster in the 1970s than in either the 1980s or the 1990s. Food stamps became a national program in 1972, and real program outlays per capita were 14 times higher in 1979 than in 1969. The percentage of low-income children in federally subsidized housing roughly doubled, and the value of the subsidy to the average tenant also rose.[8] Real per capita Medicaid outlays rose by a factor of 2.5 during these years. The Census Bureau's estimates suggest that these three programs raised low-income children's pretax household income by about a sixth in 1979. Our best guess is that they raised children's pretax household income by only 3 per cent in 1969.[9] We do not know how the distribution of taxes and other benefits changed

Table 3.2   Effect of noncash income and taxes on per capita resources of children's households, by income quintile and year (incomes in 1999 CPI-U-RS dollars)

Income concept and quintile	Year				Percentage growth by decade		
	1969	1979	1989	1999	1970s	1980s	1990s
Pretax money income per capita							
Bottom quintile	2462	2544	2378	2830	3.3	−6.5	19.0
Middle quintile	7579	9351	9967	11049	23.4	6.6	10.9
Top quintile	17620	21309	25909	33790	20.9	21.6	30.4
Ratio of top to bottom quintile	7.2	8.4	10.9	11.9			
After-tax money and nonmoney income per capita*							
Bottom quintile	NA	3226	3123	3789	NA	−3.2	21.3
Middle quintile	NA	8506	9161	10577	NA	7.7	15.5
Top quintile	NA	17121	21079	27936	NA	23.1	32.5
Ratio of top to bottom quintile	NA	5.3	6.7	7.4			

Note: *Census definition 14.

Source: Author's tabulations from the March Current Population Survey.

55

during these years, but if they remained unchanged, low-income children's real incomes would have risen by about 14 per cent between 1969 and 1979 rather than by 2 per cent, as Figure 3.2 indicates.

Changes in Household Size

In 1969 the average child's household included 2.2 adults and 2.3 other children under 18. By 1999 the average child's household included only 2.1 adults and 1.4 other children. The total number of people in children's households therefore fell by 18 per cent (from 5.5 to 4.5 individuals). Most of this change occurred during the 1970s. Figure 3.1 ignored this change. Figure 3.2 assumed that an 18 per cent reduction in household size implied an 18 per cent reduction in the household's economic needs. This adjustment is likely to overstate the material benefits of reducing household size, because it ignores economies of scale. A household composed of four does not need twice as many kitchens as a household of two. Nor does the household of four need twice as many automobiles or clothes dryers as the household of two.

Economists have devised various 'equivalence scales' that seek to determine how much money households of different sizes need to be equally well off.[10] It is easy to determine the amount of income that makes a family of four comparable to a family of two in some specific respect, such as the size of its TV set. But an equivalence scale that equalizes families on one measure of well-being is not especially likely to equalize them on other measures. If we want to construct an overall equivalence scale we need some more general criterion for comparing families of different sizes. Economists sometimes solve this problem by assuming that families of different sizes have the same tastes and then asking what income level generates similar expenditure patterns. But people often live in households of different sizes because their tastes differ. People have children, for example, because they would rather spend their income on eating at home with their children than on taking their spouse to a restaurant. People who value restaurants highly are likely to have smaller families than those who do not, so we cannot assume that families of different sizes are equally well off when they spend the same fraction of their food budget on restaurant meals.

If our goal is to predict adults' well-being, adjusting for how many children they have makes no more sense than adjusting for how many cars they have. Both children and cars are expensive, and both leave adults with less money for everything else. But we would not want to conclude that a couple with an income of $40 000 was poorer if they had two cars than if they had one, and nor should we conclude that they are poorer when they have two children rather than one.

If our goal is to predict children's well-being, however, the problem is quite different. Children do not choose to have additional siblings, and we have found no evidence that children benefit from having additional siblings. Additional siblings reduce both a child's material standard of living and the amount of time and attention the child is likely to get from his or her parents. For a child, therefore, per capita household income may be more relevant than total household income. In the absence of solid evidence, however, the best strategy is to track trends in both total and per capita household income and use the two measures to place upper and lower bounds on changes in economic well-being.

Consumption versus Income

The Census Bureau's measure of pretax money income can also provide a misleading picture of changes in the material standard of living if the ratio of personal consumption to income is changing. This can happen when the government finances a growing fraction of personal consumption through noncash benefits like Medicare and Medicaid. It can also happen when tax rates, saving rates, or interest rates change.[11] Table 3.3 compares NIPA estimates of total personal consumption in the nation as a whole to Census Bureau estimates of total pretax money income in the nation as a whole. This ratio has risen steadily since 1969.[12]

Conclusions about Income and Consumption

None of the problems discussed in this section has a definitive solution. There is no general agreement about how one should adjust income for changes in prices, changes in household size, or changes in noncash benefits. Conclusions about changes in households' material living standard therefore need to be tested against other sources of evidence. The next section uses data on changes in the material standard of living to see whether Figure 3.1 or Figure 3.2 tells a more accurate story about changes in children's economic resources over the past generation.

TRENDS IN CHILDREN'S LIVING CONDITIONS

If low-income children's real income declined between 1969 and 1989, as Figure 3.1 implies, children should have experienced more material hardship and should have had less access to luxuries of various kinds in 1989 than in 1969. If low-income children's real income was relatively flat between 1969 and 1989, as Figure 3.2 suggests, we should not see much

Table 3.3 Growth in income, consumption, and population, 1969–1999 (all estimates are in 1999 dollars, using the PCE chain-price index)

Type of measure	Year				Percentage growth by decade		
	1969	1979	1989	1999	1970s	1980s	1990s
Resources per capita in 1999 PCE dollars							
Pretax money income (Census)	11 689	14 746	17 628	20 571	26.2	19.5	16.7
Personal consumption expenditure (NIPA)	11 696	14 903	18 599	22 391	27.4	24.8	20.4
Ratio (Row 2/Row 1)	1.001	1.011	1.055	1.088	1.0	4.4	3.2
Population (in millions)							
Individuals[a]	202.7	225.1	247.4	279.1	11.0	9.9	12.8
Households	63.4	80.8	93.3	104.7	27.4	15.6	12.2
Individuals/households[b]	3.20	2.79	2.65	2.67	−12.8	−4.9	0.6

Notes:
a. Includes the institutional population and members of the armed forces living on bases and overseas.
b. Because the count of individuals includes those who did not live in households, the ratio of individuals to households exceeds the size of the average household.

Sources: Consumption and population data and the PCE price index are from Council of Economic Advisers (2002). Numbers of households and their mean income are from US Bureau of the Census (2000a).

change in material hardship or in the availability of luxuries. Likewise, if children's income rose faster in the middle of the distribution than at the bottom, as both Figures 3.1 and 3.2 suggest, living conditions should have improved more among middle-income than low-income children.

To investigate these questions we look at changes in housing conditions, automobile ownership, air conditioning, telephone service, physician visits, and food consumption. We did not select these items because they seemed ideal from some theoretical perspective. We selected them because the federal government has collected data on these items at the household level since the late 1960s or early 1970s. Federal agencies tend to be more interested in the distribution of what the public regards as necessities than in the distribution of what the public regards as luxuries. As a result, the government seldom starts collecting data on the availability of a good or service until most affluent families already have it. For this reason we focus on trends among low- and middle-income children, ignoring high-income children.

We report the percentage of children in the top, middle, and bottom income quintiles whose household has a given problem or amenity. Appendix Table 3A.1 shows changes in mean income for each of these three groups. The trends are very close to those shown in Figures 3.1 and 3.2, except that the mean of the top quintile rises even more than the 90th percentile, because the biggest gains were at the very top. The official child poverty rate, which is based on the CPI-U, was 14.0 per cent in 1969, 16.4 per cent in 1979, 19.6 per cent in 1989, and 16.9 per cent in 1999 (US Bureau of the Census 2000b, Table B-2), so most children in the bottom quintile are officially poor in all periods.

Our initial analyses of living standards classified children by both per capita income and total household income. Roughly half our measures were more strongly correlated with total income than with per capita income, while the opposite was true for the other half. Because trends were very similar regardless of which measure we used, we present only the results based on total household income, which is more familiar.

To facilitate comparisons between changes in living conditions and changes in income, we report changes in living conditions for two separate periods. The first period starts in either 1969 or 1973 and runs through 1989. All our income data suggest that low-income children either lost ground or made no gains during these years. (Children's real income appears to be fairly flat between 1969 and 1973, so trends between 1973 and 1979 are quite similar to those between 1969 and 1979.[13]) Our second period starts in 1989 and runs through the late 1990s. Our income data suggest that children at all income levels made gains during these years.

Table 3.4   Characteristics of children's housing, by income quintile, 1973–1999

Measure and year	Quintile of total income			All
	Bottom	Middle	Top	
Per cent in multifamily dwellings				
1973	26.6	14.3	7.1	16.1
1979	38.1	13.0	4.3	17.1
1989	39.8	15.0	6.1	19.3
1999	37.7	13.5	4.0	17.8
Percentage point change				
1973–89	13.2	0.7	−1.0	3.2
1989–99	−2.1	−1.5	−2.1	−1.5
Per cent in rental units				
1973	56.1	24.7	9.8	29.6
1979	66.8	22.4	7.1	30.1
1989	72.7	32.8	8.9	36.9
1999	68.5	28.3	6.6	33.4
Percentage point change				
1973–89	16.6	8.1	−0.9	7.3
1989–99	−4.2	−4.5	−2.3	−3.5

Source: American Housing Survey: unweighted cell sizes are about 4000 in 1973, 4900 in 1979, 2900 in 1989, and 3400 in 1999.

Housing Conditions

We examine four attributes of children's housing: the overall character and ownership of the housing unit, whether the unit was crowded, whether it had various kinds of physical deficiencies, and whether it was located in a dangerous neighborhood. Our data come from the American Housing Survey (AHS), which began in 1973.

Type of housing and ownership
The fraction of low-income children living in rural areas and small towns declined during the 1970s and 1980s, while the fraction living in the more densely populated central cities of metropolitan areas grew. As a result, low-income children were more likely to live in apartment buildings and less likely to live in single-family homes. The fraction of low-income children living in multifamily buildings rose from 26.6 per cent in 1973 to 38.1 per cent in 1979 and then more or less leveled off (see Table 3.4). There was no clear trend in the proportion of middle-income children living in multifam-

ily units. Not surprisingly, the shift into apartment buildings was accompanied by a decline in home ownership (see Table 3.4). Home ownership also declined among more affluent parents during the 1980s, perhaps because real interest rates were unusually high.[14] During the 1990s parents at all income levels began buying homes again.

Crowding

Because of the shift to central cities, low-income children's homes had slightly fewer rooms in 1979 and 1989 than in 1973. But the number of people living in low-income children's households fell even faster than the number of rooms, so the proportion of low-income children in what the Census Bureau calls crowded conditions (more than one person per room) dropped sharply (see Table 3.5).

Neither mean household size nor the mean number of rooms changed much during the 1980s, so crowding did not change much either.[15] During the 1990s, in contrast, children's households got smaller at all income levels while their homes got larger. While many critics of the 1996 welfare reform legislation feared that it would force more single mothers to 'double up', Table 3.5 suggests that crowding declined even among children in the poorest quintile.

Housing problems

We used the AHS to examine seven housing problems: holes in the floor, cracks or holes in walls or ceilings, a leaky roof, broken plaster or peeling paint in an area of more than one square foot, not having a sewer or septic system, not having electric outlets in every room, and not having complete plumbing. Complete plumbing means having hot and cold running water, a sink, a toilet, and a shower or tub. Plumbing must be indoors and for the exclusive use of household members to count, but until the 1980s it could be down the hall rather than inside an apartment.

Table 3.6 shows that the mean number of problems in low-income children's homes declined steadily between 1973 and 1999. The decline between 1973 and 1989 was somewhat larger than the decline between 1989 and 1999 in both absolute and percentage terms. This pattern holds for most specific problems as well (see Appendix Table 3A.2). Declines during the 1970s and 1980s suggest that even Figure 3.2 may underestimate the improvement in low-income children's material standard of living during these years.

Disparities in the number of problems experienced by low- and middle-income children also narrowed between 1973 and 1999, even though both Figures 3.1 and 3.2 suggest that the income gap widened. Because the housing problems included in our index are all relatively unusual, across-

Table 3.5   Crowding in children's housing, by income quintile, 1973–1999

Measure and year	Quintile of total income			
	Bottom	Middle	Top	All
Mean household size				
1973	5.2	5.0	5.3	5.1
1979	4.5	4.7	5.0	4.7
1989	4.5	4.6	4.7	4.6
1999	4.2	4.5	4.6	4.5
Percentage point change				
1973–89	−0.7	−0.4	−0.6	−0.5
1989–99	−0.3	−0.1	−0.1	−0.1
Mean number of rooms				
1973	5.1	5.7	7.1	5.9
1979	4.9	5.8	7.1	5.9
1989	4.9	5.8	7.3	5.9
1999	5.1	6.1	7.5	6.2
Percentage point change				
1973–89	−0.2	0.1	0.2	0.0
1989–99	0.2	0.3	0.2	0.3
Per cent with more than one person				
per room				
1973	38.1	23.4	11.1	24.4
1979	29.2	17.8	10.0	19.3
1989	27.0	17.2	7.4	17.8
1999	18.2	10.9	4.4	11.7
Percentage point change				
1973–89	−11.1	−6.2	−3.7	−6.6
1989–99	−8.8	−6.3	−3.0	−6.1

Source: American Housing Survey.

the-board improvements almost inevitably imply larger absolute declines among the least affluent, because the more affluent are more likely to start off in problem-free housing. But the percentage decline in housing problems is also larger among low-income children. This result is more surprising, since the percentage increase in income is much greater for middle- than for low-income children.

Safety
Although low-income children's housing had fewer physical problems in 1989 than in 1973, Table 3.7 shows that the percentage of low-income parents who described crime as a serious problem in their neighborhood more than

Table 3.6   Mean number of housing problems experienced by children, by income quintile, 1973–1999

Year	Quintile of total income			
	Bottom	Middle	Top	All
1973	0.81	0.26	0.14	0.37
1979	0.72	0.23	0.15	0.34
1989	0.54	0.24	0.16	0.29
1999	0.39	0.22	0.15	0.24
Difference				
1973–89	−0.26	−0.02	0.02	−0.08
1989–99	−0.16	−0.02	−0.01	−0.05
Percentage change				
1973–89	−33	−7	14	−21
1989–99	−29	−8	−9	−18

Note: The seven problems included in this measure are holes in the floor, cracks or holes in the ceiling or walls, broken plaster or peeling paint, a leaky roof, not having a sewer or septic system, not having electric outlets in every room, and incomplete plumbing. See the text for details and Appendix Table 3A.2 for item by item data and for additional items not included in the index.

Source: American Housing Survey.

Table 3.7   Percentage of children in neighborhoods where parents say crime is a serious problem, by income quintile, 1973–1999

Year	Income quintile			
	Bottom	Middle	Top	All
1973	14.3	13.5	13.8	13.6
1979	24.8	18.7	17.0	19.7
1989	31.9	23.1	17.7	24.2
1999	23.0	14.5	9.3	15.6
Percentage point change				
1973–89	17.6	9.6	3.9	10.6
1989–99	−8.9	−8.6	−8.4	−8.6

Source: American Housing Survey.

Table 3.8 Victimization rates per 100000 by age and income quintile, 1979–1981 versus 1988–1990

Crime and Year	All persons over the age of 12				Persons between the ages of 12 and 20			
	Bottom quintile	Middle quintile	Top quintile	All	Bottom quintile	Middle quintile	Top quintile	All
Rape								
1979–81	205	82	58	104	467	163	117	228
1988–90	137	62	24	64	268	118	87	167
Percentage change	−33.2	−24.4	−58.6	38.5	−42.6	−27.6	−25.6	−26.8
Robbery								
1979–81	1140	600	464	672	1779	1095	844	1107
1988–90	978	383	325	520	1498	625	725	968
Percentage change	−14.2	−36.2	−30.0	−22.6	−15.8	−42.9	−14.1	−12.6
Aggravated assault								
1979–81	1323	998	775	997	2896	1770	1504	1887
1988–90	1262	779	560	823	2743	1894	1363	1933
Percentage change	−4.6	−21.0	−27.7	−17.5	−5.3	7.0	−9.4	2.4
Simple assault								
1979–81	2096	1703	1620	1748	4251	3094	3236	3300
1988–90	2153	1552	1186	1534	4587	3803	3352	3722
Percentage change	2.7	−8.9	−26.8	−12.2	7.9	22.9	3.6	12.8

Source: National Criminal Victimization Survey (tabulations by David Knutson). Unweighted cell sizes for robbery and aggravated assault are at least 20000. Cell sizes for rape are roughly half as large.

doubled during these years. Concern about neighborhood crime increased far more among low-income parents than among more affluent parents.

But while low-income parents were more likely to believe that crime was a serious problem in their neighborhood, their beliefs do not seem to have been based on their own experiences. The National Crime Victimization Survey (NCVS) asks household members whether they have been victims of rape, robbery, burglary, and assault within the past six months. Table 3.8 compares responses in 1979–81 to responses in 1988–90.[16] The first four columns cover everyone over the age of 12. The last four columns are limited to individuals between the ages of 12 and 20. The fraction of low-income households reporting a rape or robbery fell noticeably during the 1980s. There was no clear trend in assault. Thus while low-income parents clearly believed that their neighborhoods were more dangerous, it is not clear why they felt this way. Growing emphasis on violent crime in the nightly news may have been a factor.

Motor Vehicles

Physical mobility is important to both children and adults. In America, mobility depends to a great extent on motor vehicles, although this is some-what less true in central cities than elsewhere. Table 3.9 shows trends in motor vehicle ownership by household income. These data come from the decennial census.[17] The fraction of low-income children whose parents owned a car or truck did not change much during the 1970s, even though urbanization brought low-income parents closer to public transportation and the jump in gasoline prices made operating a vehicle more expensive. During the 1980s, the proportion of low-income children living in house-holds with at least one motor vehicle rose slightly, and the proportion in households with two or more vehicles jumped by almost half, from 17.6 to 25.8 per cent. The number of middle-income parents with two or more cars also jumped by almost half. These trends are hard to reconcile with the hypothesis that low-income children's households had less purchasing power in 1989 than in 1973. Indeed, they are hard to reconcile with the hypothesis implicit in Figure 3.2, namely that low-income households' purchasing power was flat during this period.

Air Conditioning

Air conditioning is one of the few luxuries on which we have data. It was far from universal in 1973, even among the affluent, and it spread rapidly during the 1970s, 1980s, and 1990s. The fraction of households without air conditioning fell by roughly three-fifths between 1973 and 1999, and the

*Table 3.9   Percentage of children in households with motor vehicles, air
conditioners, and telephones, by income quintile, 1973–1999*

Measure and year	Income quintile			
	Bottom	Middle	Top	All
At least one motor vehicle				
1970	68.1	95.6	98.8	90.1
1980	68.4	95.7	98.4	90.0
1990	69.7	97.0	99.0	91.1
Percentage point change				
1970–90	1.6	1.4	0.2	1.0
Two or more motor vehicles				
1970	16.6	44.4	74.8	45.1
1980	17.6	50.7	76.6	49.0
1990	25.8	75.3	92.9	67.4
Percentage point change				
1970–90	9.2	30.9	18.1	22.3
Air conditioning				
1973	30.5	48.0	62.0	46.8
1979	33.0	54.7	65.0	51.7
1989	48.2	67.3	75.7	65.2
1999	69.2	78.4	84.5	78.2
Percentage point change				
1973–89	17.7	19.3	13.7	18.4
1989–99	21.0	11.1	8.8	13.0
Telephone service				
Census				
1970	63.9	91.7	98.5	86.4
1980	76.2	95.8	99.0	91.6
1990	74.2	96.5	99.5	91.9
AHS				
1979	72.7	94.7	98.4	89.8
1989	74.0	95.7	98.6	91.2
1999	93.0	98.2	98.4	97.0
Percentage point change				
Census: 1970–80	12.3	4.1	0.5	5.2
Census: 1980–90	−2.0	0.7	0.5	0.3
AHS: 1979–89	1.3	1.0	0.2	1.4
AHS: 1989–99	19.0	2.5	−0.2	5.8

Sources: Decennial Census and American Housing Survey.

proportionate decline was fairly uniform across the entire income distribution. One reason for this change was that the cost of air conditioners fell relative to most other goods and services.

Telephones

Table 3.9 shows data on telephone service from both the decennial census (1970 to 1990) and the AHS (1979 to 1999).[18] The census suggests that the proportion of low-income children in households without telephones fell by a third during the 1970s. The census suggests that this trend reversed in the 1980s, while the AHS suggests that it continued, but both agree that the change was small. During the 1990s the fraction of low-income children in households without telephones fell dramatically, from 26 to 7 per cent. Middle-income children's access to telephones also increased during the 1970s and 1990s. The absolute changes were smaller than among low-income children, but the percentage reduction in the chances of not having a home telephone was about the same for both groups (roughly four-fifths between 1970 and 1999).

Doctor Visits

Most pediatricians believe that children should have a medical checkup at least once a year, especially when they are young. The proportion of young children who have seen a doctor within the past year is therefore a widely used measure of whether parents are willing and able to ensure that their children get adequate medical attention. The National Health Interview Survey (NHIS) has collected data on doctor visits since the 1950s, but the NHIS questionnaire changed between 1980 and 1982, so changes during this interval may be methodological artifacts. The survey changed again in 1998, so we have no trend data after 1996.

Table 3.10 shows that the percentage of low-income children who had not visited a doctor within the past year declined sharply between 1970 and 1980. Both the absolute and proportional declines were greater among low-income children than among the more affluent. The same pattern recurs when we look at the total number of visits during the past year (data not shown). We suspect, but cannot prove, that this improvement was partly attributable to broader Medicaid coverage, which made it easier for doctors and clinics to survive in poor neighborhoods. This change, in combination with urbanization, made medical care more physically as well as economically accessible in 1980 than in 1970.

Doctor visits continued to become more common among low-income children between 1982 and 1989, but the change was tiny, both in absolute

*Table 3.10   Percentage of children who had not visited a doctor in the past
year, by income quintile: 1970–1996*

Year and child's age	Income quintile		
	Bottom	Middle	Top
1970–80			
Children under 7			
1970	26.5	15.9	9.4
1980	11.9	10.2	7.2
Percentage point change	−14.6	−5.7	−2.2
Ratio of 1980 to 1970	0.45	0.64	0.77
Children aged 7–17			
1970	45.1	36.9	25.7
1980	32.7	30.8	26.0
Percentage point change	−12.4	−6.1	0.3
Ratio of 1980 to 1970	0.73	0.83	1.01
1982–89			
Children under 7			
1982	14.4	11.8	8.4
1989	14.0	10.9	5.6
Percentage point change	−0.4	−0.9	−2.8
Ratio of 1989 to 1982	0.97	0.92	0.67
Children aged 7–17			
1982	32.6	32.3	23.0
1989	31.4	27.3	17.5
Percentage point change	−1.2	−5.0	−5.5
Ratio of 1989 to 1982	0.96	0.85	0.76
1989–96			
Children under 7			
1989	14.0	10.9	5.6
1996	12.7	10.9	6.8
Percentage point change	−1.3	0	1.2
Ratio of 1996 to 1989	0.91	1.00	1.21
Children aged 7–17			
1989	31.4	27.3	17.5
1996	29.0	27.9	18.0
Percentage point change	−2.4	0.6	0.5
Ratio of 1996 to 1989	0.92	1.02	1.03

Source: National Health Interview Survey (tabulations by David Knutson). Cell sizes for
bottom deciles range from 1000 to 1400 for children under seven and from 1600 to 2500 for
children aged 7–17.

terms and relative to changes among more-affluent children. Low-income children's chances of seeing a doctor improved more during the 1990s than during the 1980s, but not much more. The improvement among low-income children during the 1990s was, however, a contrast with the trend among more-affluent children, whose chances of visiting a doctor declined slightly between 1989 and 1996.[19]

Food Consumption

We do not have good data on changes in what children eat. The National Food Consumption Survey (NFCS), which asked homemakers what they served their families in 1955, 1965, and 1977, found that the diets of the poor and the affluent became more alike between 1965 and 1977 (Jencks and Mayer 1987, Table 3.2). The NFCS was repeated in 1987, but the response rate was less than 40 per cent, so we did not analyze the 1987 data.

Parents' reports of what they spent on food are also quite problematic. Few households keep detailed accounts, and many respondents round their estimates of grocery spending to numbers like $50 a week.[20] Nor do all surveys interview the individual with primary responsibility for grocery shopping. Even when a survey does interview the primary shopper, he or she seldom knows how much other members of the household spend on the food, especially if they consume it away from home. Survey estimates of poor households' grocery spending are also problematic because survey questions seldom include clear instructions about how respondents should treat food stamps. This problem was especially severe during the 1970s, when poor families had to make copayments for food stamps.

The quality of households' reports on food expenditure also appears to have deteriorated over time. When we compared the data collected from the Gallup Survey, the Consumer Expenditure Survey (CES), and the Panel Study of Income Dynamics (PSID) to the estimates of total food expenditure in the NIPA, which are based on sales figures, the household surveys appeared to miss at least a quarter of total food consumption, and the ratio fell between the early 1970s and the early 1990s. Nonetheless, we present household data from two sources: the PSID and the CES. Our measure of food expenditure is the sum of a family's reported expenditures at home and away from home.

The PSID began in 1968 and tracks households (including new households formed by members of the initial sample or their descendants) over time. It has asked about grocery spending in most years.[21] The data for 1969 to 1971 differ from the data for later years, because the PSID asked respondents whether their estimate had included any money spent on alcohol or cigarettes, and if so, how much was spent on those items. The

PSID subtracted these items to get a 'pure' food measure. These questions were dropped in later years. The data for the 1970s are compromised by a series of changes in the treatment of food stamps. The only two internally consistent time series, in our judgment, run from 1969 to 1971 and from 1981 to 1991.[22]

The US Department of Agriculture (USDA) has found that when large and small families spend the same amount per person (which they seldom do), the large families achieve higher levels of nutritional adequacy than the small families. Putting the same point slightly differently we can say that there appear to be some economies of scale in food consumption, so that a couple with four children do not need to spend twice as much as a single parent with two children to achieve the same level of nutritional adequacy. Households have become smaller since 1969, so these economies of scale have diminished slightly. As a result, households need to spend slightly more per capita to attain the same level of dietary adequacy. To correct for this, we compare each family's total food spending to the USDA 'thrifty' food budget for a family of the relevant size. (This is also the budget used to calculate food stamp allotments.) The elasticity of the thrifty budget with respect to family size is 0.84, which comes from an analysis of the expenditure levels required to ensure that households of different sizes purchase diets of equal nutritional value (Kerr and Peterkin, 1975).[23]

In 1991 the thrifty food budget for two adults, a teenager, and a 10-year-old was $21.35 per person per month. NIPA data indicated that per capita food expenditures averaged $49.47 per person per month, so the thrifty budget was a bit less than half the per capita mean. The USDA adjusts the thrifty food budget for price changes using the BLS fixed-weight index for food consumed at home, which rose by an average of 6.0 per cent a year between 1969 and 1991. Like any fixed-weight index, this one overstates the increase in expenditure required to buy food of constant palatability or nutritional adequacy, because it ignores the fact that consumers can substitute foods whose price has risen relatively slowly (such as chicken) for foods whose price has risen more rapidly (such as beef). To avoid (or at least minimize) this source of bias we adjust the 1991 thrifty budget using the NIPA chain-price index for food, which rose only 5.7 per cent a year between 1969 and 1991.

Table 3.11 shows the ratio of PSID respondents' estimated monthly expenditure to the thrifty food budget for a household of the relevant size. The first two columns suggest that low-income children ate about 10 per cent better in 1971 than in 1969. There appears to be a sharp decline in low-income parents' food spending between 1971 and 1981, but this could be due to changes in the questionnaire. There was no change between 1981

Table 3.11   *Food expenditures in children's households as a proportion of the 1992 thrifty food budget, by quintile of total income in the PSID*

Income or consumption quintile*	PSID–I		PSID–II		CES	
	1969	1971	1981	1991	1972–73	1989–90
Bottom	0.94	1.04	0.87	0.86	0.87	0.87
Middle	1.13	1.16	1.11	1.08	1.36	1.29
Top	1.53	1.53	1.52	1.50	2.03	2.05
All	1.17	1.20	1.15	1.12	1.39	1.36
Ratio of reported food expenditure per capita to NIPA	0.754	0.761	0.756	0.734	0.711	0.656

Note: *PSID households are allocated to income quintiles on the basis of their mean income for the year in which food expenditures were reported and the previous calendar year. CES expenditures are allocated to quintiles on the basis of their total consumption during the same 12 months for which they reported their food expenditures. CES expenditures are reported quarterly. PSID expenditures are reported annually. The thrifty food budget was adjusted for inflation using the NIPA chain-price index for food, not the CPI index used by the USDA for food stamps.

Source: Tabulations by Tim Veenstra, Judith Levine, and Scott Winship.

and 1991. Food spending followed the same pattern for middle-income families, rising between 1969 and 1971, falling between 1971 and 1981, and changing little between 1981 and 1991. But the changes were less marked for middle- than for low-income families.

To check our PSID results we also compared food expenditures in the 1972–73 CES to expenditures in the 1989–90 CES. Table 3.11 shows that in the CES there is no clear trend in the ratio of food expenditure to need for low-income children. This finding reinforces our suspicion that the change in the PSID between 1971 and 1981 is attributable to changes in the questionnaire. Note, too, that both the PSID and the CES show that the ratio of food expenditure to need fell after 1971 among middle-income children. This decline is unlikely to reflect income constraints. It seems more likely to reflect underreporting.

After many years working with these data we have reluctantly concluded that there is no way of knowing whether the trends shown in Table 3.11 are real. We have included these results only because they constitute one of the few instances in which poor children's material standard of living does not appear to rise and suppressing results at odds with our basic thesis would be hard to defend.

CONCLUSIONS

The CPS suggests that children at all income levels gained ground during the 1990s. Our direct measures of material welfare tell the same story. Children at all income levels gained during the 1990s on almost every measure where improvement was possible. The principal exception was that middle- and high-income children showed no increase in doctor visits during the 1990s.

The CPS presents a much gloomier picture of the 1970s and 1980s. In Figure 3.1 low-income children's real household income declines sharply between 1969 and 1989, while middle-income children's real income stagnates. Even in Figure 3.2 low-income children's real income stagnates during the 1970s and falls somewhat during 1980s, although middle-income children make significant progress.

Direct measures of material welfare present a more optimistic picture than either Figure 3.1 or Figure 3.2. Income data suggest that low-income children's living standards should either decline or stagnate between 1969 and 1989. We do observe declines in home ownership and living in a single-family dwelling. These changes are, however, linked to improvements in most measures of housing quality. Housing problems declined, and so did crowding. Air conditioning and telephones also became more common. Low-income parents felt that their neighborhoods were more crime-ridden, but the proportion who said they had been raped or robbed fell, while the proportion who said they had been assaulted remained constant. The proportion of low-income children in households that owned a motor vehicle was flat, but the proportion in households with two vehicles rose sharply. The percentage of low-income children who had seen a doctor within the past year rose. Food consumption remains a puzzle.

The story for middle-income children in the 1970s and 1980s is also full of ambiguities. Figure 3.1 suggests that middle-income children's real incomes stagnated during the 1970s and 1980s, while Figure 3.2 suggests a substantial increase. When we look at direct measures of the standard of living, we see many improvements during the 1970s but relatively few during the 1980s. Home ownership among middle-income parents rose slightly in the 1970s but declined significantly in the 1980s. Crowding declined in the 1970s and remained unchanged in the 1980s. Housing problems diminished in the 1970s but increased slightly in the 1980s. Air conditioning became more common in both decades, but telephone service rose more in the 1970s. Almost all middle-income parents had motor vehicles by 1970, but the fraction with two vehicles rose modestly in the 1970s and dramatically in the 1980s. Doctor visits for middle-income children increased at all ages in the 1970s but only for children over six in the 1980s. These results suggest that middle-income families' purchasing power rose more during the 1970s than during the 1980s, which is consistent with Figure 3.2 but not with Figure 3.1.

Taken as a whole our findings suggest that census statistics on household income were not a reliable guide to changes in the material standard of living during the last three decades of the twentieth century. Middle- and low-income families made more progress during the 1970s and perhaps even the 1980s than census reports implied. These inconsistencies can be reduced by using the CPI-U-RS rather than the CPI-U, as the Census Bureau now does when it publishes historical statistics on income.[24] Inconsistencies between income statistics and direct measures of material well-being during the 1970s can also be reduced by using per capita household income instead of total household income, but the rationale for this change is weaker.

While income statistics and direct measures of material well-being moved up together during the 1990s, it would be rash to assume that this linkage will persist in the years ahead. Instead, the Census Bureau needs to keep checking the validity of estimated changes in real income by establishing a parallel program to monitor changes in material well-being.

NOTES

*　This chapter was prepared with the support of the Levy Economics Institute of Bard College and the American Academy of Art and Science's Initiative on Children. It was completed while Jencks held a Hewlett Fellowship at the Center for Advanced Study in the Behavioral Sciences supported by the William and Flora Hewlett Foundation. Juliet Schor and the other participants in the Levy Institute conference, 'What Has Happened to the Quality of Life in America and Other Advanced Industrial Nations?' made helpful comments and suggestions. David Knutson, Judith Levine, Ankur Sarin, Timothy Veenstra, and Scott Winship provided valuable research assistance.

1.　For statistics on gross domestic product (GDP) and per capita consumption, see Council of Economic Advisers (2002, Tables B-2 and B-31).

2.　Because of the spread of cohabitation, all our analyses treat households rather than families as the unit of analysis. We weight each household by the number of children under 18 living in it. This means that our results are representative of children, not parents. Suppose, for example, that we observe two couples, one of which has one child and one of which has three children. The average parent in this sample has two children. But the average child lives in a household that includes $[(1)(1)+(3)(3)]/4=2.5$ children. We report the household incomes of children at the 10th, 50th, and 90th percentiles because of CPS changes in the top-coding of income sources during this 30-year interval. Estimates of mean household incomes by quintile can be found in Appendix Table 3A.1.

3.　For a strong statement of this argument see Boskin et al. (1996). For a good introduction to the CPI and its critics, see Schultze and Mackie (2002).

4.　Stewart and Reed (1999) describe the CPI-U-RS in more detail.

5.　Even after excluding medical services the PCE and CPI market baskets are not exactly comparable, but as far as we know the remaining differences are unlikely to have a major impact on estimated price trends.

6. In the early 1980s the Census Bureau estimated the market value of an insurance policy that provided coverage equivalent to state Medicaid programs. In some states, however, Medicaid was worth so much to the elderly that they could end up with an imputed income above the poverty line even if they had no cash income, no food stamps, and no housing subsidy, so this method was dropped.

7. Table 3A.1 shows that the ratio of after-tax money and nonmoney income to pretax money income is essentially the same for total and per capita income. When we calculate trends in per capita household income by quintile we allocate households to quintiles based on their per capita income rather than their total income.

8. Jencks et al. (2002) estimate that the fraction of low-income families receiving some kind of rent subsidy rose from 6.0 per cent in 1969 to 13.5 per cent in 1979.

9. This guess assumes that the value of benefits to the bottom quintile of households with children grew at the same rate as real per capita government outlays on the programs.

10. For a good general review of the large literature on equivalence scales, see Michael and Citro (1995).

11. Both NIPA and BLS exclude taxes and interest payments from 'personal consumption'.

12. We also investigated the ratio of reported consumption to reported income in the CES, but after many years of working with these data we concluded that neither the income data nor the consumption data were of high enough quality to be useful for our purposes.

13. The official child poverty rate rises by 2.4 points between 1969 and 1979. Five-sixths of this increase (2.0 points) occurs after 1973 (US Bureau of the Census 2000b, Table B-2).

14. In the 1970 decennial census 60.6 per cent of low-income children lived in rented housing. This figure rose to 63.1 per cent in 1980. This increase was considerably smaller than the increase observed in AHS data. In the 1990 decennial census 71.9 per cent of low-income children lived in rented housing, so the increase over this decade is similar in the AHS and the census.

15. The decennial census also asks about household size and number of rooms. In 1970, 41.7 per cent of low-income children lived in a home with more than one person per room. This figure dropped to 26.8 per cent in 1980 and was 27.0 per cent in 1990. Thus there appears to have been a decline in crowding in low-income children's homes between 1970 and 1973, after which the trend is the same in census and AHS data.

16. The NCVS began in 1973, but we were unable to make the pre- and post-1979 data consistent with each other.

17. Micro data from the 2000 Census were not yet available when we completed this paper.

18. AHS data on telephone service is not available for 1973.

19. Parents were somewhat more likely to say that their children had been sick enough to stay home from school or stay in bed in 1989 than in 1970. These reports are hard to interpret in light of the decline in mortality. Staying home from school or going to bed was not a strong predictor of children's doctor visits in any year, and the increase in visits was far larger than one would predict based on the increase in reported sickness (Mayer 1991). Reports of chronic and acute conditions increased faster among low-income than among middle-income children between 1970 and 1980 but the gap stayed constant during the 1980s (Pamuk et al. 1998). The increase in reports of ill health could account for the rise in doctor visits among low-income children or the increase in reports of ill health could be a byproduct of the increase in doctor visits.

20. Rounding means that spending at a given percentile of the distribution, such as the median, can remain unchanged for long periods even though the distribution as a whole is shifting. Rounding can also generate small random errors in quintile means.

21. We omit years in which the PSID did not ask about food expenditure or in which we have no estimate for the value of food stamps. We also omit 1968, because the question was not repeated.

22. A memo describing the many changes in the PSID questions since 1968 is available from the authors on request.

23. In the real world the observed elasticity of food expenditure with respect to family size is always less than 0.84. We have not seen any evidence on whether children in larger families suffer adverse health effects as a result of this shortfall.

24. The Census Bureau still uses the CPI-U to calculate historical trends in poverty, so these remain suspect (see Jencks et al. 2002).

REFERENCES

Boskin, M., E. Dulberger, R. Gordon, Z. Griliches and D. Jorgenson (1996), *Final Report of the Advisory Commission to Study the Consumer Price Index*, Washington, DC: US Government Printing Office.

Bryan, M., and S. Cecchetti (1993), 'The CPI as a measure of inflation', *Economic Review*, **29** (4), The Federal Reserve Bank of Cleveland, pp. 15–24.

Buhmann, B., L. Rainwater, G. Schmauss and T. Smeeding (1998), 'Equivalence scales, well-being, inequality, and poverty: sensitivity estimates across ten countries using the Luxembourg Income Study database', *Review of Income and Wealth*, **34**, 115–42.

Council of Economic Advisers (2002), *Economic Report of the President*, Washington, DC: US Government Printing Office.

Cutler, D., M. McClellan, J. Newhouse and D. Remler (1998), 'Are medical prices declining? Evidence for heart attack treatments', *Quarterly Journal of Economics*, **113** (4), 991–1024.

Jencks, C., and S.E. Mayer (1987), 'Poverty and material hardship: How we made progress while convincing ourselves that we were losing ground', Working paper, Center for Urban Affairs and Poverty Research, Northwestern University, Evanston, IL.

Jencks, C., S.E. Mayer and J. Swingle (2002) 'Why official poverty rates provide no useful information about changes in children's economic welfare', Working paper, Malcolm Wiener Center for Social Policy, Harvard University, Cambridge, MA.

Kerr, R., and B. Peterkin (1975), 'The effect of household size on the cost of diets that are nutritionally equivalent', Washington, DC: US Department of Agriculture, Consumer and Food Economics Institute, CFE (adm) 325.

Mayer, S.E. (1991), 'Are there economic barriers to seeing the doctor?', Working Paper, Harris School of Public Policy Studies, Chicago: University of Chicago.

Michael, R., and C. Citro (eds) (1995), *Measuring Poverty: A New Approach*, Washington, DC: National Academy Press.

Pamuk, E., D. Makuk, K. Heck, C. Reuben and K. Lochner (1998), *Socioeconomic Status Health Chartbook. Health, United States*, Hyattsville, MD: National Center for Health Statistics.

Schultze, C., and C. Mackie (eds) (2002), *At What Price? Conceptualizing and Measuring Cost-of-Living and Price Indexes*, Washington, DC: National Academy Press.

Stewart, K., and S. Reed (1999), 'CPI research series using current methods, 1978–98', *Monthly Labor Review*, June, 29–38.

US Bureau of the Census (2000a), 'Money income in the United States: 1999', *Current Population Reports*, Series P60-209, Washington, DC: US Government Printing Office.

US Bureau of the Census (2000b) 'Poverty in the United States: 1999', *Current Population Reports*, Series P60-210, Washington, DC: US Government Printing Office.

US Bureau of the Census (2002), 'Detailed historical income and poverty tables from the March Current Population Survey 1947–1998', available at: http://www.census.gov.hhes/income/histinc/.

US Department of Labor, Bureau of Labor Statistics (1968), 'Revised equivalence scale for estimating equivalent incomes or budget costs by family type', Bulletin No. 1570–2, Washington, DC: US Government Printing Office.

US Department of Labor, Bureau of Labor Statistics (1999), *Consumer Expenditure Survey: 1980–99*, Internal files.

Appendix Table 3A.1   Total and per capita household income of children under 18 years, by quintile, using different income measures, 1969–1999

Price index, income measure, and year	Total household income			Per capita household income			Price index (1999 = 100)
	Bottom quintile	Middle quintile	Top quintile	Bottom quintile	Middle quintile	Top quintile	
Pretax money income							
CPI-U							
1969	15788	44129	94195	2787	8580	19947	22.0
1979	12704	45122	98691	2728	10030	22856	43.6
1989	10871	44349	109147	2451	10270	26696	74.4
1999	12342	48074	138911	2830	11049	33790	100
CPI-U-RS							
1969	13947	38982	83209	2462	7579	17620	24.9
1979	11844	42067	92010	2544	9351	21309	46.7
1989	10550	43041	105928	2378	9967	25909	76.7
1999	12342	48074	138911	2830	11049	33790	100
Ratio of 1999 to 1969							
CPI-U	0.78	1.09	1.47	1.02	1.29	1.69	4.54
CPI-U-RS	0.88	1.23	1.67	1.15	1.46	1.92	4.01

Appendix Table 3A.1   (continued)

Price index, income measure, and year	Total household income			Per capita household income			Price index (1999 = 100)
	Bottom quintile	Middle quintile	Top quintile	Bottom quintile	Middle quintile	Top quintile	
After-tax money and nonmoney income (Defn 14)							
CPI-U							
1979	15916	41042	79761	3461	9124	18360	43.6
1989	14215	40916	89122	3218	9440	21718	74.4
1999	16561	45956	115387	3789	10577	27936	100
CPI-U-RS							
1979	14839	38263	74362	3226	8506	17117	46.7
1989	13795	39710	86493	3123	9161	21078	76.7
1999	16561	45956	115387	3789	10577	27936	100
1999/1979 income using CPI-U-RS							
Pretax money income	1.04	1.14	1.51	1.11	1.18	1.59	2.14
After-tax money and nonmoney income	1.12	1.20	1.55	1.17	1.24	1.63	2.14

Sources: Author's tabulations from the March Current Population Survey. Households are weighted by the number of children under 18. The CPI-U-RS is from US Bureau of the Census (2000a). The CPI-U is from Council of Economic Advisers (2002). Topcoding varies from year to year, which exaggerates the increase in real income for the top quintile.

*Appendix Table 3A.2   Children's housing problems, by income quintile,
1973–1999*

Measure and year	Quintile of total income			
	Bottom	Middle	Top	All
Incomplete plumbing				
1973	10.8	0.9	0.2	3.0
1979	5.6	1.2	0.3	2.0
1989	3.7	1.9	1.8	2.2
1999	2.4	1.1	0.5	1.2
No sewer or septic system				
1973	7.3	0.6	0.0	2.0
1979	3.4	0.6	0.1	1.1
1989	1.1	0.0	0.0	0.3
1999	0.4	0.0	0.0	0.1
No electrical outlet in one or more rooms				
1973	14.0	4.5	2.3	6.3
1979	7.8	3.1	1.8	4.0
1989	5.2	2.5	1.1	2.8
1999	3.2	1.7	1.5	2.1
Holes in floor				
1973	6.8	1.3	0.5	2.6
1979	6.9	1.5	0.6	2.8
1989	4.7	1.1	0.6	1.8
1999	4.5	1.0	0.7	1.7
Cracks or holes in walls or ceiling				
1973	16.3	5.7	2.6	7.9
1979	17.7	4.5	3.0	7.9
1989	16.3	5.7	2.9	7.8
1999	13.5	7.0	3.6	7.9
Broken plaster or peeling paint (>1 sq.ft)				
1973	10.1	5.4	2.7	6.0
1979	15.8	5.1	3.7	7.7
1989	12.2	4.6	2.4	6.0
1999	6.7	3.9	1.6	3.8
Leaky roof				
1973	15.4	7.5	5.7	9.2
1979	14.6	7.4	5.3	8.9
1989	11.2	8.3	7.2	8.5
1999	8.0	7.6	6.6	7.4

Appendix Table 3A.2   (continued)

Measure and year	Quintile of total income			
	Bottom	Middle	Top	All
No air conditioning				
1973	69.5	52.0	38.0	53.2
1979	67.0	45.3	35.0	48.3
1989	51.8	32.7	24.3	34.8
1999	30.8	21.6	15.5	21.8
Mean age of housing unit				
1973	28.1	24.3	20.0	24.1
1979	29.8	24.6	20.1	24.7
1989	29.5	26.1	21.8	26.1
1999	33.4	30.8	24.2	29.4
Housing unit built before 1940				
1973	40.2	31.7	22.3	31.3
1979	38.0	27.3	18.1	27.6
1989	25.9	20.1	14.8	20.8
1999	23.8	20.8	12.5	18.6
Rats or mice				
1973	23.1	11.6	8.1	13.8
1979	25.1	14.2	11.7	15.9
Rats				
1989	14.0	4.8	2.0	6.2
1999	2.5	0.8	0.7	1.3

4. Reassessing the consumer price index: five years after the Boskin Commission

Dean Baker

INTRODUCTION

Federal Reserve Board Chairman Alan Greenspan started one of the more perverse national political debates in recent memory when he told the Senate Finance Committee in late 1994 that the consumer price index (CPI) substantially overstates the true rate of inflation. At the time, the country was facing large budget deficits. Greenspan pointed out that substantial areas of federal spending, most notably Social Security, and federal income tax brackets were indexed to the CPI. This meant that a reduction in the rate of inflation reported by the CPI could potentially reduce federal spending by hundreds of billions of dollars over the next decade and increase revenue by a comparable amount. According to Greenspan, much of the budget shortfall could be eliminated simply by correcting the CPI.

During the next two and a half years, methodological issues in the construction of the CPI were featured prominently in every major budget story, as changing the CPI was assumed to be the key to eliminating the budget deficit. Briefings by the Bureau of Labor Statistics (BLS) on new aggregation formulas for entry-level items and hedonic quality adjustments became 'standing-room only' press events. The Boskin Commission, appointed by the Senate Finance Committee to evaluate the accuracy of the CPI, issued a final report that was, for a brief time, the hottest book in Washington (SFC 1996).

Eventually, the attention to the CPI died down. Part of the reason was political. Cutting Social Security benefits and raising taxes are never popular measures, even if the rationale involves technical issues with the CPI. The interest groups that ordinarily oppose such changes eventually rallied against efforts to tinker with the CPI. Also, the deficit problem largely disappeared by itself, as more rapid economic growth and a surge in tax revenue shifted the deficits to surpluses in short order.

But, there were also serious questions raised about the accuracy of the claims made by the Boskin Commission and others concerning the CPI overstatement of inflation (for example, Moulton and Moses 1997; Madrick 1997; Baker 1997; and Moulton 1996a). Many of the commission's claims concerning an overstatement of inflation in the CPI were not well supported by research. In some cases, the assertion of a bias rested on no more than introspection and casual observation. It was also possible to identify important areas where the commission appeared to neglect evidence that suggested the CPI could understate inflation. In short, the case against the CPI was far less compelling than the Boskin Commission's final report implied.

Now that nearly five years have passed and the political heat around this issue has virtually disappeared, it is worth reassessing the evidence. For economists, there is still a great deal at stake. Our whole understanding of economic history and the growth process would be radically altered if the commission's assessment is largely correct. Annual economic growth in the United States would have been approximately 1.0 percentage point higher than current data indicate. This means that we were much poorer in the recent past than is generally recognized and will be far richer in the near future than current projections suggest is possible. The same would be true for all other countries as well, since few of the criticisms of the CPI would apply to the US measure alone.

A vast amount of economic research on other topics would also be called into question. For example, lifetime saving and consumption patterns would look quite different if the true rate of inflation has been 1.0 per cent less, on average, than what the current data show. Real interest rates and returns on investment would also be far higher than is generally recognized. Macroeconomic studies of the impact of inflation on growth will also have to be reassessed, if inflation has generally been reported as being far higher than its true rate. Industry studies, which examined issues such as the effects of deregulation, would also be called into question, since the reference point for such studies is usually the change in the overall price level. In fact, there would be few areas of economic research which would be left untouched by a large downward adjustment to the consumer price index. For this reason, it is important to come to grips with the Boskin Commission's claim, even if it is less relevant to the current political situation.

CATEGORIZING THE ISSUES

Most of the debate on the CPI has centered on the types of bias identified by the Boskin Commission: formula bias, substitution bias, retail-outlet substitution bias, quality bias, and new-product bias. While this categorization makes important distinctions between potential sources of bias, it tends to focus the debate too narrowly. In principle, the Boskin Commission was examining the extent to which the CPI served as an accurate measure of the change in the cost of living, the amount of money that is necessary to keep the average consumer at the same level of well-being.[1] While the types of bias identified by the commission would all be relevant to any sort of cost-of-living index, maintaining a level of well-being involves a range of factors that were largely neglected by the Boskin Commission.

One of the key assumptions in the Boskin Commission's assessment of the CPI as a measure of the cost of living is that it is possible to evaluate the cost of living by examining the price and quality of goods and services apart from the context in which they are consumed. This implies that the quality of publicly provided goods and services and the natural and social environment can be assumed to remain constant. This is a rather heroic assumption, and the failure of the commission to seriously consider this point limited the value of its analysis of the CPI as a measure of the cost of living.

There are numerous examples of situations in which changes in the natural or social environment, or the quality of publicly provided goods and services, could make large differences in the cost of living. The spread of automobiles, and the restructuring of cities to accommodate them, has made individuals who do not have an automobile unambiguously worse off than they were in years before car ownership became common. An accurate cost-of-living index would show some increase reflecting the new need for an automobile to keep one's level of well-being constant.

Similarly, the spread of the Internet as a means of communication has made households without access to the Internet worse off. They are now being excluded from an important source of communication. Information that may have previously been available through other sources now travels largely on the Internet. In addition, they may find it more difficult to maintain social contacts, if their friends come to rely on the Internet for communication, while they lack access. Again, a true cost-of-living index would show an increase in the cost of living based on the need of individuals to pay for Internet access to keep their well-being constant.

There are numerous other examples where the physical or social environment and provision of public goods can make a large impact on the cost of living, if it is defined as maintaining a level of well-being. The quality and accessibility of public schools, parks and recreational facilities, clean drinking water, and crime-free neighborhoods are all factors that would have a large impact on people's well-being. An accurate cost-of-living index would have to take account of all of these factors.

However difficult it might be to try to quantify some of the effects noted above, these effects, at least in principle, are amenable to inclusion in the construction of a cost-of-living index. They can be perceived of as individualistic, in the sense that the well-being or harm derived from these factors can in principle be assessed by examining their impact in isolation. There is a much greater problem in constructing a cost-of-living index if well-being is inherently a relative concept, in other words, if the well-being that individuals derive from consuming a bundle of goods is inherently linked to the consumption patterns of others as argued by Thorstein Veblen or Krugman (1996). In this case, there is no basis for constructing an index, since well-being for individuals would depend on their relative position in society, not an absolute level of consumption.

It is important to recognize that there is no theoretical justification for excluding relative factors, or Veblen effects, from a cost-of-living index. The only basis for such an index is some implicit concept of utility. If individuals derive utility from their relative consumption, rather than their absolute consumption, then any cost-of-living index that excludes the effects of relative consumption is not measuring the cost of living. Such an index would lack any theoretical foundation. Whether the effects of relative consumption patterns on well-being are sufficiently small that they can be ignored is an empirical matter, not something that can be determined a priori on theoretical grounds.

The questions raised concerning the physical and social environment in which consumption takes place are quite complex. The issues raised by the importance of relative patterns of consumption are even more complex. In both cases, it is questionable whether these topics can be well addressed by standard economic analysis. Clearly they have not been to date either in the construction of the CPI by the BLS, or by the critics of the CPI. This chapter will examine these issues only to establish their importance to individuals' well-being. The fact that these factors are important, and do not lend themselves easily, or at all, to standard modes of economic analysis, argues against efforts to treat the CPI as a cost-of-living index. The CPI was designed by the BLS as a price index, and this is how it is best regarded, since economists lack the expertise and possibly the theoretical basis for constructing a genuine cost-of-living index.

The remainder of this chapter is divided into four sections. First, we examine how the social and physical structure in which consumption takes place affects individuals' well-being. Second, we assess the importance of relative consumption in individuals' well-being. The next and largest section examines the types of biases noted in the Boskin Commission's report, and assesses the evidence for its claims. Finally, some concluding comments on the accuracy of the CPI as a price index are presented.

CONSUMPTION: THE PHYSICAL AND SOCIAL INFRASTRUCTURE

In order for the CPI to provide a useful measure of the cost of living, it must be the case that the changes in the physical and social infrastructure, including the changes in publicly provided goods, are sufficiently small that their impact on well-being can be ignored. There is little reason to assume that this is the case. This section briefly examines some of the ways in which the changes in infrastructure in recent years can be viewed as important. The factors discussed will exclude issues of relative consumption (although these cannot be completely separated), which will be dealt with in the next section.

Table 4.1 shows each of the major categories within the CPI, along with their relative importance in the index, and lists some of the ways in which changes in the physical and social infrastructure over the last half-century could be an important factor in the well-being derived from the consumption of the goods and services in each category. As can be seen, there is no area of consumption in which it can be assumed that these changes are not at least potentially quite large.

The discussion below is necessarily largely anecdotal. It would be difficult, if not impossible, to rigorously quantify the impact of many of these effects. The purpose of the discussion is not to argue that there has been a general pattern to these effects that would lead the CPI to either understate or overstate the true increase in the cost of living. Rather, the purpose is to establish that these effects are likely to be large, and that changes in the physical and social infrastructure cannot be ignored in a serious analysis of the cost of living.

The first category in the table is food and beverages. The two items listed here are the increased need to consume food away from home, as a result of an increase in working hours per adult, and changes in access to clean drinking water. The first effect is the result of the increasing number of two-earner households, or families headed by a single adult. The percentage of families in which the woman was not in the paid labor force fell from 67.1 per cent in 1951 to 29.5 per cent in 1998 (Mishel et al. 2001, Table 1.6). The fact that it is far less likely that a family has an adult at home who is not working for a wage means that the typical family has far less time available to prepare food. In order to maintain the same quality of food, it would be necessary to either buy more prepared foods, which are more expensive, or to eat out more frequently. The relative importance of food away from home in the CPI rose from 4.6 per cent in 1953 to 5.7 per cent in 2001, a period in which the relative importance of the rest of the food component dropped from 25.0 per cent to 9.6 per cent of the index (Bureau of Labor Statistics 1966, 2001).

Table 4.1   Impact of the physical and social infrastructure on well-being

CPI category	Relative importance	Infrastructure changes
Food and beverages	16.20	Increased family work hours – less time for food preparation – more food consumed away from home Changed availability of clean drinking water
Housing Shelter	30.25	Increased distances both within and between metropolitan areas – more time spent commuting, on shopping trips, or to visit friends and family – increased needs for communication (for example, long-distance phone calls or Internet) and short- and long-distance travel, including increased need for hotels/motels Increased crowding – less availability of open space/recreational areas Increased or decreased pollution of air/water/soil Crime – greater precautions, including restricting behavior, and added expenses (for example, car and house alarms)
Insurance	0.37	Liability laws, social norms on lawsuits
Apparel	4.45	Changing standards for work attire
Transportation New and used vehicles	7.48	Congestion, size and weight of other vehicles, safety regulations and enforcement (for example, drunk-driving laws)
Public transportation	1.41	Number of routes covered and frequency, congestion
Insurance	2.41	Congestion, size and weight of other vehicles, safety regulations and enforcement (for example, drunk-driving laws), liability laws
Motor fuel	3.48	Availability of gas stations
Medical care	5.81	Improved knowledge of factors affecting health (for example, diet, exercise, smoking, and drinking)

Table 4.1   (continued)

CPI category	Relative importance	Infrastructure changes
		Changed exposure to hazards in the physical environment
		Changed exposure to hazards in the social environment (for example, stress)
		Exposure to new diseases
Recreation	5.91	Quality of performance (for example, sports teams affected by expansion), quality of facilities (for example, replacement of old stadiums by modern facilities)
		General patterns of recreation (for example, availability of partners for sports)
		Changed television content due to factors such as the spread of cable
		New broadcast formats
Education and communication		
Education	2.80	Change in the quality of public schools
Computers	0.80	Change in software standards
Other goods and services		
Personal care goods	0.73	Changing standards of work appearance
Personal care services	0.99	Changing standards of work appearance
Tobacco	1.31	Restrictions on smoking

Source: Bureau of Labor Statistics (2001).

An analysis that measured the increased wages associated with more workers per family, but did not also make some allowance for the increased expenses associated with paying more for prepared food or eating meals out, would overstate the increase in real family income. In principle, an accurate cost-of-living index would measure the increased expenditures on buying prepared food or eating out which would leave a family just as well off as they had been previously, when they had more time available to prepare their own meals. As a practical matter, this would not be easy, since families are likely to consume more prepared foods or eat out more frequently, not just because they have less time, but as a result of the fact that they have more income.

The second item under this category, the availability of clean drinking water, may be more a question of increased concern over health than an actual change in the quality of the water provided through public water systems. However, there has been a large increase in consumption of bottled water and in purchases of water filtration devices over the last three decades. Insofar as these expenditures have been necessary simply to offset an actual deterioration in the quality of public drinking water, it would constitute a large increase in the cost of living.[2] (Two bottles of water a day, would cost approximately $700 per year, or roughly 2 per cent of the annual expenditure of a typical family.)

There are several issues with respect to the items in the housing category, which could be very important in assessing the cost of living. The most obvious is simply the question of location itself. The index never makes direct comparisons between the cost of housing in different locations, it only measures changes in the cost of specific housing units. This means that, insofar as there are gains or losses associated with the new units added to the housing stock, these will be left out of the index. To some extent, this raises quality issues of the housing itself, which will be discussed later; however, at least as important to the value of the housing unit are factors determined by its location, which is distinct from the physical quality of the house itself.

The first set of issues concerns the distances that it may be necessary to travel as a result of changes in living patterns.[3] If housing becomes increasingly dispersed, then it may be necessary for people to own cars, who may not otherwise have needed to own a car. In addition, they may have to spend more time commuting to work, traveling to and from stores, and to visit friends. The availability of open land to allow construction of new housing units is a factor that limits the increase in housing costs compared to a situation where an increased population has to be housed on a fixed amount of land. In this sense, the CPI as constructed, should pick up reasonably well the gains associated with the increased dispersion of housing. However, by excluding all the additional costs implied by greater dispersion, it would be understating the increase in the cost of living. (Of course the increased ability to work at home as a result of the Internet is an important factor going in the opposite direction.)

A comparable set of factors would apply to increasing dispersion of family members across the nation or world. Economic theory implies that an increasingly mobile labor force should be a source of greater efficiency, since workers can find jobs in locations where their skills can be most fully utilized. The gains from this greater mobility should be picked up in more rapid real wage growth than would otherwise have been possible. However, costs that could result from such dispersion, such as the increased travel and communication expenses that are necessary for families to stay in contact, do not get included in the CPI.

There is a range of other factors that can significantly affect the utility that individuals derive from a particular housing arrangement. The population density and the availability of open spaces for recreation could have a very large impact on people's well-being. People often travel long distances and/or spend large amounts of money to have access to open space. Similarly, the cleanliness of the air, water, and soil will affect people's enjoyment from living in a particular location, as well as their health. Crime and the fear of crime also can be tremendously important factors in determining individuals' well-being.[4]

The well-being that individuals derive from clothing will depend to an overwhelming extent on the social norms governing fashion. The expense of purchasing sufficient material for body warmth is trivial compared with the expense of buying clothes that conform to accepted standards within society. Clearly, the CPI makes no effort to factor in the impact of changing norms on clothing patterns, nor is it obvious how it possibly could. In addition, workers generally have to maintain certain standards of attire on their jobs. This can lead to increases or decreases in the cost of living as these standards change. For example, if more casual clothing becomes common, there could be less of a need for spending on business suits and dry cleaning. Since work clothes are generally paid for by workers (except for uniforms), changes in expectations concerning work clothes can significantly affect the cost of clothing to workers.

There are numerous infrastructure factors that would affect the utility that an individual can derive from owning a car. At the top of the list would be traffic congestion and the quality of roads. The regulations governing driving, such as speed limits or restrictions on off-road driving, and the extent of their enforcement, could also have an important impact on the utility derived from car ownership. In addition, the risks associated with driving will depend to a large extent on the type and number of other vehicles on the road. For example, the proliferation of sports utility vehicles in recent years has increased the dangers faced by drivers of other types of cars.

With public transportation, the frequency of train, bus, or plane trips would be an important factor in determining their usefulness, as would the number of routes covered. The latter is a difficult issue to assess, since it may be necessary for the number of routes to expand through time in order to maintain the same quality of service, if residential patterns are increasingly dispersed. The CPI makes no effort to account for any of these factors.

Crowding of public transportation is also a significant issue affecting well-being. In an airplane that is one-third empty, every passenger can have an empty seat next to them. Passengers pay a large premium for the extra space that goes with a business- or first-class seat. If higher capacity utilization significantly reduces the probability that passengers will have an empty seat next to them, then this is a major deterioration in service quality. Travel delays also have a large impact on quality.

The social influences on medical care are likely to be very large. In general, health is probably far more dependent on diet, exercise, and environmental factors than the medical care provided by the health-care system. Yet these factors, whether positive or negative, are not in any way picked up in the CPI. In fact, the CPI measures of inflation in this sector could easily go in the opposite direction of an accurate measure of health-care costs. For example, if anti-smoking campaigns led to a large enough reduction in some kinds of diseases, it is possible that the treatment for these diseases would rise, as the cost of drug research or expensive equipment would be spread over a smaller number of patients. Conversely, a decline in the price of the drugs developed to treat a new disease, such as AIDS, would be recorded only as fall in the price of medical care, even though the cost of medical care would obviously be still lower if the disease had never appeared in the first place. It is worth noting that the CPI measures the cost of specific procedures, such as treating knee injuries, or specific drugs. If the cost of health insurance rises because individuals are on average receiving more tests or more drugs, this would not appear as an increase in the cost of medical care in the CPI. For this reason, the price changes measured by the CPI in the medical-care sector may have relatively little relationship to how most people experience rising health-care costs.

In the area of recreation, social norms play a very large role in determining costs. It becomes impossible to engage in many types of recreation, if it is not possible to find partners. If people increasingly choose individualistic types of entertainment, such as watching television or playing video games, then it would become increasingly difficult for someone who preferred to play baseball or basketball, or to just sit on a porch talking to neighbors, to pursue their chosen form of recreation. Such a loss would not be taken into account in the CPI. Similarly, the CPI obviously does not attempt to assess the quality of sports or events (for example, movies, concerts, and plays) that people pay to see. If there is a systematic improvement or deterioration in quality through time, this will not be picked up in the CPI.

Public schools are a very important publicly provided good. If there is a deterioration in the quality of these schools, so that more people feel a need to send their children to private schools, then this could be a large increase in the cost of living, which would not be picked up in the CPI. Similarly, insofar as parents need to pay for daycare for their children, because they do not have a nonworking parent at home, this would be an important cost not picked up in the CPI. Child care now accounts for an average of nearly 0.4 per cent of consumption expenditures (Bureau of Labor Statistics 2001).

The CPI has shown an extraordinary rate of price decline for computers in recent years. While this may reflect real improvements in computer technology, to some extent these improvements are needed to operate ever more complex software. New software may offer real advantages to many consumers, but others may feel the need to buy it simply to stay in communication with individuals and websites that use the more complex software. The cost of upgrading software, simply to be able to stay in contact with others, could be a significant unmeasured cost associated with computer ownership.

The other goods and services category includes personal-care items, such as hair cuts and styling. The need for this would be dependent to a very large extent on social norms, including grooming requirements at workplaces. This category also includes legal and accounting services. The need for legal services would depend on social norms and the complexity of the legal system. For example, if laws are written so that it is very simple to write a will or buy a house, then the demand for lawyers would be significantly reduced. Expenditures for legal and financial services now account for 0.7 per cent of consumer spending, with auto and home insurance accounting for another 2.8 per cent (Bureau of Labor Statistics 2001).[5] Insofar as an increase in spending on these items is attributable simply to the greater complexity of society, this could be a source of substantial increase in the cost of living. Tobacco also appears in the other goods and services category. While restrictions on smoking may have increased the well-being of nonsmokers, and those who are trying to quit, they would reduce the utility that individuals derive from smoking. The CPI does not attempt to pick up either of these effects.

To summarize, the list of changes in the social and physical environment that would have affected the utility that individuals derive from consuming a particular bundle of goods over the last 50 years is quite extensive. The ones noted above are at best a very small subset of the factors that would be relevant to individuals' utility. It is likely that the cumulative effect of these changes is large, although it is impossible to determine without more careful investigation whether the net impact is positive or negative on individual well-being. A true measure of the cost of living would have to assess the quantitative importance of these changes along with the changes in the prices of market goods and services.

RELATIVE CONSUMPTION

The standard assumption in nearly all economic work is that individuals only derive utility from the goods they directly consume, not what they consume relative to what others consume. In many situations this may be a fine working assumption, even if it is not entirely accurate. Measuring changes in the cost of living is not one of those situations.

The *only* reference point for a cost-of-living index is individual utility. It involves comparing different bundles of goods and services of varying quality through time. There is no common metric, except individual utility, against which these bundles can be measured. If individuals view their relative consumption as an important factor in their well-being, economists have no justification whatsoever not to take this into account. If an identical bundle of goods and services leaves a person feeling worse off in a situation in which their relative position has deteriorated, then a cost-of-living index that failed to measure this impact is inaccurate. If relative patterns of consumption are actually quite important to individual well-being, a cost-of-living index that ignored relative consumption patterns would not really be measuring anything at all.

The actual importance of relative consumption to individual well-being is, of course, an empirical question, not a theoretical one. It is not clear how the importance of relative consumption to well-being can be determined or if economists even possess tools that readily lend themselves to this sort of assessment. In any case, it is clear that few economists have attempted to take issues of relative consumption patterns seriously or tried in any serious way to quantify such effects.[6] This section will examine the major categories of the CPI to note areas in which relative consumption patterns are likely to be important to the utility derived. The discussion is intended to be suggestive, since a comprehensive analysis of the impact of relative consumption patterns is beyond the scope of this chapter.

Before directly considering specific categories of goods and services, it is worth again noting the distinction between the nature of the problem posed by relative consumption affecting individuals' utility and the type of problems noted in the previous section. That section noted changes in the social and physical infrastructure that would affect individuals' well-being. A genuine cost-of-living index would have to take these changes into account. The CPI makes no effort to include these sorts of factors, nor are there any serious proposals to incorporate such effects in the future, but in principle, it should be possible to measure their impact on well-being. On the other hand, it is not clear how an index could even theoretically include the impact of changes in relative consumption, even if this could somehow be measured. In other words, if relative consumption patterns are actually important to individuals' well-being, it is not clear that a cost-of-living index is a meaningful concept.

Table 4.2 lists the major categories of the CPI, along with their relative weights and the ways in which relative consumption patterns may prove to

Table 4.2   Importance of relative consumption to utility

CPI category	Relative importance	Nature of potential impact
Food and beverages		
Foods	9.56	Utility derived from various types of food may be affected by the status associated with them
Alcoholic beverages	0.62	Utility derived from various types of beer, wine, or hard liquor may be affected by the status associated with them
Food away from home	6.02	Utility associated with specific restaurants depends on status and location
Housing		
Rent	7.08	The value attached to a particular location depends on the status attached to living or visiting a specific area
Owners' equivalent rent	20.46	
Hotels and motels	2.10	
Household furniture (including appliances)	4.61	Utility depends in part on relative quality
Apparel	4.45	Utility depends on conforming to style changes
Transportation		
New and used vehicles	7.48	Utility is a function of relative quality and newness of vehicle
Public transportation	1.41	Segregating travel by class provides utility apart from the qualitative features associated with the differences
Medical care	5.81	Standards of health and appearance could be relative
Recreation	5.91	Desirability of specific types of recreation could be affected by the social status associated with them
Education and communication		
Education tuition and fees	2.80	Quality of schools is a relative measure
Total	78.31	

Source: Bureau of Labor Statistics (2001).

be important to individual's utility. Most of the major items in the CPI do appear on the table, although it is not easy to determine the extent to which relative factors are important to individuals' utility.

For example, in the case of food, it is not clear to what extent a preference for lobster over mackerel is attributable to intrinsic human characteristics, as opposed to the relative expense and status associated with lobster. The same sort of issue arises with a wide variety of foods, in addition to quality upgrading within a food type. It is at least plausible that status is a very important factor in the utility that individuals derive from the food they consume. The view that status plays an important role in the utility from consuming various types of beer, wines, and spirits seems even more plausible.

There are huge differences in prices charged by restaurants that may outwardly appear to be comparable in the quality of service and food. These differences may in part be explained by the status associated with the particular restaurant and the status associated with the location. (A restaurant overlooking a river in rural Pennsylvania will not command the same premium for its river view as a restaurant overlooking the Hudson River in New York City.)

It is reasonable to believe that status considerations play an enormous role in the utility derived from housing. There are enormous price differentials for comparable housing in different parts of the country or different parts of the same metropolitan area (Moulton 1995). A small apartment near Central Park in Manhattan can easily be rented for a higher price than a large house in a rural part of the country. Since housing is such a large part of consumption spending (the shelter component has a 30.3 per cent relative importance in the CPI (Bureau of Labor Statistics 2001)), this issue can pose very large problems in assessing living standards. For example, rents can rise rapidly in an area either because of pure inflation, or because the area becomes relatively more desirable. (As noted earlier, the CPI only measures price changes for the same units of housing, it does not make comparisons across units.)

There is no obvious way to distinguish between these two phenomena, but it does raise a very important issue. Everyone cannot live in Manhattan. If most people do not necessarily want to live in Manhattan, then this is not a problem. However, if through time it becomes increasingly important to more people to live in Manhattan, there is greater sense of deprivation caused by the limited housing space there. A cost-of-living index has to assume that the latter sort of shifts in taste do not occur, or at least that they are relatively unimportant.

The claim that the utility derived from clothes is in part relative should not be too contentious. It would be difficult to imagine that the desire to change clothing styles with fashion changes is intrinsic to the human psyche. Similarly, the point at which clothes are considered too old to wear is probably less dependent on their physical usefulness than clothing standards within different social strata. The situation with cars and trucks is similar. The claim that people select a luxury car (or almost any car) at least in part for the status it conveys is probably not too controversial.

Some types of public transportation, such as air travel and now trains, are explicitly segregated by class of travel. It is at least plausible that part of the premium for a first-class ticket on an airplane is attributable to the status it conveys, and the desire to be among a higher class of traveler. Informal types of segregation in travel are probably at least as important as the formal types, for example, choosing trains rather than buses, or cabs rather than shuttles.

Relative factors could be quite important to the types of medical care that people receive. If social norms change so that higher standards of health become common, individuals may expect more from their medical care. For example, if it becomes common to engage in strenuous physical activity later in life, there will be an increased demand for doctors that specialize in sports medicine. Similarly, if certain types of largely cosmetic medical procedures become common (for example, braces for children with ill-formed teeth), then those who do not get these procedures will suffer as a result.

The utility derived from many types of recreational events is probably to a large extent a function of relative factors. For example, it is certainly plausible that the value that individuals will attach to a ticket to a rock star's concert is in part attributable to the fact that he or she is popular. Seeing the same star would provide less utility, if he or she were less popular. Similarly, for some people, part of the attraction of a sport like racquetball, instead of sports like bowling, probably stems from the relative status associated with the two sports.

The component of education that goes to tuition and fees can be viewed as heavily affected by relative factors. It is very unlikely that a parent or student would be satisfied paying the same tuition for a school that stood near the bottom in its rankings as one near the top. (Education could arguably be treated as an investment good, and therefore excluded from the CPI altogether, since much of the purpose is to increase future income.)

The items listed in Table 4.2 account for 78.3 per cent of the weight of the CPI, and even this figure could be low. For example, it is certainly plausible that status considerations affect the well-being that individuals derive from different types of tobacco, or even personal-care items, although these are not included in the table. Of course, being included in the table does not establish that relative factors are important to the utility derived from the consumption of these items. However, it is at least plausible that relative factors are important, and it would be arbitrary to assume the opposite in the absence of any supporting evidence.

ANALYZING THE CPI AS A PRICE INDEX

The purpose of the preceding discussion was to place the analysis of the accuracy of the CPI in its proper context. The CPI was not designed as a cost-of-living index, and could not easily be transformed into one. As noted above, a true cost-of-living index would have to evaluate the impact of all the changes in the social and physical infrastructure as well as the provision of publicly provided goods and services. The BLS does not even attempt to make this sort of assessment, nor have its critics. At the very least, maintaining this assessment on an ongoing basis would require an enormous expansion of the index into new realms, where it is not clear that economists have the necessary expertise.

The problem of constructing a cost-of-living index goes from difficult to impossible, if it is the case that many of the sources of utility are inherently relative, as noted in the previous section. Here also, there is no research to support the contention that relative factors are unimportant to well-being, simply a hope that reality corresponds to convenience.[7]

The focus of the CPI must be narrower than an all-encompassing measure of the cost of living. The CPI is defined as a price index for consumption goods and services, and this is the only purpose that it can reasonably be expected to serve. An index that attempts to quantify the additional convenience associated with 24-hour food stores or ATMs (automated teller machines), as some have proposed, but does not pick up the benefits lost, which are related to these developments, from changing norms under which it is less acceptable to borrow items from neighbors, or less common for stores to accept personal checks, is not more accurate than an index that ignores both sets of changes in society.

To evaluate social progress or well-being it will be necessary to look at many other factors that go beyond the measures of real wages or income obtained with the CPI. These factors could include various health-care statistics, education measures, incarceration rates, and numerous other measures that may reflect the overall progress of society. The CPI is not a comprehensive measure that can be used for this purpose, and there is no plausible way in which it can be transformed into such a measure.

This section will evaluate the evidence on the accuracy of the CPI as a price index. It will examine the types of bias that have appeared in the CPI, and the extent to which their size has varied over the last half-century.

While the main topic in this discussion is the CPI-U, the standard CPI reported in news accounts, this section will also make reference to the CPI-U-RS, an index that the BLS recently constructed which applies the current CPI methodology to the years between 1978 and 1998 (Stewart and Reed 1999).[8]

Formula Bias

The simplest form of bias that has appeared in the CPI in recent decades is formula bias. The issues here are rather straightforward. Because of the way that the BLS substitutes new items into its survey, it overweighted items that were selling at temporarily low prices and therefore likely to experience larger than average price increases, and underweighted goods that were temporarily selling at high prices and therefore likely to experience price declines. This caused the index to overstate the true rate of inflation for a wide variety of goods in the period from when it began its rotating sample method in 1978, to 1995 and 1996 when corrections to the flawed pricing procedure were put in place. BLS research estimates that this formula bias caused the CPI-U to overstate the rate of inflation by approximately 0.25 percentage points annually, with the largest effects on food and clothing (Bureau of Labor Statistics 1996; Armknecht et al. 1995).

In addition to the problem with sampling rotation, there were two other notable areas in which CPI formulas led to bias in the index. An incorrect aggregation formula used for the owner-equivalent rent component led it to rise at a rate of approximately 0.6 percentage points annually compared to a proper index, over the 1987–95 period. This would have led to an upward bias of approximately 0.12 per cent in the index as a whole over this period. On the other side, failure to impute rent increases for vacant units led to an understatement of inflation of approximately 0.1 percentage points annually in both the rent and owner-equivalent rent component in the years 1978–95, which would have biased downward the reported inflation rate in the CPI as a whole by approximately 0.03 percentage points a year over this period (Henderson and Smedley 1994). These specific sources of formula bias are no longer present in the CPI, and the CPI-U-RS has been adjusted to correct for their impact in previous years, as has the reconstructed CPI in Baker (1996).

Substitution Bias

The issue of substitution bias raises a basic methodological question about what the CPI should be trying to measure. Historically, the CPI has been constructed as a Laspeyres index, which held the consumption bundle fixed at base-level quantities. Assuming that the social and physical infrastructures remain unchanged, this is supposed to guarantee that the index would place an upper bound on the true increase in the cost of living.[9] If it is accepted that the CPI is not and cannot be a true cost-of-living index, then the question to be asked is which set of consumption items should it track? From this perspective, there is no obvious justification for maintaining a fixed basket, especially if the rate of inflation for this basket diverges significantly from the rate of inflation on the goods that households are actually consuming.

It is also worth noting that the difference between the inflation rate shown by a Laspeyres index and a superlative index will vary through time, depending on the overall rate of inflation and its evenness across sectors. In most of the last 15 years, the substitution incorporated into a superlative index has lowered the measured rate of inflation by less than 0.15 percentage points compared to the CPI (Aizcorbe and Jackman 1993, 1997). However, in some years – notably 1990, when the price of oil rose sharply – the difference has been considerably larger (0.6 percentage points in 1990). Bryan and Cecchetti (1993), using a somewhat different methodology, estimated the size of the substitution effect at close to 0.8 percentage points annually in the 1960s and 1970s and close to zero in subsequent years. (The Aizcorbe and Jackman series only goes back as far as 1983.) If there are large divergences between the rates of inflation shown by a Laspeyres index and a superlative index, the inflation rate shown by a superlative index would better reflect the rate of inflation that consumers are actually experiencing at the time. For this reason, as far as possible, it would be desirable to use the inflation rate shown by superlative indices, when examining historical inflation rates.

The above discussion refers to 'upper-level' substitution, where individuals substitute between categories of goods. There is also an issue concerning 'lower-level' substitution, where individuals substitute between items within a category. (For example, a switch from apples to oranges would be an example of a switch at the upper level. Switching between types of apples would be a switch at the lower level.) From the standpoint of constructing the index, the main distinction is that the BLS actually has data (albeit with a significant lag) on shifts in consumption patterns at the upper level, from the Consumer Expenditure Survey (CES). It never actually collects data on shifts in consumption at the lower level. Prior to 1998, it had used a Laspeyres index to aggregate the inflation rates shown at the lower level. With the 1998 revision to the CPI, the BLS began using geometric means to aggregate rates of inflation across items at the lower level in most categories of the index.[10] This had the effect of lowering the reported rate of inflation by approximately 0.2 percentage points annually (Moulton and

Smedley 1995, Reinsdorf 1996; Reinsdorf and Moulton 1995). The impact of this change has been incorporated into the CPI-U-RS for years after 1978. It is important to note that this has led to a serious inconsistency with the data for years prior to 1978. The BEA has used deflators constructed with geometric means to measure output in years after 1978. These revised output numbers have been, in turn, used by the BLS to measure productivity growth. Since the deflators used for years prior to 1978 continue to use the Laspeyres aggregation, the reported level of output and productivity growth is still biased downward for these years. Any serious effort to compare growth rates for the pre- and post-1978 periods should adjust for the impact of this methodological change.

Retail Outlet Substitution Bias

The third major source of bias identified by the Boskin Commission was retail outlet substitution bias: the failure of the index to pick up potential gains to consumers that result from buying goods at discount stores. This bias could arise because the index never makes direct comparisons of prices across outlets. It is assumed that the quality-adjusted price is identical in different outlets, so that price differences – for example between discount stores and traditional retail stores – reflect reduced service quality. The Boskin Commission and others have argued that this approach may cause the index to miss real gains associated with the switch to discount outlets. They pointed out that their share of the retail market has risen significantly in recent years which could suggest significant benefits to consumers (Senate Finance Committee (SFC) 1995, 1996; Oi 1992; Reinsdorf 1993, 1996.

While the Boskin Commission originally estimated this source of bias as adding 0.2, and possibly as much as 0.4 percentage points to the reported rate of inflation, more careful analysis indicates that its impact is almost certainly far smaller, and could even go in the opposite direction (SFC 1995). First, it is important to recognize that the bias only applies to a subset of the index that could in principle be sold in discount stores. Large areas of the index – shelter, medical care, utilities – are excluded altogether. The areas of the index that can properly be included – primarily food at home, clothes, appliances, and household items – only comprise about 30 per cent of the index. Second, the bias could only apply to the percentage of sales in these categories that switch in any given year. According to a study in the early 1990s (MacDonald and Nelson 1991, cited in Moulton 1996), approximately 0.7 per cent of the sales in these categories switched each year from traditional retail outlets to discount stores, which means that the bias could apply to approximately 0.2 per cent of the whole index.

Assuming a 10 per cent pure (quality-adjusted) price difference between discount stores and traditional stores, this source of bias would add 0.02 percentage points to the reported rate of inflation.[11]

It is also important to recognize that the bias could go in the other direction. If traditional retail stores, which are valued by consumers, close because the owners choose to abandon the business, then there could be a loss associated with the shift. In addition, traditional stores may reduce their service in order to more effectively compete in price with discount stores, a deterioration in service quality that would not be picked up in the CPI.[12] In short, there is no clear evidence concerning either the size or the direction of this bias, although it seems implausible that it is very large. Based on very little evidence, the Boskin Commission's final report estimated the size of retail outlet substitution bias at just 0.1 percentage point annually.

Quality Bias and New-goods Bias

The most controversial aspect of the Boskin Commission's report was its estimate of the size of quality and new-goods bias. The commission estimated that the combined impact of these two sources of bias led to an overstatement of inflation by 0.6 percentage points annually. While these are distinct sources of bias, the commission chose to treat them together in its final report. Following the commission, this discussion will also treat the two types of bias together. However, before examining the issues that arise in each category of the CPI, it is worth distinguishing conceptually between the basis of the two types of bias.

Quality bias could appear in the index because the BLS has failed to accurately measure changes in the quality of goods and services through time. In principle, the CPI is measuring the change in the price of goods and services of constant quality. If the price of items rises because their quality has improved through time, then this should not be counted as inflation in the CPI. It is important to recognize that the BLS has always made quality adjustments for most items. According to BLS data, quality adjustments reduced the reported rate of inflation by 1.77 percentage points in 1995, an increase of nearly 0.6 percentage points in the size of annual quality adjustments from the mid-1980s level (Smedley and Moulton 1997). The claim that the CPI has a quality bias is therefore not a claim that the quality of consumption items is improving through time. Rather, it is a claim that the quality of these items is rising more rapidly than the BLS is finding in its measures.

There are two issues that arise with new-goods bias. The first stems from the fact that new goods are not immediately incorporated into the CPI

survey. The sample rotation method in place from 1978 to 1998 would gradually have brought new items into the index on average over a five-year
period. The new rotation system put in place in 1998 should typically get
new goods into the index within a year of their appearing on the market.
This delay could be important because new items tend to fall rapidly in
price during the period just after they are introduced into the market. For
example, products like hand calculators and cellular phones both had very
rapid price declines in the first years after they appeared on the market. The
failure to include this price decline in the index leads to an overstatement
of the true rate of inflation.

While this can be a genuine source of bias in the index, there are two
important points about the size of this bias that should be noted. First, for
most items, the size of this bias is likely to be very small. Smedley and
Moulton (1997) estimate the size of the bias that resulted from excluding
cellular phones as 0.02 percentage points annually for the years from 1986
to 1994. While this bias is only from a single good, cellular phones were
both an extraordinarily important innovation, and also, by chance, fell
outside of the CPI's normal rotation system.[13] It is extremely unlikely that
the new-product bias from the late entry of any other individual items will
have an impact on the index of the same order of magnitude.

The other important point about this bias is that it is likely to be relevant
primarily to the consumption patterns of wealthier households. When new
goods are first introduced and are relatively expensive, most of the buyers
are likely to be higher-income households. The CPI is an expenditure-
weighted index, so that the consumption patterns of higher-income households have disproportionate weight in the index. Arguably, an index that
was democratically weighted, with the consumption patterns of each
household counting equally, would be a more appropriate price index for
most of the uses of the CPI. Recent research has found relatively little
difference between the inflation rate measured by an expenditure-weighted
index and a democratically-weighted index (Garner et al. 1996; Kokoski
1987). However, if new-products bias causes the CPI to significantly overstate inflation, then a correct index would probably show a substantial
difference between the inflation rate shown with expenditure weights compared with democratic weights. In this case, eliminating a bias that exists in
the CPI as it is constructed, could actually make it less appropriate as a
price index for the items purchased by typical consumers.

It is also important to note that the size of this bias has almost certainly
been reduced through time. Prior to 1978, items could only enter the index
at major revisions to the survey. The previous two revisions had taken place
in 1964 and 1951. It is likely that this earlier system, where the BLS tracked
the prices of an unchanging sample of goods and services, meant that there

would be several instances comparable to that of the cellular phone, where important consumption items did not appear in the CPI until long after they had been in common usage. For example, home air conditioners did not get included in the CPI until 1964, the same year that air travel was first part of the index. The fact that new goods entered the CPI so much more slowly in the years prior to 1978 probably means that the new-goods bias would have been considerably larger in those years than it was in the 1980s and 1990s, and far larger than it is with the methodology put in place in 1998.

There is one other aspect to the type of new goods bias cited by the commission that is worth noting. Following Hausman (1994), the commission cited increased variety itself, apart from any specific goods, as an unmeasured benefit to consumers that leads to an upward bias in the CPI. While increased variety may be a real source of gain, this is the sort of benefit that does not properly belong in a price index like the CPI. It is not measuring either the price or attributes of goods themselves. The benefits of increased variety would best be left to broader measures of the quality of life.

The following discussion examines the evidence produced by the Boskin Commission for quality and new-goods bias in each of the major categories of the CPI. Following the commission, this discussion uses the CPI categories in place in 1997. It summarizes a larger discussion in Baker (1997). Table 4.3 presents the amount of bias the commission estimated for each CPI component and the basis for the estimate.

1. *Food and beverages* The commission estimated that the CPI understates the quality improvements in this component by an average of 0.3 percentage points annually. This estimate was based entirely on introspection, the commission's belief that the rate for food and beverages, including food away from home, was on average about 10 per cent better in 1996 than it had been in 1976.[14]

    > How much would a consumer pay to have the privilege of choosing from the variety of items available in today's supermarket instead of being constrained to the much more limited variety available 30 years ago? A conservative estimate of the extra variety and convenience might be 10 per cent for food consumed at home other than produce, 20 per cent for produce where the increased variety in winter (as well as summer farmers' markets) has been so notable, and 5 per cent for alcoholic beverages where imported beer, microbreweries, and greatly improved distribution of imported wines from all over the world have improved the standard of living. (SFC 1996, pp.41–2)

    The commission's discussion of quality bias in this component gave no evidence that it recognized the size of the quality adjustments already included in the CPI for food and beverages. For the year 1995,

Table 4.3 Estimates of quality bias in the CPI

Major and selected minor components	Relative importance	Current (1995) quality imputations	Commission's estimate of bias	Source of estimate
1. Food and beverages	17.33	1.39		
Food at home other than produce	8.54		0.3	Introspection
Fresh fruits and vegetables	1.34		0.6	Introspection
Food away from home	5.89		0.3	Introspection
Alcoholic beverages	1.57		0.15	Introspection
2. Housing	41.35			
Shelter	28.29		0.25	Introspection
Other utilities, including telephone	3.22		1	Introspection
Appliances, including electronic	0.81		5.6	Gordon (1990)
Other house furnishings	2.64		0.3	Introspection
3. Apparel and upkeep	5.52	3.37	1	Gordon (1996)
4. Transportation	16.95	1.13		
New vehicles	5.03		0.59	Gordon (1990)
Used vehicles	1.34		0.59	Gordon (1990)
Motor fuel	2.91		0.25	Introspection
5. Entertainment	4.37	4.79		
Commodities	1.98		2	Gordon (1990)
6. Other goods and services	7.12	0.6		
Personal care	1.17		0.9	Gordon (1990)
Personal and education expenses	4.34		0.2	Introspection

Table 4.3 (continued)

Major and selected minor components	Relative importance	Current (1995) quality imputations	Commission's estimate of bias	Source of estimate
7. Medical care	7.36	2.51		
Prescription drugs	0.89		2	Berndt et al. (1993, 1997) Griliches and Cockburn (1994)
Nonprescription drugs and medical supplies	0.39		1	none
Professional medical services	3.47		3	Cutler et al. (1996) and
Hospital and related services	2.26		3	Shapiro and Wilcox (1996)
Total	100	1.76	0.612	

Source: Baker (1997).

these adjustments lowered the rate of inflation reported for this component by 1.39 percentage points (Smedley and Moulton 1997). If this year was typical, then the commission's introspective assessment of the rate of quality improvement in this category would imply that the CPI was substantially overstating the rate of quality improvement and understating the rate of inflation. At the very least, the commission has provided no evidence that the actual rate of quality improvement for food and beverages was more rapid than indicated by the CPI.

2. *Housing*   The commission estimated that the shelter component of the CPI, the largest component of the housing category, understated the rate of quality improvement by 0.25 percentage points annually. It based this estimate on the fact that the average unit rent in the Census Bureau's housing survey had risen by 1.0 percentage point a year more than the shelter index in the CPI, over the previous 20 years. It noted that the average size of a unit had risen by 1.0 per cent annually during this period. Based on this calculation it concluded that the index had accurately measured the increase in housing size, but had missed improvements in average housing quality, which it estimated at 0.25 percentage points annually.

As with the estimate of bias in the food component, it is difficult to evaluate a claim based on introspection. It is worth noting that much of the cost of housing depends on location. There was a nationwide shift of population during this period from the northeast, a relatively expensive region, to the south, the least expensive region. There was also a large shift of population from inner cities and inner suburbs to relatively inexpensive outer suburbs. This means that an index that held location constant probably would have risen far more rapidly than the Census Bureau's index. The Boskin Commission's estimate also depends on the counterintuitive assumption that square footage is priced at a constant marginal cost.

Among other items in the housing category, the commission assumed that there was a 1.0 percentage point bias in the reporting of telephone prices based on its belief that there were unmeasured improvements in the quality of telephone service over the last two decades. It is worth noting that the CPI would pick up the price declines associated with the introduction of competition to the industry, but none of the search costs that consumers face as a result of the fact that there is no longer a monopoly in the industry.

The commission also estimated a substantial amount of quality bias in the pricing of household appliances. It relied on Gordon (1990) for this estimate.[15] In fact, the evidence in this study is far more ambiguous. Compared to one of the indices constructed, the CPI does show a substantial bias, however, when compared to an index constructed from Sears catalogue price quotes, the CPI actually understated the true rate of inflation for much of the period examined. This study cannot be viewed as providing convincing evidence of a quality bias in the CPI in this area.

3. *Apparel* The commission estimated a quality bias equal to 3.37 percentage points a year in the apparel component based on a study that compared the CPI index with an index based on Sears catalogue prices (Gordon 1996). The CPI apparel index had serious problems in this period due to formula bias. However, it is not clear that there were also problems with quality bias. In the period after 1989, when the formula-bias problem in apparel was corrected, the CPI index actually showed a lower measured rate of inflation than the Sears catalogue index. Therefore, the Gordon study provides little reason to believe that the CPI measure of apparel prices is biased due to unmeasured quality improvements.

4. *Transportation* The commission estimated that the CPI understated quality improvements in new cars by 0.59 percentage points and used cars by 1.59 percentage points, based on its belief that it was not picking up improvements in durability. The commission noted the findings of Gordon (1990), who found that the CPI and his own hedonic index tracked each other reasonably well. However, it noted that the Gordon study did not include durability as a characteristic, and therefore concludes that it would have understated the true rate of quality improvement in cars. In fact, in its methodology, the CPI would factor in additional costs associated with improvements in durability.[16] The claim that these quality improvements are somehow being missed by the BLS really lacks any clear evidence.

The commission also concluded that the CPI overstated the rate of inflation for gasoline by 0.25 percentage points annually since it did not factor in the benefits of pay-at-the-pump credit-card readers. It estimated the benefit from these readers at 5 per cent of the purchase price, and obtained the 0.25 per cent annual inflation bias estimate by assuming a 20-year phase-in period. The commission had no evidence of the actual value that consumers place on this convenience, nor did it factor in the decreased availability of gas stations, a fact noted in its report, when assessing the net change in convenience to consumers.

5. *Entertainment* The commission attributed an annual quality bias of 2.0 percentage points to the items, such as VCRs and televisions, that were included in the CPI's entertainment component. This estimate was also based on estimates of bias in Gordon (1990). It is worth noting that the BLS has recently introduced hedonic pricing for most

major appliances. Contrary to the commission's expectation, this has had almost no effect of the measure of inflation in these items, and in some cases it may actually have led to a slightly lower measured rate of inflation than the quality adjustment system previously in place (see Liegey and Shepler 1999; Liegey 2000a,b,c; Shepler 2000; Kokoski et al. 2000; and Thompson 2000).

6. *Other goods and services*   The commission attributed a 0.9 percentage point annual bias in the personal-care component of the index, based on its estimate of the CPI's large undercounting of the rate of quality improvement in personal-care items, such as hairdryers. This estimate was also based on Gordon (1990). As noted above, recent research from the BLS indicates that there never was a large amount of quality bias in the BLS measure.

7. *Medical care*   The commission attributed an annual quality bias of 3.0 percentage points to the medical-care component of the index. This estimate relied largely on two studies that examined distinct sets of issues. The first study examined the cost of treating cataracts through time and compared it to a hypothetical CPI index (Shapiro and Wilcox 1996). It found that their index measuring the actual cost of treatment would have fallen by more than 3.0 percentage points annually measured against the hypothetical CPI index. The main reason for the difference is that the CPI index is focused narrowly on specific procedures, such as the cost of the surgery, and specific services, such as the price of a hospital room for a night. The actual cost of treating cataracts declined sharply during the period examined because it went from a type of surgery that generally required one to two weeks of hospitalization to a procedure that could be performed on an outpatient basis. The gains from this change would have been completely missed by the BLS procedures in place at the time.

While this study did expose a serious flaw in BLS methodology in pricing medical procedures, it is not clear that its impact was anywhere near as large as the findings of this study suggest. The BLS actually adopted a procedure similar to the one used in the Wilcox and Shapiro study in January 1997. There was no noticeable break in the medical services index as a result of this change. (The medical services component increased by 3.05 per cent in the year prior to January of 1997 and by 2.80 per cent in the subsequent year.) In other words, the Boskin Commission's assessment, that the different methodology would lead to a far lower measured rate of inflation, was not borne out by the evidence. Any bias that may have been introduced by a flawed procedure was clearly far smaller than the 3.0 percentage points annually assumed by the commission.

The second study cited by the commission in its estimate of bias in the CPI's medical-care component raises a qualitatively different set of issues. The study, Cutler et al. (1996), constructed a price index for treating heart attacks based on the years of expected life following a heart attack. This sort of quality adjustment brings in considerations that take it beyond a narrowly defined price index. For example, if other factors change that lead to a reduction in life expectancy following a heart attack (for example, more traffic deaths or a rise in the homicide rate), this methodology would imply that heart attack treatment should show a quality decline and therefore an increase in the price of treatment.[17]

As noted earlier, the pricing of medical care raises some very fundamental problems. In addition to the problems mentioned in the previous sections, there are also some attributable to fact that most private medical expenses are paid through insurance, and not directly by individuals. Since the CPI prices specific treatments, and not insurance premiums, it is possible that individuals' payments could increase or decrease in ways not picked up by the CPI. For example, if the cost of a typical premium rises because the average person receives more care, this would not be picked up by the CPI as an increase in medical-care costs.

This methodology can lead to some serious anomalies. The nation has a large uninsured population, many of whom are in poor health and therefore cannot afford standard insurance policies. If the government were to insure this population by directly paying for their insurance, this cost would be directly visible in the form of the necessary government expenditures and the taxes to pay for this spending. However, as an alternative, the government could require that all insurers use a system of community rating, under which all individuals pay the same premium, regardless of their health. In this situation, the average cost of insurance would almost certainly rise, since the average health of beneficiaries would have deteriorated, but there would be no price increase reported by the CPI's medical-care component as a result of this change. Clearly, this asymmetric treatment of these two policies is inappropriate.

There is a simple alternative approach that gets around this problem. Until 1964, the CPI simply priced the cost of medical insurance premiums, rather than the cost of individual procedures. This method has the advantage of simply measuring what individuals actually pay for their medical care.[18] It does not evaluate the quality of the care they are receiving. In effect, this methodology would measure the rate at which individuals' spending on health care increases independent of any assessment of what they are getting for their expenditure. The latter can better be measured by examining data on health. Presumably what people value is their health – the ability to live a long and healthy life. The quality of the medical services they receive is a secondary consideration.

By coincidence, an index that tracked the increase in out-of-pocket health-care expenditures and insurance premiums would have shown roughly the same rate of inflation as the CPI's medical-care component over the 1970–91 period: 8.12 per cent annual growth in per capita out-of-pocket health spending and 8.17 per cent annual growth in the medical-care index in the CPI (Cowen and McDonnell 1993, p. 228). This is due to the fact that a shift to employer and government-paid health care largely offsets the more rapid increase in insurance premiums over this period. However, there is no reason to expect that in general this will be the case, so in the future there could be substantial divergences between these two measures. The CPI will be a more meaningful price index if it measures what people pay for their health care – a reasonably straightforward task – as opposed to trying to assess the quality of the health care they receive.

In sum, there is remarkably little evidence to support the claim of a substantial quality bias in the CPI in the period examined by the Boskin Commission. More than a quarter of the quality bias they attributed to the index was based on nothing more than causal reflection. There was no research to support their assessment. Most of the other estimates of bias involved dubious extrapolations from a very limited body of research. In several of these cases, such as the hedonic pricing of appliances and the new procedures for pricing medical care, subsequent BLS research and changes in the index itself have shown that the commission's estimates of bias were grossly exaggerated.

There is one last point worth noting on the issue of quality adjustment. All quality adjustments, in trying to price the gains (or losses) from the changes in quality, assume that consumers are homogeneous and therefore would all place the same value on these changes (for example, Griliches 1971; Lancaster 1977). This can be an important source of overstatement of the size of quality improvements, since many consumers may value improvements little, or possibly not all. But consumers generally do not have the option to buy the 'unimproved' version of the product, so they end up paying for the quality improvement regardless of whether they want it or not.

For example, the hedonic methodology now in place for pricing computers has consistently shown quality improvements in computers of more than 30 per cent annually. As a result, there has been a reported rate of price decline in some years of close to 40 per cent. The rate of price decline reported for computers over the last six years would have reduced their cost by a cumulative total of more than 90 per cent since 1995.[19] This would imply that a 1995 computer, equipped with fully web capable Windows 95 software, could be purchased today for $150. While some consumers may prefer this option to paying three or four times this price for a much better computer, it is unlikely that they could purchase a new computer for this price.

The same situation would apply with most of the quality improvements in goods and services. The treatment of quality improvements can be seen as exactly analogous to a situation in which distinct items were sold in indivisible bundles. For example, if bacon and eggs were always sold together, consumers would have to pay for both items even if they only wanted one. Since the characteristics that are falling rapidly in price (for example, speed and memory in computers) are likely to be the ones that get added in most to products through time, the standard methods of quality adjustment are likely to lead to somewhat of a downward bias in the index. If these quality adjustments increase through time, as has almost certainly been the case, the size of the downward bias would increase.[20]

Evaluating CPI Bias through Aggregate Measures

It is worth noting another strand in the literature on CPI bias, which was not mentioned in the Boskin Commission's report. Several researchers have sought to argue that the index contains an overall bias by examining measures of aggregate living standards, rather than by finding specific areas where a bias exists. For example, Nordhaus (1998) compared changes in real median family income with positive economic assessments given by respondents in the Michigan Survey of Consumer Confidence. He showed that a CPI bias of approximately 1.0 percentage points would support the conclusion that most people will give a positive assessment of the economy in years in which the real median family income is rising. Kreuger (1998) uses a more complete analysis of the income distribution to show that an assumption of zero bias in the CPI is consistent with most families providing a positive assessment when their real income is rising.

Nakamura (1995) uses very broad consumption categories in an Engels curve analysis to argue that the shift in consumption shares between 1978 and 1994 is consistent with an upward bias in the CPI of more than 1.5 percentage points annually. This analysis ignores changes in relative prices and also the fact that most medical care is not paid for directly by consumers, with approximately half being paid by the government. Most of the shift in shares found by Nakamura was attributable to the growth in medical-care expenditures as a share of total consumption expenditures during this period.

Costa (2000) makes a similar argument based on the decline in food and entertainment shares in total consumption. However, Bils and Klenow (2001a) show that this argument depends on using only these two broad categories in the analysis. When they replicated the methodology using 106 more narrowly defined consumption categories, their results showed a significantly slower rate of share shifts than would be predicted by the measured rise in income, thereby implying that the CPI understates inflation. They therefore reject this sort of Engels curve analysis.

This study instead notes that the largest increase in spending shares took place in the CPI categories with the greatest rate of noncomparable product substitution in the CPI survey. The study considers the rate of noncomparable product substitution a measure of a sector's dynamism.[21] Therefore, they take their result to imply that consumers are switching their spending to the sectors which have the greatest dynamism in terms of new product offerings. They note that these are also the categories of the CPI that show the largest rate of price increase, and infer that the CPI is missing much of the quality improvement in goods in its substitution process.

This analysis is carried further in Bils and Klenow (2001b). This study constructs measures of quality income elasticity for 66 categories of durable goods based on an analysis of the price of the goods that households reported purchasing in the CES over the years 1980–96.[22] The study found that these quality elasticities were good predictors of the rate of price change in goods over this period, with the goods with the highest-quality elasticities showing the most rapid rate of price increase. The study then regressed the predicted rate of price increase on the rate of price increase reported for these categories in the CPI to get an estimate of unmeasured quality improvement and therefore CPI overstatement of inflation. This exercise produced an estimate of an average overstatement of inflation in the CPI of 2.2 percentage points annually in the goods examined.

While this analysis is a rather ingenious use of the data in the CES, there are some obvious problems with the methodology. First, the analysis would pick up all forms of bias in the CPI's measure of inflation in these goods, not just quality bias. For example, any bias attributable to the CPI's sample rotation procedure during this period would be picked up as quality bias. Similarly, if consumers were achieving savings on goods as a result of buying at discount outlets, this would be picked up as quality bias in this analysis, even if the savings were attributable to actual declines in service quality.

A more serious problem is the possibility that the measures of quality income elasticity may be biased by the actual price increases in the goods in the study. The CES has a relatively small cross-section sample of 5000 households a year. This means that much of the income variation in the study would be taking place through time as reported incomes rise, rather than simply across time. This would be especially true of goods that are infrequently purchased, such as playground sets, since the cross-sections of the households purchasing these items in any given year are small.[23] It is worth noting that most of the goods categories with a quality elasticity that it is at least one standard deviation from the mean calculated for the sample, have sample sizes that are smaller than the median (15 of 22), exactly the relationship that would be predicted if the measures of quality elasticity were biased by actual changes in price during the period.

It is also worth noting that there is a simple alternative explanation to the correlation between categories with an increase in expenditure shares and the number of noncomparable substitutions, found in Bils and Klenow (2001a). If firms tend to alter products in ways that make price increase less apparent to consumers, then it would be expected that categories of goods that had the largest increases in prices, would also have the most instances of product substitutions in the CPI. If demand for goods generally is inelastic, then these categories would also experience the largest increase in expenditure shares.

In conclusion, the evidence in these studies that the CPI has overstated the true rate of inflation in consumer goods is at best questionable. Furthermore, it would be difficult to know how to assess the meaning of evidence of an overall overstatement of inflation, apart from evidence of bias in the measure of inflation in specific categories of goods and services. If there are gains to well-being not directly embodied in the consumption basket, for example as a result of increased variety, this would be an issue that gets beyond a measure of prices. As argued earlier, making this sort of larger assessment of well-being requires an evaluation of a broad set of issues that are far beyond the scope of the CPI as it is presently constructed. In short, these aggregate studies can be suggestive of the existence of a bias and the possible mechanisms responsible. However, before this evidence can be taken as conclusive, it is necessary to actually show where the bias is affecting the measurement of inflation in specific areas of the CPI.

MEASURING CONSUMER PRICES: IS THE CPI THE RIGHT YARDSTICK?

The CPI has had a number of serious flaws through time. These include problems of formula bias, an inaccurate treatment of owner-occupied housing, and varying degrees of attentiveness to quality change through time. While these problems make it less than an ideal measure of the rate of inflation, as the previous discussion demonstrates, there is no compelling evidence for the claim that it has a large upward bias in its measure of the rate of inflation. It is worth noting that almost none of the economists or policy experts who have advanced this argument has been willing to embrace the implications of this view for other areas of economics or for policy debates – other than indexing benefits and tax brackets.

The CPI-U-RS series constructed by the BLS corrects many of the problems in the CPI in the period from 1978 to 1998. It provides a relatively consistent measure of inflation over this period. Unfortunately, this series has not been applied to years prior to 1978. The largest and most consistent difference in the inflation rate reported with the methodology used in the CPI-U-RS and the CPI-UX1 is a gap of approximately 0.2 percentage points annually due to the use of geometric means to aggregate inflation rates at lower levels in the CPI. To maintain as consistent series as possible, it would be appropriate to subtract 0.2 percentage points from the rate of inflation reported in the CPI-UX1 in years prior to 1978.

It is likely that the other changes that result from using the CPI-U-RS methodology would be of less consequence, and would be harder to backcast through time. The CPI-U-RS does not treat pollution abatement costs as quality improvements, as the BLS did in the CPI prior to 1998. Extending the RS series backward before 1978 would have led to some increase in the measured rate of inflation in some items, notably autos and gasoline, since additional costs attributable to catalytic converters and lead-free gas were treated as quality improvements in the CPI. However, in general, less attentiveness to quality improvements during this earlier period and the fact that new products were never brought into the index, except during revisions to the CPI, should have caused the CPI to show a somewhat higher measured rate of inflation. In other words, for periods prior to 1978, it is likely that the CPI was higher relative to the true rate of inflation than it has been during the more recent period, although there is little basis for an accurate measure of this difference.[24]

While there is a widely held view that greater product variety, increased innovation, and an increased focus on quality by producers has had a greater impact in the last two decades than in prior periods, there is little real evidence for this position. The prior three decades also saw the spread of extremely important innovations such as home air conditioning, television, and air travel. There were also large improvements in product quality, as shown in an earlier generation of studies of the CPI (Griliches 1961; Triplett and McDonald 1977; Gordon 1990). In addition, there was also a significant increase in the variety of goods and services available in the years prior to 1980. It is important to recognize that the issue here, even in the context of a cost-of-living index, is the value to consumers of increased variety, not any absolute measure of the rate of growth of variety. For example, there is no a priori reason to assume that an increase in the number of breakfast cereals from 40 to 400 would provide more benefit than an increase from 20 to 40. It is entirely possible that relatively small increases in the number of items available when the selection is very small, provide more benefits to consumers than large increases in a period in which there is already significant variety.

It is also worth noting that the size of the CPI's substitution bias has varied over time, depending on the rate and evenness of inflation. The substitution bias would almost certainly have been significantly larger in the late 1960s and 1970s than it was through most of the 1950s, 1980s, and 1990s. Ideally, a measure of the rate of inflation should take this into account. Unfortunately, there is not a consistent series measuring substitution bias in the CPI for years prior to 1982. It would be a valuable project to attempt to piece such a series together, with the best data presently available.

The Boskin Commission rushed out its report in the heat of a political battle over the budget deficit. As the members of the commission acknowledged, their estimate of a 1.1 percentage point bias involved a considerable degree of speculation, since there was relatively little hard evidence available. In the last five years, new studies, in addition to changes in the index itself, have provided a firmer basis for assessing bias in the CPI. The surviving members of the Boskin Commission recently estimated that the changes implemented in the last five years have had the effect of lowering the measured rate of inflation by approximately 0.3 percentage points annually (General Accounting Office 2000).[25] The BLS had a sound basis for implementing most of the changes that led to this lowering in the measured rate of inflation. There is very little economic research that can be cited to support the rest of the 0.8 percentage points of bias identified by the commission.

In short, researchers can feel reasonably comfortable in using the CPI-U-RS series as a measure of the rate of inflation faced by consumers in the years since 1978. The CPI-U-X1 series for the years prior to 1978 does not use the same methodology and therefore may show a rate of inflation that is slightly higher (approximately 0.2 percentage points annually) relative to the true rate of inflation. However, it is important that economists be humble and recognize that these are measures of price inflation, not the cost of living. The construction of a true cost-of-living index would require procedures that are well beyond what economists have developed to date. Those who are interested in the question of whether there has been an increase or a decrease in well-being over time will want to use measures of real wages and incomes as starting points, but they will also have to turn to other indices – life expectancy, the availability of leisure time, crime rates, and so on – to get an accurate view of social progress. Economists do not have a simple number that will provide an answer to this question.

NOTES

1. Whether the CPI should be thought of as a cost-of-living index is itself a matter for debate. The official documentation for the CPI describes it as a price index for consumption goods, as opposed to a cost-of-living index (BLS 1995; Fixler 1993). The former would not imply any claims about a direct relationship between the measure shown by the index and consumers' well-being, whereas the latter is defined exclusively in reference to a measure of consumers' welfare.
2. It is possible that people switch to consuming other fluids as well, because they view the drinking water as being unsafe.
3. Two researchers at the Texas Transportation Institute estimated that average commuting cost per family had increased by $85 a year (1993 dollars) between 1986 and 1993 (Schrank and Lomax 1996). This is equal to approximately 0.3 per cent of the average family's annual expenditure.
4. In its assessment of the accuracy of the CPI as a measure of the cost of living, the Boskin Commission briefly examined trends in crime rates over the previous three decades. This at best only gives part of the picture. Insofar as crime has gone down, or remained stable in part as a result of additional spending on security measures, such as alarm systems or security guards, the CPI would be missing a rise in the cost of living. More importantly, if people have been forced to change their behavior as a result of crime, for example not taking evening walks, then the CPI would be missing an important source of deterioration in living standards, and by implication, a large increase in the cost of living.
5. It is difficult to know exactly how much of this spending is an increase from prior years. The personal business expenditure category rose as a share of total consumption expenditures in the NIPA from 3.6 per cent in 1953 to 9.4 per cent in 1999 (NIPA Table 2.4). But this includes spending that is explicitly investment related, such as brokerage fees, which does not belong in a consumption index.
6. This issue has been examined to some extent by sociologists, perhaps most notably by Hirsch (1976).
7. It is interesting to note that Krugman (1996) asserted that status considerations are the primary determinants of well-being in the context of the debate over the accuracy of the CPI as a measure of the cost of living. This assertion was an effort to reconcile the fact that a substantial overstatement would imply widespread poverty (by the current measure) in the United States in the very recent past. Krugman argued that although people in the 1950s and 1960s might have been very poor by current standards, most people did not perceive themselves to be living in poverty because they were keeping pace with the prevailing living standards of the time.
8. Baker (1996) constructs a historical index dating back to 1953, although it relies on the methodology that was in use in the CPI at the time.
9. Actually a Laspeyres index does not necessarily show a higher rate of inflation than a superlative index for any specific period. Over time, it should be expected that an index that allows for substitution will rise less rapidly than an index that holds the consumption bundle fixed at the base-year levels, but in any specific year, it is entirely possible that the prices of the goods and services consumed in the base year will rise less rapidly than the goods and services actually consumed that year. The BLS was recently given funding so that it could update its sample every second year, instead of at 10–15-year intervals

as had been the case in the past. While this more frequent updating is desirable from the standpoint of producing a more accurate index, it appears as though Congress may have approved the funding under the mistaken view that a newer basket will generally report a lower rate of inflation, and therefore reduce spending on indexed programs (see SFC 1995; General Accounting Office 1997).

10. In CPI strata where the sort of substitution implied by geometric means seemed implausible, such as medical procedures, the Laspeyres methodology continues to be used.

11. The assumption of a 10 per cent pure price difference is quite large, since it means that after adjusting for any quality differences, discount store prices average 10 per cent less than prices in traditional stores, yet enough consumers still shop at the traditional stores to keep them in business.

12. A survey of retail store analysts suggested that exactly this type of service decline was occurring in the 1990s ('Whatever Happened to Service', *New York Times*, 4 March 1997; p. B1).

13. Cellular phones were not rotated over a five-year cycle as ordinarily would have happened, apparently because the CPI specialists in electrical appliances had assumed that cellular phones would be covered under phones, whereas the specialists in the phone division expected them to be covered as an electrical appliance.

14. The commission did cite Hausman (1994) for evidence of the benefit of increased variety in breakfast cereals – a benefit that it was argued does not properly belong in a price index.

15. Gordon (1990) is by far the most important source for the commission's estimates of quality bias in various categories of the CPI. This study contrasted inflation rates measured by the CPI with hedonic indices constructed for a variety of durable goods using price data and descriptions from Sears catalogues and Consumer Reports. Depending on the good, the series go as far back as the late 1940s, and they end in 1983. The most striking feature in most of the estimates is the reduction in the gap between the Sears catalogue index and the CPI over the period. In most cases, the CPI rose substantially against the Sears index in the 1950s and early 1960s, whereas the two indices tend to move at close to the same rate after the late 1960s. In fact, in the years after 1970, the Sears index shows a slightly higher rate of inflation than the CPI for the goods examined in the study. For this reason, it provides a rather dubious basis for the commission's estimates of quality bias.

16. The CPI methodology for evaluating the quality improvements in new cars relies on cost estimates of improvements provided by the manufacturers. It seems unlikely that this method would lead to an understatement of quality improvement.

17. The Boskin Commission cited several papers to support its assessment that the CPI overstated the rate of inflation in prescription drugs by 2.0 percentage points annually in the years after a change in procedure in 1995, and by 3.0 percentage points in prior years (Griliches and Cockburn 1994, 1996; Berndt et al. 1996). The main argument of these papers was that new classes of drugs being developed were qualitatively better than the existing drugs in ways that were not being picked up by the CPI. The new generation of anti-depressant drugs was the prime focus of two of these studies. Subsequent BLS research found that the impact of the change in BLS procedures instituted in 1995 on the rate of inflation in the prescription drug component, was only 0.4 percentage points annually, less than half the size estimated by the commission (Stewart and Reed 1999). More important for the commission's claim of unmeasured quality improvement in drugs has been new medical research which found that the new generation of anti-depressants was no more effective than the earlier generation, and possibly no more effective than placebos (Kahn et al. 2000).

18. The CPI only measures the cash expenditures by individuals for medical care, it does not attempt to measure the payments by employers to insurers or from the government. The Boskin Commission argued that all medical expenditures should be included in the CPI, which would approximately double their weight in the index. This change would make the index less accurate as a deflator of cash expenditures by households, which is its main purpose.

19. This figure combines the price decline in the GDP deflator for computers in 1995–97 with the decline in the CPI computer component since 1998, because prior to that date, the CPI did not use a hedonic pricing method for computers.
20. The BLS has not kept records on the extent to which measured quality improvements have lowered the reported rate of inflation each year, but it did have data that showed that quality improvements lowered the reported rate of inflation by an average of 1.17 percentage points in the years 1983 and 1984, as compared to 1.77 percentage points in 1995 (Armknecht and Weback 1992; Smedley and Moulton 1997).
21. Noncomparable substitutions arise in the CPI when a price collector cannot find the identical product, and no replacement product is considered close enough to be treated as identical for purposes of the survey. It is therefore necessary to make an implicit or explicit quality adjustment to assess the quality difference between the two items.
22. Quality elasticity is defined as the percentage increase in the average price of the goods purchased within a category (conditional on a purchase being made) relative to a 1 percentage-point increase in income.
23. If the price of a good rises more than average, this would lead to a higher measured rate of quality income elasticity, since the higher reported nominal incomes in later years would be associated with larger price increases. By contrast, in the case of goods that had relative price declines, the higher reported incomes in later years would be associated with the purchases of less expensive items, thereby biasing the estimate of quality elasticity toward zero. This bias would be limited if the study properly controlled for inflation in its measure of household income over the period, but it is questionable whether this is the case.
24. The convergence of the rates of inflation shown by Gordon's (1990) Sears catalogue indices and the CPI suggests a diminishing degree of quality bias during the period from the 1950s to the late 1970s.
25. Zvi Griliches, one of the members of the commission, died in 2000.

REFERENCES

Aizcorbe, A.M., and P.C. Jackman (1993), 'The commodity substitution effect in CPI data, 1982–91, *Monthly Labor Review*, December, 25–33 (see also Bureau of Labor Statistics updates).
Aizcorbe, A.M., and P.C. Jackman (1997), 'Update of "The commodity substitution effect in CPI data, 1982–91"', unpublished data prepared for the Senate Finance Committee Advisory Commission to Study the Consumer Price Index, Bureau of Labor Statistics, Washington, DC.
Armknecht, P.A., B.R. Moulton and K.J. Stewart (1995), 'Improvements to the food at home, shelter, and prescription drug indexes in the US consumer price index', Bureau of Labor Statistics working paper no. 263, Washington, DC: Bureau of Labor Statistics.
Armknecht, P.A., and D. Weyback (1992), 'Adjustments for quality change in the U.S. consumer price index', *Journal of Official Statistics*, **5**, 129–47.
Baker, D. (1996), *Getting Prices Right: A Methodologically Consistent Consumer Price Index 1953–94*, Washington, DC: Economic Policy Institute.
Baker, D. (1997), *Getting Price Right: The Debate Over the Consumer Price Index*, Armonk, NY: M.E. Sharpe.
Berndt, E., I. Cockburn and Z. Griliches (1996), 'Pharmaceutical innovations and market dynamics: tracking effects on price indexes for anti-depressant drugs', *Brookings Papers on Economic Activity (Microeconomics)*, pp. 140–200.
Berndt, E., I. Cockburn and Z. Griliches (1997), 'Pharmaceutical innovations and

market dynamics: tracking effects on price indexes for anti-depressant drugs', *Brookings Papers on Economic Activity*, (1), 133–99.

Berndt, E., Z. Griliches and J. Rosset (1993), 'Auditing the producer price index: micro evidence from prescription pharmaceutical preparations', *Journal of Business and Economic Statistics*, **11** (3), 251–64.

Bils, M., and P. Klenow (2001a), 'The acceleration in variety growth', *American Economic Review Papers and Proceedings*, May, 274–80.

Bils, M., and P. Klenow (2001b), 'Quantifying quality growth', *American Economic Review*, September 1006–30.

Bryan, M., and S. Cecchetti (1993), 'The CPI as a measure of inflation', Federal Reserve Bank of Cleveland, *Economic Review*, **29** (4), 15–24.

Buhmann, B., L. Rainwater, G. Schmauss and T. Smeeding (1988), 'Equivalence scales, well-being, inequality, and poverty: sensitivity estimates across ten countries using the Luxembourg Income Study database', *Review of Income and Wealth*, **34**, 115–42.

Bureau of Labor Statistics (1966), 'The Consumer Price Index: History and Techniques', bulletin 1517, Washington, DC: Bureau of Labor Statistics.

Bureau of Labor Statistics (1995), *Report from the Bureau of Labor Statistics for the House Budget Committee*, Washington, DC: US Congress.

Bureau of Labor Statistics (1996), 'Extending the improvements in CPI sample rotation procedures and improving the procedures for substitute items', BLS Press Release, Washington, DC.

Bureau of Labor Statistics (2001), 'Consumer price index detailed report', accessed at: www.stats.bls.gov.cpihome.htm.

Costa, D. (2000), 'American living standards, 1988–1994: evidence from consumer expenditures', NBER working paper no. 7650, Cambridge, MA: National Bureau of Economic Research, April.

Council of Economic Advisers (2002), *Economic Report of the President*, Washington, DC: US Government Printing Office.

Cowan, C. and P. McDonnell (1993), 'Business, households, and governments: health spending, 1991', *Health Care Financing Review*, **4** (3), 227–48.

Cutler, D., M. McClellan, J. Newhouse and D. Remler (1996), 'Are medical prices declining?', NBER working paper no. 5750, Cambridge, MA: National Bureau of Economic Research.

Cutler, D., M. McClellan, J. Newhouse and D. Remler (1998), 'Are medical prices declining? Evidence for heart attack treatments', *Quarterly Journal of Economics*, **113** (4), 991–1024.

Fixler, D. (1993), 'The consumer price index: underlying concepts and caveats', *Monthly Labor Review*, December, 3–12.

Garner, T.I., D.S. Johnson and M.F. Kokoski (1996), 'An experimental consumer price index for the poor', *Monthly Labor Review*, September, 32–43.

General Accounting Office (1997), 'Consumer price index: more frequent updating of market basket expenditure weights is needed', Washington, DC: GGD/OCE 98–2.

General Accounting Office (2000), 'Consumer price index: update of Boskin Commission's estimate of bias', Washington, DC: GAO/GGD 00–50.

Gordon, R. (1990), *The Measurement of Durable Goods Prices*, Chicago: University of Chicago Press.

Gordon, R. (1996), 'The Sears catalog revisited: apparel and durable goods', unpublished paper, Northwestern University, Evanston, IL.

Griliches, Z. (1961), 'Hedonic price indexes for automobiles: an econometric analysis of quality change', *The Price Statistics of the Federal Government*, Washington, DC: Bureau of Labor Statistics, pp. 137–96.

Griliches, Z. (1971), *Price Indexes and Quality Change: Studies in New Methods of Measurement*, Cambridge, MA: Harvard University Press.

Griliches, Z., and I. Cockburn (1994), 'Generics and new goods in pharmaceutical price indexes', *American Economic Review*, December, 1213–32.

Griliches, Z., and I. Cockburn (1996), 'Generics and the producer price index for pharmaceuticals', in *Competitive Strategies in the Pharmaceutical Industry*, Robert Helms (ed.), Washington, DC: American Enterprise Institute Press, pp.19–34.

Hausman, J. (1994), 'Valuation of new goods under imperfect competition', NBER working paper no. 4970, Cambridge, MA: National Bureau of Economic Research.

Henderson, S., and K. Smedley (1994), 'Improvements in estimating the shelter indexes in the CPI', Consumer Price Index Detailed Report to the Congressional Joint Economic Committee, Washington DC: Bureau of Labor Statistics, October, pp. 5–6.

Hirsch, F. (1976), *The Social Limits to Growth*, New York: Twentieth Century Fund.

Kahn, A., H.A. Warner and W.A. Brown (2000), 'Symptom reduction and suicide risk in patients treated with a placebo in antidepressant clinical trials: an analysis of the Food and Drugs Administration database', *Archives of General Psychiatry*, April, 311–17.

Kokoski, M.F. (1987), 'Consumer price indexes by demographic group', BLS working paper no. 167. Washington, DC: Bureau of Labor Statistics.

Kokoski, M., K. Waehrer and P. Rozaklis (2000), 'Using hedonic methods for quality adjustment in the CPI: the consumer audio products component', draft paper, Washington, DC: Bureau of Labor Statistics.

Kreuger, A. (1998), 'Using survey data to assess bias in the consumer price index', *Monthly Labor Review*, April, 24–33.

Lancaster, K. (1977), 'The measurement of changes in quality', *Review of Income and Wealth*, June, 157–72.

Liegey, P.L. (2000a), 'Hedonic quality adjustment methods for clothes dryers in the U.S. CPI', draft paper, Washington, DC: Bureau of Labor Statistics.

Liegey, P.L. (2000b), 'Developing an hedonic regression model for DVD players in the U.S. CPI', draft paper, Washington, DC: Bureau of Labor Statistics.

Liegey, P.L. (2000c), 'Hedonic quality adjustment methods for microwave ovens in the U.S. CPI', draft paper, Washington, DC: Bureau of Labor Statistics.

Liegey, P., and N. Shepler (1999), 'Using hedonic methods to quality adjust VCR prices: a study using hedonic methods', *Monthly Labor Review*, September, 23–4.

Madrick, J. (1997), 'The cost of living: a new myth', *New York Review of Books*, 6 March, 19–24.

Mishel, L., J. Bernstein and J. Schmitt (2001), *The State of Working America, 2000–2001*, Ithaca, NY: Cornell University Press.

Moses, K., and B. Moulton (1997), 'Addressing the quality change issue in the consumer price index', *Brookings Papers on Economic Activity*, 1997 (1), 305–66.

Moulton, B.R. (1993), 'Basic components of the CPI: estimation of price changes', *Monthly Labor Review*, December, 13–24.

Moulton, B.R. (1995), 'Interarea indexes of the cost of shelter using hedonic quality adjustment techniques', *Journal of Econometrics*, **68** (1), 181–205.

Moulton, B.R. (1996a), 'Bias in the consumer price index: what is the evidence?', *Journal of Economic Perspectives*, **10** (4), 159–77.

Moulton, B.R. (1996b), 'Estimation of elementary indexes of the consumer price index', unpublished paper, Washington, DC: Bureau of Labor Statistics.

Moulton, B.R., and K.E. Smedley (1995), 'A comparison of estimators for elementary aggregates of the CPI', unpublished paper, Washington, DC: Bureau of Labor Statistics.

Moulton, B.R., and K.E. Smedley (1997), 'Addressing the quality change issue in the consumer price index', *Brookings Papers on Economic Activity*, 305–66.

Nakamura, L. (1995), 'Measuring inflation in a high-tech age', *Business Review of the Federal Reserve Bank of Philadelphia*, November–December, 13–26.

Nordhaus, W. (1998), 'Quality change in price indexes', *Journal of Economic Perspectives*, **12**, 1 (winter), 59–68.

Oi, W.Y. (1992), 'Productivity in the distributive trades: the shopper and economies of massed resources', in Zvi Griliches (ed.), *Output Measurement in the Service Sector*, National Bureau of Economic Research Conference on Research in Income and Wealth, vol. 56, Chicago: University of Chicago Press, pp. 161–93.

Reinsdorf, M. (1993), 'The effect of outlet price differentials in the U.S. consumer price index', in M.F. Foss, M.E. Manser and A.H. Young (eds), *Price Measurements and Their Uses*, National Bureau of Economic Research Conference on Research in Income and Wealth, vol. 57, Chicago: University of Chicago Press, pp. 227–54.

Reinsdorf, M. (1996), 'Formula bias and seller substitution', unpublished paper, Washington, DC: Bureau of Labor Statistics.

Reinsdorf, M., and B.R. Moulton (1995), 'The construction of basic components of cost of living indexes', Bureau of Labor Statistics working paper no. 261, Washington, DC: Bureau of Labor Statistics.

Schrank, D., and T. Lomax (1996), *Urban Roadway Congestion – 1982 to 1993, Volume 2: Methodology and Urbanized Area Data*, College Station, TX: Texas Transportation Institute.

Senate Finance Committee (SFC) (1995), *Toward a More Accurate Measure of the Cost of Living*, interim report to the Senate Finance Committee from the Advisory Commission to Study the Consumer Price Index, Washington, DC: US Senate.

Senate Finance Committee (SFC) (1996), *Toward a More Accurate Measure of the Cost of Living*, final report to the Senate Finance Committee from the Advisory Commission to Study the Consumer Price Index, Washington, DC: US Senate.

Shapiro, M., and D. Wilcox (1996), 'Mismeasurement in the consumer price index: an evaluation', National Bureau of Economic Research working paper no. 5590.

Shepler, N. (2000), 'Developing a hedonic regression model for refrigerators in the U.S. CPI', draft paper, Washington, DC: Bureau of Labor Statistics.

Smedley, K., and B. Moulton (1997), 'Replication of Armknecht–Weyback analysis for 1995: summary of results', unpublished paper, Washington, DC: Bureau of Labor Statistics.

Stewart, K., and S. Reed (1999), 'CPI research series using current methods, 1978–98', *Monthly Labor Review*, June, 29–38.

Thompson, W. (2000), 'Developing a hedonic regression model for VCRs in the U.S. CPI', draft paper, Washington, DC: Bureau of Labor Statistics.

Triplett, J., and R. McDonald (1977), 'Assessing the quality error in output measures: the case of refrigerators', *Review of Income and Wealth*, June, 137–56.

PART II

International Comparisons of Living
Standards

5. Has economic well-being improved in Canada and the United States?

Lars Osberg and Andrew Sharpe*

INTRODUCTION

By standard measures of economic well-being, the year 2000 was the best yet in North America. Inflation and unemployment were both down, while gross domestic product (GDP) per capita was up. Although Canadians were a bit unhappy because growth was much stronger in the United States than in Canada in the early 1990s, the 30 years from 1970 to 2000 saw substantial growth in GDP in both countries. Admittedly, both the US and Canadian economies experienced sharp recessions in the early 1980s, but over the entire period between 1970 and 1990, they both grew by about the same amount (per capita real GDP was up 56.6 per cent in Canada and 53.8 per cent in the United States). In the early 1990s, both countries went into recession, but a growth-oriented monetary policy in the United States produced rapid recovery and enabled GDP per capita to grow by a further 24.8 per cent from 1990 to 2000. Because the Bank of Canada was willing to sacrifice growth for inflation aversion, it took until 1995 for Canadian GDP per capita to recover to its level of 1989 – by which time US GDP was 7.6 per cent above its 1989 level. Since then Canadian growth in per capita GDP has been comparable to US growth, but much of the early 1990s gap remained. Still, in both countries GDP per capita was, in the year 2000, at historic highs. So what? Does growth in GDP per capita imply greater economic well-being?

In 1980 Ronald Reagan asked the American people a seemingly simple question: 'Are you better off today than you were four years ago?'. Although US real GDP per capita, was, in 1980, 8.8 per cent higher than in 1976, his audiences answered 'No!'. In 1998, when Canadians were asked how the overall financial situation of their generation compared to that of their parents at the same stage of life, less than half (44 per cent) thought that there had been an improvement – despite an increase of approximately 60 per cent in real GDP per capita over the previous 25 years.[1] Evidently, national income accounting

123

measures may not necessarily be a good guide to popular perceptions of trends in economic well-being.

Are such popular perceptions unreasonable? National income accounts omit consideration of many issues (for example, leisure time, the length of life) that are clearly important to the well-being of individuals. For many years, the System of National Accounts (SNA) has been the accounting framework within which most discussions of trends in economic well-being have been conducted, and GDP per capita has been an often used summary measure of economic trends.[2] The compilers of the national accounts have often protested that their attempt to measure the aggregate value of marketed economic output was never intended as a full measure of economic well-being, but it has often been used as such.

Although GDP per capita has many deficiencies as a measure of economic well-being, it is at least a quantity of output measure. Trends in the unemployment rate and hourly wages are also often used to indicate economic performance, but the hourly wage rate is a price (the price of labor), from which individuals derive no direct utility. The unemployment rate measures utilization of an input in the production process. Their widespread use as evaluative criteria cannot be because they indicate directly the utility that individuals enjoy, but because they are indirect indicators of something else, like potential consumption or insecurity.

Summarizing the economic well-being of a complex society inevitably requires a series of ethical and statistical judgments. There are many different dimensions to well-being, which are valued to different degrees by different observers. With a single index number, it may be difficult to disentangle the relative importance of value judgments and technical measurement choices in the construction of the index. Osberg (1985a), therefore, proposed that an index of economic well-being should be based on indices of consumption, accumulation, inequality, and insecurity.[3] This basic framework is consistent with a variety of theoretical perspectives. We, therefore, avoid a specific, formal model.[4]

This chapter is divided into three main sections. First, we present evidence on trends in standard measures, such as GDP per capita and the unemployment rate. Second, we develop estimates of the four key components or dimensions of the index of economic well-being – consumption flows, stocks of wealth, inequality, and insecurity; and develop preliminary estimates of the overall index and its components for the United States and Canada. Third, we discuss the 'productivity' of GDP growth for trends in economic well-being.

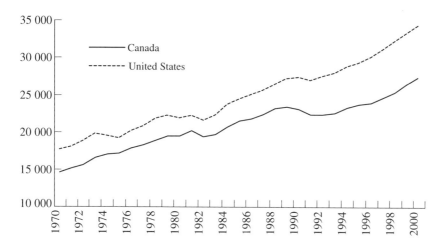

Sources:
Canada   GDP: 1981–2000, CANSIM II 380-0002; 1970–1980, CANSIM D15721. Price
deflator: CANSIM D15689. Population: CANSIM P200000.
United States   GDP & price deflator: Bureau of Economic Analysis (see: http://www.bea.
doc.gov/bea/dn/gdplev.htm). Population: *Economic Report of the President*, 2000.
PPPs: 1997 GDP PPP exchange rate estimate 0.83 $US/$CAN, from Statistics Canada,
CANSIM II, v647808, August 2001.

*Figure 5.1   Real GDP per capita, 1970–2000 (1997 US dollars at
purchasing power parity)*

RECENT TRENDS IN CONVENTIONAL ECONOMIC AND LABOR MARKET VARIABLES

GDP Per Capita

Figure 5.1 presents the trend in real GDP per capita in Canada and the
United States since 1970. Three slowdowns in growth can be discerned. In
1974–75 the United States experienced a more severe recession than
Canada, but in 1981–82 the recession was sharper in Canada. In 1988,
Canadian monetary authorities embarked on the pursuit of 'price stability', and ensuing high interest rates meant that Canada led the United
States into the recession of 1990–91, and produced a considerable lag in
emerging from that recession. Nevertheless, by 2000 both countries had
realized impressive gains in the level of real GDP per capita and both were
growing strongly – and both experienced a considerable growth slowdown
in 2001.

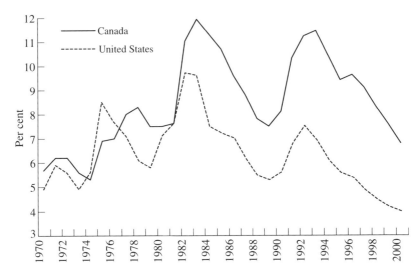

Sources:
Canada: *Labour Force Historical Review 2000* and CANSIM D44950.
United States: *Economic Report of the President*, 2000, and US Bureau of Labor Statistics.

Figure 5.2   Unemployment rates in Canada and the United States, 1970–2000

Unemployment and Employment

Figure 5.2 presents long-term trends in the official unemployment rate in Canada and the United States.[5] As Riddell (1999) has documented, the divergence between Canadian and US unemployment rates in the 1980s can primarily be ascribed to the supply side; in Canada the labor force participation rate increased faster than in the United States. In the 1990s, however, the main event has been strong growth of aggregate demand and jobs in the United States, but a very delayed recovery in Canada. Figure 5.3 presents the employment/population ratio for the two countries. The recessions of the early 1980s and 1990s can easily be identified – and the difference in the recovery paths can also clearly be observed – as Canadian monetary policy in the 1990s remained subservient to the objective of 'price stability' (officially defined as a rate of core inflation in the range of 1 to 3 per cent, with the actual objective below the mid-point of the target band and average annual CPI inflation from 1994 to 2000 at 1.5 per cent).

Trends in Average Hourly Real Wages

Figure 5.4 presents average direct hourly real wages for production workers in Canada and the United States. For many workers, and for many years,

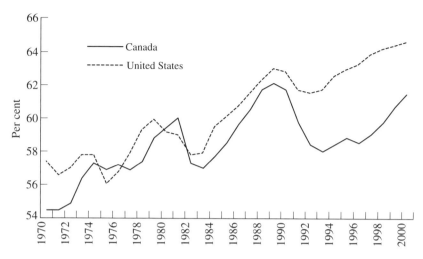

Sources:
Canada: *Labour Force Historical Review 2000*.
United States: *Economic Report of the President*, 2000, and US Bureau of Labor Statistics.

*Figure 5.3   Employment/population ratio for Canada and the United
States, 1970–2000*

hourly real wages have been fairly flat in North America. Although there
has been substantial growth in incomes at the top end of the income distribution (which has pulled up the average income of the population as a
whole), the middle part of the income distribution has seen little progress
(Osberg 1999). Figure 5.4 also illustrates the fact that Canadian and
American production workers have, if jobs are available, similar earning
possibilities. However, the difference between expressing Canadian wages
in purchasing power parity (PPP)-adjusted US dollars, or converting at the
current exchange rate, also illustrates the competitive advantage that
Canadian firms obtain when the Canadian dollar is undervalued relative to
its estimated PPP value.

So What Does All This Have To Do With Economic Well-being?

Economists often start by assuming that individuals derive utility from
consumption and from leisure. But GDP per capita includes many items
(such as exports or investment) that are not part of consumption, while it
excludes completely any leisure enjoyed by individuals. The employment
rate measures labor supply, which is often thought of by economists as a
cost that people incur in order to enable consumption – it is not clear why

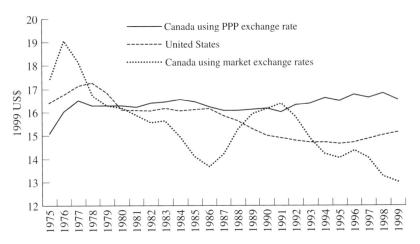

Note: Hourly direct pay includes (a) pay for time worked (basic time and piece rates plus overtime premiums, shift differentials, other premiums and bonuses paid regularly each pay period, and cost-of-living adjustments) and (b) other direct pay (pay for time not worked (vacations, holidays, and other leave, except sick leave), seasonal or irregular bonuses and other special payments, selected social allowances, and the cost of payments in kind), before payroll deductions of any kind. Direct pay is also measured on an hours-worked basis for every country.

Source: US Bureau of Labor Statistics (ftp://ftp.bls.gov/pub/special.requests/ ForeignLabor/supptab.txt).

Figure 5.4   Hourly direct pay for production workers in manufacturing, Canada and the United States, 1975–1999 (1999 US dollars)

working more is, by itself, a 'good thing'. The wage rate is useful as an indicator of the price of labor (that is, the rate at which people trade time for goods), but it is not inherently a source of utility. None of the above measures really corresponds to anything that individuals would actually want. The difference between trends in average hourly real wages for production workers (in PPP terms, fairly flat in both countries, but somewhat higher in Canada by 1999) and trends in GDP per capita (up strongly, but more so in the United States) is a clue to the fact that indicators of economic performance may disagree. But saying that these indicators are unsatisfactory is one thing; can a better measure of economic well-being be constructed?

AN INDEX OF ECONOMIC WELL-BEING

GDP is a measure of the aggregate marketed income of a society, however 'income' is a flow variable that does not directly consider the aggregate value of the bequest this generation will leave to its descendants. Although those now alive clearly care about the level of their own consumption, they also care (in varying degrees) about the well-being of future generations. Furthermore, trends in average income do not reveal the chances that individuals have to share personally in the general prosperity. Individuals are justifiably concerned about where they might sit in the distribution of income, and the degree to which their personal economic future is secure. This chapter therefore identifies four dimensions of economic well-being:

- *effective per capita consumption flows*   consumption of marketed goods and services; and effective per capita flows of household production, leisure, and other unmarketed goods and services;
- *net societal accumulation of stocks of productive resources*   net accumulation of tangible capital, housing stocks, and consumer durables; net changes in the value of natural resources stocks; environmental costs, net change in level of foreign indebtedness; accumulation of human capital; and research and development (R&D) investment;
- *distribution*   the intensity of poverty (incidence and depth) and the inequality of income; and
- *economic security*   economic security from job loss and unemployment, illness, family breakup, poverty in old age.

A fuller discussion of the rationale for this framework of consumption, accumulation, distribution, and insecurity can be found in Osberg (1985a). We distinguish these four main dimensions of economic well-being to enable persons with differing value judgments (for example, a greater or lesser preference for intergenerational bequest, or for the reduction of poverty, compared to increases in average consumption) to account explicitly for those values. Each dimension of economic well-being is itself an aggregation of many underlying trends, on which the existing literature is sometimes spotty.[6]

We recognize that the SNA has, thanks to many years of development effort by international agencies, produced an accounting system for GDP that is rigorously standardized across countries. Internationally comparable statistics on other dimensions of economic well-being are far less complete. However, using GDP per capita as a measure of well-being would implicitly: (i) assume that the aggregate share of income devoted to accumulation (including the value of unpriced environmental assets) is automatically optimal, and (ii) set the weight of income distribution or economic insecurity to zero, by ignoring their influence entirely. Neither assumption seems justifiable.

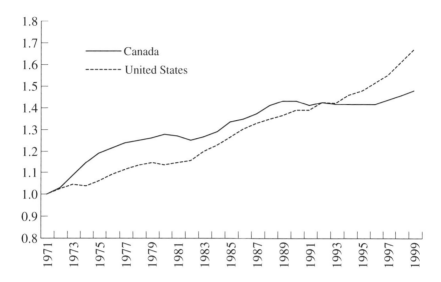

Figure 5.5   Trends in per capita consumption in the United States and Canada

Average Consumption Flows

Current consumption is certainly an important component of economic well-being, but a better measure than GDP per capita is required. The objective of this subsection is to outline our methodology for calculating average effective consumption in order to show specifically how GDP can be improved on as a measure of economic well-being. Figure 5.5 presents our final calculation of trends.

The starting point is aggregate real personal consumption per capita in constant prices.[7] The SNA provides a strong basis for estimating the consumption of marketed goods and the cost of providing government services, and there have been enough studies of the value of household production to enable some confidence as to the range of reasonable values.[8] Estimates are more imprecise when one considers the value of a number of other factors that also influence consumption flows, such as leisure, regrettables, the underground economy[9] and life expectancy. At this stage in the development of the index of economic well-being, our preference (wherever possible) is to include, rather than exclude. Since omitting a variable would implicitly set its value to zero, an imprecise measure is likely to embody a smaller error than omitting a variable. However, when there is no estimate available at all, omission is unavoidable.

Life expectancy has increased significantly in recent years in North

America, and we have every reason to believe that having a long life is an important component of well-being. The economic value of these extra years of life should be included in the total consumption flows of individuals, since presumably people care about both how much they consume per year, and how many years they get to consume it.[10] For this chapter, we adopt the simple expedient of considering an increase in consumption per year and consumption for an increased number of years to be equivalent; that is, we add to consumption flows in each year the percentage increase in average life expectancy.[11] However, we do recognize the crudity of this measure of an existential issue. Between 1971 and 1999, Canadians enjoyed an 8.1 per cent increase in life expectancy while Americans experienced an 8.0 per cent rise. Personal consumption per capita is adjusted upward by the percentage increase in life expectancy relative to base.[12]

When individuals cohabit in households, they benefit from economies of scale in household consumption. There is a large literature on the estimation of 'equivalence scales', which attempt to account for the magnitude of such economies of scale in households of different sizes.[13] When comparing the average effective consumption of individuals over time, the implication is that as households have shrunk in average size, economies of scale have been lost. Trends in average per capita consumption should, therefore, be adjusted for the average loss over time of economies of scale in household consumption.[14] All Western countries have experienced a long-term decline since the 1970s in average family size; in the United States, the decline was 10.9 per cent, from 3.57 in 1971 to 3.18 in 1999. The 'LIS' (Luxembourg Income Study) equivalence scale (that is, the square root of family size) has been applied to average family income to construct an index of equivalent family income (1971 = 100), which is used to adjust personal consumption per capita.

Some of the economic activity included in GDP does not contribute to economic welfare, but rather measures defensive expenditures – or intermediate inputs – that individuals make in order to be able to produce or consume. The costs households pay in order to commute to work are considered in the GDP to be part of household consumption, but the expenses which firms incur to bring materials to the work site are seen as an intermediate input in production. Since intermediate inputs in the business sector are netted out in the calculation of value added, we argue that similar expenditures by households should be subtracted from marketed consumption to obtain a better estimate of true consumption flows. Similarly, if the good that individuals want to consume is 'a crime-free street', but it now takes a greater expenditure on police services to produce that good, an increase in police expenditure that only serves to maintain the crime rate unchanged should not be counted as an increase in (public sector) consumption. This chapter uses the estimates of costs of commuting, crime, house pollution abatement, and auto accidents constructed by Anielski and Rowe (1999) and subtracts these from the value of current consumption.

A major defect of GDP as a measure of well-being is that because it counts only market income, it effectively assigns a zero value to leisure time. Among OECD countries there are major differences in both the initial level and trends over time in the average annual number of hours worked. Therefore, we standardize for changes in hours of paid work relative to the average annual hours worked per adult of working age in the United States in 1971. Unlike the measure of economic welfare developed by Nordhaus and Tobin (1972), no attempt is made here to define leisure activities, estimate the amount of leisure enjoyed, and place a value on this total leisure time. We avoid placing a monetary value on inframarginal hours of leisure, which might be highly problematic. Rather, we adjust the value of consumption for differences in paid hours relative to a benchmark, namely, the United States in 1971. When average annual hours worked is less than the benchmark we make a positive adjustment to consumption and a negative adjustment when there is more working time than the benchmark.

Our methodology is equivalent to saying that at the margin, individuals ascribe a value equal to the after-tax average wage to changes in nonworking time that are not due to unemployment fluctuations. Estimates of relative working time per person employed are adjusted for the employment/working-age population ratio to provide estimates of relative nonworking time on a working-age population (15–64) basis to account for differences in employment/population ratios. These estimates are then valued at the after-tax[15] wage rate to provide estimates of the value of relative nonworking time per working-age person, adjusted by the working-age population/total population ratio to control for differences in demographic structure. This amount, expressed in constant prices, is then added to consumption flows to produce a working-time-adjusted estimate of consumption relative to the US benchmark.

However, unemployment does not constitute leisure. Many authors have noted that there are psychological costs to unemployment (for example, Clark and Oswald 1994). We cannot, in this chapter, provide estimates of the negative utility of unemployment time, or any partial value of such time. However, in the imputations for the value of nonworking time, we deduct hours of unemployment,[16] that is, assign such hours zero value.[17] To account for involuntary leisure we subtract average annual hours of unemployment per working-age person from the relative nonworking time estimate.

By 1999, working hours per adult (15–64) in the United States were 141 hours above their 1971 level, but only up 54 hours in Canada. Since 141 hours is equivalent to around 2.7 hours per week, this represents a substantial change in well-being that should be reflected in a reasonable measure of economic progress. However, since leisure hours receive zero valuation in GDP accounting, these changes do not show up in GDP per capita.

The provision of nonmarketed or heavily subsidized services by the government is also part of the flow of effective consumption. Current expenditure data (for all levels of government including defense and capital consumption allowances, but excluding debt service charges and transfer payments) are taken from the national accounts, expressed in constant prices. The importance of government final consumption expenditures relative to personal adjusted consumption in 1999 was 19.9 per cent in the United States, lower than in Canada (29.3 per cent).

The components of per capita consumption flows (adjusted personal consumption, government consumption, the cost of regrettables, and the imputation for nonworking time) are summed to total consumption flows adjusted for hours worked.

Accumulation, Sustainability, and the Intergenerational Bequest

If individuals alive today care about the well-being of future generations, measurement of trends in current well-being should include consideration of changes in the well-being of generations yet unborn. This consideration of future generations can also be justified on the grounds that a concept of 'society' should include both present and future generations. Either way, wealth accumulation by this generation will increase the bequest left to future generations, and is an important component of well-being.[18]

Figure 5.6 provides our estimates of trends in the accumulation of productive assets. We emphasize that this component of economic well-being consists of those stocks of real productive assets that can generate real income for future generations, not the financial instruments that will determine the allocation of the returns from those assets. As Osberg (1998a) discusses in more depth, financial 'generational accounting' techniques focus on the distributional impact of government debt; in this subsection we are concerned with the real accumulation of productive assets that will generate the income flows that are allocated by financial claims. It is the stocks of 'wealth' left to the next generation, broadly conceived to include environmental and human resources as well as physical capital stock, that will determine whether a society is on a long-run sustainable trajectory of aggregate consumption, irrespective of the distribution of those consumption flows at the individual level.

The physical capital stock includes residential and nonresidential

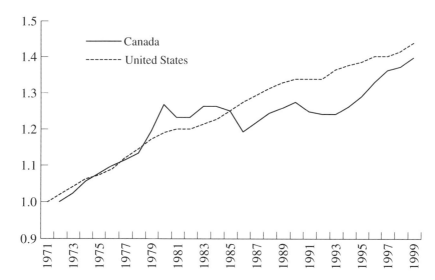

Figure 5.6   Trends in per capita wealth accumulation in the United States and Canada

structures, machinery, and equipment in both the business and the government sector. The greater the capital stock, the greater is the future productive capacity and future potential consumption flows and economic well-being. The capital stock data are based on the perpetual inventory method where investment flows are accumulated over time, with depreciation rates applied to the different assets. Data for the current net fixed capital stock, expressed in constant prices of national currency units, have been taken from national sources. It is assumed that their growth rates are internationally comparable, although the use of different depreciation rates by statistical agencies may reduce comparability for both level and rate of growth comparisons.[19] Between 1971 and 1999, the increase in the fixed capital stock, on a per capita basis, was higher in Canada (71.0 per cent) than in the United States (62.6 per cent).

Closely related to the physical capital stock is the concept of the R&D capital stock. In an era of rapid technological change, expenditure on R&D is a crucial ingredient in the ability of society to innovate and create wealth. Statistical agencies do not produce R&D stock data, but OECD data on annual flows of total business enterprise expenditure on research and development can be accumulated into a stock of R&D capital valued at cost of investment; a depreciation rate of 20 per cent on the declining balance is assumed.[20]

Current consumption levels could be increased by running down stocks of nonrenewable natural resources or by exploiting renewable resources in a nonsustainable manner, but this would be at the cost of the consumption of future generations. A key aspect of the wealth accumulation is net changes in the value of natural resources (which depends on both changes in resource prices and the estimated stocks of resources). From an intergenerational perspective, it is the value of the natural resources, not their physical extent, which counts. The valuation of these resources poses serious conceptual problems.[21] Statistics Canada (1997) has provided estimates for both physical and value estimates of natural resources such as forests, energy reserves, and minerals and the Bureau of Economic Analysis (*Survey of Current Business*, April 1994) has provided estimates for oil and gas, coal, metals, and other minerals. These were used in the construction of the index of economic well-being for Canada and the United States (Osberg and Sharpe 1998, 1999).

The human capital accumulated by the workforce generates both current and future income. Trends in the stock of human capital, including both formal educational attainment levels and on-the-job training, are important determinants of current and future economic well-being. School retention and participation in post-secondary education have increased dramatically in Canada over the last three decades, and there is a strong relationship between educational attainment and individual income.[22] This chapter uses an admittedly crude and incomplete (but feasible) input cost method: the cost per year of education expenditures at the primary, secondary, and post-secondary levels. Yearly estimates of the distribution of education attainment in the population were then used to compute the total cash cost of production of human capital in education. Data on the educational attainment of 25–64-year-olds and expenditure per student for the early childhood, primary, secondary, non-university tertiary, and university-level education were used to estimate the per capita stock of human capital. In order to clearly distinguish intercountry differences in the quantity of education obtained, as opposed to differences in its cost of production, we apply a common cost base (the cost of education in the United States) to both countries.

We do not count the gross level of government or corporate debt as a 'burden' on future generations, and we do not count as part of the intergenerational bequest the value of paper gains in the stock market. In general, financial instruments represent both assets to their holders and liabilities to their issuers. The distribution of such assets/liabilities will play a major role in allocating the real returns to the future capital stock, but the issue at this point is the aggregate value of the real intergenerational bequest.

However, net debt to foreigners is another issue. Since interest payments on the net foreign indebtedness of citizens of one country to residents of other countries will lower the aggregate future consumption options of those citizens, increases in the level of foreign indebtedness reduce economic well-being within a given country. Estimates of the net investment position are from national sources and are deflated by the GDP deflator and adjusted for population to obtain real per capita estimates in the net international investment position.

Like the excess depletion of natural resources, current consumption can be increased at the expense of the degradation of the environment, reducing the economic well-being of future generations. Consequently, changes in the level of air and water pollution should be considered an important aspect of wealth accumulation. Countries pass on from generation to generation both a natural and a man-made national heritage. If this heritage were damaged, the economic well-being of future generations would be reduced. Since it is very difficult, if not impossible, to put a monetary value on, for example, the pristine condition of national parks, or historic buildings, there will be no attempt to set an aggregate value to these assets.[23]

However, the issue of trends in well-being is the change in such assets, which is easier to measure and for which indicators of environmental quality can be developed. Probably the best-known environmental change is global warming arising from increased emissions of greenhouse gases, the most common of which is carbon dioxide emissions. Fortunately, data are available on these emissions and their estimated costs can be subtracted from the stock of wealth to obtain an environmentally adjusted stock of wealth. The conceptual issues to be dealt with in estimating the costs of CO_2 emissions include whether the costs should be viewed from a global, national or subnational perspective, whether the costs increase linearly with the levels of pollution, whether the costs should be borne by the producer or receptor of transborder emissions, and whether costs should vary from country to country or be assumed the same for all countries. Since global warming affects all countries, we estimate world total costs of emissions and allocate these costs on the basis of a country's share of world GDP. Fankhauser (1995) has estimated the globalized social costs of CO_2 emissions (with no adjustment for different national costs) at US$20 per ton in 1990. Since world CO_2 emissions in 1997 were 22636 million metric tons this implies a global social cost of $452720 million. This amount was allocated on the basis of share of real world GDP, expressed in US dollars, then converted into national currency at the PPP exchange rate and divided by population. As these costs represent a loss in the value of the services provided by the environment, they can be considered a deduction from the total stock of wealth of the society. For example, in 1999, per capita stocks of wealth in Canada were reduced by Can$364 because of the social costs imposed by CO_2 emissions according to this methodology.

As the estimates of the physical capital stock, the R&D capital stock, natural resources, human capital, net foreign debt, and environmental degradation are expressed in value terms, they can be aggregated and presented on a per capita basis. Net foreign debt per capita and the social costs of CO_2 emissions are negative entries and subtracted from the stocks of wealth. For the 1971–99 period, estimates for the six components of the wealth stock are found on the website tables containing the data underlying this chapter. The rate of change for per capita real wealth stocks in national currency at constant prices was 43.7 per cent in the United States, higher than in Canada (39.5 per cent).

Income Distribution: Inequality and Poverty

Would economic well-being in a society in which everyone has an income of $500 remain the same if income were redistributed so that half the population had $999 and the other half had $1? Both societies would have the same average income, but the more equal society is likely to generate more aggregate utility.[24] The idea that 'social welfare' depends, in general, on both average income and the inequality of incomes has a long tradition in welfare economics. However, in measuring the level of social welfare, the exact relative weight to be assigned to changes in average incomes, compared to changes in inequality, cannot be specified by economic theory. Since Atkinson (1970), it has been recognized that the measurement of inequality itself depends on the relative value which the observer places on the utility of individuals at different points in the income distribution. For a 'Rawlsian', only changes in the well-being of the least well-off matter, but others will admit some positive weight for the income gains of the nonpoor,[25] and will assign some negative weight to inequality among the nonpoor.

Since the economic well-being of the population is affected both by inequality in the distribution of income and by the extent of poverty, there are two issues: (i) the importance of inequality/poverty compared to trends in average income, and (ii) the relative weight to be placed on poverty compared to inequality. We suggest that a compound subindex should place some weight (β) on a measure of inequality in the aggregate distribution of income (summarized here by the Gini coefficient of after-tax household income[26]) and some weight $(1 - \beta)$ on poverty intensity.

In 1999 the Gini coefficient was considerably larger in the United States (0.457) than in Canada (0.403); although poverty intensity was also higher in the United States than in Canada, the differential shrank during the late 1990s (Osberg 2000; Osberg and Xu 2000). The overall index of equality is a weighted average of the indices of poverty intensity for all units or

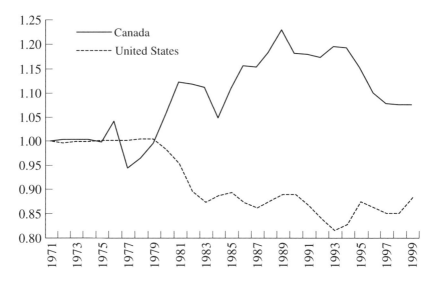

Figure 5.7   Trends in income equality in the United States and Canada

households and the Gini coefficient, with the weights 0.75 and 0.25, respectively. The index is multiplied by –1 in order to reflect the convention that increases are desirable. Figure 5.7 presents the trend in economic equality from 1971 to 1999.

Insecurity

If individuals knew their own economic futures with certainty, their welfare would depend only on their actual incomes over their lifetimes, since there would be no reason to feel anxiety about the future. However, uncertainty about the future will decrease the economic welfare of risk-averse individuals. Individuals can try to avoid risk through social and private insurance, but such mechanisms do not completely eliminate economic anxieties, which have to be considered a subtraction from well-being.

Although public opinion polling can reveal that many feel themselves to be economically insecure, and that such insecurity decreases their subjective state of well-being, the concept of economic insecurity is rarely discussed in academic economics.[27] Consequently, there is no generally agreed definition of economic insecurity. Osberg (1998b, p. 23) has argued that economic insecurity is, in a general sense, 'the anxiety produced by a lack of economic safety; that is, by an inability to obtain protection against subjectively significant potential economic losses'. In this sense, individuals' perceptions of insecurity are inherently forward looking, the result of their expectations of the future and their current economic context, hence only imperfectly captured by measures such as the *ex post* variability of income flows.[28] Ideally, one would measure trends in economic security with data that included (for example) the percentage of the population who have credible guarantees of employment continuity and the adequacy of personal savings to support consumption during illness or unemployment. However, such data are not widely available. For these reasons, rather than attempt an overall measure of economic insecurity, this chapter adopts a 'named risks' approach, and addresses the change over time in four key economic risks.

Over 50 years ago, the United Nations' Universal Declaration of Human Rights (Article 25) stated:

> Everyone has the right to a standard of living adequate for the health and well-being of himself and of his family, including food, clothing, housing and medical care and necessary social services, and the right to security in the event of unemployment, sickness, disability, widowhood, old age or other loss of livelihood in circumstances beyond his control.

For this chapter, we construct measures of the percentage change over time in the economic risks associated with unemployment, illness, 'widowhood' (or single-female parenthood), and old age. In each case, we model the risk of an economic loss associated with the event as a conditional probability, which can itself be represented as the product of a number of underlying probabilities. We weight the prevalence of the underlying risk by the proportion of the population that it affects. Figure 5.8 presents the results. The core hypothesis underlying the measure of economic insecurity proposed here is that changes in the subjective level of anxiety about a lack of economic safety are proportionate to changes in objective risk.

The economic risk associated with unemployment can be modeled as the product of the risk of unemployment in the population and the extent to which people are protected from the income risks of unemployment. We have taken as a proxy for the risk of unemployment changes in the employment rate (employment/population ratio). Changes in this ratio reflect changes in the unemployment rate and changes in the participation rate (both cyclical and structural). The extent to which people have been protected by unemployment insurance (UI) from the financial impacts of unemployment can be modeled as the product of: (i) the percentage of the unemployed who claim regular UI benefits,[29] and (ii) the percentage of average weekly wages replaced by UI.

Viewed from a longer-term perspective, the economic insecurities associated with illness in Canada certainly dropped considerably with the introduction of universal health insurance in 1968–70 (that is, prior to the period

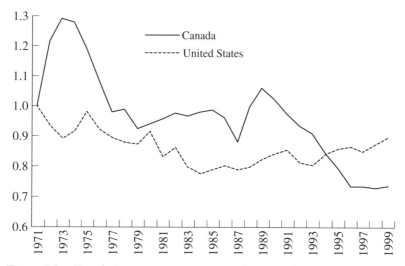

Figure 5.8   Trends in economic security in the United States and Canada

of analysis of this chapter). However, a full estimate of the trend in economic anxieties associated with ill health should also include the risk of loss of earnings. Historically, a portion of the labor force has had some income loss protection through sick-leave provisions in their individual or collective employment contracts. In Canada, self-employment increased substantially in the 1990s and is now roughly twice the US level. One implication of a trend to short-term contract employment and self-employment is an increase in the fraction of the population whose employment income ceases totally in the event of ill health. Data limitations prevent us from modeling such risks. Instead, we focus on the risk of health-care costs and assume that risk is proportional to the share of uninsured private medical-care expenses in disposable income (which has risen in Canada with the increase in uninsured drug costs).

Medical-care expenses as a proportion of disposable income (excluding medical insurance premia and net of insurance reimbursement for medical expenses) were in 1999 much higher in the United States than in Canada. However, to follow the convention that increases in the subcomponents of the index of economic security are improvements, we want an index of 'security' and not an index of 'insecurity', hence we multiply the risk of illness, where increases are negative for economic well-being, by −1.

When the UN Universal Declaration of Human Rights was drafted in 1948, the percentage of single-parent families was relatively high in many countries, partly as a result of World War II. At that time, 'widowhood' was the primary way in which women and children lost access to male earnings. Since then, divorce and separation have become the primary origins of single-parent families. However, it remains true that many women and children are 'one man away from poverty', since the prevalence of poverty among single-parent families is extremely high. To model trends in this aspect of economic insecurity, we multiply (the probability of divorce)* (the poverty rate among single-female-parent families)[30]* (the average poverty gap ratio among single-female-parent families).[31] The product of these last two variables is proportional to the intensity of poverty.

We stress that in constructing a measure of the economic insecurity associated with single-parent status, we are *not* constructing a measure of the social costs of divorce. Economic well-being is only part of social well-being, and divorce has emotional and social costs (for example, for the involved children) that are not considered here. Arguably, over time the social costs associated with divorce (for example, stigma) have changed, as the institution of marriage itself has changed, but such issues lie well beyond the scope of this chapter. The annual divorce rate in 1999 was 2.05 per cent of legally married couples in the United States but lower in Canada (0.95 per cent). The poverty rate for single-female parents was 45.2 per cent in the United States and 43.0 per cent in Canada in 1997 (the most recent year comparable data for the two countries were available). The average poverty gap ratio for single-female parents was greater in the United States (39.8 per cent) than in Canada (31.2 per cent).

Again, to follow the convention that increases in the subcomponents of the index of economic security are improvements, we want an index of 'security' and not an index of 'insecurity', hence we multiply the risk of single parenthood, where increases are negative for economic well-being, by -1. A negative sign, therefore, indicates that an increased negative value represents a decline in well-being (and a decreased negative value, an increase in well-being).

Since income in old age is the result of a lifelong series of events and decisions, which we cannot hope to disentangle in this chapter, we model the idea of 'insecurity in old age' as the chance that an elderly person will be poor, and the average depth of that poverty. The poverty rate for the elderly in 1997 was 24.4 per cent in the United States and 5.4 per cent in Canada. The average poverty gap ratio for the elderly was higher in the United States (28.3 per cent), than in Canada (15.8 per cent).

Again, to follow the convention that increases in the subcomponents of the index of economic security are improvements, we want an index of 'security' and not an index of 'insecurity'. Hence we multiply the risk of elderly poverty by -1.

Overall Index of Economic Security

The four risks discussed above have been aggregated into an index of economic security using as aggregation weights the relative importance of the four groups in the population:

- for unemployment, the proportion of the population aged 15–64 in the total population;
- for illness, the proportion of the population at risk of illness, which is 100 per cent;
- for single-parent poverty, the proportion of the population comprising married women with children under 18; and
- for old-age poverty, the proportion of the population in immediate risk of poverty in old age, defined as the proportion of the population aged 45–64 in the total population.

The above proportions have been normalized for all years to one. For example, the weights for Canada in 1999 were the following: unemployment (0.2784), illness (0.4149), single parenthood (0.2134), and old age (0.0934).[32] Implicitly, by expressing changes as proportionate to an initial base, we are assuming that individuals habituate to a given level of background stimulus, but respond similarly to proportionate changes in stimulus.

Based on the above weights, the overall index of economic security for Canada and the United States is shown in Figure 5.8. The decline in economic security in Canada in the 1990s is notable.

ESTIMATES OF TRENDS IN THE OVERALL INDEX OF ECONOMIC WELL-BEING

Weighting of Components

Trends in any index are determined by the choice of variables that are included in the index, the trends in those variables, and the weights these variables receive. Since the four main dimensions of average consumption, intergenerational bequest, inequality/poverty, and insecurity are separately identified, it is easy to conduct sensitivity analyses of the impact on perceived overall trends of different weightings of these dimensions; we think that this is a major advantage of the index. We therefore present two examples; first, a simple average of the four components of well-being that assigns equal weight to each component, and second, a

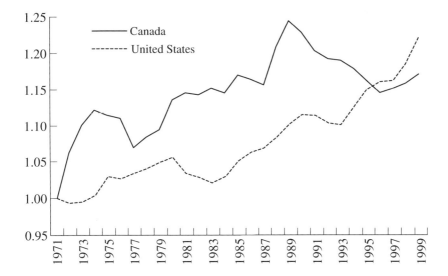

*Figure 5.9   Trends in economic well-being in the United States and
Canada (equal weighting of consumption, accumulation,
distribution, and economic security)*

'consumption-oriented' weighting that assigns relatively heavy weight
(0.7) to per capita effective consumption and relatively little weight to
accumulation (0.1), equality (0.1), and security (0.1).

Trends in the Overall Index of Economic Well-being

Figure 5.9 compares trends in economic well-being in Canada and the
United States under the 'equal-weighting' assumption. The contrast
between the two countries in the early 1970s, when well-being rose much
more strongly in Canada than in the United States, and in the 1990s, when
well-being declined in Canada but rose in the United States, is particularly
striking. Generally, the more heavily current average consumption is
emphasized the closer the index of economic well-being mirrors trends in
GDP per capita. Figures 5.10–12 illustrate the point by comparing trends
in GDP per capita, the 'consumption-oriented' weighting, and equal
weighting, for both the United States and Canada. However, in every
instance the consideration of a wider range of issues than those recognized
in GDP accounting reduces the measured increase in economic well-being.

In the United States, GDP per capita increased by 84.1 per cent over the
1971 to 1999 period, but our equally weighted index of economic well-being

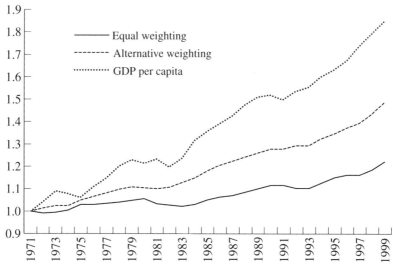

Note: Alternative Weighting = 0.7* Construction + 0.1 *Wealth + 0.1 *Equality +0.1 *Security.

Figure 5.10   Trends in economic well-being in the United States (equal

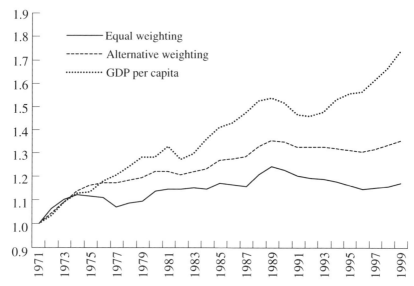

Note: Alternative Weighting = 0.7* Construction + 0.1 *Wealth + 0.1 *Equality +0.1 *Security.

Figure 5.11   Trends in economic well-being in Canada (equal weighting,
alternative weighting, and GDP per capita)

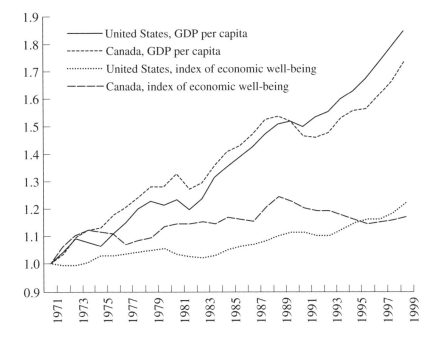

Figure 5.12   Trends in economic well-being (equal weighting) and GDP per capita in the United States and Canada

was up only 21.8 per cent. The United States has been marked by a substantial increase in economic inequality over this period, as seen in Figure 5.7, and increases in money income have been limited to the top end of the income distribution (see Osberg 1999). Increases in money income have also been obtained at the cost of substantial increases in working hours. Hence, this is not an unreasonable finding. In Canada, GDP per capita rose 73.0 per cent between 1971 and 1999, while the index of economic well-being based on an equal weighting scheme advanced only 17.0 per cent. As Figures 5.7 and 5.8 indicate, the 1990s saw a substantial decrease in economic equality and economic security in Canada, with insufficient counterbalancing gains in average consumption and aggregate wealth (see Figures 5.5 and 5.6). The result is shown in Figures 5.9 and 5.11: a decline in overall economic well-being in Canada for much of the 1990s.

Level Comparisons of Economic Well-being

Comparisons of the level of well-being across countries are inherently much more problematic than comparisons of the trends in various components of economic well-being within countries. In describing trends, one can focus on changes at the margin (such as the *change* in environmental quality) and finesse the valuation of infra-marginal units (such as the total value of environmental amenities enjoyed by Canadians and Americans). In cross-country comparisons, the institutional context of economic data differs to a far greater extent than in within-country, over time comparisons. Calculations of PPP equivalence across several countries have greater uncertainty than comparisons of within-country consumer price levels. Statistical agencies in different countries differ in their data availability and data-gathering practices to a greater degree than they change those practices over time in the same country. For all these reasons, this chapter avoids direct commentary on comparative levels of economic well-being.

CONCLUSION AND IMPLICATIONS

Early economists were fairly broad in their conception of 'prosperity', but were in no doubt that it had many positive implications. More recently, the measure of economic success has been narrower, and it falls to critics of the System of National Accounts to show that alternative measures to GDP per capita are possible, plausible and make some difference. This chapter has, therefore, developed an index of economic well-being based on four dimensions or components of economic well-being – consumption, accumulation, income distribution, and economic security.

In general, a key finding of this chapter is that economic well-being has increased at a much slower rate over the last 30 years than real GDP per capita. Although GDP per capita is a widely used indicator, it is best seen as an *input* into economic well-being. Hence, if 'productivity' is the ratio between 'outputs' and 'inputs', and if the output we want (economic well-being) is growing more slowly than the input we supply (GDP per capita), then in a very real sense social productivity is declining.

Historically, the 'welfare state' of advanced capitalist countries aimed at mitigating the extent of economic insecurity and economic inequality, two key dimensions of economic well-being. Recent years have seen substantial revisions to social policy in both Canada and the United States, and it is precisely the inequality and insecurity dimensions of well-being in which there have been the strongest adverse trends (particularly in Canada). If growth in GDP no longer translates into as great an increase in economic well-being, these recent changes in social policy may well be responsible for this decline in social productivity.

Social policy clearly operates within the context set by macroeconomic policy and by broader social, economic and technological change, and each particular social policy needs to be evaluated on its own merits. Nevertheless, the general implication of this chapter is that policy design should consider the impacts of economic and social policy on *all* the dimensions of economic well-being – consumption, accumulation, distribution and insecurity.

NOTES

*   We would like to thank Lynn Lethbridge, Dmitry Kabrelyan, and Jeremy Smith for their exemplary work on this project and the Social Sciences and Humanities Research Council of Canada for its support to Osberg under Grant 010-97-0802. An earlier version of this chapter was presented at the Conference, 'Labor in a Globalising World: The Challenge for Asia', City University of Hong Kong, Hong Kong, China, 4–6 January, 2001. The underlying data are posted at www.csls.ca under the Projects/Index of Economic Well-being. Comments are welcome. Revised versions will be posted at http://is.dal.ca/~osberg/home.html.This paper also draws on material from Osberg and Sharpe (1998, 1999).

1.   For real GDP per capita see CANSIM D14606; for poll details see Angus Reid Globe/CTV poll of July 1998, available at: www.angusreid.com.

2.   Keuning (1998) reviews the contributions in Dawson (1996) and Kendrick (1996) and the most recent (UN 1993) revisions to the SNA.

3.   We argue for the explicit recognition that the weights attached to each component will vary, depending on the values of different observers. By specifying additive subindices, we are implicitly assuming that preferences for social outcomes are separable into their components (for example, that the weight placed on consumption does not depend on the weight placed on inequality). We do not explicitly constrain the weights to be assigned to each component of well-being, since we think of them as the preferences of different observers. However, some observers may, if they are consistent, have linked preferences. For example, if attitudes about insecurity are driven solely by risk aversion (but see Osberg 1998b), the weight an individual places on inequality, and the weight he/she places on insecurity, will both depend on the second derivative of his/her utility function.

4.   However, a sufficient, but not necessary set of conditions for the index of economic well-being that we propose would be that societal economic well-being can be represented as the well-being of a 'representative agent' if: (i) such an agent has a risk-averse utility function (that is, diminishing marginal utility); (ii) from behind a 'veil of ignorance' as to his/her own characteristics, each person draws an individual stream of equivalent income (and prospects of future income) from the actual distribution of income streams; (iii) each person has a utility function in which both personal consumption and bequests to future generations are valued; (iv) individual income streams are exposed to unpredictable future shocks; and (v) capital markets and public policies do not always automatically produce a socially optimal aggregate saving rate.

5.   The definition of the unemployed used by Statistics Canada for the official Canadian unemployment rate differs somewhat from that used by the Bureau of Labor Statistics for the US unemployment rate. The BLS now publishes a series for Canada based on US definitions. Adjustments are made to exclude (i) those aged 15 years; (ii) passive job seekers, defined at those whose only job search method is looking at help wanted ads in newspapers; (iii) persons waiting to start a new job who did not seek work in the past three weeks; and (iv) those unavailable for work due to personal or family responsibilities. An adjustment is made to include full-time students looking for full-time work. The passive job seeker adjustment is the most important. The net impact of the adjustments is to lower the annual average Canadian unemployment rate 0.4–1.0 percentage points in the 1990s. See Sorrentino (2000) for further information.

6. For example, since a great deal of work has been done on the valuation of household production, there is at least a clearly defined range of estimates. However, economists have paid very little attention to the measurement of insecurity (Osberg 1998b), and the measures of economic insecurity are correspondingly underdeveloped.
7. In this chapter, no adjustment is made for potential consumer price bias (Boskin et al. 1999).
8. Because of the lack of time-series estimates of the value of household and volunteer production in the United States, this variable has been omitted from this chapter. In an earlier paper on the index of economic well-being for Canada (Osberg and Sharpe 1998), it was possible to include this variable, as Statistics Canada produces such data.
9. Earlier versions of this chapter presented estimates of the underground economy, based on benchmark estimates by Statistics Canada, the Bureau of Economic Statistics, and the trend in the share of the self-employed in total employment, on the argument that the self-employed have greater opportunity to hide income than paid workers. (Since there has always been some level of 'underground' activity, the issue for the measurement of trends in well-being is whether or not the prevalence of the underground economy has changed substantially over time. When tax rates are rising, there may be increased incentives to go underground, but the secular trend to increased penetration of franchise systems in the small business sector and the greater computerization of business records may also have made it more difficult to escape detection by tax authorities.) We do not include these estimates in this chapter, because they make very little difference to measured output trends. Because the base level of underground activity is a relatively small share of GDP, the trend in a small number is an even smaller fraction of GDP.
10. Dan Usher (1980) of Queen's University has developed a methodology for the estimation of the value of increased longevity.
11. Implicitly, this procedure ignores both the differential values that individuals might place on changes in mortality probability at different ages, and the distribution, by age, of actual changes in mortality probability.
12. Longer life and a more affluent retirement may interact in their impacts on well-being. To some extent, we capture these interactions: below we note that economic insecurity depends partly on the level of poverty among the elderly, which has declined in most countries. However, no account is taken in this chapter of any relative increase in well-being of the nonpoor elderly.
13. See, for example, Phipps and Garner (1994) or Burkhauser et al. (1996).
14. Even though the impact on average household size is the same, the impact on average living standards of (for example) a five-person household splitting will differ from the impact of a two-person household splitting, since the latter change will imply a greater loss of economies of scale.
15. To compare the gains, at the margin, from additional market work compared to either leisure or home production, we estimate the total 'tax wedge' between taxed returns to time in the market and untaxed returns to leisure or home production as the sum of sales and income taxes. The share of general government current receipts in nominal GDP is used as the tax rate in the calculation of after-tax wages of labor compensation.
16. Total annual hours of unemployment are calculated as the product of the number of unemployed and average annual hours per employed person on the assumption that an unemployed person wants to work average hours. Total unemployed hours are then divided by the working-age population to determine average annual hours of unemployment per working-age person.
17. Unpaid work contributes to economic welfare and thus in principle should be included in an index of economic well-being. Unpaid work consists of both household work and volunteer work. Statistics Canada (1996) has produced estimates of unpaid work for Canada, and these estimates were incorporated into the original index of economic well-being developed for Canada (Osberg and Sharpe 1998b). Because of the unavailability of internationally comparable estimates of the value of unpaid work for countries other than Canada, this component has not been incorporated into the index of economic well-being developed in this chapter.

18.   If one could assume that income flows were always optimally divided between consumption and saving, one could omit separate consideration of consumption and wealth accumulation and concentrate on trends in average income. However, aggregate accumulation of private assets depends heavily on tax policy, and accumulation of public assets depends on spending decisions of government. Because both depend heavily on the political process, and because capital markets have significant imperfections, the assumption of automatic optimality seems too hopeful by far (for further discussion, see Osberg 1985b). Note that in aggregating over different forms of capital and environmental assets we are implicitly following the 'Hartwick rule' for resource depletion, and assuming that accumulation and depletion of stocks of particular types of assets can be offset.

19.   See Coulombe (2000), who notes that the average depreciation rate for Canada's business sector capital stock over the 1961–97 period was 10 per cent compared to 4.4 per cent in the United States.

20.   The R&D investment series starts in 1971; the stock of R&D in 1971 is therefore equal to the R&D investment that year and the series has a base of zero in 1970.

21.   The estimated market value is the price the resources would bring if sold on the open market, and is based on the difference between the annual cost of extraction of a given resource and the revenue generated from the sale of the resource. In other words, the total value or wealth associated with a stock is calculated as the present value of all future annual rent that the stock is expected to yield. The quality of the resources, the state of extraction technologies, the price of the resource, and factor costs determine this amount of rent.

22.   Like these other assets, the value of the human capital of living persons represents the future consumption that possession of such assets enables. The endogenous growth perspective has argued that the benefits of societal learning are partly the output such learning enables in the current generation and partly the fact that future generations can start learning at a higher level. As a consequence, higher levels of education produce a higher long-run growth rate, as well as a higher current level of income (Galor and Zeira 1993; Eckstein and Zilcha 1994). If this is correct, a production cost valuation of human capital may underestimate considerably the value of human capital stock investments.

23.   Osberg (1985b) argued that heritage preservation laws can be seen as an optimal intergenerational contract, which constrains the present generation not to despoil irreplaceable assets. In the presence of such constraints, the current generation still has to decide how large a bequest to future generations to leave in the form of replaceable assets, but the 'national heritage' remains untouched. As a consequence (like the family heirloom that is never priced because it will never be sold), trends in economic well-being can be evaluated without placing an explicit monetary value on irreplaceable environmental and cultural assets. Note, however, that international comparisons of the *level* of well-being (which we avoid making in this chapter) would require some estimate of the value of such assets.

24.   Because an additional dollar means less to a millionaire than to a pauper, economists tend to agree that 'diminishing marginal utility' is a reasonable assumption.

25.   Jenkins (1991) surveys the issues involved in measurement of inequality.

26.   Since there are no data available on inequality and poverty within families, we have no option but to follow the standard pattern of assuming that equivalent income is equally shared among family members. Phipps and Burton (1995) have demonstrated that if children do not in fact share equally in household resources, inequality within the family can make a very big difference to perceptions of the level of child poverty, and the same implications would hold for gender inequalities. However, since the issue for this chapter is the *trend* of poverty, our conclusions will hold unless there has been a systematic trend over time in the degree of inequality within families (for example, if senior citizen families, whose share of the poverty population has fallen over time, have systematically different levels of within-family inequality than younger families).

27.   To be precise, there are nine matches to the term 'economic insecurity' in the ECONLIT database for the years 1969–97. A search of the Social Sciences Index from 1983, and the

PAIS International and PAIS Periodicals/Publisher Index from 1972, yields 11 matches. The Social Sciences Citation Index for the years 1987–97 was similarly unproductive.

28. For example, a tenured professor with occasional consulting income may have a variable income stream, but feel little insecurity. Further, data only on individuals' income streams cannot reveal who had a credible long-term employment guarantee (like tenure), and who sweated out a series of short-term contract renewals.

29. Osberg and Sharpe (2000a,b) develop estimates of the index of economic well-being for a number of OECD countries. In those papers a measure of gross replacement rates for UI produced by the OECD is used in the variable for the risk associated with unemployment as data on the UI coverage ratio was unavailable for OECD countries. Thus the economic security variable in this chapter for Canada and the United States is not comparable with estimates in our OECD paper. As the number of countries is expanded, the problem of international data comparability increases.

30. However, RATE = INCIDENCE × AVERAGE DURATION. Since the poverty rate among single parents is equal to the conditional probability that a single parent will enter poverty and the average duration of a poverty spell, we implicitly account jointly for the duration of poverty spells and for their likelihood.

31. This procedure effectively ignores single-male parents. Although the authors of this chapter feel that this is an important group, males comprise only about 10 per cent of the single-parent population, and their income loss on divorce is considerably less than that of women.

32. In order that the base year for the indices of all risks of economic security be the same at 1.000 in Figure 5.9, the constant 2 has been added to the indices of risk of illness, single parenthood, and old age, whose original base was −1.

REFERENCES

Anielski, Mark, and Jonathan Rowe (1999), *The Genuine Progress Indicator: 1998 Update*, San Francisco, CA: Redefining Progress, March.

Atkinson, Anthony B. (1970), 'On the measurement of inequality', *Journal of Economic Theory*, **2**, 244–63.

Boskin, M.J., E.R. Dulberger and Z. Griliches (1999), *Toward A More Accurate Measure of the Cost of Living*, Final Report to the Senate Finance Committee from the Advisory Commission to Study the Consumer Price Index, Collingdale: DIANE Publishing Company.

Burkhauser, Richard V., Timothy M. Smeeding and Joachim Merz (1996), 'Relative inequality and poverty in Germany and the United States using alternative equivalence scales', *Review of Income and Wealth*, **42** (4), 381–400.

Clark, Andrew, and Andrew Oswald (1994), 'Unhappiness and unemployment', *Economic Journal*, **104** (424), 648–59.

Coleman, James S. (1988), 'Social capital in the creation of human capital', *American Journal of Sociology*, **94**, S95–S120.

Coulombe, Serge (2000), 'The Canada–US productivity growth paradox', working paper no. 12, Industry Canada, Ottawa, March.

Dawson, J.C., (ed.) (1996), *Flow-of-Funds Analysis*, Armonk, NY: M.E. Sharpe.

Eckstein, Z., and I. Zilcha (1994), 'The effects of compulsory schooling on growth, income distribution and welfare', *Journal of Public Economics*, **54** (May), 339–59.

Fankhauser, S. (1995), 'Evaluating the social costs of greenhouse gas emissions', *Energy Journal*, **15**, 157–84.

Galor, O., and J. Zeira (1993), 'Income distribution and macroeconomics', *Review of Economic Studies*, **60** (January), 35–52.

Jenkins, S. (1991), 'The measurement of income inequality', in L. Osberg (ed.), *Economic Inequality and Poverty: International Perspectives*, Armonk, NY: M.E. Sharpe, pp. 3–38.

Kendrick, J.W. (ed.) (1996), *The New System of National Accounts*, Boston, MA: Kluwer Academic Publishers.

Keuning, Steven (1998), 'A powerful link between economic theory and practice: national accounting', *Review of Income and Wealth*, **44** (3), 437–46.

Nordhaus, William, and James Tobin (1972), 'Is growth obsolete?', in *Economic Growth*, Fiftieth Anniversary Colloquium V, New York: National Bureau of Economic Research.

Osberg, Lars (1985a), 'The measurement of economic welfare', in David Laidler (coordinator), *Approaches to Economic Well-Being*, vol. 26 of the Royal Commission on the Economic Union and Development Prospects for Canada (MacDonald Commission), Toronto: University of Toronto Press, pp. 49–87.

Osberg, Lars (1985b), 'The idea of economic well-being', Paper presented at the 19th General Conference of the International Association for Research in Income and Wealth, Noordwijkerhout, Netherlands, 25–31 August, and mimeo, Dalhousie University, June.

Osberg, Lars (1998a), 'Meaning and measurement in intergenerational equity', in Miles Corak (ed.), *Government Finances and Intergenerational Equity*, Ottawa: Statistics Canada and Human Resources Development Canada, pp. 131–9.

Osberg, Lars (1998b), 'Economic insecurity', discussion paper no. 88, Sydney, Australia: Social Policy Research Centre, University of New South Wales.

Osberg, Lars (1999), 'Long-run trends in economic inequality in five countries: a birth cohort view', paper presented at the conference Macro Dynamics of Inequality, Levy Economics Institute of Bard College, 28 October, accessed at: http://is.dal.ca/~osberg/home.html.

Osberg, Lars (2000), 'Poverty in Canada and the USA: measurement, trends and implications', *Canadian Journal of Economics*, **33** (4), 847–77.

Osberg, Lars, and Andrew Sharpe (1998), 'An index of economic well-being for Canada', research paper R-99-3E, Applied Research Branch, Strategic Policy, Human Resources Development Canada, December.

Osberg, Lars, and Andrew Sharpe (1999), 'An index of economic well-being for Canada and the United States', paper presented to the annual meeting of the American Economic Association, New York, 3–5 January.

Osberg, Lars, and Andrew Sharpe (2000a), 'Estimates of an index of economic well-being for OECD countries', paper presented at the 26th General Conference of the International Association for Research in Income and Wealth, Cracow, Poland, 27 August–2 September.

Osberg, Lars, and Andrew Sharpe (2000b), 'International comparisons of trends in economic well-being', LIS discussion paper no. 242, Luxembourg Income Study, Center for Policy Research, Syracuse University, Syracuse, NY.

Osberg, Lars, and Kuan Xu (2000), 'International comparisons of poverty intensity: index decomposition and bootstrap inference', *Journal of Human Resources*, **35** (1), 51–81.

Phipps, S., and Peter Burton (1995), 'Sharing within families: implications for the measurement of poverty among individuals in Canada', *The Canadian Journal of Economics*, **28**, (1) (February), 177–204.

Phipps, S., and T.I. Garner (1994), 'Are equivalence scales the same for the United States and Canada?', *Review of Income and Wealth*, **40** (1), 1–18.

President of the United States (various years), Annual Economic Report of the President, Washington, DC: US Government Printing Office.

Riddell, C. (1999), 'Canadian labour market performance in international perspective', *Canadian Journal of Economics*, **32** (5), 1097–134.

Sorrentino, Constance (2000), 'International unemployment rates: how comparable are they?', *Monthly Labor Review*, June, 3–20.

Statistics Canada (1996), *Households' Unpaid Work: Measurement and Valuation*, Studies in National Accounting no. 3 cat. no. 13–603.

Statistics Canada (1997), *Environment-Economy Indicators and Detailed Statistics 1997*, Econnections: Linking the Environment and the Economy, cat. no. 16–200, December.

United Nations (1993), *System of National Accounts 1993*, Series F, No. 2, Rev. 4, New York: Eurostat, International Monetary Fund, Organization for Economic Cooperation and Development, and World Bank.

Usher, Dan (1980), *The Measurement of Economic Growth*, Oxford: Basil Blackwell.

6. Comparing living standards across nations: real incomes at the top, the bottom, and the middle

Timothy M. Smeeding and Lee Rainwater[*]

INTRODUCTION

The types of yardsticks used by economists to measure living standards (or economic well-being across nations) are basically two. Macroeconomists use aggregate GDP per capita – a single value summary of economic output per person in a nation – to measure economic well-being. By converting currencies into comparable dollars (into real 'purchasing-power adjusted' terms) one creates a 'one number per country' measure of economic well-being. In contrast, microeconomists compare the distribution of disposable income across households to assess the distribution of economic well-being, expressed in terms of income per equivalent adult (or per equivalent child). Here the comparisons of well-being are almost always relative 'within-nation' comparisons of many points in the income distribution, including measures of central tendency such as the median or mean, but also the spread of incomes among people.

These analyses lead to dissatisfying results from both perspectives. Real GDP per capita includes much more than is actually consumed by households, and by definition ignores the distribution of income among households (within countries). Distributions of income measure differences in sustainable consumption across the population within a country, but they are only relative and thereby ignore differences in 'real' standards of living across countries.

The usual exchange over these differences as they concern the United States runs something like this: the first analyst suggests that 'the United States is the richest nation on earth', the second retorts that 'income inequality is also highest in the United States'. The first then responds: 'Yes, but the United States is so rich that being poor in the United States is better than being middle income in other rich countries'. Thus, the conundrum is presented and the question posed, what is the distribution of real income within as well as across countries?

The purpose of this chapter is to try to answer this question by presenting estimates of the real purchasing power parity-adjusted distribution of disposable income for a number of countries. This is not an easy task, as we shall argue below. The major tool for converting (relative) nominal national incomes into real incomes is 'purchasing power parities' or PPPs (for example, OECD 2000). While these PPPs are designed for aggregate macroeconomic statistics, not for microdata-based measures of disposable income, careful comparisons can yield approximate answers to the questions posed. And, in fact, we find that comparisons of 'real' economic well-being or 'living standards' look very different across countries depending on where in the income distribution one decides to make these comparisons.

The next section introduces the issue by defining terms, measurement issues, and data. Then we move to comparing macroeconomic 'average' incomes and microdata-based 'relative' incomes across countries, before moving to PPP-adjusted distributional measures of living standards for all households and for households with children. We include children as a separate group here because most analysts argue that children are a particularly scarce resource in modern rich societies, and we agree with others that nations may be fairly judged by the way they treat their children (Carlson 1993).

METHODOLOGY: MEASURES, DATA, TERMINOLOGY, AND PPPs

Economic well-being is the primary indicator of living standards for most economists and the only one we rely on here. At its broadest, economic well-being refers to the material resources available to households.[1] The concern with these resources is not with consumption *per se* but rather with the ability to consume and with the capabilities they give household members to participate in their societies (Sen 1992). These capabilities are inputs to social activities, and participation in these activities produces a given level of well-being for adults and for other household members (Coleman et al. 1978; Rainwater 1990). They also allow families to invest in their children, using private resources to supplement publicly-provided goods and services such as education or health care.

All advanced industrial societies are highly stratified socially. The opportunities for social participation are vitally affected by the differences in resources that the family has at its disposal, particularly in nations like the United States where there is heavy reliance on the market to purchase goods such as health care, education and childcare services (Rainwater 1974). But even in other rich nations that provide higher levels of social goods from tax dollars and not from personal resources, money income is the central resource. In this chapter, we are concerned not only with the distribution of disposable money income (as described more fully below) but also with its noncash components.

Unfortunately, we cannot take a direct account of the major in-kind benefits that are available in most countries – for example, health care, education, day care and preschool, general subsidies to housing and the like. To the extent that the level and distribution of these resources are different in different countries our analysis of money income must be treated with some caution. However, such differences would be unlikely to change the conclusions reached in this chapter. In fact, as we later argue in a secondary analysis of health and education benefits alone, inclusion of these benefits may even exacerbate these differences (see Smeeding et al. 1993 for an analysis that includes more of these benefits; see also Smeeding et al. 2001).

Measuring Economic Inequality: The Basic Dimensions

Here we briefly review the sources of our evidence and their strengths and weaknesses. There are currently no international standards for income distribution that parallel the international standards used for systems of national income accounts.[2] Hence, researchers need to decide what they want to measure and how far they can measure it on a comparable basis. The Luxembourg Income Study (LIS), which underlies much of this chapter, offers the reader many choices of perspective in terms of country, income measure, accounting unit, and time frame.[3]

Our attention is focused here on the distribution of disposable money income, that is, income after direct taxes and including transfer payments and refundable tax credits. The period of income measurement is the calendar year, with income measured on an annual basis.[4]

Two important points should be noted about this choice:

- the definition of income falls considerably short of a comprehensive definition, typically excluding much of capital gains, imputed rents, home production, and most of income in-kind (with the exception of near-cash benefits, such as food stamps and housing allowances); and
- no account is taken of indirect taxes or of the benefits from public spending (other than cash and near-cash transfers) such as those from health care, education, or most housing subsidies.

For example, one country may help low-income families through money benefits (included in cash income), whereas another provides subsidized housing, child care, or education (which is not taken into account). While one study (Smeeding et al. 1993) finds that the distribution of housing, education, and health care benefits reinforces the general differences in income distribution for a subset of the Western nations examined here, there is no guarantee that these relationships hold for alternative countries or methods of accounting (Gardiner et al. 1995). Because noncash benefits are more equally distributed than cash benefits, levels of inequality within high-noncash-spending countries are lessened (as mentioned above), but the same rank ordering of these countries, with respect to inequality levels that is found here using cash alone, persists when noncash benefits are added in (Smeeding et al. 1993). And while we use income, not consumption, as the basis for our comparisons, due to the relative ease of measurement and comparability of the former, there is strong evidence that consumption inequalities are similar to, but less than, income inequalities in major European nations and in the United States (de Vos and Zaidi 1996; Johnson and Smeeding 1998).

The distribution of disposable income requires answers to both the 'what' and the 'among whom' questions. Regarding the former, earned income from wages and salaries and self-employment, cash property income (but not capital gains or losses), and other private cash income transfers (occupational pensions, alimony, and child support) or 'market income' are the primary sources of disposable income for most families. To reach the disposable income concept used in this chapter, governments add public transfer payments (social retirement, family allowances, unemployment compensation, and welfare benefits) and deduct personal income tax and social security contributions from market income. Direct tax subsidies such as refundable tax credits, the US Earned Income Tax Credit (EITC), and the United Kingdom's Family Tax Credit are also included. Near-cash benefits, those that are virtually equivalent to cash (food stamps in the United States and housing allowances in the United Kingdom and Sweden), are also included in the disposable income measure used here.

The question of distribution 'among whom' is answered: among individuals, either all persons or persons living in households with children, including children *per se* as separate individuals. When assessing disposable income inequality, however, the unit of aggregation is the household: the incomes of all household members are aggregated and then divided by an equivalence scale to arrive at individual equivalent income (EI).

Complete intrahousehold income sharing is assumed, despite the fact that members of the same household probably do not equally share in all household resources. However, to assume that unrelated individuals living with others do not at all share in common household incomes or household 'public goods' (such as heat, durables) and should therefore be treated as separate units is a worse assumption in our judgment. Similarly, we assume that children share equally in the resources controlled by their parents or by other adults in the household. Thus, our unit of account is the household.

Income and Needs

Families differ not only in terms of resources but also in terms of their needs. We take account of differing needs, based on household size and on the head's stage in the life course, by adjusting income for family size, using three different equivalence scales (one for the macro measure of living standards, and two for the micro-based measures). The equivalence adjustment for household size is designed to account for the different requirements families of different sizes have for participating in society at a given level. Different equivalence scales will yield different distributions of well-being, depending on differences in household size and structure within and across nations.[5]

Several studies in Europe, the United States, and Australia point to an equivalence scale that implies rather dramatic economies of scale in the conversion of money incomes to social participation among families with children (Buhmann et al. 1988; Bradbury 1989; Rainwater 1990; Burkhauser et al. 1996). Analysis of some of these surveys also suggests that there are important variations in need as a function of the head of the household's age.

Drawing on these studies, we use two equivalence scales for the microdata-based analyses. The equivalence scale used to make the relative income comparison in the next section is the square root of household size. This initial 'equivalent income' or 'adjusted disposable income' (*EI*) concept is produced by dividing (unadjusted) disposable income (*Y*) by family size (*S*) raised to the power of 0.5. This is the same scale used in Atkinson et al. (1995) and by numerous other analysts (see also Buhmann et al. 1988). It produces the following computation for equivalent income:

$$EI = Y/S^{0.5}. \tag{6.1}$$

For the real income comparisons of children (or adults) that follow, we use a scale that defines need as the product of the cube root of family size multiplied by a factor which sees need as increasing roughly 1 per cent per year for head's age up to 45 years and then decreasing at the same rate. Hence, we define equivalent income in the following way:

$$EI = Y/(S^{33}*0.99^{|A-45|}). \tag{6.2}$$

That is, equivalent income (*EI*) here is defined as an individual family disposable income (*Y*) divided by the product of the cube root of the family's size (*S*) and multiplied by 0.99 compounded by the number of years difference between the head's age (*A*) and 45 (see also Rainwater and Smeeding 2000). The reader should keep in mind that all of the real income estimates in this chapter are based on adjusted or equivalent income calculated according to formula (6.2) above.[6]

Having defined equivalent income in these ways, we determine the median of all individuals in each country. We first examine the distribution of incomes of all households in relation to the median for all individuals *within* each nation in our relative analyses. In the 'real' analyses we express the incomes of all persons (or all children) relative to the median EI of all US persons, expressed in 1997 PPP dollars. In the final figures for children, we tabulate the well-being of children who live at various points in the income distribution. In technical terms, our calculations are weighted by the number of persons in each household in the initial analyses, and by the number of children in our final set of figures.

Real Incomes: PPPs and Microdata

If we are to convert nominal national incomes into 'real' incomes of comparable value we have two choices: current exchange rates or purchasing power parities. Most economists prefer the latter for these comparisons since they price out 'equivalent' market baskets of goods and services in each nation, thereby converting incomes into units of equal purchasing power (for example, Summers and Heston 1991; OECD 2000). In contrast, current exchange rates may be influenced by a large number of factors that are independent of the cost of living in a nation, for example, capital market flows, currency markets, and related factors that only indirectly affect 'real' living standards. However they are conceptualized, PPPs were developed to permit accurate comparison of aggregate domestic product and national consumption across countries rather than disposable incomes or the consumption expenditures of households. This means that, even though PPPs are appropriate for comparing national output (or output per capita), they are less appropriate for establishing consistent microdata-based disposable income distributions comparisons.

The Penn World Tables Mark V PPPs were judged to be accurate and consistent for the 1980s for all nations except Italy (Summers and Heston 1991). However, they have not been systematically updated. The OECD and the World Bank have finally taken up this task and developed their own sets of PPPs. We do not present comparisons of real income distribution over time due to the intertemporal inconsistency of

PPPs compared to household income data dating back to the early 1980s or earlier.[7]

Our estimates of real income distributions are based on a single set of PPP rates, the most recent set benchmarked by the OECD for year 1996, extended back or forward to cover the period from 1992 to 1997. This is the most recent OECD base year for estimating such PPP rates (OECD 2000) and limits our calculations to those OECD nations for which we have LIS data for the same period.[8] We use the OECD estimates of PPP exchange rates to translate household incomes in each country into 1997 US dollars and then compare income distributions relative to the US median disposable income per equivalent adult using the equivalence scale formula outlined above in equation (6.2). For 1997, this figure is $28 005 per equivalent US adult.

The OECD's estimates of PPP exchange rates are particularly far from ideal for comparing the well-being of low-income households in different countries. In principle, the PPPs permit us to calculate the amount of money needed in country A to purchase the same bundle of consumption items in country B. If relative prices on different consumption items differ widely between the two countries, however, the PPP rate may only be correct for one particular collection of items. Some analysts worry about the market basket for the 'poor' compared to the market basket for the 'average' household. However, this is not our primary concern here, and most early studies of this phenomenon indicate that the differences caused by different relative weights for consumption items at low levels of income compared to average levels are not very great (Smeeding 1974; Heston 1986). But this is not our only concern.

The PPP rates calculated by the OECD are accurate for overall aggregate national consumption including consumption spending by governments as well as by households (Castles 1996). Thus, the PPP rates are appropriate for comparing market baskets of all final consumption, including government-provided health care, education, and housing. These goods are paid for in different ways in different nations, however. In most countries, health care as well as some rental housing, child care, and education are subsidized more generously by those governments than is the case in the United States. Thus, disposable incomes in countries with publicly financed health and higher education systems reflect the fact that health and education costs have already been subtracted from households' incomes (in the form of direct tax payments to the government). One implication is that in countries where in-kind benefits are larger than average, real incomes may be understated because citizens actually face a lower effective price level for privately purchased goods than is reflected by the OECD's estimates of the PPP rate.[9] The opposite is true for those countries whose citizens must pay larger amounts for health care and

Table 6.1   Cash and noncash social expenditures as a percentage of GDP, 1995

Country	Health	Education	Health plus education	Cash	Total	Health plus education/total
Sweden	5.90	6.31	12.21	25.28	37.49	0.33
Netherlands	6.74	4.57	11.31	21.32	32.63	0.35
France	7.98	5.94	13.92	20.43	34.35	0.41
Germany	8.13	4.49	12.62	20.39	33.01	0.38
UK	5.73	4.84	10.57	14.82	25.39	0.42
Canada	6.58	6.22	12.80	12.12	24.92	0.51
United States	6.53	4.99	11.52	9.69	21.21	0.54
Australia	5.74	4.46	10.20	9.51	19.71	0.52
Average	6.67	5.23	11.89	16.70	28.59	0.42

Sources: OECD (2000, 2001).

Table 6.2   Average living standards from a macro perspective (real GDP per capita for 1999/converted to US dollars using PPPs or exchange rates)

Country	Amount (US dollars)		Index (USA=100)	
	PPPs	Exchange	PPPs	Exchange
France[1]	22067	23764	65	70
Finland	22723	25046	67	74
United Kingdom	22861	24228	68	72
Sweden	23017	27256	68	81
Germany	23819	25729	70	76
Belgium	24845	24347	73	72
Australia	25590	21432	76	63
Netherlands	25923	24906	77	74
Canada	26424	20822	78	62
Denmark	27073	33124	80	98
Norway	28133	34277	83	101
Switzerland[2]	28672	36247	85	107
United States	33836	33836	100	100
Average	25768	27309	76	81

Notes:
1. Figures include overseas departments.
2. Country still using SNA 68.

Source: OECD (2002b).

education out of their disposable incomes. Since on average other nations spend slightly more on noncash benefits than does the United States (Table 6.1), US real incomes are likely to be overstated in the comparisons that follow. In contrast, European countries (Sweden, France, and Germany) provide higher levels of tax-financed health-care and education benefits, and so their real incomes are likely to be understated. On the other hand, Canada, the United States and Australia spend more on noncash benefits than on cash benefits (Table 6.2). Therefore, noncash benefits may have a significant effect on well-being comparisons across income groups.

A different problem for comparing real income distribution across countries arises because of differences in the quality of the household income survey data used to measure income distribution. For example, the LIS survey for the United States is the Current Population Survey (or CPS). The CPS captures about 89 per cent of the total household incomes that are estimated from other sources (national income accounts data and government agency administrative records). Most, but not all, of the other surveys used by LIS capture approximately the same percentage of total income (Atkinson et al. 1995). The household surveys of the Scandinavian countries capture between 93 and 94 per cent of the incomes reflected in the aggregate statistical sources, while the Australian survey captures 83 per cent of the total, about the same as Germany and France. Unfortunately, not all countries have performed the calculations that would allow us to determine the overall quality of their household survey data. We used a rough methodology to compare the quality of survey data for the different LIS countries. Only those countries with LIS household surveys that captured a large percentage of national income are included in our comparisons of real income distributions.[10]

Assuming that the household surveys from different countries yield information about disposable incomes with comparable reliability, we should expect that once incomes are converted into a common currency unit, we can do a fairly good job of comparing real disposable cash incomes across nations at points other than the average or 'median', despite the fact that noncash incomes will not be included.

Noncash Benefits

While we are not able to distribute noncash government benefits across the disposable incomes here, we can at least see if noncash benefits vary directly or indirectly with cash benefits (Table 6.1). First, we see that noncash benefits, on average, are 70 per cent as large as cash benefits in these nations. In fact, we find that the 1995 distribution of cash and noncash benefits is similar to those found earlier for the 1980s in Smeeding et al. (1993). The countries in Table 6.1 are ordered according to cash social expenditures (OECD 2001). Public health and education benefits are included, but housing is excluded.[11] While noncash benefits as a percentage of GDP are far more equal across nations than are cash benefits, we find that the nations that spend the most in cash incomes (Sweden, Germany, France) also spend the most on health and education combined. Australia and the United States are low spenders on noncash benefits and cash benefits. The two anomalies are Canada, where noncash benefits are bigger than average, and the Netherlands, where noncash benefits are lower relative to cash benefits.

However, we also note that noncash public spending exceeds governmental cash spending in Canada, Australia, and the United States. Thus, tax-financed noncash benefits are very important in most nations, most especially in low-cash-benefit nations, and may affect the distributional comparisons of real income offered below.

Because the United States spends less than the average country on noncash benefits, while its consumers pay the most out of pocket for these services (Smeeding and Freund 2002), one can argue that the real income comparisons presented below are liable to overstate real incomes in the United States and understate them in other nations (Smeeding et al. 2001). However, some counterarguments can also be made, particularly for low-income households. More than 85 per cent of Americans are covered by some type of health insurance. They do not pay for most of the health care they consume out of the disposable income measured here, though they do pay more out of pocket for health care, on average (see Rainwater et al. 2001, note 4; Smeeding and Freund 2002, Table 3). In other words, the average insured American does not pay the full 'price' of medical services reflected in the OECD's PPP estimates for the United States, but they do pay more out of pocket than do their counterparts in other nations. For a large majority of low-income Americans, insurance is provided gratis through the Medicaid program or at reduced cost under Medicare. For others, it is subsidized by an employer's contribution to a company-sponsored health plan. Employer benefits are roughly an additional 1.1 per cent of GDP. While low-income people in most, if not all, LIS nations pay lower net prices for medical care than do residents of the United States, the United States probably has the highest final consumption prices for medical care of all OECD countries. The OECD's PPP estimates should therefore show that the United States has a high cost of living (at least for medical care).

Second, nearly one-quarter of low-income Americans receive housing subsidies, either directly, through vouchers to cover some fraction of rents, or indirectly, through below-market rents on publicly subsidized apartments. Still, on a comparative basis European subsidies for rental housing vary by country, but they are generally larger than in the United States as

US public housing benefits are less than 0.25 per cent of GDP (OECD 2001).

Third, some consumption items that are more important to low-income than to high-income families are dramatically cheaper in the United States than they are in most other OECD countries. Food is one such item. Because it is likely that food consumption has a greater weight in the consumption of the poor than it does in aggregate consumption, the OECD's PPP exchange rates are biased against the United States.

In summary, while we could develop better PPP exchange rates for purposes of comparing low-income families across OECD countries, it is not obvious that a superior set of PPPs would reveal a systematically different pattern of income distribution. Hence, we feel that our comparisons are about as good as any that could be done at this time.

Database

The data that we use for this analysis are from the Luxembourg Income Study (LIS) database, which now contains more than 100 household income data files for 29 nations covering the period 1967 to 2000 (LIS 2003). We can analyze both the level and trend in poverty and low incomes for a considerable period across a wide range of nations. To compute the level of relative inequality, we have selected 21 nations. For the real income comparisons we use 13 OECD nations with incomes measured between 1992 and 1997. The 21 countries are the largest and richest in the world and include all of the G-7 nations, Scandinavia, Canada, Australia, and most of Europe. We include all of Germany in our analysis, including the eastern states rejoined to West Germany in 1989.

LIS has overcome some, but not all, of the problems of making comparisons across countries that plagued earlier studies. Some problems, such as the use of data from different types of sources, still remain. But all of the data are drawn from household income surveys, or their equivalent, and in no cases are synthetic data used. One major advantage of LIS is the availability of microdata. Access to the microdata means that it is possible to produce results on the same basis, starting from individual household records, and to test their sensitivity to alternative choices of units, definition, and other concepts. The data all cover, at least in principle, the whole noninstitutionalized population, though the treatment of immigrants may differ across nations. These data are supplemented here by data provided by one major nation not yet a member of LIS (Japan) where a national expert calculated income inequality measures with the consultation of the LIS staff (Ishikawa 1996). The rest of the calculations were made by the authors and the LIS project team.[12]

Measuring Living Standards: A Conceptual Interpretation

Our measure of living standards is based only on disposable incomes, but that allows us the luxury of examining incomes for not only the middle or average person in society (median person), but also those at other percentiles of the income distribution. Comparing points in the distribution allows us to examine differences across persons within nations as well as across nations, all expressed in 1997 US PPP dollars and all relative to the median EI in the United States in 1997.

In addition to the median person, we also compute the real income of a low-income person (or child) and a high-income person (or child) in each nation. The low-income person (or child) is measured at the 10th percentile (median of bottom quintile) while the high-income person (or child) is measured at the 90th percentile (median of the top quintile).

We refer to the difference between persons with high and low incomes as 'social distance' in making both relative and absolute comparisons here. This distance can be measured in ratio format (for example, the decile ratio or P_{90}/P_{10}), in bar graph format, or with the real income distance between these points measured in PPP-adjusted dollars per equivalent person (or per equivalent child).[13]

Particularly when we refer to children in the second half of the chapter, we like to think of the measure of social distance as a measure of equality of opportunity within each nation. Nations with smaller social distances (or smaller decile ratios) have higher levels of 'equal opportunity' across the population of parents and children. We also like to focus on the distance between the middle- and the low-income child as a measure of 'fair chance'. Our measure of equality of opportunity captures only the real economic distance between the high- and low-income child. We are also vitally interested in the absolute level of resources available to the low-income child, relative to similar children in other nations. Children in nations with relatively higher real income levels for 'low-income children' have more of a 'fair chance' in that nation, when compared to similar children in other nations. In an era when the US president invokes the slogan 'leave no child behind' it will be useful to see which nations leave their children behind, which ones give them a good start, and by how much.

TRADITIONAL RESULTS FROM MACRO AND MICRO PERSPECTIVES

We begin where traditional measures of living standards begin – 'real' GDP per capita (Table 6.2). We present both PPP-based and exchange rate-based estimates here to compare the two sets of results.[14] Countries are ranked from lowest to highest according to PPP-adjusted GDP per capita in 1999.[15] On this basis, the United States is the richest nation of all, with a real 1999 income of \$33 836 per person. Other nations are bunched between 65 and 85 per cent of the US average in Table 6.2. In contrast, the exchange rate-based figures run from 63 to 107 per cent of the US average and with somewhat different rankings of nations. Clearly there is a major difference depending on whether one uses PPPs or exchange rates, and we choose the former.[16]

While these results give some idea of the overall living standard in a nation, they are far less than satisfying because they are void of distributional content. In fact, one cannot even interpret these as the income of the 'average' person in a nation. The average person is the median person, while the overall national average income per person may not, in fact, accrue to any one person. In fact, the greater the level of inequality in a nation, the larger the difference between the mean income amount and the median person's income (Gottschalk and Smeeding 1997; Smeeding 2000).

Relative income distributions are the second traditional measure of well-being. The LIS data sets are used here to compare the distribution of disposable income in 21 nations around 1995 and in earlier periods where 1995 data are not yet available. We focus here on relative (Figure 6.1), not absolute, income differences. As has been demonstrated, the relative inequality patterns found here correspond roughly to the results found in Atkinson et al. (1995), which uses LIS data from earlier years in most cases (Smeeding 2000). Our choice of inequality measures are the three mentioned earlier: the ratio of the income of the person at the bottom and top 10th percentile to the median – P_{10} and P_{90}, respectively – and the ratio of the income of the person at the 90th percentile to the person at the 10th percentile – the decile ratio – (one measure of 'social distance'). We also present a bar chart to visualize social distance.

At the bottom of Figure 6.1 we find that in the United States a low-income person at the 10th percentile in 1997 (P_{10}) has an equivalent (or adjusted) income that is 38 per cent of the median equivalent income. While this figure is low, the 1997 estimate is above that found in either the 1995 or 1991 US LIS database (Smeeding 2000). A high-income person at the 90th percentile (P_{90}), in contrast, has 214 per cent of the median. The US decile ratio is 5.64, meaning the income of the typical high-income person is more than five-and-a-half times larger than the income of the typical low-income person, even after we have adjusted for taxes, transfers, and family size. In contrast, the average low-income person has 51 per cent of the income of the middle person in the average country; the average rich person has 184 per cent as much, and the decile ratio shows an average 'social distance'

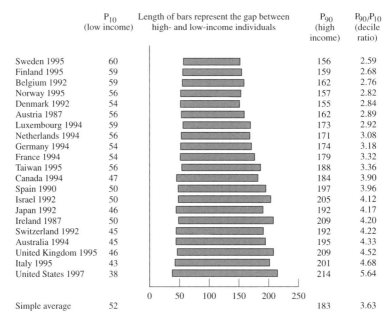

	P_{10} (low income)	Length of bars represent the gap between high- and low-income individuals	P_{90} (high income)	P_{90}/P_{10} (decile ratio)
Sweden 1995	60		156	2.59
Finland 1995	59		159	2.68
Belgium 1992	59		162	2.76
Norway 1995	56		157	2.82
Denmark 1992	54		155	2.84
Austria 1987	56		162	2.89
Luxembourg 1994	59		173	2.92
Netherlands 1994	56		171	3.08
Germany 1994	54		174	3.18
France 1994	54		179	3.32
Taiwan 1995	56		188	3.36
Canada 1994	47		184	3.90
Spain 1990	50		197	3.96
Israel 1992	50		205	4.12
Japan 1992	46		192	4.17
Ireland 1987	50		209	4.20
Switzerland 1992	45		192	4.22
Australia 1994	45		195	4.33
United Kingdom 1995	46		209	4.52
Italy 1995	43		201	4.68
United States 1997	38		214	5.64
		0 50 100 150 200 250		
Simple average	52		183	3.63

Source: Authors' calculations from Luxembourg Income Study (various years), and Japan taken from Ishikawa (1996).

Figure 6.1   *'Social distance': relative income comparisons across 21*
                nations in the 1990s (decile ratios for adjusted disposable
                income; numbers are per cent of median in each nation)

between rich and poor of 3.6 times P_{10}. At the other end of the chart, a Swedish citizen at P_{10} has 60 per cent of the median, the P_{90} is 156, and the decile ratio is 2.59, less than one-half as large as the US value. This evidence suggests that the range of inequality and relative social distance between rich and poor in the rich nations of the world is rather large in the mid-to-late 1990s.

Countries in Figure 6.1 fall into clusters, with inequality the least in Scandinavia (Finland, Sweden, Denmark, and Norway) and Northern Europe (Belgium, Denmark, and Luxembourg). Here the P_{10} values average 58 per cent of the median and the decile ratios are less than 3, ranging from 2.59 to 2.92. Central Europe comes next (the Netherlands, Germany, Austria, and France) with decile ratios from 2.89 to 3.32. Taiwan is an anomalous entry in the middle of the table, with a decile ratio (3.36) in the middle European range. Canada appears next with a lower decile ratio (3.90) than any other Anglo-Saxon nation and with less inequality than is found in Southern Europe. Spain, Israel, Japan, Australia, Switzerland, and Ireland come next with decile ratios from 3.96 to 4.33. Finally, Italy (4.68) and the English-speaking countries of the United Kingdom (4.52), and the United States (5.64) come last with the highest levels of inequality and the greatest social distances.

The United States has the highest decile ratio due in large part to its low relative incomes at the bottom of the distribution. The closest ratios to their P_{10} value of 38 are the United Kingdom (46), Italy (43), Australia (45), Switzerland (45), Canada (47), and Japan (46). No other nation has a value below 50. At the top of the distribution, incomes in the United States are less different from those in other high-inequality nations. The P_{90} of 214 is highest, followed by Ireland and the United Kingdom (209), Israel (205), and Italy (201). But we find no others above 200.

In sum, there is a wide range of inequality among rich nations. Measures of social distance and overall disposable income inequality indicate that the United States has the most unequal distribution of adjusted household income among all 21 countries covered in this study, while Sweden has the most equal. In terms of groupings, the Scandinavian and Benelux countries have the most equal distributions, Central Europe is in the middle of the groupings, and the United Kingdom and Italy come closest to the degree of inequality found in the United States.

But these rankings are incomplete in other ways. While we now have distributional measures that are based on variance in incomes relative to the middle person in each nation, comparisons across nations are limited to relative incomes only. There is no absolute measure of living standards. Thus, we are left with some questions, especially concerning low-income persons in the United States, which is both the richest and the most unequal nation of those studied here. In the next section, real income distribution comparisons will allow us to examine both relative and absolute standards of living at one time.

REAL INCOME DISTRIBUTION MEASURES OF LIVING STANDARDS

Combining PPPs and relative income data for 13 countries, we can compare the distribution of real incomes across nations and over the income spectrum.[17] Before we look at the distributions, however, consider the differences in ranking by 'average' economic status alone when moving from macrodata to microdata measures of 'average' economic well-being.

The first two columns of Table 6.3 compare the average standards of living using macro-based GDP per capita and microdata-based equivalent income (EI, or disposable personal income) per equivalent adult from

Table 6.3   Average economic well-being of all persons and of children for 13 nations compared to the average person in the United States (in US dollars)

Country	Macrodata[1]	Microdata[2]		
	Average overall GDP per capita	Average person relative to US person (US = 100)	Average child relative to US person (US = 100)	Within-nation ratio of child to overall[3]
Sweden 1995	68	67.8	70.1	1.03
United Kingdom 1995	68	69.2	61.5	0.89
Finland 1995	67	70.7	72.1	1.02
Australia 1994	76	79.0	72.1	0.91
France 1994	65	79.2	76.6	0.97
Germany 1994	70	79.2	72.4	0.91
Netherlands 1994	77	79.6	72.0	0.90
Denmark 1995	80	80.9	83.2	1.03
Belgium 1997	73	87.3	78.0	0.89
Canada 1994	78	88.7	89.5	1.01
Norway 1995	83	92.3	87.5	0.95
Switzerland 1992	85	98.4	94.9	0.96
United States 1997	100	100.0	87.9	0.88

Notes:
1. GDP figures and rankings based on 1999 OECD PPPs from Table 6.1, columns 1 and 3, expressed as a percentage of 1999 US GDP per capita of $33 896.
2. Equivalent income, or disposable income per equivalent adult using equation (6.2), and OECD PPPs to bring all nations to 1997 US dollars. Figures expressed as a percentage of 1997 US median equivalent income or $28 005 per equivalent adult.
3. Ratio of column 3 to column 2.

Source: OECD (2000) and Luxembourg Income Study (various years).

equation (6.2) for the same countries. Despite the differences in years (1999 for GDP versus 1997 dollars for the micro-based measures), in income measures (GDP versus LIS), and in equivalence scales (per capita versus adult equivalent income), the two rankings of the 'average' living standard are very similar. The more heavily taxed countries (for example, Sweden, Denmark, Belgium, and Norway) have a slightly lower ranking according to EI compared to GDP per capita, but the rankings are not that dissimilar. While the range of GDP per capita is only from 65 to 85 per cent as large as the United States, the range of EI for all persons is from 68 to 98 (or to 92, leaving out Switzerland). By both rankings, the US citizens enjoy the highest average standard of living.

Children's equivalent incomes vary from 62 to 95 per cent of the US overall median, on average (column 3), and 70 to 95 per cent (excluding the United Kingdom), which is not very different from the overall range of incomes in column 2. But, on average, children are worse off than the overall population (see column 4). The average child in a nation has a higher level of real income compared to the population as a whole in that nation, in only four countries: Sweden, Denmark, Finland, and Canada.

In the United States, the United Kingdom, and Belgium, children's real incomes are 89 per cent or less of the overall average real EI of an American person, with US children having the lowest average real incomes at 88 per cent of the overall average income. Note also that on a per child basis the United States no longer has the highest living standard. Swiss and Canadian children are slightly better off, and Norwegian children are equally as well off as are American children using this measure of real living standards per person.[18]

Real Income for All Persons

Moving to our distributional measures of PPP-adjusted EI, we find quite different levels of real income at various points in the income distribution. The measures of social distance in Figure 6.2 are similar to Figure 6.1 though they differ slightly because of the flatter second equivalence scale used in Figures 6.2–6. However, we can now compare real, not just relative, incomes at both the P_{10} and P_{90} income levels, because all percentiles are given as a fraction of the median US equivalent disposable income per person ($28005 in 1997 dollars).

At the 10th percentile, the United States has the third lowest real income level relative to the median. Only in Australia and the United Kingdom (with average incomes that are 67 and 79 per cent of the US median, respectively) do low-income persons have a lower real living standard (in money terms) compared to that in the United States. All other nations have higher living standards for the average low-income person measured in equivalent disposable cash income terms, despite the fact that all have average real incomes (and average GDP per capita) far below those found in the United States (see Tables 6.2 and 6.3). For instance, the average Dutchman has a real income 80 per cent as large as that of an average American, but the low-income Dutchman has an income that is 110 per cent of the low-income American (that is, the Dutch real income at the 10th percentile is 43 per cent of the US median compared to 39 per cent in the United States). The United States is about 10 per cent below the 13-country average P_{10} of 43 per cent of the median.

	P_{10} (low income)	Length of bars represent the gap between high- and low-income individuals	P_{90} (high income)	P_{90}/P_{10} (decile income)	Real income gap[2]
Switzerland 1992	55		185	3.36	$36 406
Norway 1995	50		143	2.86	26 044
Belgium 1997	47		153	3.26	29 685
Germany 1994	44		139	3.16	26 604
Denmark 1995	43		123	2.86	22 404
France 1994	43		148	3.44	29 405
Netherlands 1994	43		133	3.09	25 204
Finland 1995	41		110	2.68	19 323
Canada 1994	41		167	4.07	35 286
Sweden 1995	40		103	2.58	17 643
Australia 1994	34		148	4.35	31 925
United Kingdom 1995	33		142	4.30	30 525
United States 1997[1]	39		209	5.36	47 608
		0 50 100 150 200 250			
Simple average	43		146	3.49	$29 081

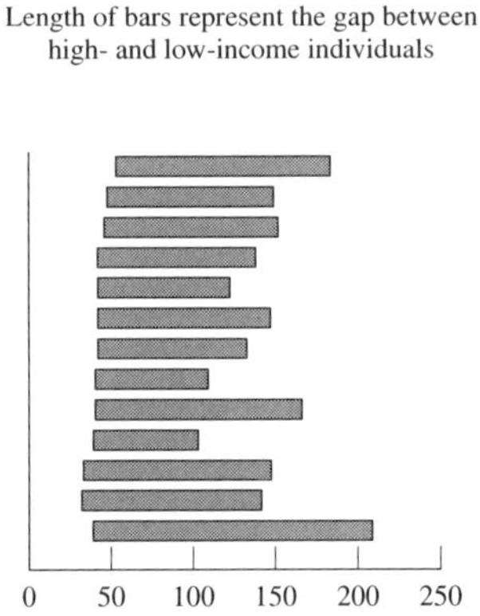

Notes:
1. US estimate differs from that shown in Figure 6.1 due to a different equivalence scale (see text). The United States median income per equivalent person in 1997 was US$28 005.
2. Figures given are expressed in 1997 US PPP-adjusted dollars per equivalent person, weighted by the number of persons per household.

Source: Authors' calculations from Luxembourg Income Study (various years).

Figure 6.2   Social distance and real standards of living (percentage of overall US 1997 median equivalent income in PPP terms)

At the other end of the spectrum, the average high-income American has a living standard that is 209 per cent of the living standard of the average American. The next nearest nation is at 185 per cent of the US median (Switzerland) and the next one 167 per cent (Canada). On average, a rich person in the United States has a living standard that is 43 per cent higher than the average rich person in the other 12 nations (that is, 209 compared to 146).

Combining these percentiles, we find two measures of social distance, the decile ratio and the real income gap between the 10th and 90th percentiles (expressed in EI 1997 US dollar terms). The gap between rich and poor in America given by the decile ratio is the largest of all the countries at 5.36. The EI of a low-income person is $10 927 (or 39 per cent of $28 005) while that of a high-income person is $58 530 (209 per cent of $28 005), producing a gap of $47 608. This amount is 1.64 times the average gap of $29 081, and is more than $11 000 higher than the next nearest gap ($36 406 in Switzerland). The smallest gap ($17 643) is found in Sweden.

Real Incomes of Children

Although we would argue that economic well-being (at least in developed countries) is most crucially a function of the individual's relative position in the distribution of income, real levels of living are also important in comparing living standards and well-being across nations. Interest in real income for children goes beyond the situation of poor children alone – in comparative studies one also wants to know about the real standard of living of average and well-off children. These measures can also be understood as measures of equality of opportunity and dollar measures of the types of life chances that parents can provide for their children. Figures 6.3–6 address the issue of real incomes for children, presenting the same information in several ways.

First of all, Figure 6.3 is constructed exactly the same as Figure 6.2, with all incomes expressed as a fraction of the 1997 US overall median EI ($28 005). The percentiles differ because the figure presents only the EIs for all persons in families with children. On average, children's real incomes at the 10th percentile are the same as all persons' real incomes at the 10th percentile (43 per cent of the median in both Figures 6.2 and 6.3), but the average incomes of families with children are less than those of all families (Table 6.2), mainly because the 90th percentile for children (132) is below that for the whole population (146, comparing Figures 6.2 and 6.3). Thus, inequality as measured by the decile ratio is less than average for children and the real income gap is also lower for children. In fact, use of the first microdata-based equivalence scale (equation (6.1) above) would produce more inequality and therefore larger real income gaps.

Looking first at our measure of 'fair chance', the nations with the highest P_{10} offer their children the best economic chance for future success. We agree with Mayer (1997) and others that income alone is a poor proxy for life chances for middle-class households with children. Another $100 or $1000 per child for middle-income or well-to-do families makes little difference to their children's overall life chances compared to other influences (such as parents, schools, communities, and peers). But we also agree with Duncan et al. (1998) that being born into a family with very low income significantly decreases a child's overall life chances.[19] Thus, we believe that the P_{10} for children is a meaningful and important indicator of a fair life chance.

On this basis, only a child in the United Kingdom has a less fair chance, at 31 per cent of the median, than does a child in the United States, at 35 per cent of the median, based on real incomes alone. Australian children are at roughly the same levels of living as US children, while the next nearest is the unified Germany at 40 per cent. All

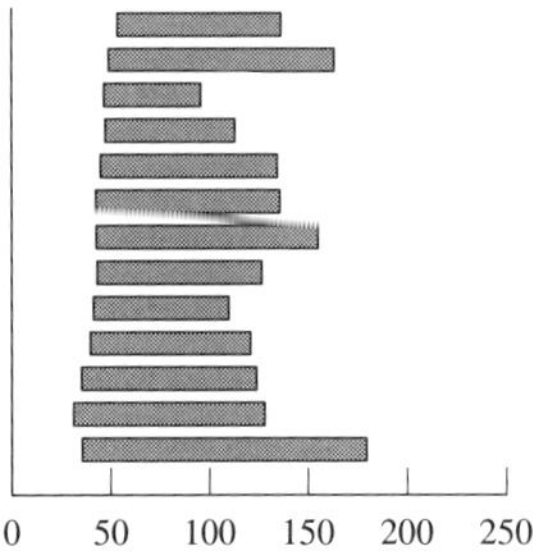

	P_{10} (fair chance or low income)	Length of bars represents the gap between high- and low-income individuals	P_{90} (high income)	Equal opportunity P_{90}/P_{10} (decile ratio)	Real income gap[2]
Norway 1995	55		126	2.29	$19 884
Switzerland 1992	51		165	3.24	31 926
Sweden 1995	48		97	2.02	13 722
Denmark 1995	48		114	2.38	18 483
Finland 1995	46		136	2.96	25 205
France 1994	44		137	3.11	26 045
Canada 1994	44		156	3.55	31 366
Belgium 1997	44		127	2.89	23 244
Netherlands 1994	42		110	2.62	19 043
Germany 1994	40		121	3.03	22 684
Australia 1994	36		124	3.44	24 644
United Kingdom 1995	31		127	4.10	26 885
United States 1997[1]	35		179	5.11	40 327
		0 50 100 150 200 250			
Simple average	43		132	3.13	$24 881

Notes:
1. Figures given are 1997 US PPP-adusted dollars per equivalent person, weighted for the number of children in each unit size.
2. Figures differ from Figure 6.1 because we weight by children, not all persons, and because we include only families with children in this table. The overall US median income per equivalent person was $28 005 in 1997; the median per equivalent was $24 620 or 87.9 per cent of the overall median.

Source: Authors' calculations from Luxembourg Income Study (various years).

Figure 6.3   Equal opportunity and fair chance: real standards of living for children (percentage of overall US 1997 median equivalent income in PPP terms)

other nations have children's living standards that are above the average standard of 43 per cent, which is 8 percentage points above the US level, or 23 per cent higher than the 35 per cent US value.

At the other end of the scale, US children in prosperous US households have living standards 179 per cent above the median US person. Swiss children are also relatively better off (at 165 per cent of the median). The average incomes of the best-off children are 135 per cent of the median, while US children are 44 percentage points above this level. In Sweden, the high-income child actually has a living standard (measured by cash income) just below that of the average US person.[20]

These percentiles translate into decile ratios and real income gaps for children that are similar to those found in Figure 6.2. Here we interpret the social distance measure as a measure of equality of opportunity. Nations with smaller social distances (or lower real income gaps) provide more equal chances for their children, both high- and low-income children. The

US gap in decile ratio (5.11) and real EI terms is again the highest. Only one other nation (the United Kingdom) has a decile ratio above 4.00. The real income gap in the United States of $40 327 is by far the largest, with Switzerland and Canada the only others above the $30 000 level, and with the other nations near or below the $25 528 average difference. The above-average gaps between poor and rich children in these three nations must be seen in light of the fact that all three have above-average P_{10} ratios as well. The real income gap of $40 327 in the United States means that low-income children have resources of $9802, assuming all resources are evenly split among household members. In contrast, high-income families have $50 129 to spend on each child.

For Every Dollar . . .

Perhaps an easier way to understand these differences across nations is to compare children at average-, low- and high-income levels directly. Figure 6.4 presents the 'supra chance' or average standard of living for the high-income US child compared to the high-income child in 12 other nations. For every dollar the average high-income US child has, other nations' children have far less. Only Swiss and Canadian children are close, with 92 and 87 cents per dollar, respectively. All other rich children have less in spendable income by a wide margin. Parents of rich children in Sweden have resources less than 55 cents per dollar compared to a well-to-do child in the United States. High-income US children are truly advantaged by this measure of living standards. Smaller family sizes, later marriage and child bearing, higher labor force participation and earnings for married women with children, and assortative mating (that is, marrying someone of the same education level with similar labor force participation – such as, 'career couples') all help raise the standard of living among high-income US children (Gottschalk and Smeeding 1997, 2000). It would seem that the United States is the best place to be born a rich child.

The average US child also fares well (Figure 6.5). For every dollar available to a US child, children in almost all other nations have less, with a Swiss child the only one more 'advantaged' on average (108 per cent) in an absolute dollar sense, and with the average Canadian child (102 per cent) at a similar living standard. Other nations are now closer to the United States, but a Swedish (80 cents per dollar) or a British child (70 cents per dollar) still has a lower level of resources by a significant amount.

Given these comparisons, Figure 6.6 should come as something of a surprise to most observers. For every dollar available to a low-income US child, the low-income children in every nation but one (the United Kingdom) have more. Swiss, Norwegian, Danish, and Swedish children are

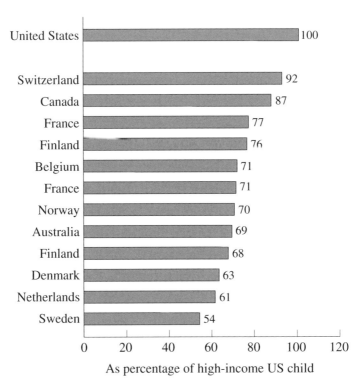

Note: Child in a household at the 90th percentile of the US equivalent income distribution for households with children, all other currencies converted to 1997 US dollars using PPPs.

Source: Figure 6.3, P_{90} column.

Figure 6.4   Supra chance: real incomes of the high-income child

37 to 57 per cent better off, while other European low-income children (Canada, Belgium, France, and the Netherlands) are at least 20 per cent better off. Even Australian children have a 3 per cent higher living standard than do US children in real spendable dollar terms.

Stated differently, if one were unsure of their economic status in childhood, or if one were a risk-averse child, there would be a considerable difference in real living standards depending on one's nation of birth. For those born to low-income families in rich nations, the United States is not such a good place to grow up.

The high overall living standards in the United States must be balanced by the fact that these advantages do not translate directly to low-income

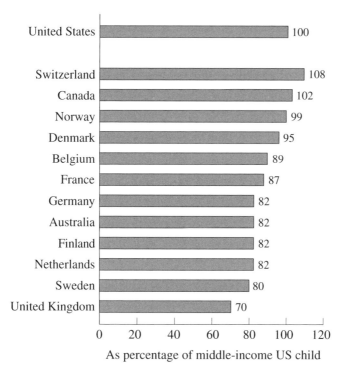

Note: Child in a household at the 50th percentile (median) of the US equivalent income distribution for households with children, all other currencies converted to 1997 US dollars using PPPs.

Source: Table 6.3, 4th column.

Figure 6.5   Average chance: real incomes of the average child

children. Race, ethnicity, and single parenthood play roles in explaining these differences, but low parental wages and lack of social income support are the two most important factors that explain this result (Smeeding, 1998; Burtless and Smeeding 2000; Smeeding et al. 2001).

Summary

While the United States has a higher real level of overall income than all of our comparison countries, it is the high- and middle-income persons (in general), and particularly the well-to-do children in our nation who reap the benefits (and much more the former than the latter). Low-income

Note: Child in a household at the 10th percentile of the US equivalent income distribution for households with children, all other currencies converted to 1997 US dollars using PPPs.

Source: Table 6.3, P_{10} column.

Figure 6.6   Fair chance: real incomes of the low-income child

American children suffer in both absolute and relative terms. The average low-income child in the other 12 countries is at least 25 per cent better off than is the average low-income American child. If we were able to add measures of the cost, quality, and access to other social goods such as primary and secondary education (including child care) and health care, we doubt that it would very much reduce the cross-national differences shown here. The inequality of access to health care in the United States is well known, as is the average to poor performance of schools and the poor educational outcomes evident in many low-income areas in this nation. We might even be able to generalize that societies with wide income disparities across families with children have less support for public and social goods such as tax-financed health care, child care, and education, because high-income families can privately purchase above-average levels of those goods with their higher incomes, rather than supporting high overall levels of tax-financed goods and sharing them with less-well-off children.

DISCUSSION AND CONCLUSION

This chapter has tried to broaden the economic concept of 'standard of living' to encompass a wider range of points than the 'average'. The advantage of microdata-based measures of living standards is that they can show variance within and across nations. And in nations with a great deal of inequality, the 'average' – be it the mean or the median – can be a poor descriptor of the living standards of the rich or the poor.

When we translate all incomes into 'real' PPP-adjusted incomes, we find that rankings of countries and living standards can be quite different depending on where in the income distribution we focus and on which group we focus (for example, overall versus children). Clearly the nation with the highest real GDP per capita and the highest real disposable equivalent income per person is also the most unequal. And this inequality manifests itself in terms of relatively and absolutely lower living standards at the bottom of the US income distribution, especially for children.

The distributions of noncash benefits are not expected to change these findings by much. While public noncash spending is relatively larger than cash spending in the three low-cash-spending nations of Australia, Canada, and the United States, we know that noncash benefits may vary according to both quality of services provided and the amount of income paid for them by consumers. Perhaps, most importantly, we do not know how low-income families value noncash benefits relative to cash benefits. While health and education benefits received below cost most certainly improve well-being, many low-cash-income families might prefer to receive the benefits in more flexible cash terms (Canberra Group 2001, Ch. 4). If this is the case, we cannot simply add noncash incomes to cash incomes without overstating the real incomes of poor families.[21]

The findings have political and policy implications as well. Children in the United Kingdom have the lowest real living standards of any of the children observed here, but they also have a prime minister who has set a national goal of improving living standards and eradicating child poverty in Britain over the next decade, and who has matched his political rhetoric with some modicum of real fiscal and community efforts (Bradshaw 2001; Micklewright 2001; Walker and Wiseman 2001). In contrast, the United States is led by a president whose slogan 'leave no child behind' is rather hollow and whose fiscal stance is to use income tax reductions for the rich and fiscal stringency for the poor to further increase the overall gap between rich and poor US children. As we have seen, the gap between American rich and poor children is already the highest, even accounting for the effect of the EITC which has increased the income of US children in the 10th percentile by a substantial amount since the early 1990s. Instead of public dollars for children, the US president prefers voluntary 'faith-based efforts' which are complementary to, but are not substitutes for, adequate public safety nets.

Unfortunately, analyses such as the one presented here have not had a substantial effect on these policies. It is often remarked that analyses of living standards and child outcomes are better and more complete for the United States than for any other nation (for example, Micklewright 2001). Unfortunately these analyses do not easily transform themselves into policy actions or into better outcomes for US children.

NOTES

*   The authors would like to thank the Levy Economics Institute, the Ford Foundation, the Research School of Social Sciences at the Australian National University, the MacArthur Network on the Family and the Economy, and the LIS member countries for their support. Excellent assistance was provided by Esther Gray, Kati Foley, Jonathan Schwabish, and Deb Tafel. Useful comments were made by Stein Ringen, Tim Colebatch, Bobbi Wolfe, Bob Haveman, Edward Wolff, and participants at the Levy Institute conference. We alone are responsible for the results and interpretations presented here.

1.   We use the terms 'household' and 'family' interchangeably. Our formal unit of aggregation is the household – all persons living together and sharing the same housing facilities – in almost all nations. In Sweden and Canada the 'household' refers to a slightly more narrow definition of the 'family' unit.

2.   However, the 'Canberra Group' of national statistical offices and organizations such as LIS, the World Bank, and the United Nations have recently produced such a standard (Canberra Group 2001).

3.   Its relatively short timeframe (1979–97 for most nations, but 1968–97 for five countries) and limited number of observation periods per country (three to five periods per country at present) currently limits its usefulness for studying longer-term trends in income distribution. Coupled with the problems of defining PPPs over time, we do not present trend data for real incomes here.

4.   The UK data are the only exception to this rule; their Family Expenditure Survey (FES) uses a bi-weekly accounting period with rules for aggregating up to annual totals. In Germany, LIS has aggregated the monthly and quarterly data into annual income amounts.

5.   In fact, the selection of per capita income (as with macroeconomic measures of living standards) is one choice of an equivalence scale, and one that suggests there are zero economies of scale for different family sizes. The cost of reaching a given level of well-being increases proportionally with family size. Thus, a family of four needs four times as much as a single person to reach the same living standard. Such a scale does not make much sense to most microeconomists, who realize that two can reach the same standard of living less cheaply by living together rather than apart, and that a family of four can reach a similar standard of living at less cost per person than four times the individual amount.

6. According to the square root formula, four persons need twice as much as one to be as well off. According to the second 'cube root' formula for a 45-year-old head, the household of four needs 1.6 times as much as a family of one. Thus, the second formula suggests a lower cost of children (assuming they are the third or fourth members of the household) than the first. The use of the second formula therefore presents our most conservative estimate of the costs of children in the final section of this chapter.

7. For additional comments on PPPs and microdata-based comparisons of well-being, see Castles (1996); Bradbury and Jäntti (1999, Appendix); Rainwater and Smeeding (1999); Gottschalk and Smeeding (2000); Smeeding et al. (2001). The OECD has a set of PPPs that go back to the 1970s but they are inconsistent with household income datasets over the same period.

8. The base year is important because PPPs are reconfigured with a different 'base' market basket only every four to five years. Between base years, price indices are used to adjust base baskets for comparisons. These price indices may differ from the consumer price index (CPI) used to adjust incomes within countries and the choice of CPI may also affect the results. Hence, we stick with 1996 base year PPPs adjusting back to 1992 PPPs or forward to 1997 PPPs using the implicit OECD price index.

9. Indirect taxes are reflected in the final prices used to adjust PPPs and therefore do not affect these comparisons.

10. We compared grossed-up LIS market incomes to OECD final domestic consumption aggregates. The one nation for which we have mid-1990s data and which differed most from the rest was Italy, which captured only about 47 per cent of OECD gross final consumption in its LIS survey, compared to 89 per cent for the United States. Most other nations were close to the US level; a few were above it.

    Underreporting of income has a large impact in comparing real income distribution across countries. The smaller the percentage of aggregate income that is reported in the household survey, the less the measured level of real income. Underreporting may also affect comparisons if income at either the bottom or the top of the income distribution is differentially underreported. Unfortunately, we cannot currently assess the relative importance of income underreporting in different parts of the income distribution.

11. Since public housing benefits are already included in cash incomes in the United Kingdom and Sweden, the major omission is for France, where public housing equals 0.85 per cent of the GDP. In all other countries, public housing benefits are less than 0.33 per cent of GDP (OECD 2002a). We also take no account of imputed rent for owner-occupiers.

12. Distributional results similar to those reported here in Figure 6.1 are directly available from the 'key figures' section of the LIS website along with the program used to generate them (http://www.lisproject.org/keyfigures.htm).

13. While we have used this measure before (for example, Smeeding 1998, 2000; Rainwater and Smeeding 2000;) others have developed more sophisticated measures of polarization and social distance. For a good introduction to these, see D'Ambrosio (2001).

14. The 13 nations mentioned here are the same 13 that are used later for the real income distribution analyses.

15. The results are about the same for 1995 GDP per capita using PPPs. See Appendix Table 6A.1.

16. For reasons why one might choose the latter, for example to determine the cost of a particular commodity such as a prescription drug available only in one country at that country's prices, see Ward (2001).

17. The eight nations that drop out from Figure 6.1 are those with income data before 1992 (Spain, Austria, and Ireland), nations without OECD PPPs (Taiwan and Israel), nations with extraordinarily low incomes as measured by their LIS surveys (Italy), nations for which we have no microdata at LIS (Japan), and one tiny nation with 400000 persons and GDP per capita 135 per cent larger than the United States (Luxembourg).

18. Canadian LIS data do not include payroll taxes paid by the employee. These vary considerably by province, income level, and program, with exemptions, deductions, and exclusions. Employee payroll taxes in Canada average about 4 per cent of wages, and overall employer and employee taxes are lower than in the United States as a percentage

of GDP. Were we able to adjust for employee payroll taxes, the average level of disposable income in Canada would decline by about 3 percentage points (Lin 2001). In Table 6.3 this would leave Canadian children slightly worse off, on average, compared to American children. Because of low-wage exemptions and other features of Canadian payroll taxes, we cannot estimate how other points in the distribution would be affected.

19. Duncan et al. (1998) find that US children who live in families with incomes at or below 75 per cent of the US poverty line (roughly 33 to 36 per cent of the median income) do less well than other US children. Similar studies have not been done for other nations. Similar figures to those found here but from an earlier period can be found in Rainwater and Smeeding (2000).

20. However, because the Swedish household treats children living at home who are aged 18 and over the same as children who live alone, the effects of this structure may be to understate the true EI of such children.

21. From a child's perspective (or that of a taxpayer) we might argue that research spending is as large as cash spending.

REFERENCES

Atkinson, Anthony B., Lee Rainwater and Timothy M. Smeeding (1995), 'Income distribution in OECD countries: evidence from the Luxembourg Income Study (LIS)', *Social Policy Studies*, **18**, Paris: Organisation for Economic Co-operation and Development (October).

Bradbury, Bruce (1989), 'Family size equivalence scales and survey evaluations of income and well-being', *Journal of Social Policy*, **18** (3) (July), 383–408.

Bradbury, Bruce, and Markus Jäntti (1999), 'Child poverty across industrialized nations', Innocenti Occasional Papers Economic Policy Series 71, Florence: UNICEF International Child Development Centre, September, accessed at http://www.unicef-icdc.org/publications/pdf/eps 71.pdf, August 2003.

Bradshaw, Jonathan (2001), 'Child poverty under Labour', in G. Fimister (ed.), *An End in Sight? Tackling Child Poverty in the UK*, London: Child Poverty Action Group, pp. 9–27.

Buhmann, Brigitte, Lee Rainwater, Gunther Schmaus and Timothy M. Smeeding (1988), 'Equivalence scales, well-being, inequality and poverty: sensitivity estimates across ten countries using the Luxembourg Income Study (LIS) database', *Review of Income and Wealth*, **34** (2), June, 115–42.

Burkhauser, Richard V., Timothy M. Smeeding, and Joachim Merz (1996), 'Relative inequality and poverty in Germany and the United States using alternative equivalence scales,' *Review of Income and Wealth*, **42** (4), 381–400.

Burtless, Gary, and Timothy M. Smeeding (2000), 'The level, trend and composition of American poverty: national and international perspective', conference paper presented at the Institute for Research on Poverty, Madison, WI, May.

Canberra Group (2001), *Expert Group on Household Income Statistics: Final Report and Recommendations*, Canberra Group, Ottawa: Statistics Canada, February.

Carlson, Olaf (1993), remarks made at a conference in honor of his birthday, Prime Minister's office, Stockholm, Sweden, December.

Castles, Ian (1996) 'Review of the OECD–Eurostat PPP program', STD/PPP (97)5, Economic Studies Branch, Paris: Organization for Economic Cooperation and Development, accessed at http://www1.oecd.org/std/ecastle.pdf.

Coleman, Richard Patrick, Lee Rainwater, and Kent A. McClelland (1978), *Social Standing in America: New Dimensions of Class*, New York: Basic Books.

D'Ambrosio, Conchita (2001), 'Household characteristics and the distribution of income in Italy: an application of social distance measures' *Review of Income and Wealth*, **47** (1) (March), 43–64.

de Vos, Klaas, and Asghar Zaidi (1996), 'Inequality in consumption vs. inequality of income in the EC, unpublished manuscript, University of Netherlands, Leiden, Netherlands.

Duncan, Greg J., Wei-Jun J. Yeung, Jeanne Brooks-Gunn and Judith Smith (1998), 'How much does childhood poverty affect the life chances of children?' *American Sociological Review*, **63** (3) (June), 406–23.

Gardiner, Karen, John Hills, Jane Falkingham, Valérie Lechene, and Holly Sutherland (1995), 'The effects of differences in housing and health care systems on international comparisons of income distribution', Welfare State Programme discussion paper no. 110, London: London School of Economics, July.

Gottschalk, Peter, and Timothy M. Smeeding (1997), 'Cross-national comparisons of earnings and income inequality,' *Journal of Economic Literature*, **35** (2) (June), 633–87.

Gottschalk, Peter, and Timothy M. Smeeding (2000), 'Empirical evidence on income inequality in industrialized countries', in *Handbook of Income Distribution*, edited by Anthony B. Atkinson and François Bourguignon, Amsterdam: North-Holland, pp.261–308.

Heston, Alan (1986), 'Some problems of comparing poverty levels across countries', Center for the Analysis of Developing Economies discussion paper no. 86–42, Philadelphia: University of Pennsylvania.

Ishikawa, Tsureo (1996), 'Data runs conducted by Japanese Ministry of Welfare,' unpublished data, November 26.

Johnson, D., and T. Smeeding (1997), 'Measuring the trend in inequality among individuals and families: consumption or income?', paper presented to the American Economic Association, 6 January.

Lin, Zhenxi (2001), 'Payroll taxes in Canada revisited: structure, statuory parameters and recent trends', Ottawa, Canada: Statistics Canada, Analytical Studies Branch research paper, no. 149, August.

Luxembourg Income Study (LIS) (2003), *LIS Database List*, Syracuse, NY: Center for Policy Research, Luxembourg Income Study, Maxwell School, accessed at www.lisproject.org/techdoc/datasets.htm.

Mayer, Susan E. (1997), *What Money Can't Buy: Family Income and Children's Life Choices*, Cambridge, MA: Harvard University Press.

Micklewright, John (2001), 'Social exclusion and children: a European view for a US debate', paper presented to the Conference on Social Exclusion and Children, Institute for Child and Family Policy, Columbia University, New York, 3–4 May.

Organisation for Economic Co-operation and Development (2000), 'Purchasing power parities for OECD countries, 1970–1999', Paris: OECD, accessed at http://www.oecd.org/std/pppoecd.xls, August, 2003.

Organisation for Economic Co-operation and Development (2001), 'Social expenditures database: 1980/1998', Paris: OECD.

Organisation for Economic Co-operation and Development (2002a), 'Education at a Glance: OECD Indicators 2002', Paris: OECD.

Organisation for Economic Co-operation and Development (2002b), *National Accounts of OECD Countries: Main Aggregates*, vol. 1, Paris: OECD.

Rainwater, Lee (1974), *What Money Buys: Inequality and the Social Meanings of Income*, New York: Basic Books.

Rainwater, Lee (1990), 'Poverty and equivalence as social constructions', LIS working paper no. 91, Syracuse, NY: Luxembourg Income Study, Center for Policy Research, Syracuse University, August.

Rainwater, Lee, and Timothy M. Smeeding (1999), 'From "relative" to "real" income: purchase power parities and household microdata, problems and prospects', *Papers and Final Report of the Third Meeting on Household Income Statistics*, Ottawa: Statistics Canada, pp. 139–63, accessed at http://www.lisproject.org/canberra/ottawareport/ottasession5.PDF.

Rainwater, Lee, and Timothy Smeeding (2000), 'Doing poorly: the real income of American children in a comparative perspective', in J. Skolnick and E. Currie (eds), *Crisis in American Institutions*, Boston: Allyn and Bacon, pp. 118–25.

Sen, Amartya Kumar (1992), *Inequality Reexamined*, Cambridge, MA: Harvard University Press.

Smeeding, Timothy M. (1974), 'Cost of living differences at low income levels', Institute for Research on Poverty discussion paper no. DP-23, Madison, WI: University of Wisconsin.

Smeeding, Timothy M. (1997), 'US income inequality in a cross-national perspective: why are we so different?', *Looking Ahead*, **XIX** (2–3), 41–50, reprinted in J. Auerbach and R. Belous (eds), *The Inequality Paradox: Growth of Income Disparity*, Washington, DC: National Policy Association, pp. 194–217.

Smeeding, Timothy M. (2000), 'Changing income inequality in OECD countries: updated results from the Luxembourg Income Study (LIS)', in R. Hauser and I. Becker (eds), *The Personal Distribution of Income in an International Perspective*, Berlin: Springer-Verlag, pp. 205–24.

Smeeding, Timothy M. and Deborah Freund (2002), *The Future Costs of Health Care in an Ageing Society, Is the Glass Half Full or Half Empty?*, Syracuse, NY: Center for Policy Research, Syracuse University.

Smeeding, Timothy M., Lee Rainwater and Gary Burtless (2001), 'United States poverty in a cross-national context', in S. Danziger and R. Haveman (eds), *Understanding Poverty*, New York: Russell Sage Foundation and Harvard University Press, pp. 162–89.

Smeeding, T.M., P. Saunders, J. Coder, S. Jenkins, J. Fritzell, A. Hagenaars, R. Hauser and M. Wolfson (1993), 'Poverty, inequality and family living standards impacts across seven nations: the effect of noncash subsidies for health, education, and housing', *Review of Income and Wealth*, **39** (3), 229–56.

Smeeding, Timothy M., Michael Ward, Ian Castles and Haeduck Lee (2000), 'Making cross-country comparisons of income distributions', paper presented at 26th General Conference of the International Association for Research in Income and Wealth, Cracow, 3 August, accessed at http://www.stat.gov.pl and http://www.econ.nyu.edu/dept/iariw.

Summers, Robert and Alan Heston (1991), 'The Penn World Table (Mark 5): an expanded set of international comparisons, 1950–1988', *Quarterly Journal of Economics*, **106** (2, May) 327–68.

Walker, Robert and Michael Wiseman (2001), 'The house that Jack built: the story of British welfare reform', *Milken Institute Review* (4th quarter), 53–62, accessed at http://www.milkeninstitute.org/publications/review2001_12/52–62mr.pdf.

Ward, Michael (2001), 'Purchasing power parity and international comparisons,' paper presented to the United Nations Human Development Report Statistical Advisory Panel, New York, 4 March.

Appendix Table 6A.1   GDP per capita in selected countries, 1995 and 1999

Countries	1995 GDP/capita		1999 GDP/capita	
	Amount ($)	Index	Amount ($)	Index
United Kingdom	18 743	67	22 861	68
Finland	18 861	68	22 723	67
Sweden	19 949	72	23 017	68
France	20 198	72	22 067	65
Netherlands	21 222	76	25 923	77
Germany	21 357	77	23 819	70
Australia	21 459	77	25 590	76
Belgium	21 840	78	24 845	73
Canada	22 951	82	26 424	78
Denmark	22 965	82	27 073	80
Norway	23 316	84	28 133	83
Switzerland	25 672	92	28 672	85
United States	27 895	100	33 836	100
Average	22 033	79	25 768	76

PART III

Wealth and Living Standards

7. Race, home ownership, and family structure in twentieth-century America

William J. Collins and Robert A. Margo[*]

INTRODUCTION

More than 35 years ago, the Moynihan Report (or *The Negro Family: The Case for National Action*) ignited a firestorm of controversy regarding allegedly detrimental changes in the structure of American families, and in particular, regarding the social implications of the rise in female-headed households among African Americans (US Department of Labor 1965). Since then, the rate of female headship and the proportion of children raised in female-headed households, has risen for both whites and blacks. In previous work, we have undertaken a series of investigations of the historical evolution of racial gaps in homeownership rates and in the value of owner-occupied housing based on samples of male household heads (Collins and Margo 2001, 2003). Concerned that the exclusion of female-headed households might have affected our interpretation of long-run racial change in housing outcomes, we have extended our analysis to consider the influence of changing household composition on housing market outcomes for household heads and also, importantly, for young children.

Although labor economists and economic historians have devoted substantial effort to measuring and understanding the evolution of racial differences in income (Smith and Welch 1989; Donohue and Heckman 1991), the historical development of racial gaps in other economic outcomes has been studied far less intensively. This relative neglect is unfortunate because income is only one of several ways to gauge economic well-being. The underlying premise of this chapter is that 'wealth matters' in that differences in wealth across households have a substantial effect on economic well-being (Wolff 1998). Throughout the century, owner-occupied housing has been a major component of private sector wealth, and the ownership of one's home has long been viewed as a central component of 'the American Dream'. Racial differences in home ownership and

housing values are important proximate causes of racial differences in
wealth which, historically and at present, are far larger than racial differences in income (Higgs 1982; Margo 1984; Long and Caudill 1992; Oliver
and Shapiro 1995; Wolff 1998).

Racial gaps in home ownership and in the value of owner-occupied
housing directly reflect gaps in well-being because they are linked to a flow
of consumption services – shelter, comfort, public school quality, proximity to work and recreation, and so on – that are embedded in housing units
and in 'neighborhood quality'.[1] In addition to private economic benefits,
there is recent evidence that home ownership may have a positive 'treatment
effect' on the owner's behavior and on the children of homeowners (Green
and White 1997; DiPasquale and Glaeser 1999). Because neighborhood
quality, including schools, may have disproportionate effects on children,
racial gaps in home ownership and home values may tend to perpetuate
themselves and to reinforce gaps in other social outcomes such as income,
employment, and criminal behavior.

In our previous work we used the various twentieth-century Integrated
Public Use Microdata Series (IPUMS, Ruggles and Sobek 1997) samples
of federal population censuses (1900–20, 1940, 1960–90) to study the long-
run evolution of racial differences in home ownership and housing values
among adult *male* household heads. However, as noted above, the proportion of black households headed by females has increased relative to the
proportion among whites. Consequently, to the extent that gender is a
numerically significant correlate of home ownership and house value,
focusing solely on male household heads may give a misleading portrait of
racial change over time. Here, we extend our previous work by expanding
the samples to include female household heads, to assess the exposure of
children to home ownership, and to observe how the rise of female headship may relate to children's exposure to ownership.

We begin by comparing levels and trends in ownership rates and housing
values across samples consisting of all household heads and of male and
female household heads separately. Since the all-household sample is
simply a weighted average of the male and female samples, we can mechan-
ically understand the all-household trends by observing the male and
female trends and changes in the implicit weight given to female heads in
forming the all-household average. We find that in levels and in trends of
ownership and value, the male and female samples are similar (within race
categories) up to around 1940. That is, white (or black) female-headed
households were about as likely to own homes as white (or black) male-
headed households, and their homes were about 90 per cent as valuable as
male-owned homes. Some time after 1940, however, the gender-specific
samples began to diverge. By 1980, male heads had ownership rates that

were about 20 points higher than those of female heads, and among owners, the average property value of female heads had fallen to about 75 per cent of that of male heads.

As the female samples diverged from the male samples, the number of female heads grew faster than the number of male heads, and consequently, the influence of females on the movement of the overall racial gap in housing outcomes became stronger. We find that racial convergence of ownership rates among male heads between 1960 and 1990 was not complemented by convergence among female heads, or by convergence of females on males. Furthermore, the proportion of female heads among blacks increased by more than it did among whites. Through both channels (the lack of racial convergence among women and the growing proportion of female heads), overall racial convergence in ownership was dampened.

Female headship's influence on our view of racial convergence in ownership and home values is small compared to its influence on our view of children's exposure to ownership. We find that over the 1960–90 period, the racial gap in the probability that young children (age 10 and under) resided in owner-occupied housing (henceforth the 'exposure index') narrowed for children living in father-headed households, but did *not* narrow for all children. This lack of convergence is partly due to especially adverse trends in the 1980s, but even so, the steady redistribution of children out of father-headed households has been a considerable drag on racial convergence in children's likelihood of living in owner-occupied housing. Later in the chapter we undertake some simple counterfactual calculations to size up the importance of rising female headship to housing market outcomes for the heads themselves and for young children. Though such calculations do not identify a true causal link, they do provide some quantitative perspectives on the issue.

We then extend the analysis to a series of regressions of housing outcomes on household characteristics, including race, from 1940 to 1990. The multivariate analyses reveal how much of the gaps in housing market outcomes can (and cannot) be accounted for by observable differences in heads' characteristics. Adding women to the sample tends to widen the 'adjusted' racial gaps (relative to the results obtained for men-only samples) and to dampen the degree of convergence after 1960.

Overall, our results clearly suggest that including female household heads in the samples influences the observed trends in racial gaps in housing outcomes. However, the importance of sample composition should not be overstated because certain other 'stylized facts' remain unchanged from our earlier studies. For example, regardless of whether female heads are included, substantial increases in the black/white ratio of housing values and of homeownership rates occurred between 1940 and

1970, a period in which blacks were moving to central cities while whites were moving to suburbs, and in which racial discrimination was pervasive in housing markets (Massey and Denton 1993; Collins and Margo 2001). Moreover, adding women to the sample does not alter a central finding of our previous work: between 1970 and 1980, the value of black-owned housing, conditional on the characteristics of the household head or the housing unit itself, declined sharply relative to white-owned housing.

The next section presents and explores the IPUMS data in detail, starting with ownership rates, then moving to children's 'exposure' to ownership, and finally measuring the gap in the value of owner-occupied housing. Drawing on our previous work, we then present a brief historical narrative that attempts to place the empirical findings in their economic and institutional contexts.

RACE, HOME OWNERSHIP, AND HOUSING VALUES: LONG-RUN EVIDENCE FROM THE IPUMS DATA

In our previous work we used the IPUMS to study long-run trends in racial differences in home ownership and, among owners, in housing values. Because of the nature of the census questions on home ownership, and because we wished to examine individual-level correlates of housing outcomes, the natural unit of observation was the household head. We further limited our analysis to male household heads, on the grounds that the vast majority of studies of long-run trends in racial differences in earnings have focused on adult males, studies that form a natural comparison to ours (see, for example, Smith and Welch 1989; Donohue and Heckman 1991).

However, there are several reasons why limiting the sample to male household heads may give a misleading portrait of racial change. First, as noted above, the share of female-headed households has increased over time, especially among black households. Second, on average, female household heads have lower incomes than male household heads and, on those grounds alone, are less likely to be homeowners. If they do become owners, they are likely to reside in homes of lower value than those of male household heads (Danziger and Weinberg 1994). Third, female-headed households were and are more likely to receive some type of public assistance. At least prior to recent welfare reforms, it is widely believed that such programs discouraged work effort and the accumulation of financial assets, both of which would reduce the likelihood of home ownership (Moffitt 1992).

With the exception of 1950, each IPUMS sample since 1900 contains information on home ownership.[2] Dwellings were classified as owner-

occupied if the owner lived there, though the census did not explicitly identify who within the household actually owned the home. Following census
convention, we assume that only household heads could be homeowners
and that if the home was owner-occupied, it was owned by the household
head. The samples in each year consist of all black and white household
heads who are over the age of 19 and who are not in school. We make an
effort to identify Hispanic household heads (generally counted as white)
as a separate category in the 1980 and 1990 censuses. We do not attempt
to explore the Hispanic experience in housing markets, though that is certainly a topic worthy of attention in future work; rather, we simply want
to ensure that combining Hispanics with other whites does not alter our
findings.

Home Ownership

For whites and blacks, Table 7.1 reports homeownership rates for all household heads, male household heads, and female household heads, along with
the proportion of all heads who are female for 1900, 1920, 1940, and
1960–90, with 1990 the last year for which IPUMS data are currently available (but see below). Also shown are the racial gaps, expressed as ratios
(black/white) and in levels (white – black).

From 1940 to 1970, the census did not permit married women to be
classified as household heads. Therefore, all female heads were single
women (with or without children), widows, divorced women, or women
whose husbands were 'absent' at the time the census was taken. Since 1980,
some married women have been identified as household heads even if their
husbands were present, and therefore, according to our algorithm, can be
counted as homeowners. Table 7.1 reports two columns (a and b) for both
1980 and 1990. Columns 1980a and 1990a simply take the census data as
given. For the sake of comparability with earlier samples, columns 1980b
and 1990b count households headed by married women as if they were
headed by men. The adjustments generally have a small impact on the
trends at the center of our investigation.[3]

At the turn of the twentieth century, only about half of all white household heads were homeowners and among blacks, less than a quarter were.
The black rate of home ownership increased between 1900 and 1920 while
the white rate remained essentially constant. Rates of home ownership for
both races fell back between 1920 and 1940. Although at present there are
no IPUMS data for 1930, there is little doubt that the fall in home ownership between 1920 and 1940 was a consequence of the Great Depression
(Jackson 1985; Collins and Margo 2001).

In the subsequent two decades, homeownership rates for both races

Table 7.1 Home ownership, by race

	1900	1920	1940	1960	1970	1980a	1980b	1990a	1990b
All household heads									
White	49.30	49.81	45.70	65.13	66.77	69.38	69.38	68.98	68.98
Black	22.34	26.14	23.06	38.44	42.09	46.22	46.22	44.84	44.84
Black/white ratio	0.45	0.52	0.50	0.59	0.63	0.67	0.6?	0.65	0.65
White – black difference	26.96	23.67	22.64	26.69	24.68	23.16	23.16	24.14	24.14
Male household heads									
White	48.75	49.59	45.18	67.58	70.47	74.50	74.57	74.04	74.03
						(75.76)	(75.85)	(75.82)	(75.85)
Black	22.51	25.94	22.50	41.22	47.76	55.47	55.?5	54.84	54.77
						(55.71)	(55.60)	(55.31)	(55.26)
Black/white ratio	0.46	0.52	0.50	0.61	0.68	0.74	0.74	0.74	0.74
White – black difference	26.24	23.65	22.68	26.36	22.71	19.03	19.22	19.20	19.26
Female household heads									
White	53.45	51.58	48.89	52.56	52.00	54.27	52.29	57.02	54.57
						(55.61)	(53.55)	(58.78)	(56.23)
Black	21.61	27.07	25.02	31.26	31.17	34.29	33.01	35.23	33.55
						(34.44)	(33.16)	(35.58)	(33.89)
Black/white ratio	0.40	0.52	0.51	0.59	0.60	0.63	0.63	0.62	0.61
White – black difference	31.84	24.51	23.87	21.30	20.83	19.98	19.28	21.79	21.02

Female proportion of household heads

White	11.72	11.15	13.98	16.33	20.04	25.34	23.31	29.71	25.94
Black	18.64	17.72	22.27	27.89	34.17	43.66	40.88	51.00	46.79
Black/white ratio	1.59	1.59	1.59	1.71	1.71	1.72	1.75	1.72	1.80
White – black difference	−6.92	−6.57	−8.29	−11.56	−14.13	−18.32	−17.57	−21.29	−20.85

Note: Samples include household heads over 19 years old who are not in school. Figures in parentheses are from samples that exclude self-reported Hispanics. From 1940 to 1970, married women were never reported as household heads, but in 1980 and 1990 married women were sometimes reported as household heads. Columns 1980a and 1990a take the census data as given and do not adjust for changes in the reporting of headship. Columns 1980b and 1990b treat households headed by married women as if they were headed by men for the sake of consistency with earlier samples. In 1980, only 2 per cent of white household heads were married women, and only 3 per cent of black household heads were married women; consequently, the reclassification does not make a large impact on the results. In 1900 and 1920, married women are sometimes, but very rarely, reported as household heads; their reclassification (not shown in table) has a very small impact.

Source: IPUMS (Ruggles and Sobek 1997).

increased sharply, in part because of important institutional innovations in mortgage finance (discussed at length below). While the increase among blacks was sufficient to produce a rise in the black/white ratio of home-ownership rates, the racial gap in levels actually widened, from 22.6 per-centage points in 1940, to 26.7 points in 1960. Elsewhere we have shown that, among male household heads, the rise in the level gap can be explained to a considerable extent by the geographic redistribution of the black pop-ulation after World War II (Collins and Margo 2001). In particular, move-ment out of the rural South into central cities, where ownership rates were relatively low, dampened the rise in the black homeownership rate.

In the 1960s, the racial gap in home ownership narrowed somewhat, as the black homeownership rate increased by about 3.7 percentage points and the white rate increased by only 1.6 points. From 1970 to 1990, however, the gap barely narrowed at all, whether measured as a ratio or as a difference in rates. In terms of the difference (white – black) in own-ership levels, the gap was narrowest *before* World War II. In terms of the black/white ratio, the bulk of racial convergence occurred between 1940 and 1970, as the black homeownership rate rose by about 83 per cent (from 23.1 to 42.1 per cent), approximately twice the percentage increase in the white rate of home ownership over the same period (from 45.7 to 66.8 per cent).

Because the 2000 IPUMS sample was not yet available at the time of writing, we do not present race-specific rates spanning the entire twentieth century. However, data from the Current Population Survey (CPS) based on a definition of home ownership equivalent to the post-1980 census defi-nition suggests a modest upward trend in the black/white ratio of homeownership rates in the 1990s along with a slight decline in the racial gap in percentage point terms.[4] Even so, it is clear that at the start of the new millennium, a large and persistent racial gap in home ownership exists in the United States, and has existed for a very long time.

Although the focus of this work is on racial differences, Table 7.1 also speaks to absolute changes in homeownership rates over time. In interpret-ing these absolute changes in home ownership, our underlying assumption is that higher levels of home ownership imply a higher standard of living. Home ownership has a direct impact on well-being because it is positively correlated with the consumption of housing services, some of which derive from the attributes of the housing unit itself and others from neighborhood effects. Additionally, investments in home ownership, which at least since the 1940s have been highly leveraged financial transactions, have generated a substantial amount of wealth for middle-class Americans.[5] Lastly, as mentioned in the above, home ownership might have important 'treatment effects' on the behavior of owners and their children.

With regard to absolute changes in ownership rates, three aspects of Table 7.1 are important to point out. First, as noted above, the absolute level of ownership rose substantially for both black and white households between 1900 and 1990. However, the timing of change was episodic rather than continuous. Among white household heads, ownership rates did not rise between 1900 and 1940, but they rose sharply between 1940 and 1960. Among whites, rates continued to increase after 1960, but the magnitude of the rise over the next two decades was only about a quarter as large as the increase between 1940 and 1960. Among black household heads, a post-1960 slowdown is also apparent, but the extent of the slowdown was smaller than among whites. For both races, the 1980s were a decade of almost no change in homeownership rates, whereas the 1990s was again a decade of rising home ownership.

Why have changes in homeownership rates in twentieth-century America been episodic rather than continuous? Some of the discussion below is relevant to this question, as is our previous work (Collins and Margo 2001), though a full answer is worthy of a separate paper. Here, we simply outline a plausible explanation. Part of the post-1940 'structural break' in the trend in home ownership after 1940 can be accounted for by the negative effects of the Great Depression in the 1930s. Had a depression not occurred, the level of home ownership in 1940 presumably would have been higher than it actually was, and so part of the large post-1940 increase in ownership reflects a bounce back from the Depression.

Even after factoring out the rebound from the Depression, a significant portion of the two-decade upsurge in home ownership after 1940 does appear to have been a genuine break with the past. Some of this upsurge may be attributable to strong real income growth, along with changes in various demographic trends. For example, after 1940, marriage and fertility rates began to rise after bottoming out during the Depression. Family size, controlling for other factors, was positively correlated with home ownership throughout the century, though the correlation with home ownership strengthened in the post-1940 period (see Collins and Margo 2001). The combination of rising marriage and fertility rates and a stronger empirical connection between those variables and ownership both contributed to the post-1940 jump in ownership.

Demographic influences aside, a portion of the post-1940 structural break can be attributed to changes in federal tax policy and housing finance that effectively subsidized home ownership. Some of these important structural reforms in housing finance, discussed below, were instituted in response to high rates of foreclosure early in the Depression. Institutional innovation in housing markets did not cease after 1960, and yet, as Table 7.1 documents, a slowdown in growth of home ownership occurred, particularly in the 1980s.

At this point, we have not completely accounted for this slowdown, or for the subsequent rise in the 1990s.[6] Presumably the answer lies in some combination of the post-1970 slowdown in the growth rate of average real wages, coupled with rising wage inequality; various demographic shifts, including the one focused on in this chapter (the rise of female-headed households), which reduced the relative demand for owner-occupied housing at given prices and incomes; and changes in housing policies and other factors that may have reduced incentives at the margin to become a homeowner, relative to those in place during the 'boom years' of the 1940s and 1950s.

Returning to the central focus of this chapter – race and family structure – the homeownership rate among all household heads is a weighted average of the gender-specific rates, with the weights equal to the male and female proportions among household heads. Disaggregating by the gender of the household head produces several important findings. First, in the pre-1960 IPUMS samples, there is little evidence that female heads of households were less likely to be homeowners than male household heads within each race category. Therefore, in terms of measuring racial differences, a sample of all household heads and a sample of male household heads essentially track each other. However, by 1960, homeownership rates among female household heads, within each racial category, were much lower than among male household heads; and historically, the proportion of female households has always been greater among African Americans. As a consequence, from 1960 forward, the racial gap in homeownership rates among all household heads exceeded the size of the gap among male heads only.

Between 1960 and 1980, ownership rates among female heads increased slightly for both races, but remained well below rates for adult males. Over the same period, the proportion of black households headed by women rose by 16 percentage points (according to column 1980a), to 44 per cent of all black households. In comparison, the proportion of female heads among white households rose by 9 percentage points, to 25 per cent of all households. Overall, black ownership rates increased substantially between 1960 and 1980, but this increase was driven primarily by the rising ownership rate among male household heads.

In the 1980s ownership rates fell very slightly among male heads of both races but rose slightly among female heads. However, because the share of female-headed households rose as well, and because female ownership rates remained well below those of men, the overall ownership rates declined. In the case of whites, the decline in levels was essentially the same in the overall and male samples while, in the case of blacks, the overall decline was larger than among males.

The upshot of these findings is that the sample's gender composition does influence the observed patterns of racial change in home ownership, at least beginning at some point between 1940 and 1960. We can illustrate the magnitude of that influence by computing what the overall home-ownership rates would have been under different assumptions about the gender-specific ownership rates and the proportion of female-headed households. For example, if the gender-specific homeownership rates are held fixed at their 1990 level (using column 1990b), but the 1960 proportions of female-headed households are substituted in computing the overall rate, the overall black homeownership rate in 1990 would have been 48.9 per cent instead of 44.8, a significant difference. Making the same calculation for whites suggests that the ownership rate would have been 70.9 per cent instead of 69.0. Together, these calculations imply that the ownership gap would have been 22.0 points rather than 24.1.

Given the nature of the census data and our analysis of them, we cannot claim that simulations such as these (and those reported below) identify causal relationships. Nonetheless, the results are consistent with the hypothesis that in the absence of the differential increase in female head-ship among black households, the racial gap in home ownership would have narrowed by more after 1960 than it actually did. At the same time, however, the calculations demonstrate that the relative increase in female headship among blacks did *not* have a very large effect on the size of the racial gap in ownership rates. In fact, the ownership gap would remain quite large even in the absence of differential changes in the proportion of female heads.

As noted above, recent work by urban economists suggests that home ownership may have positive effects on the social behavior of homeowners. For example, homeowners are more likely to participate in the local political process and in community organizations (Rossi and Weber 1996; DiPasquale and Glaeser 1999). More tantalizing are the findings reported by Green and White (1997), who claim that children of homeowners also exhibit more socially responsible behavior. For example, they are less likely to be dropouts or get in trouble with the police. Here, we do not wish to join the debate over whether these purported relationships between behavior and home ownership are true 'treatment effects' (see Rossi and Weber 1996); or, if they are, whether their intensity has shifted over time. Rather, we simply take the contemporary findings at face value and ask whether the racial difference in children's exposure to owner-occupied housing has changed over the twentieth century.

We measure exposure by computing the proportion of children under age 10 who were living in owner-occupied housing at the time of the census. The age cutoff is arbitrary, but a fairly low age is useful to avoid sensitivity to long-term changes in the age at leaving home, and it ensures that a new cohort of children are counted in each census period. The unit of observation is the child, and we sort the children into three household types: those headed by the child's father (or stepfather), those headed by the child's mother (or stepmother), and those headed by neither the father (stepfather) nor the mother (stepmother).[7] The results are shown in Table 7.2.

Over the course of the twentieth century, the proportion of young children living in owner-occupied housing increased for both blacks and whites, as one would expect given the large increases in home ownership among household heads. Among whites, the long-term increase in exposure (about 18 percentage points from 1900 to 1990) was approximately the same as the long-term increase in the homeownership rate. However, among blacks, the exposure index increased by only about 10 percentage points, a much smaller increase than in the overall homeownership rate. After a drop during the 1980s, the level of the exposure index for each race was approximately the same in 1990 as in 1960. Ultimately, despite blacks' rising average income and wealth relative to whites over the century, the racial gap in exposure in 1990 was an astonishing 30 percentage points, 8 points larger than in 1900, and the black/white ratio of exposure in 1990 stood at 0.53, identical to the level in 1900. If, as Green and White's work (1997) suggests, exposure to home ownership at an early age confers some kinds of human and social capital, then the figures in Table 7.2 indicate that enormous room for racial convergence still exists.

The samples that are conditional on parental headship shed light on why such a large racial gap in exposure has persisted throughout the twentieth century. Among children in households headed by their father (or stepfather), the racial gap in exposure declined in relative (black/white) and absolute (white – black) terms between 1960 and 1980. By 1980, the majority of young black children living in father-headed households resided in owner-occupied housing. However, the proportion of such children has declined remarkably over time, particularly among African Americans after 1960. By 1990, only about a third of all black children under age 10 lived in households headed by their father (or stepfather), less than half the corresponding figure among whites.

The opposite side of the coin has been a long-term rise in the proportion of children of both races living in households headed by their mother (or stepmother), or by neither parent (usually a grandparent). With respect to the latter category (neither parent), the long-term trend actually increased the exposure index, particularly for black children, because the odds of living in owner-occupied housing were higher than average in this household type. But for children in mother-headed households, the odds of living in owner-occupied housing have always been low for both races, and thus the increase in children residing in mother-headed households has served to dampen increases in the exposure index. Because the increase in the proportion of children in mother-headed households has been greater for blacks than whites, and because among blacks the exposure gap between father- and mother-headed households has widened, there has been a disproportionately large impact on black children's likelihood of living in owner-occupied housing.

As above, we can compute what the 1990 exposure indices would have been using the 1960 distribution of children across household types. For blacks, the implied 1990 exposure index is 43.4, almost 10 percentage points higher than the actual figure for 1990. Thus, changes in the distribution of children across household types can, in a proximate sense, explain why the exposure index for blacks remained unchanged between 1960 and 1990. Clearly, the most important factor was the rise in the proportion of young black children living in mother-headed households. The analogous calculation for whites raises the 1990 exposure index to 68.4 per cent, just 4 percentage points higher than the actual figure. Together, these calculations suggest that the exposure gap might have narrowed considerably were it not for the redistribution of children across household types after 1960.

As with Table 7.1, we stress that the correlations in Table 7.2 and the simulations based on them are entirely descriptive. We are not claiming to have identified a causal effect of household type. Nonetheless, the findings are highly suggestive and, as with Table 7.1, illustrate quite clearly the importance of sample composition in influencing one's perception of long-run racial trends in housing outcomes. An important difference between the results in Tables 7.1 and 7.2 is that although the relative rise of female-headship among blacks did not have a large impact on the overall racial gap in ownership rates, the relative rise in the proportion of black children in mother-headed households did have a sizable impact on the ownership exposure gap for children.

Housing Values

In 1940, the IPUMS provides information on house and property values for owner-occupied homes, and beginning in 1960, it reports various housing characteristics as well (for example, the number of rooms). Care must be taken in interpreting these data because the extent of coverage and method of value estimation changed somewhat over time. As above, we presume that if the home was owner-occupied, the household head was the owner. Some additional restrictions are placed on the sample in order to improve comparability over time (see the note to Table 7.3 and Collins and Margo 2003). Table 7.3 reports the black/white ratio of average house

Table 7.2 Children living in owner-occupied housing, by race and household head

	1900	1920	1940	1960	1970	1980	1990
Panel A: Proportion of children living in owner-occupied housing							
All children							
White	46.21	44.23	36.26	63.91	66.15	69.06 (72.25)	64.12 (68.75)
Black	24.26	24.22	18.55	32.53	36.62	40.77 (41.00)	33.81 (34.16)
Children in father-headed households							
White	45.66	43.43	34.59	64.73	68.28	73.38 (75.99)	69.75 (73.55)
Black	24.33	23.56	16.35	33.02	42.17	54.57 (54.86)	47.69 (48.23)
Children in mother-headed households							
White	37.22	40.83	26.74	36.03	34.19	36.55 (41.37)	36.58 (42.04)
Black	17.34	19.15	12.68	12.72	15.37	16.60 (16.69)	13.78 (13.95)
Children in nonparent-headed households							
White	62.23	57.92	58.75	71.26	70.77	68.75 (72.34)	65.36 (71.51)
Black	27.96	31.44	28.80	46.40	49.83	54.00 (54.29)	51.56 (51.92)

Panel B: Distribution of children across household headship

White, father-headed	92.31	91.17	89.40	92.02	89.27	83.60 (84.79)	76.70 (78.90)
White, mother-headed	2.90	2.48	2.79	3.79	6.56	11.07 (10.26)	16.01 (14.83)
White, nonparent-headed	4.79	6.35	7.81	4.20	4.18	5.32 (4.94)	7.29 (6.27)
Black, father-headed	78.30	79.14	72.40	66.04	58.52	44.73 (44.71)	33.42 (33.32)
Black, mother-headed	8.03	7.88	7.69	14.96	25.32	36.04 (36.02)	43.56 (43.54)
Black, nonparent-headed	13.67	12.98	19.91	19.00	16.16	19.23 (19.27)	23.01 (23.14)

Note: The samples include children under 10 years of age. 'Father' and 'mother' here include stepfathers and stepmothers. The 1990 sample is the IPUMS unweighted 1 per cent sample. No adjustments were made for the change in 1980 that allows married women to report as household heads. The figures in parentheses for 1980 and 1990 are for samples that exclude self-reported Hispanics.

Source: IPUMS (Ruggles and Sobek 1997).

Wealth and living standards

Table 7.3   Relative values of owner-occupied housing (ratios × 100)

	1940	1960	1970	1980a	1980b	1990a	1990b
All household heads: B/W	35.81	52.90	59.50	58.50	58.50	59.23	59.23
Male household heads: B/W	36.40	53.91	60.89	61.09	60.73	63.04	62.26
Female household heads: B/W	35.26	54.52	61.84	57.70	59.48	57.04	59.98
Black female/male household heads	88.92	80.43	76.19	74.84	72.97	75.14	72.54
White female/male household heads	91.79	79.53	75.02	79.23	74.51	83.06	75.31
Female proportion of black household heads in sample	26.91	22.71	24.88	31.84	28.75	39.34	34.29
Female proportion of white household heads in sample	16.73	12.78	14.89	18.99	16.69	23.41	19.31

Note: Samples include household heads residing in owner-occupied housing, over 19 years of age, who are not in school. For comparability over time, farms, condos, properties on more than 10 acres, properties used commercially, trailers, boats, and multifamily dwellings (based on the IPUMS 'unitsstr' variable) are generally excluded from the samples. In 1940 only farms can be excluded. Columns 1980a and 1990a take the census data as given; columns 1980b and 1990b count married female household heads as if they were men for the sake of comparability with previous years. Results from samples that exclude Hispanics in 1980 and 1990 are very similar to those reported above. Since 1960, house and property values have been top-coded. Approximately, the top 3 per cent of households in 1960 (above $35000), 1970 (above $50000), and 1990 (above $400000) are top-coded. The top 1 per cent in 1980 (above $200000) are top-coded. In 1940, however, values are not top-coded. The average value of the top-coded category in 1960 is estimated by multiplying the top-code by the ratio of the average value of homes in the top 3 per cent in 1940 to the value of homes at the 97th percentile (a factor of approximately 1.44). Similar multiples are formed for 1970, 1980, and 1990 on the basis of 1940s data.

Source: IPUMS (Ruggles and Sobek 1997).

values for all household heads and, separately, for male and female household heads. In addition, we report male/female value ratios and the proportion of owners who were female within race categories.

In 1940, the average value of black-owned housing was slightly more than a third of the value of white-owned housing, reflecting blacks' geographic concentration in the South where property values (for whites and blacks) were low relative to the rest of the country and where blacks' property values were low relative to whites. However, over the next 30 years, as homeownership rates were rising for both races, the black/white ratio of housing values rose by nearly 24 percentage points. Within each race category, the ratio of female/male values declined over this period, but the overall trend in racial convergence was very similar to the trend observed for male-only samples. Remarkably, racial convergence essentially halted after 1970: the value ratio increased slightly for men, declined slightly for women, and was flat for the full sample.

This suspension of convergence is surprising in that it comes after the passage of local, state, and federal fair housing initiatives intended to curb racial discrimination in housing markets. In the next section, we discuss hypotheses related to this phenomenon in some detail, including the suggestion that the anti-discrimination measures themselves (given the pre-existing effects of discrimination) might have had a perverse impact on black-owned property values. At this point, it is worth noting that our previous work (Collins and Margo 2003) indicates that the relative stagnation of the overall ratio actually hides a substantial decline in the relative value of black-owned property in central cities after 1970.

Thus, as with ownership, failure to include women in the sample yields a slightly misleading portrait of racial change in the black/white value ratio over time. The male-only sample has at least a small convergence in housing values after 1970, whereas the sample including female owners does not. Nonetheless, the magnitude of the impact is quite small relative to the size of the racial gaps that we are studying.

Regression Analysis

The racial gaps in home ownership and housing values in Tables 7.1 and 7.3 are 'unconditional'; that is, they are simply sample means. Both levels and changes over time in home ownership, housing values, and exposure are correlated with factors other than race. It is useful to control for these factors, within the limits of the data at hand, in order to ferret out the 'pure' effects of race.[8]

Toward this end, we estimated several regressions of the form:

$$h = X\beta + \delta'(\text{Black} = 1) + e$$

where h is a housing outcome (either ownership or the log of house and property value), the X's are characteristics of the household head and the household (other than race), and e is a random error term. We call δ the 'adjusted' racial gap. The full set of regression coefficients is too large to report here. Rather, in Table 7.4 we report estimates of δ for samples of all household heads and for separate samples of male and female heads. The list of X variables is the same for all census dates and includes a quadratic in age (plus a dummy for over 64 years of age), a quadratic in years of education, several dummies for family size and for marital status/gender categories (for example, single male, single female, divorced/separated male, divorced/separated female, and so on), a dummy for multifamily households, and dummies for

Table 7.4   Adjusted racial gaps in ownership and housing values

	1940	1960	1970	1980	1990
Panel A: Home ownership					
All household heads	−0.0494	−0.1131	−0.1057	−0.0808	−0.0854
				(−0.0890)	(−0.0966)
Male household heads	−0.0564	−0.1119	−0.1028	−0.0733	0.0800
				(−0.0816)	(−0.0915)
Female household heads	−0.0297	−0.1127	−0.1053	−0.0887	−0.0904
				(−0.0972)	(−0.0998)
Panel B: Housing values					
All household heads	−0.3583	−0.2438	−0.1880	−0.2835	−0.2305
				(−0.2946)	(−0.2428)
Male household heads	−0.3502	−0.2249	−0.1625	−0.2489	−0.2017
				(−0.2601)	(−0.2141)
Female household heads	−0.4249	−0.3081	−0.2690	−0.3654	0.2856
				(−0.3763)	(−0.2986)

Note: Figures are regression coefficients, from separate regressions, on an indicator
variable equal to one for African Americans. Regressions also include controls for age
(quartic and a dummy for over 64), education (quadratic), log family income, family size (a
series of dummies), a series of dummies for marital status/gender categories, dummies for
central city residence and suburban residence (in metro area, not central city), region of
residence, and dummies for migrant status (foreign-born and native-born, interregional
migrants). Family income is top-coded from 1960 to 1980; top-coded values are multiplied
by 1.4 (before logs are taken). In 1940 only wage and salary income is reported in the census,
and so in that year regressions are restricted to wage and salary workers. Treatment of top-
coded housing values and composition of housing value samples are discussed in notes to
Table 7.3. Samples in Table 7.4 are not identical to those in Tables 7.1 and 7.3 because
missing values for any of the independent variables (for example, income and metropolitan
residence) require omission from the regressions. Change in the geographic coverage of the
metro variable after 1980 (and therefore the sample composition) may tend to artificially
narrow the racial gap in housing values reported above. Though still not perfectly
comparable, the change in coverage seems to narrow the gap by 3 to 4 percentage points.
There is little impact on the racial gap in ownership. In 1980 and 1990 the figures in
parentheses are from regressions that exclude self-reported Hispanics.

Source: IPUMS (Ruggles and Sobek 1997).

region of residence, central city residence, suburban residence, and the household head's migrant status (dummies for the foreign born and for the native
born who reside in a region that differs from that of birth).

We estimated linear probability regressions of ownership and OLS
regressions of the log of housing value. Although we do not report the full
set of regression coefficients, a number of findings revealed therein are
worthy of comment. First, at all points in time, economic variables are

strongly and positively correlated with housing outcomes; that is, higher levels of education and income raise the probability of ownership and housing values. Second, the correlation between marital status and home ownership became strongly positive by 1960, and the correlation between age and ownership, though always positive in the twentieth century, became increasingly steep. Third, throughout the century, central city residents, and residents of the Northeast (relative to other regions) have been less likely to own homes. Not surprisingly, given the direction of these effects and the correlations of these variables with race, the adjusted racial gaps are smaller at all points in time than the racial gaps based on the sample means.

With respect to ownership, in fact, the 1940 racial gaps are almost entirely accounted for by differences in the observable characteristics (other than race) of household heads. The adjusted gaps increase substantially by 1960, and in fact, the magnitude of the increase in the gap is larger than in the unadjusted gap reported in Table 7.1. Thereafter, the gaps declined slowly over time, at least to 1980.[9] The adjusted ownership gap among women is generally similar in magnitude to the gap among men, though from 1960 to 1990 it is slightly larger among women and declines more slowly over the period. As with the unadjusted sample means, including women in the sample tends to dampen the degree of convergence compared to the men-only sample.

With respect to house and property values, the δ coefficient is larger and more variable over time than in the ownership regressions. Between 1940 and 1970, the adjusted racial gap in housing values declined considerably in all three samples. During the 1970s, however, the adjusted gap widened dramatically in all three samples.[10] Some of the gap's widening in the 1970s may have been reversed in the 1980s, but only partially.[11] In this case, bringing women into the analysis of racial gaps in housing outcomes tends to widen the observed gaps at any point in time (compared to the men-only sample) without significantly altering the path of convergence and divergence observed over time.

DISCUSSION

We have shown that the samples' gender composition matters to the measurement of racial gaps in housing market outcomes, at least after 1960. However, in certain key respects, the stylized facts of the racial gaps' evolution are not dependent on sample composition. In particular, the 1940–70 period stands out as one of relative gains in black home ownership and average housing values (compared to whites), whereas the 1920–40 and 1970–90 periods witnessed few, if any, gains. In fact, controlling for household and household-head characteristics, there appears to have been a sharp decline in the relative value of black-owned homes in the 1970s, again regardless of the sample's gender composition. In what follows we draw on our previous papers (Collins and Margo 2000, 2001, 2003) to sketch out a historical narrative to make sense of these stylized facts.

At the turn of the twentieth century most blacks lived and worked in the rural South, engaged primarily in agricultural production. By current standards, mortgage finance in the early twentieth century was limited and underdeveloped. Relatively few black households could afford the substantial downpayments required by institutional lenders, even if they could find one willing to lend to them. Although blacks did succeed in accumulating some real estate wealth prior to World War I, the levels of black wealth and home ownership were very low, both absolutely and relative to whites.

Over the next seven decades, millions of blacks left the rural South for metropolitan areas, many of which were outside the region. New migrants typically settled in predominantly black neighborhoods in central cities, and as the populations of those neighborhoods grew in size and density, black ghettos emerged. Middle-class black residents of these neighborhoods often sought to leave when poor migrants moved in, but they were largely thwarted by whites bent on containing the geographic spread of the urban black population. A variety of tactics were used, including racial 'restrictive covenants' and, in some cases, intimidation, fraud, and outright violence. As a result, blacks were less able to acquire owner-occupied housing, even if, in terms of their incomes or other personal characteristics, they were as 'qualified' as potential white homeowners.

In the 1930s, a series of institutional innovations dramatically altered the nature of housing finance, setting in motion a process that eventually increased homeownership rates for both races (Jackson 1985; Collins and Margo 2001). The economic free fall during the early years of the Great Depression generated unprecedented rates of home foreclosures. In response, the federal government created a series of agencies that fundamentally transformed the nature of mortgage finance. The Home Owner's Loan Corporation (HOLC), the Federal Housing Administration (FHA), and later the Veteran's Administration (VA), Fannie Mae, and Freddie Mac, promoted the self-amortizing fixed-interest 30-year (or longer) mortgage, with much lower downpayments. The loans could be insured, and later bought and sold in secondary markets, thereby lowering credit risk and interest rates.

However, the implementation of these innovations was far from race-neutral. For example, when it developed new underwriting standards for mortgage loans, the HOLC systematically divided metropolitan neighborhoods into categories according to their desirability and stability. The lowest-quality neighborhoods were shaded 'red' (hence the term, 'redlining'). Race, among other factors, was explicitly used as a criterion in redlining. The HOLC standards were adopted by the FHA, which in turn generally declined to offer mortgage insurance to such neighborhoods, making it more difficult for residents, disproportionately blacks, to obtain mortgage finance from conventional lenders.

At the same time, the federal agencies adopted policies that tended to subsidize new construction in suburban areas. Although some portion of white suburbanization after World War II would have occurred anyway (see Margo 1992), such policies, at the margin, tended to facilitate 'white flight', particularly at a time when the pressure to expand at the edges of black ghettos was intensifying. At mid-twentieth century, racial residential segregation was reinforced by virtually every significant housing industry participant. Real estate agents embedded racial segregation in their 'code of ethics'; builders marketed racially exclusive new developments; white homeowners' associations used restrictive covenants and peer pressure to keep neighborhoods all-white; and the FHA, VA, and lending institutions openly encouraged racial restrictive covenants (at least until 1948) and 'stability'.

Yet, despite the high and rising level of racial segregation, which peaked around 1970 (Cutler et al. 1999), blacks' home ownership and housing values increased relative to whites' in the 1960s. A plausible, if ironic, explanation is that the mirror image of 'white flight' was 'filtering'. Housing in central cities, formerly occupied by whites who moved to the suburbs, could now be occupied and owned by blacks.

With the advent of the civil rights movement, public awareness of the federal government's culpability in fostering racial segregation in housing was heightened. One upshot was the passage of fair housing legislation at the federal level in 1968, followed by several supplementary pieces of legislation intended to outlaw racial discrimination in the purchase or rental of housing. Despite these legislative efforts, well into the 1980s and 1990s studies reported evidence that minority applicants faced continuing discrimination in housing markets (Yinger 1995). With the evidence at our disposal, we are hardly in a position to estimate a 'treatment effect' of fair housing policy.[12] However, if such policy has been effective, we might expect it to diminish the relative importance of race as an independent correlate of ownership after 1970. We do find such a decline, although it is a very small one in the sample of all heads.

Policy aside, both the high level of racial segregation in metropolitan areas and the associated concentration of black home ownership in central cities by 1970 left black housing values extraordinarily vulnerable to adverse economic shocks that disproportionately affected urban areas in general or blacks in particular. Recent research by Massey and Denton (1993) and Cutler and Glaeser (1997) has demonstrated how such shocks might be 'magnified' in the context of racially segregated housing. In Massey and Denton's work, the key idea is that an adverse shock that disproportionately affects blacks will necessarily be concentrated geographically. As long as there are 'neighborhood effects' – that is, negative outcomes that spill over across households – the shock will have a multiplicative impact, enhancing in Massey and Denton's words 'the social problems associated with income deprivation' (Massey and Denton 1993, p. 122).

In the economics literature, Cutler and Glaeser (1997) are the best-known exponents of this line of argument. Using census data for 1990, Cutler and Glaeser show that the relative likelihoods of adverse social and economic outcomes among African Americans – in particular, single parenthood – were strongly and positively related to the level of residential segregation. However, Cutler and Glaeser did not investigate, in their language, whether ghettos were always 'bad'. We have found that the negative effects of segregation documented by Cutler and Glaeser were not similarly present in 1970; rather, they emerged in the 1970s and intensified in the 1980s (Collins and Margo 2000).

In Collins and Margo (2003) we explored the impact of residential segregation on the relative value of black-owned housing. To measure segregation, we used Cutler et al. (1999) indices, which pertain to metropolitan areas only. Specifically, we hypothesized that, if ghettos went 'bad' in the 1970s, we should have observed a strong negative correlation between the degree of segregation and the relative value of black-owned housing after 1970, but not before. In fact, this is what we observed: other factors held constant, the level of segregation had little relationship with the relative value of black-owned housing in 1970, but the correlation turned strongly negative by 1980. Importantly, controlling for the level of segregation reverses the direction of change in the racial value gap in the 1970s. That is, the increasingly negative magnitude of the segregation coefficient can fully account for the widening adjusted racial value gap. However, we found no evidence that segregation had a similar effect on the relative odds of black home ownership; if anything, the racial ownership gap was narrower in highly segregated cities, at least prior to 1990, when the coefficient was essentially zero.

The regressions also reveal that the negative correlation between segregation and relative black home values in central cities intensified between 1980 and 1990. However, with the continued movement of middle-class blacks out of central cities, the impact of 'bad ghettos' on the overall racial value gap diminished, perhaps contributing to the mean reversion evident in Table 7.4. Our narrative of the effects of segregation on home values and ownership derive from our previous analyses of samples of male heads of households. However, in light of Cutler and Glaeser's (1997) and our (Collins and Margo 2000) findings regarding the negative impact of segregation on single parenthood among African Americans, it is clear that the relationships between segregation and the various housing outcomes, particularly housing values, would be reinforced in a sample of household heads including females.

Although the 'bad ghettos' hypothesis can help explain why the relative value of black-owned housing declined in the 1970s, why ghettos went bad in the first place is an open issue. One possibility, argued by Wilson (1987), is that fair housing legislation, along with the War on Poverty, finally allowed middle-class blacks to escape central city neighborhoods for the suburbs. Although the suburban neighborhoods to which blacks moved were not necessarily well integrated, the overall level of residential segregation has fallen since 1970. This movement of middle-class blacks, according to Wilson, created a cultural and socioeconomic vacuum in predominantly black central city neighborhoods, and consequently the quality of life in those neighborhoods deteriorated.

The Wilson hypothesis is highly controversial, and the evidence from the census is not sufficient to evaluate it fully. In Collins and Margo (2003) we do show, however, that the relationship between suburban residence and income among male black household heads turns positive between 1970 and 1980, which is consistent with the Wilson hypothesis. However, we also find that there was a pre-1970 trend in this direction, and so the post-1970 change does not appear to be a structural break.

A second possibility involves the 1960s riots. Surely, the riots were by no means the sole cause of 'urban decline' or even the primary cause. However, the riots may have been far more than just coincidental events. Along with the immediate and direct destruction of property in black neighborhoods, business establishments that were looted or damaged might (and did, in many cities) have closed their doors permanently, causing additional job losses in black neighborhoods. Moreover, new investment might have been curtailed or shifted to suburban locations faster than it otherwise would have been. The riots, in other words, may have tipped the balance in black neighborhoods, accelerating a self-reinforcing cycle of decline.

To assess this possibility, we collected data on the incidence of riots from various published and archival sources, and we examined whether the emergence of a negative correlation between the black/white housing value ratio and segregation was concentrated in cities that experienced riots (see Collins and Margo 2003). We found that in such cities, a negative correlation already existed in 1970, and that the correlation became more strongly negative in the 1970s. In cities without riots, there was a (slight) positive relationship between segregation and the black/white value ratio in 1970, but this correlation, too, turned negative in the 1970s. However, the magnitude of the change in sign was smaller in the non-riot than in the riot cities. While this does not pin down a causal effect of the riots, it is suggestive evidence in that direction. Much work remains to be done, however, to measure the relative importance of the different shocks behind the emergence of 'bad' ghettos and their consequences.

CONCLUDING REMARKS

This chapter examines long-run trends in racial differences in the ownership and in the value of owner-occupied housing. In contrast to our previous work, we include female-headed households in the analysis. This extension is important, because female-headed households are less likely to own homes and conditional on owning, tend to own less valuable properties. The incidence of female headship is considerably greater among blacks than among whites, and so there are certainly implications for our measurement of racial gaps over time.

We find that, in terms of the measurement of racial gaps in housing outcomes, this extension of the sample has non-negligible effects. Both in levels and in terms of the direction of change, samples of all household heads (including women) diverge somewhat from a sample composed solely of male household heads. Where the inclusion of women really matters, however, is not in the racial gaps in ownership and property values among heads, but rather in the racial gap in children's likelihood of living in owner-occupied housing. We find that over the course of the twentieth century there has been essentially no racial convergence in the relative odds (black/white) that young black children would live in owner-occupied housing, and there has been a widening in the gap when measured as a difference in likelihoods (white – black). This lack of convergence is clearly correlated with the redistribution of children across household types, and in particular, with the enormous decline in the proportion of black children living in father-headed households after 1960.

This work can be extended in several directions. First, we have focused on adult household heads. However, not every adult is a household head, or married to one. Extending the analysis to cover all adults, regardless of headship status, would be a fairly straightforward endeavor. Second, as noted above, our historical narrative is based on analyses of samples of male household heads. Although we argued that the substantive conclusions would be strengthened by including females, it would nevertheless be useful to reestimate the multivariate analyses reported in Collins and

Margo (2003) on samples of all heads. Third, and perhaps most importantly, this study follows a time-honored tradition in labor and urban economics in its use of decompositions. These decompositions are suggestive of causal estimates, but not a substitute for them. Thus, an important task for future research is to attempt to specify and, hopefully, estimate structural models of racial gaps in housing outcomes that take account of the inherent endogeneity and influence of different household types; that is, the factors that cause the formation of different types of households, and the identification of the incentives and constraints shaping their housing choices.

NOTES

*   This chapter was written while Margo was a visiting senior scholar at the Levy Economics Institute. We are grateful to Thesia I. Garner, Ed Wolff, and participants at the Levy conference, 'What Has Happened to the Quality of Life in America and Other Advanced Industrialized Nations' for helpful comments.
1.   By 'neighborhood quality', we are referring to attributes/behavior of one's neighbors and the characteristics of their housing, local public goods, access to transportation and retail services, and so on. The IPUMS data set that we analyze in this chapter includes information on the characteristics of households, and housing (for some years), but does not include direct information on neighborhood quality.
2.   Information on home ownership was not retained in the 1950 sample. A 1930 IPUMS sample is not currently available.
3.   Similar adjustments for 1900 and 1920, which are not reported in Table 7.1, are very small.
4.   The CPS definition of home ownership is based on the concept of a 'householder' – one (and only one) person in a sample household is designated the householder, who is considered the homeowner if the housing unit is owner-occupied. According to the CPS data the black/white ratio of homeownership rates among all householders rose from 0.62 (in 1994) to 0.66 (in 2000), and the racial gap in percentage point terms fell from 25.4 points (in 1994) to 23.9 points (in 2000). See www.census.gov.
5.   Accordingly, a regression of wealth on a dummy variable for home ownership would have a positive and highly significant coefficient.
6.   See Bostic and Surette (2000), who use CPS microdata for 1989 and 1998 to study racial differences in home ownership in a regression context similar to ours. Controlling for income and other factors, they find that the racial gap in home ownership declined between 1989 and 1998. They attribute this decline primarily to a favorable macroeconomic environment and changes in the regulatory environment that improved access to mortgage finance for minority and low-income households.
7.   The majority of children who live in households in which neither parent is identified as the household head are living with grandparents. We do not adjust the 1980 and 1990 data for the counting of married women as household heads. Since married women make up only 2 per cent of white household heads and 3 per cent of black household heads in 1980, such an adjustment is unlikely to have a large impact on the trends identified in Table 7.2, though it might dampen the rise of mother-headed households.
8.   By 'pure effect' we do not mean 'true effect'. Race and racial discrimination (both current and past) may affect several of the regression's independent variables (for example, income), and therefore controlling for those observable differences may result in an understatement of the true effect of race. Rather, the estimate is 'pure' in the sense that

      it pertains narrowly to housing market outcomes, after controlling for other observable characteristics.

9. Because these are linear probability regressions, δ is analogous to the level gaps reported in Table 7.1. In ratio form, the adjusted racial gaps (that is, black/white) narrowed between 1940 and 1960.

10. The same conclusions hold if the independent variables in the value regression pertain to housing (rather than household) characteristics, or if housing and household characteristics are included. See Collins and Margo (2001b).

11. Some of the observed decline in the adjusted gap during the 1980s appears to be due to a change in the geographic coverage of the metropolitan status variable in the IPUMS. See the note to Table 7.4 for more detail.

12. In future work, we do intend to investigate those effects using sub-federal variation in fair housing laws.

REFERENCES

Bostic, Raphael W., and Brian J. Surette (2000), 'Have the doors opened wider? Trends in home ownership by rates and income', working paper No. 31, Washington, DC: Board of Governors of the Federal Reserve System.

Collins, William J., and Robert A. Margo (2000), 'Residential segregation and socioeconomic outcomes: when did ghettos go bad?', *Economics Letters*, **69**, 239–43.

Collins, William J., and Robert A. Margo (2001), 'Race and home ownership: a century-long view', *Explorations in Economic History*, **37**, 68–92.

Collins, William J., and Robert A. Margo (2003), 'Race and the value of owner-occupied housing, 1940–1990', *Regional Science and Urban Economics*, **33**, 255–86.

Cutler, David M., and Edward L. Glaeser (1997), 'Are ghettos good or bad?', *Quarterly Journal of Economics*, **112**, 827–72.

Cutler, David M., Edward L. Glaeser and Jacob L. Vigdor (1999), 'The rise and decline of the American ghetto', *Journal of Political Economy*, **107**, 455–506.

Danziger, Sheldon H., and Daniel H. Weinberg (1994), 'The historical record: trends in family income, inequality and poverty', in S.H. Danziger, G.D. Sandefur and D.H. Weinberg (eds), *Confronting Poverty: Prescriptions for Change*, Cambridge, MA: Harvard University Press, pp. 18–50.

DiPasquale, Denise, and Edward I. Glaeser (1999), 'Incentives and social capital: are homeowners better citizens?', *Journal of Urban Economics*, **45**, 354–84.

Donohue, John, and James Heckman (1991), 'Continuous versus episodic change: the impact of civil rights policy on the economic status of blacks', *Journal of Economic Literature*, **29**, 1604–43.

Green, Richard K., and Michelle J. White (1997), 'Measuring the benefits of homeowning: effects on children', *Journal of Urban Economics*, **41**, 441–61.

Higgs, Robert (1982), 'Accumulation of property by southern blacks before World War One', *American Economic Review*, **72**, 725–37.

Jackson, Kenneth T. (1985), *Crabgrass Frontier: The Suburbanization of the United States*, New York: Oxford University Press.

Long, James E., and Steven B. Caudill (1992), 'Racial differences in home owner-ship and housing wealth', *Economic Inquiry*, **30** (January), 83–100.

Margo, Robert A. (1984), 'Accumulation of property by southern blacks before

World War One: comment and further evidence', *American Economic Review*, **74** (September), 768–76.

Margo, Robert A. (1992), 'Explaining the post-war suburbanization of population in the United States: the role of income', *Journal of Urban Economics*, **31**, 301–10.

Massey, Douglas S., and Nancy A. Denton (1993), *American Apartheid: Segregation and the Making of the Underclass*, Cambridge, MA: Harvard University Press.

Moffitt, Robert (1992), 'Incentive effects of the U.S. welfare system: a review', *Journal of Economic Literature*, **30**, 1–61.

Oliver, M.L., and T.M. Shapiro (1995), *Black Wealth/White Wealth: A New Perspective on Racial Inequality*, New York: Routledge.

Rossi, Peter H., and Eleanor Weber (1996), 'The social benefits of home ownership: empirical evidence from national surveys', *Housing Policy Debate*, **7**, 1–36.

Ruggles, Steven, and Matt Sobek (1997), 'Integrated public use microdata series', Minneapolis: Historical Census Projects, University of Minnesota.

Smith, James, and Finis Welch (1989), 'Black economic progress after Myrdal', *Journal of Economic Literature*, **27**, 519–64.

US Department of Labor (1965), *The Negro Family: The Case for National Action*, Washington, DC: US Government Printing Office.

Wilson, William J. (1987), *The Truly Disadvantaged: The Inner City, the Underclass, and Public Policy*, Chicago, IL: University of Chicago Press.

Wolff, Edward J. (1998), 'Recent trends in the size distribution of household wealth', *Journal of Economic Perspectives*, **12**, 131–50.

Yinger, John (1995), *Closed Doors, Opportunities Lost: The Continuing Costs of Housing Discrimination*, New York: Russell Sage Foundation.

8. Living standard potential and the transmission of advantage in Chile

Seymour Spilerman and Florencia Torche*

INTRODUCTION

Attempts to understand the determinants of living standards and family well-being have frequently been cast, in recent years, in an asset development framework. This is the case with studies pertaining to the capabilities and functionings of poor households (for example, Sen 1987, 1993; Oliver and Shapiro 1995; Shapiro 2001), although an asset perspective – as distinct from a focus on income flows – has also received attention in assessments of the economic circumstance of working- and middle-class families (Inhaber and Carroll 1992; Wolff 1995; Ackerman and Alstott 1999). An emphasis on asset development and asset holdings, moreover, is a common theme in the literatures on family welfare in both developed and less-developed countries, although the particular asset that is stressed is often different in the two literatures.

In the United States the asset development literature has emphasized the accumulation of material resources: savings accounts, retirement funds, homes, and the like (Sherraden 1991; Edin 2001). As part of an anti-poverty strategy, the goal of asset development formulations is to redirect welfare policy from a system of means-tested income supplements to a set of programs intended to reduce dependency and empower the poor to take responsibility for their lives. Current welfare policy is viewed as discouraging household savings and entrepreneurial activity, as well as future planning and investment calculations, since it makes the accumulation of even modest assets a reason for losing eligibility. Thus, the very behaviors and dispositions that are valued in middle-class culture and are central to the economic functioning of families, are discouraged for the poor population.

In most asset-building formulations, the goal of empowerment would be accomplished by promoting the accumulation of resources in the form of individual development accounts or IDAs (Sherraden 1991, 2001). Through the provision of matching funds, poor families would be encouraged to save from their income flows with more generous matching rates for the very poor, who would have greatest difficulty putting aside even modest amounts.[1] These monies could be withdrawn only for targeted purposes – to purchase a home, start a business, further the education of the account holder or a family member, or for retirement expenses. When not exhausted by these expenditures, the accounts could be inherited, which would provide some funds to the younger generation in a population that commonly receives little in the way of intergenerational transfers. An essential point is that the mere fact of asset holdings would be expected to stimulate the sorts of financial calculations and behaviors that are critical for economic independence.

In the United States, participation in asset development programs is also encouraged for the wider population. With the contraction of public transfer supports and the growing emphasis on private sector approaches to social welfare, families increasingly need to rely on their own resources to cover the costs of medical care, nursing-home stays, the education of children, and to provide retirement income. However, the asset holdings of the majority of Americans are modest, leaving many vulnerable to financial crisis in the event of illness or job loss. Wolff (2001, p. 63), for example, estimates that some 40 per cent of American families could subsist on their financial reserves for less than one month, even at a consumption level equal to 125 per cent of the poverty line.

In light of the importance of accumulating savings to protect future consumption needs, President Bill Clinton, in 1999, proposed a program of universal savings accounts (USAs), essentially a version of IDAs targeted more broadly than to the poor population. This would have been in addition to existing 401(k) plans and Keogh accounts, which already provide tax advantaged savings for middle-class families. Senator Bob Kerry has also proposed children's savings accounts (CSAs), in which annual deposits would be made by the federal government for all children from birth through age 18; Representative John Kasich has proposed retirement savings accounts (RSAs), intended as a supplement to Social Security retirement income. While none of the proposals reached fruition in the 106th Congress, the present attempt by the Bush administration to divert a portion of Social Security accumulations into private investment accounts very much fits with the spirit of this legislative agenda.

If the asset development literature in the United States, especially the version formulated for the wider population, emphasizes material resources intended as a store of future consumption, the parallel literature in less-developed countries, especially in Latin America, identifies education and human capital as the assets of principal importance (Birdsall and Londono 1997; Attanasio and Szekely 2001). As such, this literature has adopted a broader view of assets, encompassing all potentially productive resources in a household: material assets, social capital, and human capital (Moser 1998). Also, when material assets are discussed it is the *productive role* of the asset that is stressed. Thus, while home ownership is valued in the asset literature of developed countries as a store of savings (consumption reserve), the parallel literature in less developed countries emphasizes the productive aspect of home ownership, namely the opportunity it accords a family to engage in domestic manufacturing or to open a storefront business in one of the rooms of the residence (Moser 1998).

Comparing the Formulations

One can speculate about the reasons for the difference in emphasis in the two literatures. First, the asset literature in the United States has become increasingly oriented to the well-being of the general population, stimulated by the press for privatization of welfare services and the insecurities that are attending this conversion. In Latin America, in contrast, the asset literature remains rooted in a concern about high and persistent poverty.[2] Directed at this problem, the asset approach has been raised as an alternative to safety-net strategies for combating poverty, which are regarded as palliative and as not addressing the causes of indigence and vulnerability (Katzman et al. 1999).

A consideration of material assets also provides insight into a second pervasive problem in Latin America: inequality in household income.[3] This has generally been explained by its immediate causes, especially the income generation potential of households through labor market participation. However, to the extent that material and financial assets play a role in labor market opportunity – facilitating the acquisition of a small business or entrance into the crafts and professions – or contribute directly to household income through investment returns, this heightens the importance of acquiring a detailed understanding of the distribution of various asset types in the population, as well as the mechanisms by which they are accumulated, utilized, and transferred.[4]

A second reason for the difference between the US and Latin American literatures is that the type of assets stressed in the United States – material and financial resources – are largely unavailable to the poor in Latin America. Financial assets are almost nonexistent in this population, and even access to formal credit or financial markets – in the form of credit cards, checking accounts, and small loans for productive purposes – is very limited (Mezzera 1993).

The most significant material asset in the United States, home ownership, has a very different status in Latin America. The majority of Latin American poor do not have access to government housing support. As a result, the poor use two housing strategies: illegal occupation of urban land with the self-construction of precarious residence units[5] (whose market value is minimal), or, especially in the case of newly formed families, choosing to reside with a relative, usually a parent. Even in Latin American countries where state policies have been successful in reducing housing deficits among the poor (for example, Costa Rica and Chile), the market value of the government-provided units is low. The housing projects tend to be located in the urban periphery, distant from job sources, homogeneous in poor residents, and lacking in social services. Moreover, because the housing market for the poor is largely informal, legal title is often deficient (de Soto 2000). This reduces both the market value of a residence and the consequent ability to use home equity as collateral for bank loans. Thus, while home ownership may provide shelter for the poor, it does not constitute a vehicle for savings buildup, as it does in the United States.

Third, the focus on education and the acquisition of human capital stems from the problematic nature of access to schooling and the low likelihood of completion of even the lower grades of study. As compared to the United States and Western European countries, where access to secondary education is universal, the gross enrollment rate in secondary school reaches only 62 per cent in Latin America, with sharp variations across countries and income levels (UNESCO 1999). Education and human capital are critical determinants of a family's capability to function in a modern, industrial economy. Thus, in countries in which a large proportion of the population is undereducated, a central concern must be, of necessity, with strategies for enhancing school completion, especially in the primary and middle grades (Gallart 1998).

Fourth, the emphasis in Latin America on the *productive* over the *consumption storage* function of assets emerges from the strong association between poverty and labor market variables. Empirical studies show that the main determinants of poverty in Latin America are unemployment, number of household members in the labor force, and the low returns to labor market participation (ECLAC 2001, Ch. 1). Also, decomposition of poverty rates in terms of population characteristics reveals that occupational affiliation is a major factor explaining poverty (Attanasio and Szekely 1999). Awareness of the centrality of labor market variables in accounting for poverty rates has led to a focus on productive assets; that is, resources that facilitate labor market participation, such as capital to start a small business, a room for a workshop, family assistance for child care, and the like (Birdsall and Londono 1997).

What Can Be Learned from the US Asset Literature?

The asset literature in the United States is oriented to material resources because of the concern with fluctuations in the performance of the economy, which is addressed by the 'consumption reserve' aspect of asset holdings. This orientation is also relevant to Latin American countries, not only because economic fluctuations are deeper and more sudden in this region, but because the welfare and job security systems are more limited in their ability to effectively protect families from sharp income declines due to unemployment or health events (Marquez 2001; Mesa-Lago 2001). Thus, a broadening of the notion of household assets to include material and financial resources that function as a consumption reserve would illuminate the capabilities of families to withstand at least brief periods of job loss without descending into indigence.

Further, the focus in the United States on the 'consumption reserve' function of assets has brought attention to the role of *parental* resources and transfers of resources in the transmission of inequality across generations, a theme that has received little consideration in the asset literatures of Latin America or other less-developed countries. In the United States there has been considerable research, for example, into parental decision making with respect to *inter vivos* transfers versus bequests, parental motives in allocating transfers when there are several children, the sensitivity of parental support to the availability of public assistance programs, and the contribution of parental transfers to the wealth holdings and living standards of adult children (Kotlikoff and Summers 1981, 1988; Modigliani 1988; Holtz-Eakin and Smeeding 1994; McGarry and Schoeni 1995; Spilerman 2000).

While inequality of living standards is a matter of deep concern in Latin America, because the root cause is identified with low levels of human capital and poor labor market integration – and because the bulk of material asset holdings is concentrated in a small fraction of the population – little attention has been given to the role of parental resources as a factor in the economic well-being of families. Rather, the dominant conceptual model is one that emphasizes investments in health care, public education, and other sources of human capital as the avenue for enhancing the labor force productivity of the poor, presumably, in the process, bringing about a reduction of inequality in household income and in living standards (Altimir 1998; Aninat 2000).

This strategy, however, is based on two presumptions. First, it is assumed that low rates of school completion in poor households are a result of suboptimal access to schooling or a consequence of inadequate curricula or school facilities. While the contention of underinvestment in primary and secondary education in Latin America is not in dispute (for example, Birdsall et al. 1998; Gallart 1998), a related cause of low completion rates may well be the financial burden placed on a family from maintaining a teenage child in school, forgoing the income that would otherwise flow to the household from his or her employment. Indeed, Moser (1998) argues that one way low-income households respond to economic crises is by increasing their reliance on child labor, presumably removing children from school.

This sort of problem is familiar to developmental economists (for example, Sen 1992; Solimano 2000) and relates to the formulations of moral philosophers in regard to distributive justice (Cohen 1993; Rawls 1999). A key issue in this literature is the impact of 'morally arbitrary factors' – disadvantages in initial conditions, such as parental resources, that can curtail the ability of an individual to utilize the opportunities formally available to all. Thus, even if education is a universal right, effective access to schooling may depend critically on parental income and assets. While this conditioning of opportunity is well recognized (for example, Birdsall et al. 1998), little research has been carried out to explore the dimensions of the dependence of educational attainment and, ultimately, living standards on parental resources.

A second assumption relates to the type of inequality that is worrisome and the determinants of this form of inequality. The intent of raising the educational attainment of poor children and effecting a reduction in educational inequality is not the ultimate goal. Rather, what is problematic is the presence of great inequality in *living standards*. The implicit presumption behind public investments in schooling is that living standards are largely determined by educational attainment, translated into labor market rewards, rather than by parental advantage. Yet, in actuality, the extent to which parental resources influence the economic well-being of adult children is an empirical question, with the assessment likely to differ by country. In Israel, for example, parental assets are associated with early home ownership and with other dimensions of living standards: number of household durables, car ownership, frequency of household help. Moreover, this effect is *net* of the educational attainment and earnings of adult children, suggesting the importance of direct transfers of parental resources (Spilerman 2004).

Insight into the determinants of living standards in a country is essential to the formulation of effective policies for enhancing family welfare and weakening the linkage between parental advantage and life chances. If low educational attainment is primarily due to deficiencies in school availability, it would be sufficient to focus public resources on improving access to schools and enriching the educational experiences of children. However, to the extent that a lack of parental resources is a significant contributing factor, policies that channel income supports to poor parents, encourage asset building by families, or effectively reduce liquidity constraints, thereby permitting poor families to borrow against future earnings, would be indicated (Birdsall et al. 1998; Stallings et al. 2000). Similarly, to the degree that inequality is reproduced across generations by means of direct transfers of assets, it may be necessary to entertain redistribution policies such as gift and estate taxation or an effective progressive income tax structure, as well as programs that encourage asset accumulation.

The present study is an attempt to explore the preceding issues by examining the impact of parental assets on the educational attainments and financial well-being of the Chilean population. Chile is an interesting research site because it is a relatively urban, industrialized country, with a large wage-earning sector, in comparison with other states in Latin America. It is a country in which many social welfare programs, previously funded from public monies, have been privatized, leaving families increasingly dependent on their own resources and, where available, on the assets of relatives. For this reason parental asset holdings may well be consequential to the economic welfare of adult children. We hasten to add that while parental effects of this nature are commonly expected in wealthy families, it can be the case that even modest levels of parental assistance, when carefully targeted, have a considerable impact on the life chances and living standards of the wider population, as has been reported for Israel (Spilerman 2004).

In the next section, we review some of the salient features of the socioeconomic environment and the organization of the educational system in Chile. This material provides the background for the examination of parental resource effects on educational attainment, an analysis undertaken in the subsequent section. Following that investigation, we examine the impact of the parental variables on the earnings, household income, and wealth holdings of adult children – which we view as measures of the living standard capacity of a family.

THE CHILEAN CONTEXT

The Chilean economic landscape is significantly different from what it was 30 years ago. During the 1970s and 1980s the Chilean economy underwent a deep transformation, experiencing macroeconomic stabilization, trade and market liberalization, and the privatization of social services. The social welfare system, one of the most comprehensive and advanced in Latin America but also one that is segmented and underfunded, was reformed. The reform included reduction of the state role in public spending, as well as privatization, marketization, and decentralization in the sectors of health care, education, housing, social security, and pensions. Chile's economic performance, especially in the past 15 years, can be described as a 'success story'. After a deep economic recession in the early

Table 8.1   Poverty rate in Chile, 1987–2000

	1987	1990	1992	1994	1996	1998	2000
Indigence[1] (extreme poverty)	17.4	12.9	8.8	7.6	5.8	5.6	5.7
Non-extreme poverty[2]	27.7	25.7	23.8	19.9	17.4	16.1	14.9
Total poverty	45.1	38.6	32.6	27.5	23.2	21.7	20.6

Notes:
1. The indigence (extreme poverty) line is defined by the per capita monthly cost of a basic food basket. In year 2000 the urban indigence line was Chilean $20 281/month (approx. US$31), and the rural indigence line was Chilean $15 616/month (approx. US$24).
2. The (total) poverty line in urban areas is twice the indigence line, and in rural areas it is 1.75 the indigence line. Households whose per capita income falls below the poverty line, but above the indigence line, are considered 'non-extreme' poor households.

Sources: CASEN Surveys (Ministry of Planning 2001a, 2002a).

1980s Chile has experienced sustained economic growth, with GDP per capita rising from US$2671 in 1985 to US$5501 in 1998 (Central Bank of Chile 2002; National Institute of Statistics 1998), an average annual increase of 5.5 per cent. This sustained growth has brought about a significant improvement in material living conditions and a reduction in poverty. As is evident in Table 8.1, total poverty declined from 45 to 21 per cent between 1987 and 2000, and indigence (extreme poverty) dropped from 17 to 5.7 per cent in the same period.

There is, however, a dark side to this success story, namely the continuation of very high inequality in the income distribution. After a worsening in the 1970s and 1980s, inequality improved slightly in the 1990s and has remained stable ever since. As can be seen from Table 8.2, the Gini coefficient was virtually the same in 1987 and 1998, and the ratio of the income shares received by the wealthiest and poorest quintiles remains fixed at about 15. The only notable change is a small increase in the share received by the wealthiest 1 per cent of the population, which expanded from 12 to 13.2 per cent during the 1990s.

Thus, in spite of the significant reduction in poverty, income inequality in Chile remains one of the highest in the world, surpassed in Latin America only by Brazil, Colombia, and Honduras (World Bank 2001, Ch. 3). Even though adjustments for in-kind and cash transfers to the poor reduce the Gini coefficient by about 0.05 points, the income distribution remains extremely concentrated. Economic growth has therefore led to a lessening of poverty without altering the distribution of income in the population; that is, relative living standards have remained constant.

Table 8.2   Percentage distribution of income by quintile, and various inequality measures, Chile, 1987–2000

Income quintile[1]	1987	1990	1992	1994	1996	1998	2000
1 (low)	3.8	4.1	4.3	4.1	3.8	3.7	3.7
2	7.6	8.1	8.3	8.1	8.0	8.0	8.2
3	11.5	12.3	12.2	11.9	11.8	11.7	12.2
4	19.1	18.1	18.5	18.6	19.2	19.2	18.4
5 (high)	58.0	57.4	56.7	57.3	57.2	57.4	57.5
Total	100.0	100.0	100.0	100.0	100.0	100.0	100.0
Ratio Q5/Q1	15.3	13.8	13.1	14.0	14.8	15.5	15.5
Top 1 per cent	12.0	12.4	13.7	12.4	12.7	13.2	–[2]
Gini	0.547	0.532	0.536	0.529	0.541	0.547	–[2]

Notes:
1. Quintile distribution based on income specification which includes labor market earnings, self-production, fringe benefits, rents, interest, capital gains, social security income, and pensions.
2. Data not available.

Sources: Quintile distribution: CASEN Surveys (Ministry of Planning 2001b, 2002a), top 1 per cent and Gini coefficients: World Bank (2001, Ch. 3).

Empirical studies have shown that the main determinants of poverty and inequality are household composition, years of schooling, and the different returns to schooling levels, in regard to employment rates and earnings (Larranaga and Raczinski 1995; Bravo and Contreras 1999; Contreras and Larranaga 1999; World Bank 2001, Ch. 2). Based on these findings the prevalent causal argument is the following: education determines the formation of human capital, which influences labor market participation, ultimately accounting for living standards. In the framework of this argument it is reasonable to focus on education and human capital as the generative assets. However, the disassociation between the time trends in poverty and inequality suggests that there may be other assets, differentially available to the populations at different income levels, which play a significant role in the maintenance of inequality. This could come about through two mechanisms: the contribution of material resources to the formation and utilization of human capital, and income returns to the household from investments in financial instruments. In either case, direct asset transfers across generations would contribute to the buildup of these resources and to household income flows.

In order to understand the role of parental assets in the formation of human capital, we review the characteristics of the Chilean educational system. Chile has experienced a significant educational expansion during the second half of the twentieth century. Until the 1960s the expansion was focused on primary education, with enrollment exceeding 90 per cent by 1970. Secondary school enrollment was less than 20 per cent at the beginning of the 1960s, rose to 49 per cent of the 14–18 age group in 1970, and to 84 per cent in 2000 (Cox and Lemaitre 1999; Ministry of Planning 2002b).

Our best estimates of current educational attainment are summarized in Panel A of Table 8.3, in which we have calculated (from CASEN Survey 2000) enrollment and completion rates for each educational level. Age cohorts for assessing educational attainment were selected so that we can assume that the great majority in a cohort who would ever complete the educational level had recently done so by the year 2000: the 15–19 age cohort for primary school, the 20–24 cohort for secondary education, and the 25–29 for tertiary study. In Panel B we present enrollment and completion rates for the 25–29 age group, which best conveys the differentiation in educational attainment among the income quintiles of a single cohort that has recently completed its schooling.

From these data we note that by the year 2000 primary education was almost universal, with a high completion rate for all socioeconomic strata (column 2 of Panel A), but enrollment in secondary education still varied considerably across the socioeconomic levels (column 3 of Panel A). Even though significant improvements were achieved during the 1990s (Mena and Bellei 1998), with the proportion of students in the lowest quintile attending secondary school rising to 71.9 per cent, there was still a considerable gap in the secondary-school completion rates between rich and poor, ranging from 42.6 to 94.9 per cent.

The gap between the income quintiles grows larger for tertiary education. The total post-secondary enrollment rate is 29.5 per cent, but it reaches 74.8 per cent in the top quintile while it is 5.7 per cent in the bottom quintile (column 5 of Panel A). These differential enrollment rates are important if we consider that the income returns to schooling increase substantially as we advance across educational levels: they are 6 per cent per year for primary education, about 10 per cent per year for secondary education, and more than 20 per cent per year for post-secondary study (Contreras and Larranaga 1999; Beyer 2000).[6]

Until the 1970s the Chilean education system consisted of a public sector with free primary and secondary schooling, serving the large majority of the population, and a private sector serving the wealthiest 10 per cent or so of families. The system was reformed during the 1980s, as part of the 'structural adjustment program' (Graham 1998, Ch. 2). The reform included the

Table 8.3 Schooling completion rates of selected age cohorts by income quintile, Chile, 2000[1]

Panel A Percentage of the 15–19 age cohort with primary education, of the 20–24 age cohort with secondary schooling, and of the 25–29 age cohort with tertiary education

Income quintile	15–19 Cohort		20–24 Cohort		25–29 Cohort	
	1	*2*	*3*	*4*	*5*	*6*
	Some primary	Completed primary	Some secondary	Completed secondary	Some tertiary[2]	Completed tertiary[2]
1 (low)	98.9	85.2	71.9	42.6	5.7	3.1
2	99.8	91.1	82.1	56.1	11.0	4.5
3	99.5	94.8	89.5	71.5	20.3	10.9
4	99.6	97.7	93.9	86.6	40.4	22.0
5 (high)	99.2	97.9	97.7	94.9	74.8	48.2
Total population	99.3	92.1	84.2	68.8	29.5	17.1

Panel B Schooling completion rates for the 25–29 age cohort

Income quintile	Some primary	Completed primary	Some secondary	Completed secondary	Some tertiary[2]	Completed tertiary[2]
1 (low)	97.7	71.9	53.8	30.2	5.7	3.1
2	98.7	84.3	71.4	49.7	11.0	4.5
3	99.1	92.6	84.3	67.3	20.3	10.9
4	99.4	97.1	92.8	84.0	40.4	22.0
5 (high)	99.8	99.1	97.8	94.9	74.8	48.2
Total population	98.9	88.9	80.8	64.7	29.5	17.1

Notes:
1. Excludes DK/NA (don't know/not available) comprising less than 1 per cent of the sample.
2. Tertiary includes academic, professional, and vocational higher education.

Sources: Authors' calculations based on CASEN Survey 2000 (Ministry of Planning 2000).

following components: first, reallocation of public spending from higher education to primary and secondary schooling, coupled with a reduction in the education budget, from 4.9 to 2.6 per cent of GDP. Second, schools were transferred from ministerial to local government (municipal) control. Third, the financing of education was modified to a voucher system (inspired by Milton Friedman) in which a fixed amount was paid to public schools on the basis of daily attendance rates. Private schools could receive this government subsidy in exchange for not charging students tuition fees (Cox and Lemaitre 1999).[7]

These reforms provided strong incentives for additional private agents to enter the educational sector, and the number of subsidy-based private schools (that is, chartered privately, but receiving the state voucher – what we shall term 'semi-privates') grew dramatically.[8] As public school quality deteriorated due to cuts in public spending in the 1980s, the semi-private schools became an increasingly attractive option for middle-class families, unable to access the fully-paid private institutions. The emergence of semi-private schools occurred primarily in urban areas, but not in rural and less populated locales, where the market was not profitable. Thus, between 1981 and 1999 the percentage of students attending public schools dropped from 78 to 54 per cent, while the percentage enrolled in semi-private institutions rose from 15 to 37 per cent, and the proportion in fully-paid private schools remained constant at about 9 per cent (Ministry of Education 1999, p. 118).

Educational coverage expanded in spite of a decline in resources expended on schooling: secondary enrollment grew from 49.7 to 80 per cent between 1970 and 1990, suggesting that the per-pupil subsidy was an efficient mechanism for adjusting demand to supply (Cox and Lemaitre 1999, Table 4-1). However, learning results did not improve during the 1980s. Semi-private schools have not been attracted to poor and remote areas of the country, where operational costs are higher; hence, public schools have served an increasingly homogeneous poor population. As is evident in column (1) of Table 8.4, whereas 74 per cent of the bottom-quintile children attend public schools, only 18 per cent of the top-quintile children do so; the proportion attending fully-paid private schools ranges from 1 per cent in the bottom quintile to 56 per cent in the top quintile (column 3). The semi-private schools, in comparison, primarily serve the interior segments of the income distribution.

The segmentation based on ability to pay was reinforced in 1993 when semi-private primary and secondary schools were allowed to charge a copayment fee to supplement the state subsidy. As can be seen in Panels A and B of Table 8.5 there is a monotonic decline in student performance in each of the school grades as one moves from fully private to semi-private and to public school. This decline is consistent across subjects

Table 8.4   Enrollment by school type and income quintile, 1998

Income quintile	Type of school[1]			
	(1) Public	(2) Semi-private[2]	(3) Private-paid	(4) Total
1 (low)	73.7	25.4	0.9	100.0
2	62.5	35.3	2.2	100.0
3	54.2	40.0	5.7	100.0
4	39.6	44.6	15.8	100.0
5 (high)	18.1	26.3	55.6	100.0
Total	54.8	33.5	11.6	100.0

Notes:
1. Includes primary and secondary levels. Omitted from the table are 1.1 per cent of
    students who attend Corporacion de Administracion Delegada (Delegated
    Administrative Corporation) schools.
2. State-subsidized private school.

Source: CASEN Survey 1998 (Ministry of Planning 2002b)

(mathematics and Spanish) and across time, though between 1988/89 and
1996/97 there was some contraction in the performance gap among the
school types.[9] Nonetheless, the gap remains very large in 1996/97, suggesting that, in Chile, the quality of education remains closely associated with
the ability to pay.

There is evidence that the test scores are heavily influenced by the
socioeconomic backgrounds of students and that the educational system is
structured in a way that effectively reproduces the existing pattern of social
and economic inequality in the country. Not only the amount of human
capital invested in children (measured by number of years of schooling),
but also the quality of human capital (measured by test scores) is significantly influenced by parental characteristics, with the type of school
attended serving as a mediating factor between family background and
educational attainment (Medlin 1996; Mizala and Romaguera 1998; Bravo
et al. 1999). Yet, a claim that parental resources are salient for educational
attainment hardly makes Chilean society unique. The critical question concerns how potent the linkage is, and to what extent children from poor
households are handicapped in acquiring sufficient human capital to function in a modern, wage-labor economy. This is one issue that will be
addressed in the analysis.

Parental assets can be important for living standards in a second way, by
permitting direct transfers to children, especially at key points along the life

Table 8.5   Mathematics and Spanish test scores, by school type and year

Panel A   Fourth graders

Type of school	1988		1996	
	(1) Spanish	(2) Math	(3) Spanish	(4) Math
Public	50	48	68	68
Semi-private*	58	55	74	73
Fully-paid private	79	73	86	86
Total	54	52	72	71

Panel B   Eighth graders

Type of school	1989		1997	
	(1) Spanish	(2) Math	(3) Spanish	(4) Math
Public	53	52	62	59
Semi-private*	59	56	68	65
Fully-paid private	77	76	80	81
Total	57	55	65	63

Note:
* State-subsidized private school.

Source: Generated from SIMCE data (Ministry of Education (1989 and 1997), Sistema de Medicion de la Calidad de la Educacion (System of Measurement of the Quality of Education).

cycle: labor market entry, marriage, and at times of illness or job loss. Parental resources can serve as both a capital stock for investment in the earnings capacity of offspring, and as a consumption reserve, analogous in this role to formal credit agencies and informal insurance arrangements among community members. The advantage of parental resources is that children generally have a first call on these assets, and the welfare of offspring can be assumed to be part of the utility function of parents (Becker 1991, Ch. 6).[10] Without excessive exaggeration we can think of parents and children as 'conspiring' to advance the well-being of the latter through the effective targeting of parental resources.

Moreover, in Chile, for institutional reasons, the vulnerability of the population to economic dislocation is quite high. The labor market has a large informal sector,[11] there is limited job security for much of the workforce, and programs of unemployment assistance leave substantial portions of the workforce uncovered.[12] In this circumstance, the presence of parental resources may have a strong buffering effect, compensating for the inadequacies of the limited public assistance sector. Therefore, a second issue, which is examined in the paper concerns the contribution of parental resources to household income and wealth holdings – measures, essentially, of the capacity of a family to achieve economic security and maintain a particular living standard.

PARENTAL BACKGROUND, EDUCATIONAL ATTAINMENT, INCOME AND WEALTH

With this detail about the educational system, we turn to an analysis of parental effects on educational attainment and on the living standard capacity measures. The data for the study come from a module on parental asset holdings and the economic well-being of adult children that was added to a recent survey of job histories. The year 2001 Social Mobility Survey was a nationally representative, random sample of 3544 Chilean households. Respondents were male household heads aged 24–69, who acted as informants about their own background and work experience, and about their wife's, or partner's, background. Descriptive statistics for the main variables are presented in Appendix Table 8A.1, and a comparison with values from CASEN, a national household survey comparable to the Current Population Survey in the United States, is provided in Appendix Table 8A.2.

Two caveats with regard to the data. First, while the conceptual argument emphasizes the role of parental assistance and intergenerational transfers, our observations are restricted to parental assets; a transfer process is *presumed* to account for the parental effects on living standards but the details of the transmission are not spelled out in this study. Second, low parental income and resources can affect educational attainment in three ways: through its influence on the quality of the school attended (for example, tuition and fees); through the carrying costs of maintaining a child in school, forgoing his/her labor market income; and through residence in poor neighborhoods, where schools are distant or unavailable. While we have a proxy for school quality (private school attendance), we lack a measure of school accessibility in different communities at the time the respondents were in their student years – which means that this reason for low attendance will be confounded with the parental burden of keeping a child in school, a second determinant of low attendance.

At one level the distinction in the underlying cause of low attendance is unimportant; both explanations tap parental income and resources. But the distinction is relevant if one seeks to ameliorate the problem, in that a different solution is suggested in each case. Where low rates of attainment are due to a lack of school facilities, the construction of physical plants is indicated; where the problem stems from the parental burden of supporting a dependent child, the response must be quite different. In actuality, we expect the bias from this confounding to be small, especially for respondents aged 45 and younger, because primary and secondary schooling have been available in Chile in all but the most distant rural locales since the late 1960s (Aylwin et al. 1983, Ch. 4; Gazmuri 2000, Vol. II, Chs 7, 8).[13]

Descriptive Statistics

As a preliminary to the multivariate analysis we describe the zero-order relationships among the main variables. The importance of educational attainment for various aspects of family welfare is summarized in Table 8.6. The first five rows refer to household income and financial assets; rows 6–8 describe the association between some key living standard measures (functional assets) and years of schooling. The contribution of education to financial well-being is evident: husband's earnings, total family income, and its stock of financial and investment assets show a strong dependence on years of schooling, with large increases as one moves from low to high levels of education. Not surprisingly, the living standard measures show a similar dependence on schooling; presumably the income and financial resource terms serve as intervening variables in the production of these educational effects.

If we examine the association between the parental standard of living (SOL) – a subjective measure that reflects parental assets and income – and the well-being of adult children we find a similar effect pattern (Table 8.7). The first eight rows exhibit a strong dependence of the financial and living standard measures on parental SOL, with considerably higher respondent values as one progresses along the SOL categories. It can reasonably be assumed that much of the impact of *parental* resources (indexed by SOL) comes from its effect on husband's schooling (row 9), which ranges over the SOL categories from 7.2 to 14.2 years, and from the consequent impact of husband's education on the couple's income and assets. The last three rows serve a different purpose; they document the association between parental SOL and its presumed objective components: father's education, father's occupational status, and parental wealth. This association serves to validate our contention that the SOL variable can be viewed as a summary measure of parental attainment and resources.

These results provide preliminary evidence for the importance of educational attainment and for the dependence of this variable and, ultimately, living standards on parental resources. In order to identify the mechanisms

Table 8.6 *Descriptive statistics relating measures of couple's financial well-being and standard of living to husband's educational attainment[1]*

Financial well-being/SOL	Years of schooling by husband							
	0–4	5–6	7–8	9–11	12	13–16	17+	N
Income and financial assets:								
Husband's earnings[2]	127	146	166	237	280	469	1149	2640
Family income[3]	161	186	210	283	362	595	1411	2951
Family wealth[4]	3.6	4.1	4.2	4.6	4.7	5.2	6.2	3091
Financial assets[5]	0.06	0.08	0.11	0.17	0.23	0.33	0.61	3053
Property ownership[6]	0.12	0.13	0.11	0.15	0.20	0.26	0.41	3102
Functional assets:								
Number of autos	0.24	0.37	0.39	0.41	0.59	0.78	1.19	3097
Number of household items[7]	−0.28	−0.16	−0.17	−0.06	0.10	0.34	0.90	3079
Home value[8]	12.3	11.6	13.4	14.8	19.5	30.3	54.2	2073

Notes:
1. Entries are for married and cohabitating couples. All values are for year 2001.
2. Unemployed husbands omitted from the calculation. Entry × 1000 = monthly earnings in pesos.
3. Entry × 1000 = monthly family income in pesos.
4. Subjective 10-category scale.
5. Proportion of respondents owning bonds, stock, life insurance.
6. Proportion of respondents owning land, business, real estate.
7. Sum of Z-scores from count of ownership of seven common household items.
8. Computed for homeowners. Entry × 1000000 = home value in pesos.

Source: Social Mobility Survey, 2001.

Table 8.7   Descriptive statistics relating husband's earnings, couple's financial status and standard of living, to parental standard of living[1]

	Parental standard of living[2]					
	1	2	3	4	5	N
Measures of couple's SOL:						
Husband's earnings[3]	177	269	424	854	1475	2627
Family income[4]	212	328	524	989	1693	2937
Family wealth[5]	3.9	4.5	5.2	5.8	6.2	3077
Financial assets[6]	0.10	0.16	0.31	0.46	0.46	3041
Property ownership[7]	0.12	0.17	0.24	0.32	0.41	3089
Number of autos	0.33	0.48	0.67	1.03	1.32	3085
Number of household items[8]	−0.18	−0.01	0.23	0.55	0.67	3067
Home value[9]	12.7	16.8	25.1	43.7	79.9	2063
Husband's education[10]	7.2	9.7	11.7	13.9	14.2	3083
Parental SOL components:						
Father's education[10]	3.8	6.1	8.5	11.8	13.3	2465
Father's ISEI[11]	25.1	29.7	35.8	46.5	55.7	2771
Parental wealth[12]	2.5	3.9	5.3	6.8	8.2	3080

Notes:
1. Entries are for married and cohabiting couples, year 2001 values.
2. Parental SOL is a five-category subjective assessment of husband's parents, pertaining to year when husband was 14 years old.
3. Entry × 1000 = monthly earnings in pesos.
4. Entry × 1000 = monthly family income in pesos.
5. Subjective assessment, 10-category scale.
6. Proportion of respondents owning bonds, stock, life insurance.
7. Proportion of respondents owning land, business, real estate.
8. Sum of Z-scores from count of ownership of seven common household items.
9. Computed for homeowners. Entry × 1 000 000 = home value in pesos.
10. Years of schooling by husband's father.
11. Occupational score, husband's father – International Socioeconomic Index of Occupational Status (Ganzeboom et al. 1992).
12. Subjective assessment of husband's parents, in year when husband was 14 years old, 10-category scale.

Source: Social Mobility Survey, 2001.

by which the parental terms influence living standards – especially the respective effects through education and direct assistance – we utilize a multivariate formulation. Indeed, it cannot be assumed that the various living standard components are even determined by the same transmission process; some may be heavily influenced by parental investments in schooling, others

Table 8.8   *Impact of parental characteristics on respondent's years of*
              schooling and type of school attended[1]

Explanatory variables	(1) Years of schooling[2]	(2) Attended private school[3]
Constant	8.8588***	−5.0811***
Father's education[4]	0.2447***	−0.0963***
Father's education(m)[5]	0.3245	−0.0357
Father's occupation[6]	0.0601***	0.0203***
Father's occupation(m)[5]	2.5072***	0.2270
Respondent's age	−0.0804***	0.0131*
Number of siblings	−0.1554***	−0.0554*
Parental wealth (log)	0.7495***	0.2922***
R^2 //-2LL	.433	1749
N	3483	3439
$*p<0.05, **p<0.01, ***p<0.001$		

Notes:
1. Respondents are males, married and unmarried.
2. Unstandardized coefficients from OLS regression.
3. Logistic regression. Dependent variable coded 1 if last school attended was private; 0 otherwise. Respondents without any formal education excluded from the analysis.
4. Years of schooling.
5. Variables education(m) and occupation(m) are missing data indicators. See text for details.
6. Occupation coded by ISEI status scores (Ganzeboom et al. 1992).

more tightly linked to direct asset transfers. In the present paper we examine parental effects on the determination of husband's education and on the principal measures of living standard potential – husband's earnings; the couple's income and wealth.

Years of Schooling and Type of Institution Attended

In the traditional socioeconomic achievement model (for example, Blau and Duncan 1967, Ch. 5), years of schooling by the respondent is formulated as a function of father's education and occupational status, the latter serving as a proxy for parental permanent income. In column (1) of Table 8.8 we follow this characterization, with occupation coded by its International Socioeconomic Index (ISEI) score,[14] though for a more complete depiction of the parental background effects we have added terms for parental wealth and number of siblings, the latter a measure of demands on the parental resources. As suggested earlier, parental wealth may well influence educational attainment *net* of father's education and earnings, because it can generate an income stream that is independent of employment. In times of economic crisis poor families often increase their reliance on child labor (Moser 1998), encouraging older children to enter the labor market. In this circumstance, parental asset holdings could provide a family with the resources to sustain a child in school.

Three additional variables are included as regressors: a term for husband's age and two missing data indicators, for husband's father's education and occupational status.[15] The age variable should correct for the tendency of older husbands to have less education; the missing data indicators (*m*-terms in the table) were added in order to retain observations that have considerable missing data on a variable, as is the case with the parental variables (Table 8A.1). Specifically, an indicator term was coded 1 for cases where data are absent on the substantive variable, and 0 otherwise. Where significant, an indicator term conveys the average effect on the dependent variable from observations for which data are lacking on the substantive regressor.[16]

The results in column (1) support the contention about the importance of parental background and, in particular, the contribution of parental asset holdings. Father's education and occupational status are highly significant, with strong effects on educational attainment. Each additional year of father's schooling increases respondent's education by 0.24 years. Father's occupational status also has a strong impact. Since status is measured on the ISEI scale, which lacks a concrete metric, we note that a standard deviation increase in father's status score – essentially the difference between occupations such as secretary and primary school teacher, or between unskilled farm laborer and carpenter – translates into a gain of 0.94 years in respondent's schooling. (In comparison, a standard deviation increase in father's education generates a gain of 1.18 years in schooling.) The coefficient for respondent's age, as expected, is negative; older Chileans, on average, have less schooling than their younger peers.

The final two variables, indicators of parental resources, also have substantial effects. Since parental wealth is highly skewed, it is more meaningful to report results in terms of the log(wealth) metric.[17] A one-standard deviation increase in this variable generates a return of 1.02 years in respondent's schooling, an effect that is net of the parental human capital variables. Equivalently, since change in the log(wealth) metric represents a multiplicative effect in the underlying variable, a one-standard deviation increase in log(wealth) – 1.36 points – is tantamount to a multiplicative factor of 3.9 (exp[1.36]). Thus, the difference in parental wealth between $10000 and $39000 (or between $100000 and $390000) is associated with 1.02 years of additional schooling.[18]

In short, the returns to parental wealth are roughly of the same magnitude as the returns to the human capital variables. When measured in terms of a standard deviation change (with parental wealth specified in the log metric), each has a considerable effect on educational attainment. In the United States, in comparison, the impact of parental wealth is weaker (for example, Axinn et al. 1997). Possibly because school attendance is compulsory through age 16 in much of the United States, family resources play less of a role as a deterrent to school dropout. Last, sibship size has a negative impact on years of schooling, a finding that has been noted in other studies (for example, Duncan et al. 1972, Ch. 3; Spilerman 2004). A larger family invariably means that less in the way of parental assistance is available to each child.

But the impact on years of schooling is not the only way that parental background and resources can influence the accumulation of human capital. There is evidence in Chile of an association between type of school attended (public, semi-private, private) and the quality of education. For example, Aninat (2000) reports that the school day is some two hours longer in private institutions than in public or semi-private ones; also, test scores are higher in private schools (Table 8.5). We therefore turn to an examination of the effect of parental resources on the channeling of students into one or the other of the parallel school systems.

In column (2) of Table 8.8 logit coefficients are reported from a regression of the dichotomous variable, 'last school attended was private, versus other type' on the parental background terms. Again, the parental effects are highly significant. Exponentiating the logit coefficients permits a comparison of the different background characteristics in terms of odds ratios. In particular, a one-standard deviation increase in parental education (4.76 years) raises the odds of attending private school by 58 per cent; for father's occupational status, a standard deviation shift translates into an odds change of 30 per cent. In comparison, a standard deviation increase in ln(parental wealth) produces a 48 per cent improvement in the odds of attending private school. Also worth noting is the negative effect of sibship size, which again suggests the detrimental consequence of having to divide the parental resources among multiple children.

To summarize, the effects of the parental background terms are considerable. Father's education and occupational status exert a major influence on two central components of respondent's educational attainment: years of study and quality of schooling (the latter indexed by private school attendance). Moreover, net of these effects, parental wealth makes an additional contribution to educational attainment that is roughly equal in size, as measured by a standard deviation change in each parental term. Since much wealth is inherited and remains within families, this source of advantage in access to education can be difficult to overcome solely from public investments in school facilities.

Respondent's Earnings

From the perspective of living standards, household income and wealth can be viewed as capacity measures. These resources provide the material basis that underlies a family's consumption level; in addition, a family's wealth stock constitutes a consumption reserve, to be drawn upon in the event of sickness or job loss. In the present section we examine the relation between parental background and respondent's earnings; in the following one, using an extended formulation that includes characteristics of spouse's background, we investigate the determinants of household income and wealth.

The impact of parental background on the log of respondent's earnings in year 2001 is reported in Table 8.9. Respondents without employment activity are omitted from this analysis. A Heckman-type selection model was not used because of the unavailability of suitable first-stage regressors. However, the bias in coefficient estimates due to the lack of a correction factor is not great. While some 13.3 per cent of the sample reported no income from employment, the majority of these respondents indicated that this was because they were retired or had chronic illness; in short, they were not available for work. Only 4.6 per cent of the sample reported reasons for inactivity which suggested that they would accept employment.

Column (1) of Table 8.9 presents the *total* effects of the parental variables; that is, the effects not mediated by respondent's education. The significance pattern is similar to that reported for respondent's education, presumably because years of schooling is the most potent determinant of earnings in a modern economy, and because the parental effects on educational attainment, reported in Table 8.8, are considerable. Again, each of the parental terms – father's education, occupational status, and parental wealth – shows a strong association with respondent's earnings.

The returns to the different parental variables can be summarized as follows: a one-standard deviation increase in father's schooling (4.79 years) translates into a 22 per cent improvement in respondent's earnings ($\exp[0.0417 \times 4.79] = 1.22$). With regard to father's occupational status, an increase of one standard deviation – equivalently a 41 per cent change from its mean value – augments earnings by 21 per cent. Father's wealth has a more modest effect: a one-standard deviation change in ln(wealth) – a multiplier of 3.9 in the wealth metric – can be associated with an 18 per cent increase in respondent's earnings. While each of these contributions is net of the other terms in the equation, in reality a father with higher education

Table 8.9 Effects of parental characteristics on respondent's earnings, 2001[1]

Explanatory variables	(1) Total effects of parental terms	(2) Effects net of education	(3) Effects net of education and occupation
Constant	4.2184***	3.3205***	3.2642***
Father's education[2]	0.0417***	0.0143***	0.0102**
Father's education(m)[3]	0.0127	0.0424	0.0323
Father's occupation[4]	0.0146***	0.0071***	0.0044***
Father's occupation(m)[3]	0.4414***	0.1646**	0.0850
Respondent's age	0.0019	0.0093***	0.0059***
Number of siblings	−0.0122*	0.0048	0.0048
Parental wealth (log)	0.1190***	0.0382***	0.0312**
Respondent's education[2]		0.1068***	0.0695***
Semi-private school[5]		0.0361	0.0334
Private school[5]		0.2710***	0.2159***
Respondent's occupational status[4]			0.0195***
R^2	0.264	0.440	0.498
N	2855	2855	2855

$*p < 0.05, **p < 0.01, ***p < 0.001$

Notes:
1. Unstandardized coefficients from OLS regressions. Dependent variable is ln(earnings), with earnings in pesos. Respondents are males, married and unmarried. Respondents without earnings are omitted from the analysis. See text for details on model specification.
2. Educational attainment measured by years of schooling.
3. Variables education(m) and occupation(m) are missing data indicators. See text for details.
4. Occupation coded by ISEI status scores (Ganzeboom et al. 1992).
5. Institutional type of last school attended. Public school is the deleted term.

is likely to also have higher occupational status and greater wealth, producing a cumulatively more potent parental impact on earnings.

To what extent do these parental effects operate through the determination of educational attainment? This question is addressed in column (2), where respondent's education and school type have been added to the equation. As expected, the contribution from the educational terms is considerable. An additional year of study has a multiplier effect of 1.113 (an 11.3 per cent increase in earnings), four years of study – the difference between primary school and high school – translates into an increase of 53 per cent in respondent's earnings.

Enrollment in private school, in contrast with public school attendance, is worth 31 per cent more in earnings, an effect that is in addition to years of study.

The degree to which the educational variables serve to transmit the parental effects can be ascertained by examining the reduction in the coefficients in equation (2) versus equation (1). The three parental variables remain significant, suggesting that family background and resources influence earnings in ways apart from their impact on educational attainment, but the coefficients are much smaller. The reductions vary from 51 per cent to 68 per cent; thus, the bulk of determination of respondent's earnings by the parental variables comes from their impact on the educational terms. In column (3) respondent's occupational status has been added, revealing a second avenue of parental influence on earnings. The decline in direct parental effects, relative to equation (1), now ranges from 70 to 76 per cent.

Household Income

The influence of parental background on family income and wealth holdings is formulated differently from the determination of respondent's education and earnings because it must now be assumed that the respondent's family has access to the resources of both sets of parents. Thus, we change the unit of analysis from the individual to the couple, and introduce regressors for the educational attainment and occupational status of the fathers of both members of the couple; we also restrict the analysis to the 89 per cent of the sample that is currently married or cohabitating. However, since only 31 per cent of the wives are employed either full or part time, we omit regressors for wife's human capital – that is, the determinants of her earnings – to simplify the formulation.

The parental wealth variable was collected only for respondent's (that is, husband's) family. The omission of wife's family wealth can be expected to bias the coefficient of the included wealth variable upwards, due to the likely positive correlation in net worth between the two sets of parents.[19] Similarly, data are available only for number of siblings of husband, which may introduce an analogous distortion. Other changes to the prior formulation include the introduction of terms for number of employed family members and a dummy term for cohabitation versus marriage.

The results of this analysis are reported in Table 8.10. In column (1) the total effects of the parental background terms on ln(family income) are presented. These show significant contributions for father's education and occupation (from each set of parents) and for parental wealth. Net of the other variables, four years of added schooling by husband's father is worth 12 per cent in respondent's family income (a multiplier of 1.12), while a one-standard deviation increase in father's occupational status is

Table 8.10   Effects of parental characteristics on family income, 2001[1]

Explanatory variables	(1) Total effects of parental terms	(2) Effects net of education	(3) Effects net of education and occupation
Constant	3.807***	3.083***	3.058***
Husband's father:			
Education[2]	0.0280***	0.0083*	0.0056
Education(m)[3]	−0.0695	−0.0220	−0.0326
Occupation[4]	0.0108***	0.0056***	0.0036**
Occupation(m)[3]	0.3396***	0.1321*	0.0738
Wife's father:			
Education[2]	0.0290***	0.0140***	0.0101**
Education(m)[3]	0.0345	0.0011	−0.0036
Occupation[4]	0.0121***	0.0078***	0.0060***
Occupation(m)[3]	0.3840***	0.2575***	0.2103***
Husband's age	0.0023	0.0090***	0.0059***
Number employed[5]	0.2646***	0.2638***	0.2566***
Cohabitation	−0.2321***	−0.1508***	−0.1322***
Number of siblings[6]	−0.0108*	0.0019	0.0020
Parental wealth (log)[7]	0.0840***	0.0262*	0.0220*
Husband's education[2]		0.0973***	0.0683***
Semi-private school[8]		−0.0125	−0.0146
Private school[8]		0.2954***	0.2539***
Husband's occupation[4]			0.0172***
R^2	0.370	0.496	0.534
N	2807	2807	2807

*$p < 0.05$, **$p < 0.01$, ***$p < 0.001$

Notes:
1. Unstandardized coefficients from OLS regressions. Dependent variable is ln(family income), with income in pesos. Respondents are males, married and cohabitating. See text for details on model specification.
2. Educational attainment measured by years of schooling.
3. Variables education(m) and occupation(m) are missing data indicators.
4. Occupation coded by ISEI status scores (Ganzeboom et al. 1992).
5. Number of family members employed.
6. Number of siblings of husband.
7. Estimate of husband's parents' wealth holdings. See text for details.
8. Institutional type of last school attended by husband. Public school is the omitted category.

associated with 15 per cent higher income. (The findings for wife's father's education and occupation are similar.) The parental wealth effect can be described as follows: if husband's father's wealth were doubled, husband's family income would be higher by 6.0 per cent. As to the controls, each additional employed family member, on average, augments family income by 30 per cent, while number of siblings and cohabitation have negative effects, the latter associated with 21 per cent less income in comparison with married respondents.

In the column (2) model, terms have been introduced for husband's educational attainment. First note that both years of study and private school attendance have strong effects on the dependent variable. Four years of added schooling serve to increase household income by 48 per cent, while private school attendance is worth 34 per cent in additional family income. The education terms also serve to transmit the effects of the parental background variables. In this regard, observe that the coefficients of husband's father's schooling and occupation are reduced by 70 per cent and 48 per cent, respectively, (with similar reductions for wife's father's terms), and the parental wealth variable is lessened by some 70 per cent; in short, the major part of the parental influence on income comes through its impact on educational attainment.

A further delineation of the parental effects is conveyed by equation (3), in which a term has been added for husband's occupational status. Not surprisingly, the impact of this term is considerable: a one-standard deviation increase in status is associated with 28 per cent greater family income (a multiplier of 1.28). The coefficient of the schooling variable is now smaller by 30 per cent, since much of the educational effect on earnings would come through the occupation term. What is surprising is that the reduction is modest, which suggests that there is considerable variation in education and income *within* the occupational categories. A final remark about the controls: number of employed family members and husband's age have positive effects on family income – as one would expect – while cohabitation has a negative impact. Since the last is net of husband's age, education, and occupational status, as well as of the parental background measures, it is not clear what is being tapped by this variable.

Wealth Holdings

Parental wealth can play a role in the intergenerational transmission of advantage in two ways. First, by its influence on educational attainment parental wealth facilitates the buildup of human capital in the next generation, thereby contributing to the earnings capacity and household income of offspring; indeed, we find evidence for such an effect in Tables 8.8–10.

There is also a small, but significant, parental wealth effect on earnings and
household income *net* of the controls for education and occupation
(columns (3) of Tables 8.9 and 8.10), suggesting the presence of complex
paths in the transmission of advantage, possibly the use of social capital by
wealthy and well-connected parents to help children locate a quality job
within the range of positions covered by an occupational title.

A second way that parental wealth contributes to the replication of
inequality is through direct transfers of material and financial assets. This is
the theme of the present section, in which respondent's household wealth is
examined in terms of the parental background variables and respondent's
education and occupation. Like parental wealth, information on respondent's
wealth level was collected in terms of a 10-category ordinal scale, with the category midpoints subsequently assigned interval values based on the estimates
of Chilean informants (see note 17). Some caveats in terms of model formulation: since household wealth represents an accumulation over the life
course, the use of current values of the explanatory variables as regressors is
problematic. Thus, in the case of husband's occupation – a proxy for earnings
flows to the household – we replace current occupation by occupation held
six years earlier.[20] In the case of number of employed family members, we
have available only the current value, which is used in the analysis.

The regression results for respondent's wealth holdings are reported in Table
8.11. In column (1) the total effects of the parental terms are presented, modified only by the control variables – characteristics of husband and his family
that are relevant to the analysis, but which are presumed not to be vehicles in
the transmission of parental advantage. The findings are quite clear. There are
modest effects from parental education and occupation (the former is significant for husband's father, the latter for wife's father). Also, the controls have
effects that are in line with our expectations: household wealth increases with
husband's age (a proxy for accumulation time) and with number of employed
family members, and it is lower in instances of cohabitation – on average, this
marital status is associated with 27 per cent less asset value.

If parental education and occupation have modest effects, this is de-
cidedly not the case with the parental wealth term. Whereas four years of
added study by husband's father translates into a 6.7 per cent wealth gain,
and a standard deviation improvement in wife's father's status is worth 12.1
per cent, a doubling of parental wealth is associated with a 26 per cent
increase in respondent's asset value. A comparison with the parental effects
in the income regression (equation (1) of Table 8.10) is instructive: the same
manipulations of the parental variables generated income gains of 12 per
cent from father's education, 15 per cent from occupational status, but only
6 per cent from parental wealth; the influence pattern in the earnings regression is similar. In short, the effects of the parental human capital terms

Table 8.11   Impact of parental characteristics on family wealth holdings, 2001[1]

Explanatory variables	(1) Total effects of parental terms	(2) Effects net of education	(3) Effects net of education and occupation
Constant	1.5640**	1.0041***	0.9941***
Husband's father:			
Education[2]	0.0162**	0.0034	0.0024
Education(m)[3]	−0.0582	−0.0244	−0.0299
Occupation[4]	0.0001	−0.0025	−0.0037*
Occupation(m)[3]	0.0738	−0.0640	−0.0985
Wife's father:			
Education[2]	0.0106	0.0011	−0.0003
Education(m)[3]	−0.0222	−0.0395	−0.0345
Occupation[4]	0.0084***	0.0055**	0.0044**
Occupation(m)[3]	0.2517***	0.1654*	0.1356
Husband's age	0.0066***	0.0116***	0.0090***
Number employed[5]	0.0901***	0.0900***	0.0885***
Cohabitation	−0.3104***	−0.2509***	−0.2461***
Number of siblings[6]	−0.0035	0.0057	0.0059
Parental wealth (log)[7]	0.3373***	0.2958***	0.2940***
Husband's education[2]		0.0707***	0.0537***
Semi-private school[8]		−0.0005	−0.0066
Private school[8]		0.0280	0.0173
Husband's occupation (1995)[9]			0.0109***
Husband's occupation(m)[3]			0.3125***
R^2	0.273	0.313	0.324
N	2957	2957	2957

*$p < 0.05$, **$p < 0.01$, ***$p < 0.001$

Notes:
1. Unstandardized coefficients from OLS regressions. Dependent variable is ln(family wealth), with wealth in pesos. Respondents are males, married and cohabitating. See text for details on model specification.
2. Educational attainment measured by years of schooling.
3. Variables education(m) and occupation(m) are missing data indicators.
4. Occupation coded by ISEI status scores (Ganzeboom et al. 1992).
5. Number of family members employed.
6. Number of siblings of husband.
7. Estimate of husband's parents' wealth holdings. See text for details.
8. Institutional type of last school attended by husband. Public school is the deleted term.
9. Husband's occupational status in 1995 (ISEI code). See text for details.

and parental asset holdings are reversed, with parental education and occupation having the larger impact on earnings and household income, and parental wealth having the dominant effect in the determination of the value of respondent's asset holdings.

To what extent do the parental background terms operate through their impact on the offspring's education and occupation? This question is addressed in columns (2) and (3). Note, first, from equation (2), that years of schooling by the respondent has a strong effect on asset value – four years of additional study can be associated with a 32.7 per cent increase in wealth holdings. But is this effect due to the transmission of parental advantage? Since husband's father's education is now insignificant and wife's father's occupation, while significant, is lower by 34.3 per cent, it is evident that respondent's education serves to transmit much of the influence of parental human capital.

In contrast, the coefficient for parental wealth remains massive – lessened by only 12.3 per cent from the introduction of the schooling variables – a strong indication that the parental wealth effect largely operates *outside* the educational system. Moreover, the addition of respondent's occupation (column (3)) produces no further reduction in the parental wealth term. As a consequence, an explanation of the association between the value of asset holdings in the two generations that emphasizes the parental wealth effect on respondent's education and occupational attainment does not fare well.

This last assessment need not have been the case. A strong influence of parental wealth on respondent's asset holdings could have come about through a parental wealth effect on education and earnings (indexed here by occupational status). Such a finding would suggest that respondent's asset holdings are accumulated through savings from labor market income, made possible by the parental wealth effect on human capital. But this is not what we discern. Parental wealth does impact the human capital of offspring (Table 8.8); however, this influence path does not account for the value of respondent's asset holdings. Rather, the evidence suggests that, in Chile, at the current time, wealth holdings are best explained by a process of direct transfers across generations.

CONCLUSIONS

We return to the themes that were raised in the introduction: how important are parental background and parental resources for the life chances and living standards of adult children? What is the particular contribution of parental wealth? What are the implications of this analysis for the persistence of inequality and for policy formulation on these issues?

As to parental background, the effects on the measures of living standard capacity are considerable. The parental terms, along with respondent's age and number of siblings, account for some 44 per cent of the variation in years of schooling (R^2 in column (1) of Table 8.8). The parental terms also explain 26 per cent of the earnings variation, 37 per cent of the variation in household income, and 27 per cent in household wealth (column (1) of Tables 8.9–11). These are large effects and suggest a strong transmission of advantage across generations.

From the point of view of individual opportunity, the good news is that respondent's education and occupational status account for an additional 23 and 17 per cent of the variation in earnings and household income, respectively (column (3) of Tables 8.9–10). Thus, it is not the case that education and occupational attainment are purely vehicles in the transmission of parental advantage, though they clearly serve this function. Moreover, it is likely that more refined measures of educational attainment and occupational affiliation than we have available would raise the contributions of these terms, as measured by added R^2. The key point is that the school system in Chile appears to operate in a way that provides real opportunity for children who do not come from advantaged backgrounds.

The story with respect to household wealth is less sanguine. The same formulation that showed respondent's education and occupation as uniquely accounting for 17 per cent of household income, finds that respondent's human capital explains only 5 per cent of the variance in household wealth, net of the parental terms (column (3) of Table 8.11). Admittedly, the wealth measures are crude; both parent's and respondent's asset values are based on subjective assessments. Moreover, the model specification is hardly optimal for a process in which wealth holdings are built up, at least in part, from accumulations over the life course. Nonetheless, the results for household wealth, both in regard to the small added R^2 from respondent's education and occupation, and with respect to the failure of these human capital terms to depress the parental wealth coefficient, are consistent, and therefore worrisome.

Also, this finding makes sense in light of the great difficulty that many households face in accumulating savings from earnings, especially in a country in which median income is low. Thus, the expenditures that are necessary for maintaining a minimally acceptable living standard often see little left over for savings. As a consequence, differences in parental wealth holdings become a major determinant of the variation in household wealth in the current generation, an initial condition that is difficult to alter solely by means of investments in schooling and human capital. Indeed, commenting on wealth disparities between black and white Americans, Blau and Graham (1990) make a similar point, noting that even if the racial gap in household income in the United States were eliminated, it would take several generations before the existing wealth disparity between the races was significantly eroded.

Yet, while we find strong evidence of a replication of household wealth across generations, only modestly offset by opportunities for education and earnings, there remains a question of the importance of household wealth for living standards and family well-being. It is a quite different matter if variations in wealth holdings correlate with ownership of a BMW versus a Volkswagen, than if the wealth holdings predict car ownership versus no car, or, of greater pertinence, high-school completion versus dropping out of school. The critical issue concerns the extent to which families can finance an acceptable living standard and provide for their children's future solely from labor market earnings. A related issue concerns the availability of safety-net programs in a country that can offset the need for accumulating private savings as a consumption reserve in the event of illness or job loss.

We cannot formally assess the role of household wealth as a determinant of living standards because the current study did not examine the owner-ship of functional assets (for example, home, car, household durables) or the manner of financing other lifestyle items (for example, vacation travel). But we can speculate on the likely importance of household wealth for con-sumption expenditures. In particular, it would seem that where a large sum is required, such as for the purchase of a home or starting a small business, this is likely to come from accumulated savings. In Israel, for example, it has been found that parental wealth is a critical resource for these sorts of expenditures, reducing, especially, the waiting time to home ownership by a young couple (Spilerman 2004).

Chile has made great progress since the mid-1980s, improving educa-tional attainment, raising median income, and reducing poverty. This has not been accompanied, however, by a lessening of income inequality, nor, presumably, of wealth inequality, though measures of the latter are lacking. Yet, if income inequality has proven resilient to modification, this is likely to be even more so for wealth inequality, since the latter is less a contem-poraneous variable than a historical record of intergenerational transfer receipts and long-term accumulations.

However, precisely because intergenerational transfers play a huge role in the replication of advantage and raise fundamental questions of equity, it is important for a country to avoid high and persistent inequality in initial conditions and maintain realistic possibilities for upward mobility in living standards (Cowan and De Gregorio 2000). Toward this end, the Chilean government might well contemplate strategies that create asset value for poor people, beyond investments in education and labor market skills, such as fostering pension savings among informal workers, facilitating access to credit markets, and providing good title to homes. Although the noneconomic externalities from very high inequality have not been addressed in this chapter, their political and social consequences are quite evident in many countries of Latin America.

A final comment should be made about the mechanics of intergenerational financial linkages. This chapter has examined the relevance of parental assets for living standards and the reproduction of inequality. However, we have yet to explore the characteristics of the transfer regimes in Chile. What is the relative importance of *inter vivos* assistance versus bequests, in the metric of amounts transferred? Which life course events (for example, marriage, birth, illness, job loss) and what sorts of children's characteristics (for example, gender, marital status, financial need, emotional closeness to parents) determine the timing and pattern of parental allocations? How does the availability of public assistance programs interact with family decisions in regard to *inter vivos* transfers? These are some open issues that are relevant to obtaining a refined understanding of the structure of opportunity and family welfare in the country, and the role played by household wealth in these matters.

NOTES

*   This research was supported by Ford Foundation grant no. 1010-2002 to the Center for the Study of Wealth and Inequality, Columbia University. We would like to thank Guillermo Wormald for making available sections of the Social Mobility Survey for which he was responsible. We would also like to thank Hanna Cho and Hsien-Hen Lu for their comments on an earlier draft.
1.   As a practical consideration, IDAs would have to be structured so that the asset holdings do not alter a family's eligibility to receive means-tested welfare payments.
2.   Poverty increased significantly in Latin America during the economic crisis of the 1980s, then declined moderately during the 1990s as a result of economic stabilization policies. In 1999 the poverty rate was 35.3 per cent (ECLAC 2001, Table 1.2).
3.   Inequality and poverty are closely related in Latin America. Most countries register 'excess poverty' (rates that are above what would be expected given the GDP per capita) as a result of high levels of income inequality (Attanasio and Szekely 1999).
4.   Some important, recent studies of material assets are reported in Attanasio and Szekely (2001), in which attention is given to the role of home ownership, capital, land, and household durables in investigations of economic well-being and living standards in several Latin American countries. For a discussion of the role of material assets in strategies for overcoming poverty, see Stallings et al. (2000).
5.   Neighborhoods of such homes go by various names in the different Latin American countries: *tugorio* in Colombia, *poblacion callampa* in Chile, *favela* and *villa miseria* in Brazil, and *cantegril* in Uruguay.
6.   In Europe a person with a college education receives about 1.8 times the earnings of a person with a primary education; in Chile the figure is 5.5 (Beyer 2000).
7.   Despite the absence of tuition charges, the attractiveness of this arrangement to the private sector came from the presence of considerable inefficiencies in the public school

system which permitted the new schools to be profitable with targeted student populations. Moreover, unlike the public schools they could select students, avoiding the most
troublesome and time-consuming children.

8.   While a few subsidy-based private schools existed before the 1980 reform, they received
     roughly half the per-student support given to the public schools.

9.   The reduction in this gap was mainly a result of aggressive educational policies under-
     taken by the democratic governments since 1990. These policies include higher public
     spending, an increase in hours of instruction, and an enhanced educational curriculum
     (Cox and Lemaitre 1999). However, shorter school days in the subsidized system, in com-
     parison with fully private schools, remains a problem (Aninat 2000).

10. A common way by which Chilean parents use their resources to assist children is by per-
     mitting coresidence in the years following marriage. In the data of the current survey,
     46.6 per cent of respondents report that they lived with parents for some period during
     their first three years of marriage or cohabitation.

11. Estimates of the proportion of the labor force engaged in informal employment are in
     the region of 35 per cent (International Labor Organization 1998).

12. In 1998 an unemployed worker, on average, received $300 for a full unemployment spell,
     which had a median duration of approximately four months (World Bank 2001, Ch. 4).
     In 2001 the Chilean Congress approved a new system of unemployment insurance, based
     on unemployment savings accounts, which is expected to widen the population of
     covered workers.

13. Some evidence that the problem of low educational attainment is principally one of drop-
     ping out of school can be seen in Panel B of Table 8.3. For the lowest-income group the
     'some primary' rate is 97.7 per cent; however, the completion rate for primary study is 71.9
     per cent. Thus, although virtually all in this cohort had access to primary schooling, some
     26 per cent departed before completion of study. Nor is this a recent development.
     Calculations from CASEN 2000 for the 35–39 age cohort show a similar pattern: a
     primary school enrollment rate of 97.4 per cent for the lowest quintile and a completion
     rate of 61.6 per cent. The enrollment rate in secondary school is lower and we do not know
     the extent to which this reflects access problems versus parental financial constraints, but,
     again, there is evidence of a significant dropout subsequent to beginning study.

14. A measure of occupational status developed by Ganzeboom et al. (1992).

15. The missing data indicator for father's occupational status includes armed forces service,
     a heterogeneous category with respect to military rank.

16. This treatment of missing data does not correct for bias any more than would the inser-
     tion of variable means or listwise deletion of observations unless the data are missing
     completely at random (MCAR). But it does permit the retention of observations with
     missing data and the indicator term provides information on the likely direction of the
     bias.

17. Parental wealth was measured by a subjective rating based on the following question:
     'Compare your household when you were age 14 with all Chilean households at that
     time. On a scale of 1 to 10, where 1 is the poorest and 10 the wealthiest, where would you
     place your household?'. Two analyses were carried out with different codings of this
     variable:
     (a)   We treated the ordinal scale values as measures of ln(parental wealth), thereby
     assuming that respondents replied in terms of percentage changes. This reflects the view
     that an additional $50000 has a quite different meaning to a household worth $10000
     than to one worth $500000.
     (b)   We averaged ratings from five Chileans as to the peso cutting points they would
     assign to the 10 categories, then used the midpoints as category values. (This is the for-
     mulation reported in the text tables.) If the latter estimates are logged, they yield the
     range 0 to 7.20, with a mean of 2.95 and a standard deviation of 1.36. In comparison,
     the 10-category scale, recoded as 0 to 9, has a mean of 3.10 and a standard deviation of
     1.76. In short, the two formulations are quite similar and the regression estimates from
     using the 10-point scale, considered as log values, are very close to the ones reported in
     the text.

18. An alternate calculation, based on change in unlogged parental wealth, suggests that a one-standard deviation increase translates into 1.7 additional years of schooling, with the variables evaluated at their means. As noted, because of the skewed nature of the wealth distribution the log(wealth) metric provides the more conservative estimate, and it is the one reported in the text.
19. This omission can also be expected to bias upward the coefficients of wife's father's education and occupation. However, the size of this bias can be estimated by comparing the relative effect on these coefficients, and on the corresponding terms for husband's father, from the introduction of the wealth variable for husband's parents. Calculated in this way, the bias is about 15 per cent.
20. An alternative choice of occupation, available in the data set, is 'first occupation after completion of schooling'. Since the rate of job changing is highest in the early years of the work career, first occupation is expected to be a poor indicator of long-term occupational affiliation, and we used, instead, the reported measure. In point of fact, the results are not sensitive to whether first occupation, occupation six years ago, or current occupation is used as a regressor.

REFERENCES

Ackerman, B., and A. Alstott (1999), *The Stakeholder Society*, New Haven, CT: Yale University Press.

Altimir, O. (1998), 'Inequality, employment and welfare in Latin America: challenges and opportunities', in V. Tokman and G. O'Donnell (eds), *Poverty and Inequality in Latin America*, Notre Dame, IN: University of Notre Dame Press, pp. 3–35.

Aninat, E. (2000), 'Economic growth, social equity, and globalisation: the Chilean case', in A. Solimano, E. Aninat and N. Birdsall (eds), *Distributive Justice and Economic Development. The Case of Chile and Developing Countries*, Ann Arbor, MI: University of Michigan Press, pp. 119–26.

Attansio, O., and M. Szekely (1999), 'An asset-based approach to the analysis of poverty in Latin America', IADB working paper R-376, Washington, DC: Inter-American Development Bank.

Attansio, O., and M. Szekely (2001), *Portrait of the Poor. An Assets-Based Approach*, Washington, DC: Inter-American Development Bank.

Axinn, W., G. Duncan and A. Thornton (1997), 'The effects of parents' income, wealth and attitudes on children's completed schooling and self-esteem', in G. Duncan and J. Brooks-Gunn (eds), *Consequences of Growing Up Poor*, New York: Russell Sage, pp. 518–40.

Aylwin, M., C. Bascunan, S. Correa, C. Gazmuri, S. Serrano and M. Tagle (1983), *Chile en el Siglo XX* (Chile in the Twentieth Century), Santiago: Emission.

Becker, G. (1991), *A Treatise on the Family*, Cambridge, MA: Harvard University Press.

Beyer, H. (2000), 'Educacion y desigualdad de ingreso: una nueva mirada' (Education and income inequality: a new approach), *Estudios Publicos*, **77**, Santiago: Centro de Estudios Publicos.

Birdsall, N., C. Graham and R. Sabot (1998), *Beyond Tradeoffs. Market Reforms and Equitable Growth in Latin America*, Washington, DC: IADB/Brookings Institution Press.

Birdsall, N., and J.L. Londono (1997), 'Asset inequality does matter: lessons from Latin America', working paper, Washington, DC: Inter-American Development Bank.

Blau, F., and J. Graham (1990), 'Black–white differences in wealth and asset composition', *Quarterly Journal of Economics*, **105**, 321–40.

Blau, P., and O.D. Duncan (1967), *The American Occupational Structure*, New York: John Wiley & Sons.

Bravo, D., and D. Contreras (1999), *La Distribution del Ingreso en Chile 1990–1996: Analisis del Impacto del Mercado del Trabajo y las Politicas Sociales* (Income Distribution in Chile 1990–1996: Analysis of the Impact of the Labor Market and Social Policies), Santiago: Department of Economics, Universidad de Chile.

Bravo, D., D. Contreras and C. Sanhuenza (1999), *Rendimiento Educacional, Desigualdad y Brecha de Desempeno Privado/Publico: Chile 1982–1997* (Educational Performance, Inequality and the Private/Public Gap: Chile 1982–1997), Santiago: Department of Economics, Universidad de Chile.

Central Bank of Chile (2002), *Indicadores Economicos*, accessed at: www.bcentral.cl/indicadores/indicadores.htm.

Cohen, G.A. (1993), 'Equality of what? On welfare, goods and capabilities', in M. Nussbaum and A. Sen (eds), *The Quality of Life*, Oxford: Clarendon Press, pp.9–29.

Contreras, D., and O. Larranaga (1999), 'Los Activos y Recursos de la Poblacion Pobre en America Latina: El Caso de Chile' (Assets and resources of the poor in Latin America: the Chilean case), IADB working paper R-358, Washington, DC: Inter-American Development Bank.

Cowan, K., and J. de Gregorio (2000), 'Distribution and poverty in Chile today: have we gained or lost ground?', in A. Solimano, E. Aninat and N. Birdsall (eds), *Distributive Justice and Economic Development. The Case of Chile and Developing Countries*, Ann Arbor, MI: University of Michigan Press, pp. 127–54.

Cox, C., and M.J. Lemaitre (1999), 'Market and state principles of reform in Chilean education: policies and results', in G. Perry and D. Leipzinger (eds), *Chile: Recent Policy Lessons and Emerging Challenges*, Washington, DC: World Bank, pp. 149–88.

De Soto, H. (2000), *The Mystery of Capital*, New York: Basic Books.

Duncan, O.D., D. Featherman and B. Duncan (1972), *Socioeconomic Background and Achievement*, New York: Seminar Press.

ECLAC (2001), *Panorama Social de America Latina 2000–2001* (Social Panorama of Latin America), Santiago: ECLAC.

Edin, K. (2001), 'More than money: the role of assets in the survival strategies and material well-being of the poor', in T. Shapiro and E. Wolff (eds), *Assets for the Poor*, New York: Russell Sage, pp. 206–31.

Friedman, M. (1962), *Capitalism and Freedom*, Chicago: University of Chicago Press.

Gallart, M.A. (1998), 'Restructuring, education and training', in V. Tokman and G. O'Donnell (eds), *Poverty and Inequality in Latin America*, Notre Dame, IN: University of Notre Dame Press, pp. 91–118.

Ganzeboom, H., P. de Graaf and D. Treiman (1992), 'A standard international socio-economic index of occupational status', *Social Science Research*, **21**, 1–56.

Gazmuri, C. (2000), *Eduardo Frei Montalva y su Epoca* (Eduardo Frei Montalva and his Epoch), Vol. II, Santiago: Aguilar.

Graham, C. (1998), *Private Markets for Public Goods*, Washington, DC: Brookings Institution Press.

Holtz-Eakin, D., and T. Smeeding (1994), 'Income, wealth and intergenerational economic relations of the aged', in L.G. Martin and S.H. Prestion (eds), *Demography of Aging*, Washington, DC: National Academy Press, pp. 102–45.

Inhaber, H., and S. Carroll (1992), *How Rich is Too Rich?*, New York: Praeger.

International Labour Organization (1998), *Chile, Crecimiento, Empleo y el Desafío de la Justicia Social* (Chile: Growth, Employment and the Challenge of Social Justice), Santiago: OIT.

Katzman, R., L. Beccaria, F. Filgueira, L. Golbert and G. Kessler (1999), 'Vulnerabilidad, Activos y Exclusion Social en Argentina y Uruguay (Vulnerability, Assets and Social Exclusion in Argentina and Uruguay), working document 107, Santiago: ILO/Ford Foundation.

Kotlikoff, L.J., and L.H. Summers (1981), 'The role of intergenerational transfers in aggregate capital accumulation', *Journal of Political Economy*, **89**, 706–32.

Kotlikoff, L.J., and L.H. Summers (1988), 'The contribution of intergenerational transfers to total wealth: a reply', in D. Kessler and A. Mason (eds), *Modelling the Accumulation and Distribution of Wealth*, Oxford: Clarendon Press, pp. 53–67.

Larranaga, O., and D. Raczinski (1995), 'Caracteristicas y determinantes la pobreza y la distribucion de ingresos en Chile' (Characteristics and determinants of poverty and income distribution in Chile: diagnostics and policy lessons), unpublished manuscript, Santiago: ILADES-CIEPLAN.

Marquez, G. (2001), 'Social protection in the unemployed: programs in Latin America', in N. Lustig (ed), *Shielding the Poor: Social Protection in the Developing World*, Washington, DC: Brookings Institution Press/IADB, pp. 41–62.

McGarry, K., and R. Schoeni (1995), 'Transfer behavior in the health and retirement study', *Journal of Human Resources* (supplement), **30**, S184–225.

Medlin, C.A. (1996), *Applying Economic Logic to Education Finance: Chile's Experiment with the Per-Student Subsidy*, Santiago: ECLAC.

Mena, I., and C. Bellei (1998), 'El desafío de la calidad y la equidad en educacion' (The Challenge of Quality and Equality in Education), in C. Toloza and E. Lahera (eds), *Chile en los Noventa* (Chile in the Nineties), Santiago: Dolmen, pp. 353–403.

Mesa-Lago, C. (2001), 'Social assistance on pensions and health care for the poor in Latin America and the Caribbean', in N. Lustig (ed.), *Shielding the Poor: Social Protection in the Developing World*, Washington, DC: Brookings Institution Press/IADB, pp. 175–216.

Mezzera, J. (1993), *Credito Informal: Acceso al Sistema Financiero* (Informal Credit: Access to the Financial System), Geneva: Regional Employment Program for Latin America and the Caribbean, International Labour Organization.

Ministry of Education, Chile (1999), *Compendio de Informacion Estadistica* (Yearbook of Statistical Information), Santiago: DIPLAP-MINEDUC.

Ministry of Planning, Chile (2001a), *Pobreza e Indigencia e Impacto del Gasto Social en la Calidad de Vida. Informe Ejecutivo* (Poverty, Indigence and the Impact of Social Spending on Life Quality. Executive Report), Santiago: Mideplan.

Ministry of Planning, Chile (2001b), *Impacto Distributivo del Gasto Social 2000. Informe Ejecutivo* (Redistributive Impact of Social Spending 2000. Executive Report), Santiago: Mideplan.

Ministry of Planning, Chile (2002a), *Series Encuesta CASEN. Cuadros Estadisticos 1998* (CASEN Survey Series. Statistical Tables 1998), accessed at: http://www.mideplan.cl/casen3/index.html.

Ministry of Planning, Chile (2002b), *Educacion Encuesta CASEN. Cuadros*

Estadisticos 1998 (Education in the CASEN Survey. Statistical Tables 1998), accessed at: http://www.mideplan.cl/casen3/index.html.

Mizala, A., and P. Romaguera (1998), *Desempeno y Eleccion de Colegios* (Performance and school selection) working paper no. 39, economics series, Santiago: Department of Industrial Engineering, Universidad de Chile.

Modigliani, F. (1998), 'Measuring the contribution of intergenerational transfers to total wealth', in D. Kessler and A. Masson (eds), *Modelling the Accumulation and Distribution of Wealth*, Oxford: Clarendon, pp. 21–52.

Moser, C. (1998), 'The asset vulnerability framework: reassessing urban poverty reduction strategies', *World Development*, **26** (1), 1–19.

National Institute of Statistics, Chile (1998), *Anuario de Demografia* (Demographic Yearbook), Santiago: INE.

Oliver, M.L., and T.M. Shapiro (1995), *Black Wealth/White Wealth: A New Perspective on Racial Inequality*, New York: Routledge.

Rawls, J. (1999), *A Theory of Justice*, Cambridge, MA: Harvard University Press.

Sen, A. (1987), *The Standard of Living*, Cambridge: Cambridge University Press.

Sen, A. (1992), *Inequality Reexamined*, Cambridge, MA: Harvard University Press.

Sen, A. (1993), 'Capability and well-being', in M. Nussbaum and A. Sen (eds), *The Quality of Life*, Oxford: Clarendon Press, pp. 30–53.

Shapiro, T. (2001), 'The importance of assets', in T. Shapiro and E. Wolff (eds), *Assets for the Poor*, New York: Russell Sage, pp. 11–33.

Sherraden, M. (1991), *Assets and the Poor*, Armonk, NY: M.E. Sharpe.

Sherraden, M. (2001), 'Asset-building policy and programs for the poor', in T. Shapiro and E. Wolff (eds), *Assets for the Poor*, New York: Russell Sage, pp.302–23.

Solimano, A. (2000), 'Beyond unequal development: an overview', in A. Solimano, E. Aninat and N. Birdsall (eds), *Distributive Justice and Economic Development. The Case of Chile and Developing Countries*, Ann Arbor, MI: University of Michigan Press, pp. 17–36.

Spilerman, S. (2000), 'Wealth and stratification processes', *Annual Review of Sociology*, **26**, 497–524.

Spilerman, S. (2004), 'Young couples in Israel: the impact of parental wealth on early living standards', *American Journal of Sociology,* **110** (1).

Stallings, B., N. Birdsall and J. Clugage (2000), 'Growth and equality: do regional patterns redeem Kutznets?', in A. Solimano, E. Aninat and N. Birdsall (eds), *Distributive Justice and Economic Development. The Case of Chile and Developing Countries*, Ann Arbor, MI: University of Michigan Press, pp. 98–118.

UNESCO (1999), *Statistical Yearbook 1999*, Paris: United Nations Educational, Scientific and Cultural Organization.

Wolff, E. (1995), 'The rich get increasingly richer: latest data on household wealth during the 1980s', in *Research in Politics and Society*, **5**, Greenwich, CT: JAI Press, pp. 33–68.

Wolff, E. (2001), 'Recent trends in wealth ownership from 1983 to 1998', in T. Shapiro and E. Wolff (eds), *Assets for the Poor*, New York: Russell Sage, pp.34–73.

World Bank (2001), 'Chile poverty and income distribution in a high growth economy', documents of the World Bank, Poverty Reduction and Economic Management Sector Unit, Latin America and the Caribbean Region.

*Appendix Table 8A.1   Descriptive statistics for variables in the analysis,
Social Mobility Survey, 2001*

Variable	Mean	Standard dev.	N
Husband's parents:			
Father's education(*m*)[1]	0.21	0.41	3544
Father's education	6.76	4.79	2811
Father's occupation(*m*)[1]	0.11	0.31	3544
Father's occupation[2]	31.40	13.03	3157
Parental wealth (ln)	2.95	1.36	3504
Wife's parents:			
Father's education(*m*)[1]	0.41	49	3544
Father's education	6.70	4.75	2080
Father's occupation(*m*)[1]	0.27	0.45	3544
Father's occupation[2]	31.17	13.67	2575
Respondent:			
Number of siblings	4.44	3.03	3539
Age	46.52	11.77	3543
Married/cohab. vs. single	0.88	0.32	3542
Cohabitating vs. married	0.11	0.31	3544
No. family members employed	1.59	0.76	3470
Years of schooling	9.83	4.43	3528
Attended public school[3]	0.79	0.41	3484
Attended semi-priv. school[3]	0.12	0.33	3484
Attended private school[3]	0.09	0.28	3484
Occupation status, 1995(*m*)[1]	0.11	0.32	3544
Occupation status, 1995[2]	36.82	14.47	3144
Occupation status, 2001[2]	36.93	14.34	3490
Earnings (ln)	5.30	0.87	2991
Household income (ln)	5.47	0.91	3348
Household wealth (ln)	3.33	1.15	3522

Notes:
1. Proportion of sample with missing data.
2. ISEI status score (Ganzeboom et al. 1992).
3. Institutional type of last school attended.

Appendix Table 8A.2   *Comparison of the 2001 Social Mobility Survey with the year 2000 Chilean National Household Survey (percentage distributions)*[1]

	2001 SMS[2]	2000 CASEN[3]
Gender:		
Male	100.0	62.9
Female	–	37.1
Area of residence:		
Santiago	41.2	44.1
Rest of country	58.8	45.9
Education:		
0–4 years of schooling	15.2	8.9
5–6	13.7	8.9
7–8	13.8	12.6
9–11	17.9	16.1
12	19.1	27.9
13–16	12.0	15.9
17+	8.0	9.7
Age:		
15–23	–	11.9
24–34	18.5	29.8
35–45	29.7	30.4
46–56	28.9	18.5
57–69	22.9	8.1
70+	–	1.3
Occupation:		
Armed forces	1.3	0.5
Legislators, senior officials & managers	5.8	6.1
Professionals	7.1	9.0
Technicians and associated professions	7.0	7.6
Clerks	5.4	9.3
Service and shop/market sales workers	8.3	14.7
Skilled agricultural & fishery workers	2.4	6.0
Craft & related trades workers	27.7	15.0
Plant & machine operators/assemblers	16.0	9.0
Elementary occupations	18.8	22.5
Earnings (pesos/month)		
Less than 120 000	32.2	37.5
120 000–210 000	29.5	27.2
210 000–390 000	19.9	18.8
390 000–1 000 000	16.9	12.2
More than 1 000 000	2.5	4.3
N	3544	182 885

Notes:
1. CASEN (Encuesta de Caracterizacion Socioeconomica Nacional) is a national household survey, conducted every two years by the Chilean Ministry of Planning. The year 2000 version contains 252 748 cases.
2. Percentages weighted to correct for stratification. Representation differences from CASEN are due to the sampling design: the SMS survey was restricted to male heads of household in the age range 24–69.
3. CASEN data refer to the economically active population aged 15 and older.

PART IV

Other Dimensions in Measuring Well-being

9. Historical perspective on the standard of living using anthropometric data

Richard H. Steckel

INTRODUCTION

Long-standing scholarly attempts to define and measure the standard of living eventually led to the national income and product accounts of the twentieth century. Although economists recognize the great achievements of the accounts, research momentum has shifted to alternatives or supplements that address shortcomings in GDP as a welfare measure or indicate living standards in time periods or among groups for which conventional measures cannot be calculated. Stature is an example now used extensively in the fields of economic history and economic development.

Readers unfamiliar with anthropometric history should not be side-tracked by genetic issues. Genes are important determinants of individual heights, but genetic differences approximately cancel in comparisons of averages across most populations, and in these situations height accurately reflects health status.

Many studies show that measures of health are positively correlated with income or wealth. Less well known are the relationship between stature and conventional measures, such as per capita income, and the ways that stature addresses certain conceptual inadequacies in gross national product as a measure of human welfare. Stature adeptly measures inequality in the form of nutritional deprivation; average height in the past century is sensitive not only to the level of income but also to the distribution of income and the consumption of basic necessities by the poor. Unlike conventional measures of living standards based on output, stature is a measure of consumption that incorporates or adjusts for individual nutritional needs; it is a net measure that captures not only the supply of inputs to health but demands on those inputs. Moreover, heights are available in settings, such as eighteenth-century America, where income data are lacking (or of low quality), and for groups, such as slaves, for which income or wage concepts do not apply. Because growth occurs largely in childhood, stature also provides valuable insights into resource allocation within the family, an interesting phenomenon obscured from household-level data on income or earnings, much less aggregate statistics on output or inequality.

After a brief review of the evolution of the field and its methodology, this chapter considers long-term trends in average height in the United States. The height of Americans has fallen behind those of several European countries in the late twentieth century, and I suggest a research agenda for exploring the causes of the shortfall.

EVOLUTION OF THE FIELD

A distinguished intellectual tradition of height studies existed prior to the mid-1970s, but the research was conducted mainly by human biologists or physical anthropologists, and its contributors largely ignored questions of interests to economics, history, and other social sciences. The 1970s witnessed a revival of interest in social accounting, created by moderation of business cycles and high rates of economic growth accompanied by urban sprawl, pollution, congestion, and crime. In this vein the United Nations created the human development index, which weighs life expectancy, literacy, and income; subsequent refinements incorporated a broader definition of education and adjustments for both gender discrimination and the income distribution. Thus, interest in stature was boosted by disaffection with national income accounting and a return to the debate over measures of human welfare.

The fortunes of anthropometric research in the formative period depended heavily on engaging debates of interest to historians and economists, and its success hinged on novel and credible results (Steckel 1998, pp. 803–21). The four areas of important applications were slavery, the standard of living during industrialization, inequality, and mortality. Slavery was the most contentious, at least in the United States. Heights recorded on slave manifests added much to the understanding over demography and quality of life. Scholars have long debated the quality of life during industrialization, and despite considerable effort using traditional sources such as per capita income and real wages, they have failed to reach anything approaching a consensus. Despite great interest, measures of inequality are often difficult to acquire and when available they often pose problems of interpretation. Height data did not resolve the problems of measuring inequality in historical settings; they merely added new, useful information. Anthropometrics also clarified explanations for the substantial long-term improvement in life expectancy that began in Europe after the middle of the nineteenth century.

METHODS AND SOURCES

Modern studies establish that two periods of intense activity characterize the growth process following birth (Tanner 1978; Eveleth and Tanner [1976] 1990). Figure 9.1, which is based on height data from the National Health and Nutrition Examination Survey (Kuczmarski et al. 2000), shows that the increase in height, or velocity, is greatest during infancy, falls sharply and then declines irregularly into the pre-adolescent years. During adolescence, velocity rises sharply to a peak that equals approximately one-half of the velocity during infancy, then declines rapidly and reaches zero at maturity. The adolescent growth spurt begins about two years earlier in girls than in boys and during their spurt girls temporarily overtake boys in average height. As adults, males are taller than females primarily because they have approximately two additional years of growth prior to adolescence.

Although genes are important determinants of individual height, studies of genetically similar and dissimilar populations under various environmental conditions suggest that differences in average height across most populations are largely attributable to environmental factors. Important for interpreting stature in the United States is the fact that Europeans and

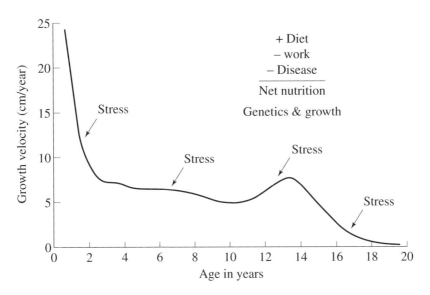

Source: Calculated from NHANES data discussed in Kuczmarski et al. (2000).

Figure 9.1   Growth velocity of boys under good environmental conditions

people of European descent, and Africans and people of African descent who grew under good nutritional circumstances have nearly identical stature (Eveleth and Tanner [1976] 1990, appendix).

Average height at a particular age reflects a population's history of net nutrition, or diet minus claims on the diet made by work (or physical activity) and disease. Metabolic requirements for basic functions such as breathing and blood circulation while at rest also make claims on the diet. The synergy between malnutrition and illness may further reduce the nutrition left over for growth. Poorly nourished children are more susceptible to infection, which reduces the body's absorption of nutrients. The interaction implies that analyses of stature must recognize not only inputs to health such as diet and medical care, but also work effort and related phenomena such as methods of labor organization. Similarly, it is important to realize that exposure to infectious disease may place claims on the diet. Toxins or environmental poisons can also stunt growth. It is well known, for example, that modest amounts of alcohol or tobacco ingested by the mother during pregnancy can retard growth *in utero*, from which it is difficult or impossible to recover, even if good net nutritional conditions return.

The sensitivity of growth to deprivation or biological stress depends upon the age at which it occurs. For a given degree of deprivation, the adverse effects may be proportional to the velocity of growth under optimal conditions (Tanner 1966). Thus, young children and adolescents are particularly susceptible to environmental insults. The return of adequate nutrition following a relatively short period of deprivation may restore normal height through catch-up growth. If conditions are inadequate for catch-up, individuals may still approach normal adult height by an extension of the growing period by as long as several years. Prolonged and severe deprivation results in stunting or a reduction in adult size.

Because GDP per capita is the most widely used indicator of living standards, it is particularly useful to compare and contrast this measure with stature (Steckel 1983). Income is a potent determinant of stature that operates through diet, disease and work intensity, but one must recognize that other factors such as personal hygiene, public health measures and the disease environment affect illness, while work intensity is a function of technology, culture and methods of labor organization. Extremely poor families may spend two-thirds or more of their income on food, but even a large share of their very low incomes purchases inadequate calories. Malnutrition associated with extreme poverty has a major impact on height, but at the other end of the income spectrum, expenditures beyond those needed to satisfy calorie requirements purchase largely variety, palatability and convenience.

At the individual level, extreme poverty results in malnutrition, retarded growth and stunting. Higher incomes enable the parents of growing children to purchase a better diet and height increases correspondingly, but once income is sufficient to satisfy caloric requirements, individuals often consume foods that also satisfy many vitamin and mineral requirements. Height may continue to rise with income because a more complete diet or better housing and medical care are available. As income increases, consumption patterns change to realize a larger share of genetic potential, but environmental variables are powerless after individuals attain the maximum capacity for growth. The limits to this process are clear from the fact that people who grew up in very wealthy families are not physical giants.

While the relationship between height and income is nonlinear at the individual level, the relationship at the aggregate level depends upon the distribution of income. Average height may differ for a given per capita income depending upon the fraction of people with insufficient income to purchase an adequate diet or to afford medical care. Because the gain in height at the individual level increases at a decreasing rate as income rises, one would expect average height at the aggregate level to increase with the degree of equality of the income distribution (assuming there are people who have not reached their genetic growth potential).

Before examining trends in anthropometric data in the United States, it is useful to consider the relationship of average height to two well-known measures of the standard of living. The data given in Figure 9.2, which are based on national height studies in 15 countries from 1963 to 1987, confirm that height is nonlinearly related to per capita GDP as estimated by methods of purchasing power parity.[1] The diagram depicts the height of boys, but the equations below show that a similar pattern applies to girls (*t*-values in parentheses):

Boys aged 12: Height $= 107.61 + 4.48 \ln$ (GDP per capita), $N = 18$, $R^2 = 0.70$
(17.07) (6.18)

Girls aged 12: Height $= 108.00 + 4.66 \ln$ (GDP per capita), $N = 17$, $R^2 = 0.68$
(15.13) (5.65).

Simple correlations between the average height of boys and the log of its per capita GDP are in the range of 0.82 to 0.88 (Steckel 1995). One should be cautious in trying to infer per capita GDP from average height, however, because many other factors can affect the relationship, including the degree of inequality, the technology of public health, food prices and cultural aspects of resource distribution within the family.

Life expectancy is also widely used as a measure of health, but historical information for the United States is limited by the lack of a complete

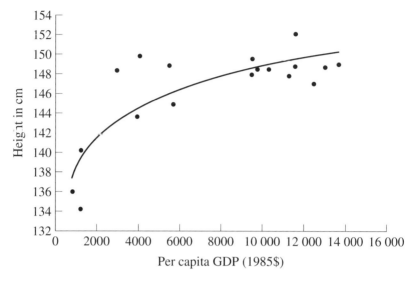

Sources: Calculated from data in Eveleth and Tanner ([1976], 1990) and Summers and
Heston (1991).

Figure 9.2   Per capita GDP and height of boys at age 12

system of death registration until the second quarter of the twentieth
century. Average height is a good proxy for health (particularly for that of
children) that is available as far back as the eighteenth century. The connection between average height and life expectancy can be studied using data
from developing and developed countries in the mid- and late-twentieth
century. Figure 9.3 presents a scatter diagram involving average height of
boys at age 12 and life expectancy at birth for the same countries as depicted
in Figure 9.2 (the countries are listed in note 1). Unlike the relationship of
height and per capita GDP, which was clearly nonlinear, the pattern in
Figure 9.3 is approximately linear, and the average tradeoff may be estimated using linear regression analysis (*t*-values in parentheses):

Boys aged 12: Height $= 106.57 + 0.601$ (Life expectancy), $N = 18$, $R^2 = 0.80$
                         (21.53) (8.09)

Girls aged 12: Height $= 110.99 + 0.521$ (Life expectancy), $N = 17$, $R^2 = 0.84$
                          (26.30) (8.87).

An increase in life expectancy of one year is associated with an increase in
average stature of about 0.56 centimeters.

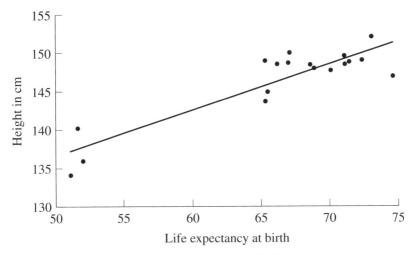

Sources: Calculated from data in Eveleth and Tanner ([1976], 1990) and from World Bank, *World Development Report* (various years).

Figure 9.3   Life expectancy at birth and height of boys at age 12

Figure 9.4 is a useful organizing device for understanding the relationship of height to living standards. Stature is a function of proximate determinants such as diet, disease and work intensity during the growing years, and as such it is a measure of the consumption of basic necessities that incorporates demands placed on one's biological system. Because family income heavily influences purchases of basic necessities such as food and medical care, stature is ultimately a function of access to resources. It is noteworthy that stature recognizes or adjusts for consumption of products (such as alcohol or drugs) that are harmful to health, but excessive consumption of food, while leading to rapid growth, may impair health in later life. Public health measures, personal hygiene and the disease environment affect the incidence of disease that claims nutrition. In addition, human growth may have functional consequences for health, labor productivity, mental development, and personality, which in turn may influence socioeconomic conditions.

TRENDS IN THE STATURE OF NATIVE-BORN AMERICANS

Table 9.1 presents evidence on height trends of adult men in various countries. Military records are the main source up to 1900 and systematic height

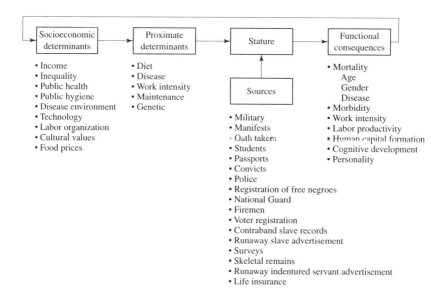

Source: Steckel (1995, p. 1908).

Figure 9.4   Relationships involving stature

studies enter the picture in the twentieth century. The most surprising feature of the table is the tall stature in the United States compared with European countries during the eighteenth and nineteenth centuries. American soldiers who fought in the French and Indian War (1754–63) attained a mean height of about 172 centimeters, or 5 feet 7 inches. In this era, residents from other countries were smaller by several centimeters and the gap persisted until the late nineteenth century and in some cases closed or narrowed only in the twentieth century. A secular increase in stature occurred in many countries in the past century but the data disguise important fluctuations such as the prominent downturns that occurred in some countries in earlier eras (for a discussion of these time trends, see papers in Steckel and Floud 1997).

Although the data of Table 9.1 suggest that stature in America was approximately constant over two centuries, if the heights are arranged by birth cohort, as shown in Figure 9.5, then cycles or fluctuations are a better characterization than is the high plateau evident from the table. Note that the heights are for the native born, so that immigration did not affect the pattern.[2] Heights were approximately constant at 171 to 172 centimeters for those born between 1720 and 1740, which corresponds to roughly the 20th

Table 9.1   Long-term trends in the stature of adult men (cm)

Approximate date	Country						
	US	UK	Sweden	Norway	Netherlands	France	Austria/Hungary
1750	172	165	167	165			166
1800	173	167	166	166		163	163
1850	171	166	168	169	164	167	
1900	171	167	172	171	169	165	
1950	175	175	177	178	178	170	171

Sources: Kiil (1939); Komlos (1989); Floud et al. (1990); Drukker and Tassenaar (1997); Sandberg and Steckel (1997); Weir (1997); Steckel (2002).

to 25th percentile of modern US height standards (Steckel 1996). But those born in the mid-1750s had gained about 1.0 centimeter over their predecessors, reaching about the 30th percentile. The gains of the mid-1700s were followed by a plateau of 172.5 to 173.5 centimeters for birth cohorts of 1780 to 1830. Thereafter heights declined irregularly to a low of approximately 169 centimeters (or the 10th percentile of modern US standards) among births in the late 1800s, an episode followed by the more familiar secular increase of the twentieth century.

Why were Americans so tall relative to Europeans in the mid-1700s? The large differences in stature by social class within Europe before the end of the nineteenth century indicate that the European's climb to modern height standards involved very large gains for the lower and middle classes. Regarding the United Kingdom, for example, Roderick Floud and Bernard Harris (1997) report that the class differences in average height were 10 to 15 centimeters, but they were no larger than one to three centimeters in the United States (Sokoloff and Villaflor 1982; Margo and Steckel 1983). The available evidence points to several possible causes of the American height advantage, including a good diet, infrequent epidemics that were associated with low population density, and widespread access to land and other resources (in other words, relatively low inequality). The abundance of good land in America enabled farmers to choose only the most productive plots for cultivation, resulting in less physical effort (after clearing the land) for a given amount of output, compared with European farmers. In addition, most of the population nestled along the coast between two sources of protein – fish from the Atlantic and game from the forests – and ample land was available to support livestock.

Before considering explanations for the nineteenth-century decline in

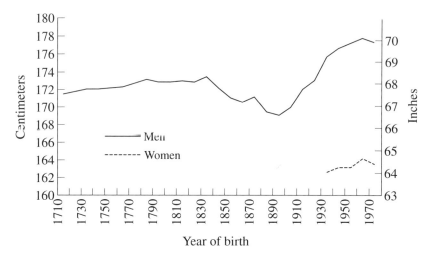

Source: Steckel (2004).

Figure 9.5   Height of native-born American men and women, by year of birth

average heights, it is useful to examine results on real GDP per capita, which are given in Table 9.2. Over the entire period from 1800 to 1970, real per capita GDP grew at an annual rate of 1.62 per cent. While average heights were declining during the heart of the American industrial revolution in the middle of the nineteenth century, the growth rate was even higher than the long-term trend, amounting to 1.91 per cent from 1830 to 1880.

The nineteenth-century height decline has been called the 'antebellum puzzle' (Komlos and Coclanis 1997; Komlos 1998) because the pattern diverges from what is known about the material standard of living. One should recognize, however, that traditional national income accounting measures and average heights focus on different aspects of living standards. The former emphasizes market behavior and various imputations for productive activity while average height reflects net nutrition and the distribution of income or wealth. Thus, a particular type of prosperity accompanied America's industrialization while other aspects of the standard of living deteriorated. *Ceteris paribus*, the measured economic prosperity of the mid-1800s should have increased average stature. The height decline suggests that other things must not have been equal. Specifically, nutritional liabilities (claims on nutrition or lower nutritional intake) that more than offset the advantages bestowed by higher incomes must have accompanied the economic prosperity.

Table 9.2   Real per capita GDP

Year	Per capita GDP (1970 prices)	Year	Per capita GDP (1970 prices)
1800	302	1890	1113
1810	318	1900	1395
1820	326	1910	1747
1830	349	1920	1743
1840	391	1930	2025
1850	430	1940	2370
1860	523	1950	3133
1870	659	1960	3623
1880	909	1970	4774

Sources: Costa and Steckel (1997, Table 2.6), compiled from Weiss (1992, Table 1.3) and US Bureau of the Census (1975).

The height–income relationship was probably weaker in the mid-nineteenth century compared with the modern period. In the absence of the germ theory of disease to guide decision making, those with higher incomes had less accurate information on expenditures that would enhance health. The finding that wealth conveyed little advantage for child survival in the mid-nineteenth century is consistent with this point of view (Steckel 1988). Thus, the beneficial aspects of income growth *per se* for stature may have been small and easily offset by claims on the diet imposed by other factors associated with income growth.

The search for understanding should recognize that most of the height decline occurred in rural areas. The United States urbanized slowly in the decades after 1830 and rural–urban differences in stature were modest. Also implicated in deteriorating health is the greater spread of communicable diseases affiliated with the transportation revolution, growing migration, increased interregional trade, employment in factories and the rise of public schools after 1830. The American population, long protected from exposure to communicable diseases by low population density, may have been especially vulnerable to the byproducts of growing interpersonal contact. Hardships associated with the Civil War no doubt added to the health woes of those born near the middle of the century.

Among additional explanations under study, one emphasizes the sensitivity of average heights to the distribution of income or wealth. Based on a statistical analysis of country-level data on per capita income, inequality and stature, scholars have suggested that growing inequality from 1830 to 1890 might have offset the rise in per capita income and may account for a small decline in average stature. That the height of upper-class men (students at Amherst and Yale, see Murray 1997) rose from 171 to 173 centimeters, while that of the Ohio National Guard declined by several centimeters is consistent with growing inequality in the second half of the nineteenth century (Steckel and Haurin 1994).

Another point of view argues that dietary deterioration influenced the height decline through a sectoral shift in production that occurred during industrialization. According to this position, urbanization and the expansion of the industrial labor force increased the demand for food and simultaneously productivity per worker and the agricultural labor force grew slowly, causing a decline in food production (especially meat) per capita (Komlos 1998).

Numerous explanations can be found for the secular growth in stature that occurred from the late 1800s to the mid-twentieth century. Understanding of the germ theory of disease and the rise of the public health movement in the 1880s, with accompanying investments in purified water supplies, vaccinations, and sewage disposal were crucial for preventing contagious diseases and improving health in the cities. Higher standards of personal hygiene and improved pre- and post-natal care led to better health for children. Economic growth and higher incomes enabled families to purchase better diets and housing. The emergence of antibiotics in the 1930s improved the chances of cures for diseases, while health insurance and public health programs increased the access to modern medicine by the public.

The average height of American men has stagnated, increasing by only a small fraction of an inch over the past half century. Figure 9.5 refers to the native born, so recent increases in immigration cannot account for the stagnation. In the absence of other information, one might be tempted to suppose that environmental conditions for growth are so good that most Americans have simply reached their genetic potential for growth. But data on the height of military conscripts in Europe (Figure 9.6) shows that this is not the case. Heights have continued to grow in Europe, which has the same genetic stock from which many Americans descend. By the 1970s Americans had fallen behind Norway, Sweden, and Denmark, and were on a par with Germany. While the height of Americans was essentially flat after the 1970s, heights continued to grow significantly in Europe. The Dutch are now the tallest, averaging six feet, about two inches more than American men.

Note that significant differences in health and the quality of life follow from these height patterns. The comparisons are not part of an odd contest that emphasizes height, nor is big *per se* assumed to be beautiful. Instead, we know that on average, stunted growth has functional implications for longevity, cognitive development and work capacity. Children

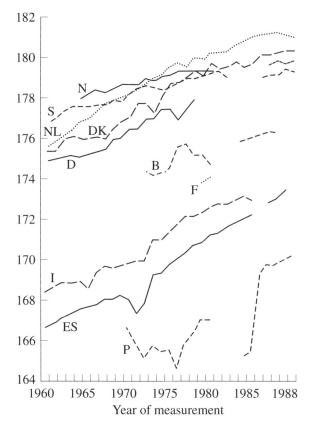

B = Belgium; DK = Denmark; F = France; D = Germany; I = Italy;
NL = Netherlands; N = Norway; P = Portugal; ES = Spain; S = Sweden

Source: Schmidt et al. (1995)

Figure 9.6   Height of military conscripts in Europe

who fail to grow adequately are often sick, suffer learning impairments
and have a lower quality of life. Growth failure in childhood has a long
reach into adulthood because individuals whose growth has been stunted
are at greater risk of death from heart disease, diabetes and some types of
cancer. Therefore it is important to know why Americans are falling
behind.

It is unlikely that the lagging height of Americans stems from low
resource commitments to health care. Figure 9.7 (Steckel 2004 and sources
therein) places American expenditures on medical care as a share of GDP

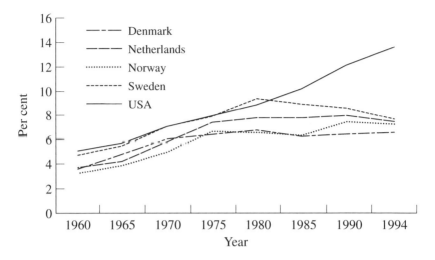

Source: Steckel (2004).

Figure 9.7   Health-care expenditure as a percentage of GDP, by country

in comparative international perspective. The figure shows that substantial growth occurred in the past several decades. In 1960 American medical expenditures as a share of GDP were about 5 per cent, only slightly above the share in Western European countries that have relatively good health such as Denmark, Norway, Sweden, and the Netherlands.[3] Between 1960 and the mid-1970s, the share rose in all these countries to the range of 6 to 8 per cent. But unlike the others, the resources devoted to medical care in the United States continued rising and in 1995 absorbed 13.5 per cent of GDP, nearly twice that of the other countries shown in Figure 9.7. Thus, it is appropriate to ask whether medical resources are being efficiently and effectively allocated in the United States.

Given the sensitivity of average height to inequality, one may suspect that basic needs are not being met for some growing children. Insurance coverage is effectively universal in northern Europe, but somewhat more that 40 million Americans lack coverage. Moreover, Figure 9.8 indicates that the share with coverage has been declining since the late 1980s. Of course, 'coverage' has many aspects, including deductibles or co-pays, out-of-pocket limits, procedures that are included, waiting times for treatment, the quality of care once it is obtained and so forth. Some people who lack insurance pay directly for their medical care, and some with insurance are not particularly effective in using it to improve their health. Generalizations are fraught with difficulties, but it seems reasonable to believe that less

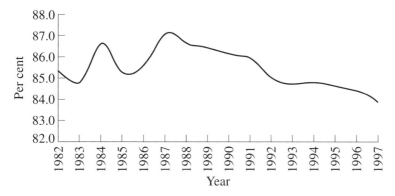

Source: Steckel (2004) and sources therein.

Figure 9.8 Percentage of US population covered by health insurance

access or use of medical care could be a factor in growth failure in the United States. In particular, the percentage of blacks and Hispanics covered by medical insurance is several points below that of whites. Therefore, biological inequality may be reducing average height in the United States relative to northern European countries.

Health insurance coverage is not the end of the story, however. Success requires knowledge and motivation to use coverage wisely, whereby early detection of disease limits physiological damage and the ensuing expense of more extensive treatment. Moreover, life-style choices that prevent disease are growing in importance for health in our contemporary world, where public health measures have substantially reduced contagious diseases such as whooping cough, diphtheria and scarlet fever, which seriously afflicted health prior to the mid-twentieth century. Personal decisions regarding smoking, alcohol consumption, use of drugs, practice of safe sex, and extent of exercise are interwined with education and peer pressure in ways that increasingly affect health via pathways that are beyond the reach of health insurance or traditional public health measures. The social sciences may have much to offer on these problems.

RESEARCH AND POLICY NEEDS

The new anthropometric history has reached the quarter-century mark with publication of several books and over 50 articles. Yet, ample research opportunities exist. Abundant data are available from military records and other sources to document historical patterns of height. Often, some socioeconomic variables are also available for analysis of historical height patterns. While very few measurements were taken before the eighteenth century, when height was widely used for identification purposes, the time frame can be extended backward for several millennia by using skeletal remains. Much cross-section height data are available for comparative research in the modern period, including the National Health and Nutrition Examination Surveys in the United States and the conscript muster rolls in Europe. An analysis of these sources at small geographic levels of analysis such as states, counties or provinces would be a good way to explore possible causes of the height differences that have emerged between the United States and Europe.

In the area of methodology, much more work is needed on the functional implications of stature. This measure will be understood by social scientists only after its relationship has been thoroughly mapped to more familiar measures. Some work has been done on height and income, and height and longevity, but research opportunities exist on height as a predictor or explanatory factor in health quality of life while living, educational attainment, and social and economic mobility. Progress in this area will require longitudinal data, which are often difficult to obtain.

Given the huge literature on poverty and inequality, it is encouraging to see interest expand in using height to monitor living standards, to investigate inequality and to evaluate social policy. A UNICEF project recently used anthropometric data to express detailed baseline measurements of child malnutrition against which progress can be measured. An ongoing children's growth surveillance program (National Study of Health and Growth) for this purpose has existed in England since 1972, but few systematic efforts are in place in industrialized countries (Rona 1989). Even in wealthy societies disadvantaged groups lack insurance coverage or are exposed to fluctuations in socioeconomic circumstances that affects health, which creates a need for assessing nutritional status. Such a program has a sound methodological base, and I expect would be sensible given the ease of collecting anthropometric data. The chapter calls for study of the costs and benefits of incorporating measures of the biological quality of life into our social accounting apparatus.

NOTES

1.   The height data are from Eveleth and Tanner ([1976] 1990), and the GDP data are from Summers and Heston (1991). The countries are Argentina, Australia, Belgium, Czechoslovakia (2 studies), Denmark, Egypt, Hungary, India, Italy, Japan (2 studies), the Netherlands (2 studies), New Zealand, South Korea, United States, and West Germany.

2. At least, there were no direct effects. Immigrants were shorter than the native born, and since small mothers are more likely to have small children, it is likely that there were some intergenerational effects of immigration on average height. Because net nutrition was good in the United States, these effects were likely to have been small. Intercontinental migration also helped to churn the disease environment, which could have diminished the growth of the native born.
3. Life expectancy at birth in each of these countries exceeds that in the United States.

REFERENCES

Blöndal, S., and M. Pearson (1995), 'Unemployment and other non-employment benefits', *Oxford Review of Economic Policy* **11** (1), 136–69.

Costa, Dora L., and Richard H. Steckel (1997), 'Long-term trends in health, welfare, and economic growth in the United States', in Richard H. Steckel and Roderick Floud (eds), *Health and Welfare during Industrialization*, Chicago: University of Chicago Press, pp. 47–89.

Davenport, H.W. (1981), 'Signs of anxiety, rage or distress', *The Physiologist*, **25** (5).

Drukker, J.W., and Vincent Tassenaar (1997), 'Paradoxes of modernization and material well-being in the Netherlands during the nineteenth century', in Richard H. Steckel and Roderick Floud (eds), *Health and Welfare during Industrialization*, Chicago: University of Chicago Press, pp. 331–77.

Eveleth, Phyllis B., and J.M. Tanner (1976), *Worldwide Variation in Human Growth*, 2nd edn (1980), Cambridge: Cambridge University Press.

Floud, Roderick, and Bernard Harris (1997), 'Health, height, and welfare: Britain, 1700–1980', in Richard H. Steckel and Roderick Floud (eds), *Health and Welfare during Industrialization*, Chicago: University of Chicago Press, pp. 91–126.

Floud, Roderick, Kenneth W. Wachter and Anabel S. Gregory (1990), *Height, Health, and History: Nutritional Status in the United Kingdom, 1750–1980*, Cambridge: Cambridge University Press.

Kiil, Vilhelm (1939), *Stature and Growth of Norwegian Men During the Past Two Hundred Years*, Oslo: I Kommision hos Jacob Dybwad.

Komlos, John (1989), *Nutrition and Economic Development in the Eighteenth-Century Habsburg Monarchy*, Princeton, NJ: Princeton University Press.

Komlos, John (1998), 'Shrinking in a growing economy? The mystery of physical stature during the industrial revolution', *Journal of Economic History*, **58**, 779–802.

Komlos, John, and Peter Coclanis (1997), 'On the puzzling cycle in the biological standard of living: the case of antebellum Georgia', *Explorations in Economic History*, **34**, 433–59.

Kuczmarski, Robert J., Cynthia L. Ogden, Lawrence M. Grummer-Strawn, Katherine M. Flegal, Shumei S. Guo, Rong Wei, Zugo Mei, Lester R. Curtin, Alex F. Roche and Clifford L. Johnson (2000), 'CDC growth charts: United States', advance data from *Vital and Health Statistics*, **314**, 1–28.

Margo, Robert A., and Richard H. Steckel (1983), 'Heights of native-born whites during the antebellum period', *Journal of Economic History*, **43**, 167–74.

Murray, John E. (1997), 'Standards of the present for people of the past: height, weight, and mortality among men of Amherst College, 1834–1949', *Journal of Economic History*, **57**, 585–606.

Rona, R.J. (1989), 'A surveillance system of growth in Britain', in James Tanner (ed.), *Auxology 88: Perspectives in the Sciences of Growth and Development*, London: Smith-Gordon, pp. 111–19.

Sandberg, Lars G., and Richard H. Steckel (1997), 'Was industrialization hazardous to your health? Not in Sweden!', in Richard H. Steckel and Roderick Floud (eds), *Health and Welfare during Industrialization*, Chicago: University of Chicago Press, pp. 127–59.

Schmidt, I.M., M.H. Jorgensen and K.F. Michaelsen (1995), 'Heights of conscripts in Europe: is postneonatal mortality a predictor?', *Annals of Human Biology*, **22**, 57–67.

Sokoloff, Kenneth L., and Georgia C. Villaflor (1982), 'The early achievement of modern stature in America', *Social Science History*, **6**, 453–81.

Steckel, Richard H. (1983), 'Height and per capita income', *Historical Methods*, **16**, 1–7.

Steckel, Richard H. (1988), 'The health and mortality of women and children, 1850–1860', *Journal of Economic History*, **48**, 333–45.

Steckel, Richard H. (1995), 'Stature and the standard of living', *Journal of Economic Literature*, **33**, 1903–40.

Steckel, Richard H. (1996), 'Percentiles of modern height standards for use in historical research', *Historical Methods*, **29**, 157–66.

Steckel, Richard H. (1998), 'Strategic ideas in the rise of the new anthropometric history and their implications for interdisciplinary research', *Journal of Economic History*, **58**, 803–21.

Steckel, Richard H. (2004), 'Health, nutrition and physical well-being', in Susan Carter, Scott Gartner, Michael Haines, Alan Olmstead, Richard Sutch and Gavin Wright (eds), *Historical Statistics of the United States: Millennial Edition*, New York: Cambridge University Press.

Steckel, Richard H., and Roderick Floud (eds) (1997), *Health and Welfare during Industrialization*, Chicago: University of Chicago Press.

Steckel, Richard H., and Donald R. Haurin (1994), 'Health and nutrition in the American midwest: evidence from the height of Ohio national guardsmen, 1850–1910', in John Komlos (ed.), *Stature, Living Standards, and Economic Development*, Chicago: University of Chicago Press, pp. 117–28.

Summers, Robert, and Alan Heston (1991), 'The Penn World Table (Mark 5): an expanded set of international comparisons, 1950–1988', *Quarterly Journal of Economics,* **106**, 327–68.

Tanner, J.M. (1966), 'Growth and physique in different populations of mankind', in Paul T. Baker and J.S. Weiner (eds), *The Biology of Human Adaptability*, Oxford: Oxford University Press, pp. 45–66.

Tanner, J.M. (1978), *Fetus into Man: Physical Growth from Conception to Maturity*, Cambridge, MA: Harvard University Press.

US Bureau of the Census (1975), *Historical Statistics of the United States, Colonial Times to 1970*, Washington, DC: US Government Printing Office.

Weir, David R. (1997), 'Economic welfare and physical well-being in France, 1750–1990', in Richard H. Steckel and Roderick Floud (eds), *Health and Welfare during Industrialization*, Chicago: University of Chicago Press, pp. 161–200.

Weiss, Thomas (1992), 'U.S. labor force estimates and economic growth', in Robert E. Gallman and John Joseph Wallis (eds), *American Economic Growth and Standards of Living before the Civil War*, Chicago: University of Chicago Press, pp. 19–75.

10. Time intensity and well-being: what we can learn from time-use data

Thomas L. Hungerford and Maria S. Floro

To do two things at once is to do neither.
Maxim 7 (Publilius Syrus 1st Century BC)

INTRODUCTION

Time intensity or performing two or more tasks at a time is an important dimension of people's well-being. It depicts the manner in which people function, particularly the way they perform their work and spend their time. After all, engagement in work – whether producing for one's own consumption or for the market – constitutes an essential element of life. Thus any inquiry into people's well-being must involve not only asking how much people earn to acquire goods and services, but also how they conduct their lives. But existing standard-of-living measurements fail to take account of this important qualitative dimension of time use. The possession of material goods and services – whether measured in terms of money income or real GDP per capita – still constitutes the primary basis for assessing well-being.

The occurrence of 'double day' for working women and the incidence of time intensity have generally been validated by the results of time-use surveys. These surveys have provided one of the most useful sets of data on women's and men's participation in activities at home, in the labor market, and in communities. While varying in form and method of collection, time-use surveys typically record the various activities (such as work, child care, domestic chore, leisure, travel, personal care, and sleep) in which an individual engages in a given period (usually a day) and the amount of time spent per activity.

Since the mid-1960s, several time-use studies have been undertaken in both developed and developing countries (Szalai 1972; Juster and Stafford 1991; Goldschmidt-Clermont and Pagnossin-Aligisakis 1995).

However, the notion of time use has yet to be routinely incorporated in our understanding of individual well-being, with the exception of leisure time.

In recent years, several social welfare policy reforms have been proposed or implemented in industrialized countries including the United States and Australia. For example, welfare reform has led to time limits on the receipt of benefits in the United States and to an increased emphasis on moving poor single mothers into the workforce in both Australia and the United States. The success of these reforms is generally measured in terms of the number of (former) recipients working or the labor income received by these women. But there may be good reasons as to why the current efforts of policy makers and policy analysts in assessing and measuring the effects of the cuts in welfare programs and social services are grossly inadequate.

While most working women are likely to be 'time-poor' (that is, working a double day and sacrificing their leisure time), working single mothers are likely to be both 'time-poor' and money-poor (Vickery 1977; Douthitt 1994). The effects of welfare reforms influence the well-being of households by affecting not only their money incomes and consumption expenditures but also the demand for nonmarket labor time. Cuts in public provision of basic services eventually become part of household maintenance (for example, child care) for time-poor and money-poor households that cannot afford the costs of private daycare centers and other market-purchased services. This can increase the likelihood for time intensification and even lengthening of working hours, especially by poor women. In so doing, women internalize the costs of poverty. The effects may be long term and even intergenerational in nature.

Although there has been significant progress in the documentation of paid and unpaid work, there is still much to be done in terms of developing new methods of measuring and studying the processes of work and nonwork activities that convey more complete information on the quality of life. This chapter addresses this by taking into account the extent to which individuals perform overlapping activities and to identify which individuals are likely to engage in such activities and for how long. Using the 1992 Australian Time Use Survey data the study also provides a means of ranking activities by the effort involved in order to determine the relation between overlapping activities and individual well-being. Since some overlapping activities can actually be pleasing while others can be stressful, classifying activities according to the level of effort (mental or physical) expended is an important task as well. The remainder of this chapter is organized as follows. We first discuss the concept of time intensity. Second, the data and methodological issues are described. Third, we provide a brief theoretical background. Fourth, tabular results are presented, followed by the multivariate analysis results. Last, we offer concluding remarks.

TIME INTENSITY: CONCEPT AND MEASUREMENT ISSUES

Over the last few decades, increasing numbers of women have taken on the role of income earners (paid work). In Australia, the labor force participation rate of prime-aged women increased from 41 per cent in 1975 to 65 per cent by 1999. Yet at the same time women continue to perform their traditional roles as household managers and childcare providers (unpaid work). Although a number of time-use studies (Juster and Stafford 1991; Robinson and Godbey 1997) indicate that men in some societies seem to be taking on more household chores, much of the unpaid work at home and in the community (such as domestic chores, child care, care of the sick, and backyard gardening) still falls on women.

Although time-use data are becoming recognized as a key source of vital information about nonmarket (unpaid) work and market (typically paid) work, there are some dimensions and aspects of well-being that have yet to be examined using such data. For example, with the exception of a few studies the measurement and documentation of time intensity has received little attention partly as a result of the methodological limitations of existing time-use methods and analysis (Juster and Stafford 1991; Floro 1995). One reason for our lack of knowledge is the relative scarcity of data on this dimension of time. Many time-use surveys still fail to take account of the fact that individuals can (and do) do more than one thing at a time. In conventional techniques of time-use data collection, such as the time diary and recall methods, interviewers are usually instructed to account for only one activity at a time, thereby precluding the possibility of overlapping activities. If someone is mending clothes while waiting for the pot roast to cook, what is that person doing? This creates a dilemma since the individual may not know whether to report the activity at a particular moment as cooking or mending clothes.

Juster and Stafford (1991, p. 482) note that primary and secondary activities may be performed one at a time or sequentially, rather than in parallel: overlapping of activities may just be frequent switches between activities and 'if the time grid were fine enough, the issue of secondary activities would then effectively disappear'. The psychology literature suggests that tasks can be and are performed in parallel, but bottlenecks may exist in processing part of the simultaneous tasks. There is a debate as to whether the bottlenecks are due to some neural limitations (Ruthruff et al. 2001) or due to strategic postponement of the less important task (Meyer and Kieras 1997).

The omission of secondary activities performed at the same time as the recorded primary activity has been acknowledged in several studies and considered a serious methodological problem. It has also created a systematic bias in the reporting of unpaid work. For example, the amount of labor devoted to certain nonmarket work such as child care tends to be underestimated. As some have found (Ironmonger 1994, 1996; Bittman and Matheson 1996; Robinson and Godbey 1997), adding secondary activity child care time increased the total amount of time devoted to child care. Australian time-use data suggest that as much as three-quarters of all time spent in child care may be accompanied by another activity (Bittman and Pixley 1997). Although an increasing number of time-use surveys now collect data for primary as well as secondary activities, little systematic study of the nature of overlapping activities has been conducted.[1] This has resulted in the time intensiveness of unpaid or nonmarket work being little recognized as a component of well-being.

Time intensity may involve varied combinations of two work activities such as house cleaning and child care. Several time-use studies in the United States and Australia show that the overlapping of activities particularly involving child care is quite common among women, more so than among men (Hill 1985; Bittman and Pixley 1997; Folbre 1997). Likewise, the findings of feminist studies on household strategies during economic crisis show that time intensification is an important coping mechanism for many women. Studies on homeworking and informal sector activities show a high incidence of combining market work and domestic activities (for example, cleaning, cooking, and child care) among women workers in Bangladesh, Mexico, the United States, and Spain (Roldan 1985; Hossain 1988; Benton 1989; Lozano 1989).

Time intensity may also take the form of combining work and nonwork such as child minding and strolling in the park, or it may combine two nonwork activities such as reading and listening to music. Some time allocation studies, such as those by Robinson (1985) on the United States and Szebo and Cebotarev (1990) on St. Lucia, find that some housework activities are intertwined with activities such as listening to the radio or socializing with relatives or friends. The practice of combining leisure with a domestic activity suggests that there is no strict demarcation between work and leisure, especially in societies where life is not so compartmentalized. Social intercourse and labor are intermingled – the working day lengthens or contracts according to the necessity of tasks at hand. It also indicates that an individual may claim very little discretionary pure leisure time.

But how does time intensity affect a person's well-being? The effect of time intensity on one's well-being depends on several factors including the regularity and length of time a person performs overlapping activities and on the nature of the activities combined such as the amount of physical energy expended and the level of concentration required. The pleasantness associated with simultaneously performing child care and gardening or going to a park, for example, is partly due to the nature of the overlapping activities – neither requires prolonged or continued high level of concentration. In addition, an interruption in a given activity can be a welcome diversion, since it breaks the monotony of the task. Overlapping of activities can also potentially increase the level of efficiency and quality of work. Listening to music while working on a manuscript may in fact contribute to improvement in a person's well-being as well as the quality of the paper. On the other hand, conducting business while having to look after young children, or having to cook and clean at the same time requires a greater amount of energy to be expended and can be stressful. When one or both of the combined activities require considerable energy (whether physical or mental), uninterrupted attention, a deadline, or some other condition(s) that needs to be fulfilled, then the level of time intensity is likely to bring about adverse effects such as stress.

The length of time one performs overlapping activities is also an important determinant of the well-being effects. The longer an individual has to, say, mind the children while performing other activities, the greater is the amount of stress. A person may not mind performing two tasks simultaneously for half an hour or so, but if one has to engage in them throughout the day or for several hours on a daily basis, then such a manner of working cannot possibly be satisfying or pleasing. Prolonged performance of combined activities can be problematic in the sense that it can have deleterious consequences for the individual's health. This is confirmed by the findings of several medical and psychology studies such as those by Baruch et al. (1987), which show that the quality of experience in roles are more powerful predictors of various stress indices than merely the case of role occupancy. Several studies such as those by Roldan (1985) on Mexican rural homeworkers, Sichtermann (1988) on women workers in Germany, Redclift and Mingione (1985) on self-employed women in Southern Italy, and Benton (1989) on homeworkers in Spain show that long hours of work coupled with prolonged periods of high levels of time intensity can have negative effects on the physical and mental well-being of women. Roldan (1985) found in her study that the increasing incidence of emotional and psychological disorders suffered by Mexican rural homeworkers is due largely to the increased intensity of their work time. Sichtermann's (1988) study of German women workers also showed that a major source of stress for women is an increase in working-time intensity. In this sense, the intensity dimensions of time use, and not just the monochronic aspects, are critical to understanding the processes affecting a person's well-being.

DATA AND METHODOLOGY

The source of our time-use data is the national representative 1992 Australian Time Use Survey (TUS). Of the 8298 persons in 4948 households selected to be in the sample, 6875 persons aged 15 years or older (82.9 per cent) completed both the questionnaire and time-use diaries (Australian Bureau of Statistics 1993). The diary days in the TUS are approximately equally distributed over the days of the week and the four quarters of the year. Diary respondents were instructed to record activities (primary, secondary, and tertiary activities) over five-minute intervals covering the 24 hours of the diary day. The primary or main activity is recorded in the first column of the time diary. The secondary activity is the response to the question 'What else were you doing at the same time?', and is recorded in the second column of the time diary.

Our analysis sample is limited to 'prime-aged' individuals between the ages of 20 and 64 who were not full-time students or retired.[2] We also eliminated people who report sleeping over 14 hours on the diary day or who are visitors to the dwelling on the diary day. Time diaries were collected for two different days. We use the information from only one of the diary days for each person in our sample. For each person we chose the first day that the individual identified as a normal day (that is, a day described as normal for the day of the week). After eliminating 326 individuals who did not report income data, our analysis sample contains demographic, economic and time-use information for 3615 prime-aged individuals in 2356 households.

Several researchers (Hill and Stafford 1985; Robinson 1985; Juster and Stafford 1991; Robinson and Godbey 1997) report that time-use diaries yield higher-quality time-use data than other methods. The TUS has been described as especially high-quality time-use data (Bittman and Wajcman 2000) and this appears to apply to our analysis sample as well. Juster (1985) suggests that the number of reported activities per day in time-use data is a good, albeit indirect, indicator of data quality. The individuals in our analysis sample report, on average, 32.1 primary activities and 14.8 *different* primary activities during the diary day. As a further check of data quality, we calculated time spent sleeping and time spent on work activities to make sure the data 'make sense'. On average, individuals in our sample sleep 488.4 minutes (8.1 hours) on the diary day. Furthermore, individuals who are full-time workers report spending 561.4 minutes (9.4 hours) on labor force activities (for example, working at main job, commuting, taking breaks) on a weekday diary day.

The relevant individual and household characteristics of our sample are listed and defined in Appendix Table 10A.1. Sample means are also reported for each variable. Slightly over half of the individuals in our sample are female, three-quarters are married (or 'defacto' married) and about 40 per cent have children under the age of 15. The average age of the sample members is 39.3 years. About 38 per cent have less than a secondary school education, 12 per cent completed secondary school, another 38 per cent have a trade certificate,[3] and 12 per cent have completed college.[4] About 70 per cent of the sample report they are employed (56 per cent report full-time employment and 17 per cent report part-time employment), 7 per cent are unemployed, and 20 per cent are not in the labor force.

The activity classification system used by the 1992 Australian TUS is based on the classification used in the 1960s Multinational Time Budget Study (see Szalai 1972). There are 10 major activity categories (one-digit codes) such as labor force activities, child care and minding, purchase of goods and services, and passive leisure. These categories are further broken down into two-digit and then into three-digit activity codes. At the three-digit level, the categories are as detailed as, for example, work-related conversation (071), making soft furnishings (155), and enjoying memorabilia (950).

To make our task manageable, we used two dimensions of time use to collapse the activities into four categories. The first dimension is how stressful or unpleasant the activity is and we divided the activities into what we felt is an unpleasant/stressful category and a pleasant/unstressful category. Our choices were guided by the work of Robinson (1993) with US time-use data as well as the medical, work physiology, and sociology literature, but there is also a subjective component to our classification. The categories vary in the level of physical and/or mental effort expended as well as in the monotony involved. Emotional and mental stress are encountered not only in commuting and in the workplace but also at home, as many years of stress research have pointed out (Rodahl 1989). High-stress activities (for example, caring for ill or disabled older adults) have been linked to higher blood pressure levels and greater mortality (Schulz and Beach 1999; Atienza et al. 2001), as they often embody social and moral obligation as well as emotional connections (Folbre 2001). At the other extreme, Ellison et al. (2001) find that religious involvement, especially church attendance, has a positive effect on well-being and a negative effect on distress.

The other dimension is whether or not someone else could do the activity for the respondent (the third-person criterion). We refer to our two categories along this dimension as 'work' and 'nonwork'. Our implicit definition of work is something that one is doing but could be done by someone else. An activity is a work activity if someone else (hired or volunteer) could do the activity of producing a good or service (for example, housework), and it is a nonwork activity if it has to be done by the respondent, including the consumption of a good or service (for example, eating) or strolling in the park. Appendix Table 10A.2 shows how the Australian time-use activities (and codes) are divided into our four categories.

The focus of our chapter is on overlapping activities or 'multitasking' and the TUS records the respondent's primary and secondary activity.[5] Nearly all of our sample (95 per cent) report overlapping activities and, on average, sample individuals spend 451 minutes (7.5 hours) engaging in multitasking. One approach to a study of overlapping activities would be to examine total time spent on overlapping activities. While this approach shows the prevalence of overlapping activities and which individuals perform them and for how long, it ignores the differences in the nature of the combined activities and the likely impact on individual well-being. For example, listening to music while reading is a very different set of overlapping activities from cleaning the house and reprimanding a child. Taking into account the two dimensions of time use (pleasant/unpleasant and work/nonwork), we have 16 possible combinations of primary and secondary activities. The average amount of time (in minutes) spent on each combination plus the number of sample members engaging in the particular combination of activities are listed in Appendix Table 10A.3. Clearly some combinations are not particularly relevant since so few people engage in the combination and/or so little time is spent doing these overlapping activities. We have chosen to focus our attention on seven combinations, which are italicized in the table. On average, these seven combinations account for 98 per cent of the time spent 'multitasking' (the median is 100 per cent).

There is some question about how to measure time spent engaged in overlapping activities. As an example, consider an individual who spends one hour (60 minutes) cooking (the primary activity) and minding the children (the secondary activity). Should this time be counted as 60 minutes of cooking plus 60 minutes of child minding for a total of 120 minutes of activities, or should it be counted as just 60 minutes of overlapping activities? Another possible measure would be to count this combination as, say, 60 minutes of cooking plus 30 minutes of child minding to reflect bottlenecks in performing two tasks simultaneously. Results from a study by Williams and Donath (1994) suggest that these two tasks should be equally weighted. In our tabular and multivariate analyses we measure the clock time spent engaged in overlapping activities by the total number of minutes devoted to the two activities together.[6]

The seven overlapping activity categories as well as the four nonoverlap-

Table 10.1   Number of minutes per day spent in overlapping and
nonoverlapping activities

Primary activity	Secondary activity	Average time (minutes)		
		Total sample	Men	Women
Unpleasant work	Unpleasant work	8.28	4.12	12.47
Unpleasant work	Pleasant work	26.56	8.75	44.46
Pleasant nonwork	Unpleasant work	10.78	6.84	14.75
Pleasant nonwork	Pleasant work	76.27	51.56	101.11
Unpleasant work	Pleasant nonwork	122.13	113.08	131.23
Pleasant work	Pleasant nonwork	15.79	18.04	13.54
Pleasant nonwork	Pleasant nonwork	180.37	175.94	184.82
Unpleasant work		323.08	368.25	277.70
Pleasant work		23.04	24.81	21.27
Unpleasant nonwork		5.95	5.70	6.19
Pleasant nonwork		636.95	655.48	618.34
Total time on the activities listed above		1429.20	1432.57	1425.88
Total time spent on overlapping activities		450.98	385.76	516.51

Note: Sample weights used. There are 1440 minutes in one day.

ping primary activities are listed in Table 10.1. On average, individuals
spend 451 minutes per day multitasking (31 per cent of the day), 323
minutes on nonoverlapping, unpleasant work activities (of which 229
minutes are devoted to labor market activities), and 637 minutes on nonoverlapping, pleasant, nonwork activities (of which 490 minutes are
devoted to sleeping). Most of the time devoted to multitasking is spent on
pleasant nonwork/pleasant nonwork activities (180 minutes) and unpleasant work/pleasant nonwork activities (122 minutes).

The seven overlapping activities can be roughly ordered based on whether
the overlapping activities detract from or enhance individual well-being.
The first two rows of overlapping activities (unpleasant work/unpleasant
work and unpleasant work/pleasant work or group A activities) reflect high
work intensity and can be thought of as multitasking in its purest sense –
two activities requiring physical exertion and/or concentration are performed at the same time. Time spent on high work-intensity activities is
likely to increase stress and have negative consequences for an individual's
health (Wolfe and Haveman 1983). Panel A of Figure 10.1 illustrates the
expected relation between time spent on group A overlapping activities and

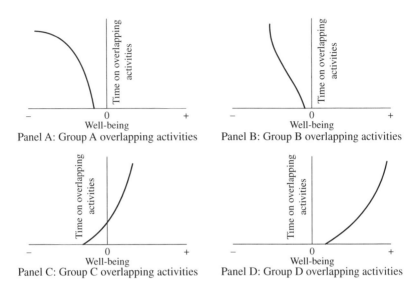

Figure 10.1   Time spent on overlapping activities versus well-being

well-being. As time spent on these intense overlapping activities increases, well-being declines at an accelerating rate.

The next two categories (pleasant nonwork/unpleasant work and pleasant nonwork/pleasant work or group B overlapping activities) reflect a primary relaxing activity (such as leisure) being performed with some kind of work. This suggests that there is a large non-discretionary and 'on-call' component to the pleasant activity (such as minding the children while watching television) – there may be no choice in location of the pleasant nonwork activity and attention may be diverted from that activity at any time. These overlapping activities may be one way to deal with time pressure and the time spent on these overlapping activities can also significantly affect well-being. As Bittman and Wajcman (2000) point out, overlapping another activity with leisure activities may lessen the enjoyment of the leisure activity. The second panel (B) of Figure 10.1 shows the hypothesized relation between time spent on these overlapping activities and well-being. Note that as the time spent on these activities increases, well-being declines slowly at first and then accelerates to decline rapidly.

However, not all overlapping activities have adverse consequences for well-being. The next two overlapping activity categories in rows 5 and 6 (unpleasant work/pleasant nonwork and pleasant work/pleasant nonwork or group C overlapping activities) are a primary work activity combined with a secondary pleasant nonwork activity which is likely to enhance the pleasantness of work or at least counters the drudgery of work. Examples would be listening to the radio while working at the office or watching television while cooking dinner. Lastly, combining a primary pleasant nonwork with a secondary pleasant nonwork activity (group D overlapping activities) may be performing two complementary leisure activities such as reading and listening to music which raises the level of satisfaction derived from the experience. Panels C and D of Figure 10.1 show the relation between time spent on these overlapping activities and well-being for group C and group D overlapping activities, respectively. In both cases, the relation is a positive one – increasing time on these overlapping activities enhances well-being.

The amount of time men and women spend on each of the overlapping activities and nonoverlapped activities is shown in Table 10.1. There are four notable differences between men and women. First, on average, women spend more time on overlapping activities than do men (516 minutes versus 386 minutes). Second, women spend roughly four times the amount of time on high work-intensity, or group A overlapping activities than men (see rows 1 and 2 of the table). Third, women spend twice the time engaged in nondiscretionary and 'on-call' pleasant nonwork (group B) activities (rows 3 and 4). Lastly, men spend 1.3 times the amount of time engaged in non-overlapped unpleasant work activities than women.

THEORETICAL FOUNDATION

We apply the decision-making model of overlapping activities proposed by Floro and Miles (2001). In their examination of secondary work activities, they argue that an individual will weigh the costs and benefits of engaging in overlapped work activities. For this study, the benefits could include such things as the increased output (goods and services as well as leisure) per unit time, the satisfaction in getting a task done within a given timeframe, or simply avoiding the consequences of not getting a task done. The costs could include increased stress levels and lower-quality outputs as a result of multitasking. If the net benefits are positive, the individual will engage in overlapping activities. The costs and benefits, reflecting the interaction of economic and social/culture-based constraints, productivity differences and social as well as personal preferences, will be influenced by demographic, economic and sociocultural factors.

Social and gender-based norms, for example, influence the division of labor and hence the allocation of time. In most societies (including Australia) it is commonly understood that 'men take out the garbage' and 'women are responsible for the kids'. These social perceptions could create time pressures for women as they are confronted with changing (and additional) roles as labor force participant, household maintenance worker, community member, and care provider. Furthermore, men and women may have different perceptions of time. Lane et al. (1989, p. 123) argue that men 'have been socialized and trained to focus on doing one thing at a time'. Floro and Miles (2001) argue that because of the interplay of economic and demographic factors with prevailing gender norms women may have developed the ability to perform multiple activities simultaneously to deal with the multiple roles that they are compelled or expected to perform.

Individuals in different stages of the life cycle will have different demands on their time. Parents with young children are likely to experience greater time pressures than childless individuals (young and old). Single parents probably experience the greatest time pressures (Vickery 1977; Douthitt 1994), especially if they work. This increased time pressure could increase the likelihood of multitasking. Educational attainment could affect the importance an individual places on the quality of the output from household production. Floro and Miles (2001, p. 10) note that this 'could manifest itself as higher standards of cleanliness, better care for the sick or elderly, more nutritious meals, or more involvement in their children's activities'.

Economic factors could also influence overlapped activities such as economic status (household income), employment status and whether or not the individual has a working spouse. Purchasing services and labor-saving goods is a way to cope with time pressures (Zick et al. 1996). Higher family income is related to the purchase of durable items (Strober and Weinberg 1977, 1980) as well as domestic services. Consequently, individuals in higher-income families may decrease the amount of time spent multitasking. Also, the extent to which an individual participates in the labor force may influence time pressure. It is not hard to imagine that a full-time worker would be more likely to face 'time squeeze' than persons not in the labor force, other things equal. Furthermore, the presence of a working spouse could change an individual's time demands. On the one hand, the additional income allows for more purchases of 'time-saving' goods and services. On the other hand, however, it enables for negotiation and bargaining on the division of labor within the household.

Cultural norms may also affect time pressures (Floro and Miles 2001). Unlike individual-oriented Western culture, many non-western cultures maintain extended kinship ties and individuals are able to draw on other family members to deal with increased time pressures. Whether or not a language other than English is spoken at home is included as a proxy variable for cultural norms. Social welfare policies may also affect time pressures and we include two binary variables indicating receipt of unemployment insurance and family allowance benefits. Lastly, Hill (1985) suggests that there may be regional, seasonal, and day of the week variations in time use. Consequently, we include a series of binary variations indicating weekdays, quarters of the year, suburban residence, and rural residence.

Our empirical strategy for the multivariate analysis is to estimate a series of tobit models of time spent in the seven categories of overlapping activities. Let T^* be individual i's desired time spent in overlapping activity j which depends on the level of net benefits to engaging in a particular set of overlapped activities. Concretely, each T^* is a linear function of the vector of independent variables and a random error term:

$$T^*_{ji} = \beta'_j X_i + \varepsilon_{ji}$$

where β_j is the vector of parameters to be estimated. The observed time is:

$$T_{ji} = \begin{cases} T^*_{ji} & \text{if } T^*_{ji} > 0 \\ 0 & \text{otherwise.} \end{cases}$$

Since our sample includes individuals from both single- and multi-person families the error terms are unlikely to be independent, thus biasing the standard errors of the parameter estimates. Consequently, Huber–White robust standard errors are estimated to correct for this bias.

TABULAR RESULTS

Time spent engaging in multitasking differs widely by income level. Table 10.2 presents the average time spent on the various overlapping activity categories by equivalence-adjusted family income quartile. The first noteworthy finding is that time spent on multitasking declines monotonically with income – those in the lowest income quartile spend, on average, about two hours more per day on overlapping activities than those in the highest income quartile. This is true whether we look at time on all overlapping activities (first row) or on overlapping activities that exclude television watching and listening to the radio as the secondary activity (second row). It is also noteworthy that the same declining pattern is apparent for the four well-being-detracting or group A and B overlapping activity categories (see rows 3–6 of Table 10.2). For the three categories that enhance well-being (groups C and D), there is either no clear pattern or a slight increasing pattern in the amount of time spent on overlapping activities as income rises.

The last four rows in Table 10.2 report the time spent on nonoverlapping

Table 10.2 Number of minutes per day spent on various overlapping and nonoverlapping activities by equivalence-adjusted income quartile

			Lowest	Second	Third	Highest
Average time in overlapping activities			513.42	463.01	435.58	384.48
Average time in overlapping activities (television & radio excluded)			336.46	292.10	261.58	211.91
Group	Primary	Secondary				
A	Unpleasant work	Unpleasant work	11.36	10.30	5.88	5.32
	Unpleasant work	Pleasant work	43.81	33.41	18.94	8.28
B	Pleasant nonwork	Unpleasant work	13.41	10.56	10.22	8.66
	Pleasant nonwork	Pleasant work	113.28	89.31	66.52	31.57
C	Unpleasant work	Pleasant nonwork	116.77	122.35	123.46	126.57
	Pleasant work	Pleasant nonwork	15.14	15.22	17.66	15.10
D	Pleasant nonwork	Pleasant nonwork	184.89	169.75	184.19	181.88
Unpleasant work			232.64	305.44	356.46	407.60
Pleasant work			24.24	25.38	23.66	18.66
Unpleasant nonwork			6.81	6.33	6.04	4.47
Pleasant nonwork			662.88	639.84	618.26	624.79

Note: Sample weights used.

or single activities. Time spent on unpleasant work activities monotonically increases with income from about four hours (232.6 minutes) for individuals in the lowest income quartile to almost seven hours for individuals in the highest income quartile. This pattern may be reflecting the correlation between hours worked and income. The pattern is somewhat different for time spent on pleasant nonwork single activities – individuals in the lowest-income quartile spend 20 to 40 minutes more time on these activities than people in higher-income quartiles.

The tabular analysis is repeated for employment status and these results reported in Table 10.3. There is no obvious monotonic pattern in time spent multitasking as there was with income. However, the differences between full-time workers and those not in the labor force are particularly large. Generally, individuals not in the labor force (for example, housewives) spend about 2.7 hours more per day engaging in multitasking than full-time workers. These individuals who are not in the labor force not only spend more time in well-being-enhancing or group C and D overlapping activities but also in well-being-detracting or group A and B overlapping activities.

Table 10.3 Number of minutes per day spent on various overlapping and nonoverlapping activities by employment status

			Full-time worker	Part-time worker	Unemployed	Not in the labor force
Average time in overlapping activities			391.81	514.92	484.57	553.57
Average time in overlapping activities (television & radio excluded)			225.21	332.75	313.37	365.41
Group	Primary	Secondary				
A	Unpleasant work	Unpleasant work	6.10	11.89	8.11	11.75
	Unpleasant work	Pleasant work	10.68	45.98	28.37	55.40
B	Pleasant nonwork	Unpleasant work	8.42	14.55	10.69	14.61
	Pleasant nonwork	Pleasant work	52.83	107.90	88.89	112.71
C	Unpleasant work	Pleasant nonwork	123.00	132.37	105.00	119.35
	Pleasant work	Pleasant nonwork	18.76	12.43	11.76	11.72
D	Pleasant nonwork	Pleasant nonwork	163.96	178.02	215.75	212.68
Unpleasant work			412.66	287.60	170.80	164.75
Pleasant work			19.94	23.13	29.30	28.95
Unpleasant nonwork			4.76	6.64	8.74	7.56
Pleasant nonwork			610.83	607.71	746.59	685.17

Note: Sample weights used.

289

*Table 10.4   Number of minutes per day spent on various overlapping and
nonoverlapping activities by age*

Group	Primary	Secondary	20–34	35–44	45–54	55–64
	Average time in overlapping activities		511.89	461.10	375.29	358.31
	Average time in overlapping activities (television & radio excluded)		333.16	295.30	209.25	172.37
A	Unpleasant work	Unpleasant work	9.97	8.54	7.59	3.70
	Unpleasant work	Pleasant work	43.21	29.73	5.04	1.67
B	Pleasant nonwork	Unpleasant work	12.24	12.17	8.45	7.04
	Pleasant nonwork	Pleasant work	106.26	100.67	28.62	6.68
C	Unpleasant work	Pleasant nonwork	126.00	126.48	120.19	104.54
	Pleasant work	Pleasant nonwork	17.98	16.25	12.32	13.40
D	Pleasant nonwork	Pleasant nonwork	184.68	154.64	186.25	210.84
	Unpleasant work		305.31	349.46	352.96	279.19
	Pleasant work		18.31	23.13	22.86	37.42
	Unpleasant nonwork		3.82	6.10	7.83	9.30
	Pleasant nonwork		600.68	600.21	681.06	755.78

Note: Sample weights used.

As would be expected, full-time workers spend considerably more time
on nonoverlapping unpleasant work activities than part-time workers and
especially nonworkers since unpleasant work activities includes labor
market activities. The results in the table suggest that individuals in the
sample tend to not multitask during paid or market work time. Full- and
part-time workers tend to spend less time (about 1.5 hours less) on nonoverlapping, pleasant, nonwork activities than those with no job.

Age differences in the amount of time spent engaging in multitasking are
also significant. The first row of Table 10.4 shows that those in the oldest
age group (55–64 years) spend about 2.5 hours less per day on overlapping
activities than those in the youngest age group (20–34 years). In general,
there is a monotonically declining pattern in multitasking. The primary
overlapping activities categories that displays this declining pattern are the
group A and B overlapping activities, which tend to detract from well-being
(see rows 3–6). Furthermore, the oldest age group (nearing retirement)
devotes slightly more time to group D overlapping activities (that enhance
well-being). Individuals in their prime work years (ages 35–54) spend more
time on nonoverlapping unpleasant work activities than either the young-

est or oldest groups in the sample. Also, time spent on singular pleasant nonwork activities increases monotonically with age. While there are clear age patterns it is impossible to tell if these are lifecycle effects or cohort effects (that is, different generations behave differently).

To further examine lifecycle differences, the sample was divided based on sex, marital status, and the presence of younger children aged 0–14 years. The results are displayed in Tables 10.5 and 10.6. In Table 10.5, four findings stand out. First, women with children (married and unmarried) spend at least three hours more per day on overlapping activities than the next highest group (married men with younger children). Second, married women with no younger children report spending more time on overlapping activities than individuals with no younger children (married or unmarried). Third, married men (with and without children) spend the most time on nonoverlapped unpleasant work activities and women with children (married and unmarried) spend the least. Fourth, individuals with children spend considerably less time on nonoverlapping, pleasant, nonwork activities than people with no children.[7]

Table 10.6 reports the results for each of the seven overlapping activity categories. The clearest result is that women with younger children (married and unmarried) spend more time on well-being-detracting overlapping activities and less time in overlapping activities in the pleasant nonwork/pleasant nonwork category than other individuals.

In summary, the tabular results in Tables 10.2–6 show three discernible patterns regarding overlapping activities. First, individuals in lower-income households tend to spend more time on well-being-detracting overlapping activities than other individuals. Second, younger adults tend to spend more time on well-being-detracting overlapping activities than other individuals, but it is impossible to distinguish lifecycle effects from cohorts effects. Lastly, married and unmarried women with younger children spend more time on well-being-detracting overlapping activities and less time in well-being-enhancing overlapping activities than other individuals.

MULTIVARIATE ESTIMATION RESULTS

We present the results of two model specifications. The results from the more basic model are presented in Table 10.7. In the table we report the coefficient estimates, the robust standard errors in round brackets, and the marginal impacts in square brackets.[8] The overlapping activity categories are arranged in the table so that the well-being-detracting (group A first and then group B) categories are shown first (see columns 1–4), followed by the well-being-enhancing (groups C and D) categories (see columns 5–7).

Table 10.5 Number of minutes per day spent on overlapping and nonoverlapping activities by sex, marital status, and presence of children

	Average time in overlapping activities	Average time in overlapping activities (TV & radio excluded)	Non-overlapping primary activities			
			Unpleasant work	Pleasant work	Unpleasant nonwork	Pleasant nonwork
Married men with no children	329.98	165.60	379.03	27.69	6.42	696.88
Married women with no children	414.53	211.02	291.83	22.68	8.37	702.59
Unmarried men with no children	367.96	169.48	317.31	17.36	4.99	732.38
Unmarried women with no children	376.69	181.88	337.93	16.93	5.28	703.16
Married men with children	449.32	297.78	390.64	26.62	5.24	568.19
Married women with children	667.67	515.48	245.06	22.60	4.53	500.14
Unmarried men with children*	324.93	153.41	296.96	19.68	9.91	788.52
Unmarried women with children	631.31	465.18	223.63	17.40	5.08	562.58

Note: Sample weights used.   *   There are only 38 unmarried men with children in the sample.

Table 10.6 *Number of minutes per day spent on various overlapping activities by sex, marital status, and presence of children*

Group:	A		B		C		D
Primary:	Unpleasant work	Unpleasant work	Pleasant nonwork	Pleasant nonwork	Unpleasant work	Pleasant work	Pleasant nonwork
Secondary:	Unpleasant work	Pleasant work	Unpleasant work	Pleasant work	Pleasant nonwork	Pleasant nonwork	Pleasant nonwork
Married men with no children	3.76	0.17	4.34	2.18	111.78	15.36	187.06
Married women with no children	6.51	3.72	10.27	8.46	140.87	11.64	222.44
Unmarried men with no children	1.85	1.66	5.06	6.08	114.02	15.95	216.90
Unmarried women with no children	4.36	1.35	9.59	10.70	114.91	13.20	214.21
Married men with children	5.77	20.61	10.16	123.59	115.91	21.28	142.82
Married women with children	20.49	101.37	21.16	221.32	130.86	14.56	138.24
Unmarried men with children*	2.88	5.90	5.78	13.45	71.54	24.70	180.44
Unmarried women with children	23.04	77.64	18.64	204.61	120.54	19.25	148.94

Note: Sample weights used. * There are only 38 unmarried men with children in the sample.

Table 10.7   Tobit results: basic model

Group:	A		B		C		D
	1	2	3	4	5	6	7
Primary:	Unpleasant work	Unpleasant work	Pleasant nonwork	Pleasant nonwork	Unpleasant work	Peasant work	Pleasant nonwork
Secondary:	Unpleasant work	Pleasant work	Unpleasant work	Pleasant work	Pleasant nonwork	Peasant nonwork	Pleasant nonwork
Constant	−1498.8832	−3804.2128	−564.2386	−7289.8343	−287.5345	−141.3734	578.3214
Female	53.3387**	134.3005**	36.8850**	179.2794**	30.4231**	−13.5883**	14.9281**
	(6.9111)	(10.0250)	(4.3231)	(18.6803)	(5.9388)	(3.4593)	(5.4454)
	[10.3529]	[23.9798]	[8.5565]	[36.4200]	[16.0808]	[−3.6539]	[9.8651]
Married	5.0619	33.2653*	6.2006	66.5515*	11.3135	−5.7751	7.8079
	(8.3293)	(16.0095)	(6.0528)	(33.0171)	(9.2244)	(5.8466)	(9.8366)
	[0.9777]	[5.7571]	[1.4260]	[13.1864]	[5.9353]	[−1.5661]	[5.1350]
Children <15 yrs	42.7957**	248.2512**	23.8934**	623.2546**	−15.9796	20.0757**	−72.3168**
	(7.3157)	(15.2901)	(5.3719)	(32.5904)	(8.2050)	(4.9058)	(8.1511)
	[8.5025]	[49.1663]	[5.6363]	[143.0736]	[−8.4365]	[5.4425]	[−47.1643]
Age	1445.5284**	3597.3197**	457.6392	6877.2912**	373.8496	89.0755	−247.6358
	(457.4073)	(801.8510)	(324.6712)	(1753.6734)	(418.5277)	(221.9578)	(463.4313)
	[281.4117]	[642.3857]	[106.5168]	[1401.4940]	[198.0672]	[23.8800]	[−163.8243]
Age²	−561.3612**	−1311.7132**	−155.4125	−2513.5448**	−144.5860	−28.2560	69.5640
	(177.4539)	(312.6595)	(127.6384)	(684.9510)	(163.1748)	(105.4819)	(179.8668)
	[−109.2843]	[−234.2371]	[−36.1727]	[−512.2246]	[−76.6023]	[−7.5751]	[46.0203]
Age³	92.9946**	201.4078**	22.6354	387.9703**	24.0353	3.1305	−8.7415
	(29.6004)	(52.4580)	(21.5441)	(115.0827)	(27.1814)	(7.5025)	(29.8977)
	[18.1040]	[35.9661]	[5.2684]	[79.0628]	[12.7340]	[0.8392]	[−5.7830]

Age⁴	−5.5738**	−11.1397**	−1.2145	−21.6060**	−1.4835	−0.0885	0.4312
	(1.7944)	(3.1955)	(1.3194)	(7.0199)	(1.6361)	(1.0507)	(1.7997)
	[−1.0851]	[−1.9893]	[−0.2827]	[−4.4030]	[−0.7859]	[−0.0237]	[0.2853]
Other language	−26.1557**	−45.5930**	−15.4953*	−125.8980**	−23.4387*	−9.6041	−12.4085
	(9.2503)	(15.2080)	(7.2908)	(34.8347)	(9.6646)	(5.7380)	(10.2022)
	[−4.8061]	[−7.6509]	[−3.4544]	[−23.7708]	[−12.0551]	[−2.5055]	[−8.0979]
UI	5.0696	−20.2315	5.0032	23.4079	−29.5853	−26.5704*	33.3377
	(16.3672)	(22.4278)	(11.9472)	(49.1393)	(16.2695)	(13.0587)	(20.7198)
	[1.0009]	[−3.4914]	[1.1848]	[4.8566]	[−14.9734]	[−6.5059]	[23.0202]
Fam Allow	5.8530	35.4374*	−5.6629	39.1892	−12.4416	−10.1465	−16.1460
	(13.9570)	(17.3614)	(9.5570)	(38.3295)	(15.2027)	(9.6365)	(18.3460)
	[1.1585]	[6.7399]	[−1.2922]	[8.2360]	[−6.4638]	[−2.6243]	[−10.4476]
Sec School	11.5146	22.1281	13.7234*	40.7680	3.7336	−4.7462	19.6455
	(9.6138)	(14.8688)	(6.7496)	(32.8181)	(10.2825)	(5.9577)	(10.0532)
	[2.3024]	[4.0796]	[3.3242]	[8.5282]	[1.9875]	[−1.2551]	[13.2770]
Trade	18.7284**	14.0688	9.6545*	43.8383	13.4684	3.0378	5.4685
	(6.3958)	(9.8173)	(4.3123)	(23.1823)	(7.1971)	(4.3741)	(6.8022)
	[3.6966]	[2.5281]	[2.2668]	[9.0124]	[7.1735]	[0.8166]	[3.6243]
Bachelor	33.9197**	36.2170*	22.7114**	91.5619**	1.1472	8.2911	16.2091
	(8.4748)	(14.5594)	(6.9693)	(34.4505)	(9.6234)	(5.8067)	(9.6996)
	[7.1504]	[6.8135]	[5.6467]	[19.7914]	[0.6087]	[2.2768]	[10.9124]
Educ Missing	11.8032	−69.1250	−5.6498	6.1544	−39.4411	−20.2350	−37.9778
	(26.7279)	(58.4675)	(23.2972)	(113.8670)	(27.9262)	(19.6129)	(28.9348)
	[2.3805]	[−10.9238]	[−1.2879]	[1.2605]	[−19.5658]	[−5.0344]	[−23.7615]

Table 10.7 (continued)

	1	2	3	4	5	6	7
Group:	A		B		C		D
Primary:	Unpleasant work	Unpleasant work	Pleasant nonwork	Pleasant nonwork	Unpleasant work	Peasant work	Pleasant nonwork
Secondary:	Unpleasant work	Pleasant work	Unpleasant work	Pleasant work	Pleasant nonwork	Peasant nonwork	Pleasant nonwork
Incquart2	−10.9704	−19.4724	−11.1960	−9.9304	−3.4237	4.1816	−21.8927*
	(7.7209)	(12.2427)	(5.7531)	(27.8940)	(9.0127)	(5.3338)	(9.1928)
	[−2.1357]	[−3.4773]	[−2.6059]	[−2.0237]	[−1.8139]	[1.1210]	[−14.4832]
Incquart3	−21.2373**	−39.0477**	−4.6480	−37.0928	−0.6969	12.8048*	−14.1578
	(7.8643)	(12.6472)	(5.8349)	(30.2166)	(9.4589)	(5.5319)	(9.4837)
	[−4.1344]	[−6.9729]	[−1.0818]	[−7.5590]	[−0.3692]	[3.4328]	[−9.3662]
Incquart4	−16.1582	−49.9515**	−6.9299	−51.1223	−3.1163	7.7003	−31.7557**
	(9.0872)	(16.9191)	(6.6892)	(38.1901)	(10.5159)	(6.5211)	(10.8266)
	[−3.1456]	[−8.9200]	[−1.6129]	[−10.4180]	[−1.6510]	[2.0643]	[−21.0081]
Spousewrk	13.7827*	6.2272	−2.8426	−19.1757	18.9552*	4.2197	−9.9067
	(7.0098)	(11.1603)	(4.9591)	(24.4550)	(7.8605)	(4.8807)	(7.7927)
	[2.6826]	[1.1119]	[−0.6617]	[−3.9088]	[10.0390]	[1.1310]	[−6.5550]
δ	97.3771	154.9265	79.8507	354.5286	159.8724	79.6676	154.1660
	(8.2833)	(6.0409)	(4.9820)	(9.0274)	(3.5412)	(3.5337)	(2.9440)
χ²	110.93	531.96	138.92	721.19	143.18	123.62	309.10

Notes: Robust standard errors in round brackets. Marginal impacts in square brackets. Other variables included are weekday and quarter of the year indicators, and suburban/rural indicators.
* Significant at 5 per cent level; ** Significant at 1 per cent level.

296

Women generally devote more time (8–36 minutes) to well-being-detracting overlapping activities than men. Each of the coefficient estimates are positive and statistically significant at the 1 per cent level. Women also devote slightly more time to well-being-enhancing overlapping activities than men. Married individuals appear to be no different from unmarried individuals for most overlapping activity categories (the coefficient estimates are typically small and not statistically significant). Individuals with younger children, however, devote considerably more time (5–143 minutes per day) to well-being-detracting categories and generally less time to overlapping activities in well-being-enhancing categories.

To allow for nonlinearities, age was entered into the equation in a flexible manner as a quartic function. In three cases (see columns 1, 2, and 4 – all group A or B overlapping activities), the coefficient estimates are statistically significant. The effect of age reaches a maximum in the late 20s for all categories, which is consistent with the results reported in Table 10.4. However, the variation is fairly small (less than 60 minutes between the maximum and minimum) in all cases except in column 4 (260 minutes from the minimum at age 20 to the maximum at age 29).

The effect of speaking a language other than English at home (*Other Language*) has the predicted effect. The coefficient estimate in each case is negative and is statistically significant in many cases. Generally, other things equal, individuals in non-English speaking households spend 3–24 fewer minutes per day on group A and B well-being detracting overlapping activities (see columns 1–4) but also spend 2–12 fewer minutes on group C and D well-being enhancing overlapping activities (see columns 5–7).

Two types of income variables are used. The first type is two binary variables indicating whether or not the main source of income is from unemployment insurance (*UI*) or from family allowance payments (*Fam Allow*), a means-tested benefit for families with dependent children. The employment status variables were omitted due to correlation with these two variables, though the results are little changed when the employment status variables are included. Overall, these two variables have little impact on time spent engaging in overlapping activities: the marginal impacts are small and the coefficient estimates are not statistically significant in most cases.

The second type of income variables is a series of binary variables indicating equivalence-adjusted total family income quartile (*Incquart2–Incquart4*). The pattern of marginal impacts conforms to the results from Table 10.2 – individuals in higher-income households devote less time to overlapping activities. The impacts, however, are fairly modest in most instances – generally less than 10 minutes but up to 20 minutes in the case of group D well-being-enhancing overlapping activities. The coefficient estimates are not statistically significant in many instances.

The results for education show that the most educated group (labeled *Bachelor* in Table 10.7) devote 6–20 minutes more per day to well-being-detracting group A and B overlapping activities than the least-educated group. The coefficient estimates are statistically significant in each case. This suggests that more educated people may be under more time pressures than less-educated people and cope by increasing time to multitasking. On the other hand, the coefficient estimates for the education variables are not statistically significant for overlapping activities in the well-being-enhancing group C and D overlapping activity categories (see columns 5–7).

Table 10.8 presents the results of the extended model. In these models the three sex, marital status, and younger children variables are interacted to create seven binary variables (the omitted category is married men with no younger children). In addition, the unemployment insurance and family allowance variables were replaced by three employment status variables. For the most part, the magnitudes and statistical significance of many coefficient estimates and marginal impacts are similar to those reported in Table 10.7.

The pattern of coefficient estimates for the sex, marital status, and younger children interaction terms conforms to the evidence presented in Table 10.6. Holding other things equal, women with children (married and unmarried) spend considerably more time (up to almost five hours per day in one category) on well-being-detracting group A and B overlapping activities. Furthermore, men with younger children (married and unmarried) spend significantly more time on overlapping activities in two of the four well-being-detracting group A and B categories (see columns 2 and 4: unpleasant work/pleasant work and pleasant nonwork/pleasant work). Individuals with children, especially women, spend more time on group B overlapping activities, which suggests that these individuals have considerably less discretionary leisure time than others which is consistent with research by Bittman and Wajcman (2000). In addition, individuals with younger children devote less time (up to an hour per day) to pleasant nonwork/pleasant nonwork overlapping activities (see column 7).

Full-time workers tend to spend less time on the well-being-detracting group A and B overlapping activities (see especially columns 2 and 4) and on pleasant nonwork/pleasant nonwork (group D) overlapping activities (see column 7), other things equal. Working individuals may purchase more services and labor-saving durable goods as one way to cope with time pressures. With the addition of the employment status variables, the coefficient estimates of the income quartile variables are smaller and in most instances no longer statistically significant.

The extended models were reestimated (results not shown), first with the income quartile variables omitted and the employment status variable

Table 10.8 Tobit results: extended model

Group:	A		B		C		D
	1	2	3	4	5	6	7
Primary:	Unpleasant work	Unpleasant work	Pleasant nonwork	Pleasant nonwork	Unpleasant work	Pleasant work	Pleasant nonwork
Secondary:	Unpleasant work	Pleasant work	Unpleasant work	Pleasant work	Pleasant nonwork	Pleasant nonwork	Pleasant nonwork
Constant	−1291.1546	−3365.8768	−461.6502	−6684.4045	−341.7604	−188.1242	645.4702
Married female – no children	25.7585*	138.5893**	26.4488**	191.6846**	46.7887**	−4.3589	13.1645
	(10.5315)	(27.8392)	(6.6831)	(53.4229)	(9.4972)	(5.7304)	(8.5419)
	[5.2453]	[28.8365]	[6.5312]	[42.5762]	[25.9700]	[−1.1552]	[8.8507]
Unmarried male – no children	−16.3545	90.3308**	−7.3561	64.8072	5.2950	3.9165	3.6524
	(12.5720)	(34.9642)	(8.7165)	(73.4271)	(14.3713)	(7.7463)	(14.0444)
	[−3.0558]	[18.2759]	[−1.6729]	[13.6016]	[2.8267]	[1.0607]	[2.4384]
Unmarried female – no children	8.8123	55.7265	20.8948*	153.1186*	17.9326	−1.8000	−0.0384
	(13.0489)	(37.4305)	(8.8512)	(69.8046)	(13.3428)	(8.4041)	(13.6839)
	[1.7498]	[10.6883]	[5.1879]	[34.3305]	[9.7435]	[−0.4790]	[−0.0256]
Married male – children	8.8247	281.5212**	18.9197*	709.3396**	−4.7651	17.0025**	−46.7209**
	(9.9359)	(29.8698)	(7.3702)	(57.3560)	(12.2430)	(6.4645)	(10.6212)
	[1.7427]	[73.2657]	[4.5997]	[220.1001]	[−2.5136]	[4.7407]	[−29.7467]
Married female – children	85.7092**	386.1177**	52.8208**	801.4160**	19.7825	17.0004*	−91.3151**
	(12.5147)	(30.7685)	(8.5144)	(61.0401)	(12.4702)	(7.0326)	(12.0613)
	[19.7977]	[118.2744]	[13.9665]	[263.1900]	[10.7010]	[4.7377]	[−55.7701]

Table 10.8 (continued)

	1	2	3	4	5	6	7
	A		B		C		D
Group:							
Primary:	Unpleasant work	Unpleasant work	Pleasant nonwork	Pleasant nonwork	Unpleasant work	Pleasant work	Pleasant nonwork
Secondary:	Unpleasant work	Pleasant work	Unpleasant work	Pleasant work	Pleasant nonwork	Pleasant nonwork	Pleasant nonwork
Unmarried male – children	−44.2118	150.6965**	0.4515	307.5099**	−52.9248	28.9923	−49.7440
	(44.8285)	(57.5384)	(22.8566)	(103.2708)	(30.3106)	(18.3265)	(35.9902)
	[−7.5686]	[35.7764]	[0.1051]	[80.8020]	[−25.6976]	[8.6669]	[−30.7181]
Unmarried female – children	90.6135**	345.9195**	45.7027**	753.6944**	22.9340	28.1507**	−88.3511**
	(18.2037)	(34.0972)	(11.6325)	(67.6490)	(17.3387)	(10.7177)	(17.7012)
	[23.0930]	[122.0716]	[12.5235]	[290.2453]	[12.5927]	[8 3375]	[−51.7808]
Age	1251.2601**	3112.8469**	356.3033	6225.3070**	432.9059	147 1454	−359.6148
	(453.7419)	(796.7629)	(326.2024)	(1725.1061)	(424.5896)	(272.4857)	(451.4316)
	[243.0052]	[545.3616]	[82.8085]	[1250.6550]	[229.4906]	[39.3800]	[−239.0754]
Age²	−487.1965**	−1132.4499**	−117.4256	−2280.3524**	−167.8632	−50.0739	113.8376
	(175.9676)	(310.6952)	(128.0989)	(674.2754)	(165.3763)	(105.5021)	(175.3694)
	[−94.6176]	[−198.4019]	[−27.2909]	[−458.1194]	[−88.9871]	[−13.4011]	[75.6803]
Age³	80.9881**	173.4906**	16.6057	352.9262**	27.9427	6.5875	−16.1016
	(29.3224)	(52.1459)	(21.5962)	(113.3387)	(27.5218)	(17.4801)	(29.1585)
	[15.7286]	[30.3950]	[3.8593]	[70.9023]	[14.8129]	[1.7630]	[−10.7045]

	(1)	(2)	(3)	(4)	(5)	(6)	(7)
Age^4	-4.8734**	-9.6009**	-0.8737	-19.7594**	-1.7171	-0.2791	0.8504
	(1.7744)	(3.1778)	(1.3209)	(6.9160)	(1.6548)	(1.0480)	(1.7547)
	[-0.9465]	[-1.6820]	[-0.2031]	[-3.9696]	[-0.9103]	[-0.0747]	[0.5654]
Other Language	-25.7877**	-44.1277**	-14.5484*	-121.8267**	-23.4095*	-9.0123	-13.2005
	(9.2488)	(15.1533)	(7.3304)	(34.2151)	(9.7451)	(5.7651)	(10.1793)
	[-4.7289]	[-7.2692]	[-3.2468]	[-22.7181]	[-12.0474]	[-2.3507]	[-8.6484]
Part-time	0.5178	51.4954**	9.6885	71.7294**	-0.0925	-20.0794**	44.0880**
	(8.2936)	(12.3378)	(5.5991)	(27.2894)	(8.9090)	(5.2260)	(8.7134)
	[0.1007]	[9.6514]	[2.3074]	[15.0092]	[-0.0490]	[-5.1126]	[30.5444]
Unemployed	-3.8119	41.7340*	0.2460	81.5549*	-12.8768	-44.1442**	61.5662**
	(12.4779)	(16.5514)	(8.7648)	(38.4076)	(12.4312)	(9.6829)	(14.3666)
	[-0.7330]	[7.8398]	[0.0572]	[17.3911]	[-6.7011]	[-10.2854]	[44.0018]
NILF	-1.4120	92.3007**	14.9104*	163.9034**	-4.3309	-31.3656**	79.6901**
	(9.1257)	(14.0014)	(6.0733)	(30.4327)	(8.8259)	(6.0203)	(10.3368)
	[-0.2735]	[18.0923]	[3.5856]	[35.8911]	[-2.2859]	[-7.8352]	[56.5521]
Sec School	12.8726	26.5836	14.4695	44.1832	4.1426	-5.9442	23.7618*
	(9.6223)	(14.4867)	(6.7688)	(32.3956)	(10.2644)	(5.9256)	(9.9093)
	[2.5765]	[4.8443]	[3.5077]	[9.1340]	[2.2077]	[-1.5636]	[16.2124]
Trade	19.7267**	22.0703*	10.8835*	52.8048*	14.3397*	1.0592	11.5964
	(6.2563)	(9.7278)	(4.3615)	(23.4205)	(7.3122)	(4.3826)	(6.8430)
	[3.8877]	[3.9062]	[2.5545]	[10.7228]	[7.6447]	[0.2837]	[7.7397]
Bachelor	37.2372**	49.8332**	24.9418**	104.9114**	2.2039	5.7533	23.1537
	(8.3901)	(14.1220)	(7.0577)	(34.8516)	(9.7334)	(5.8052)	(9.7425)
	[7.8994]	[9.4020]	[6.2339]	[22.5662]	[1.1716]	[1.5657]	[15.7832]
Educ Missing	9.7899	-71.7215	-6.5687	-0.8390	-38.6261	-21.0187	-34.8473
	(27.2617)	(58.5448)	(23.5894)	(115.1742)	(28.0581)	(19.2663)	(30.3502)
	[1.9582]	[-11.0400]	[-1.4901]	[-0.1684]	[-19.1985]	[-5.2036]	[-22.0028]

301

Table 10.8 (continued)

	1	2	3	4	5	6	7
	A		B		C		D
Group:							
Primary:	Unpleasant work	Unpleasant work	Pleasant nonwork	Pleasant nonwork	Unpleasant work	Pleasant work	Pleasant nonwork
Secondary:	Unpleasant work	Pleasant work	Unpleasant work	Pleasant work	Pleasant nonwork	Pleasant nonwork	Pleasant nonwork
$Incquart2$	−10.1864	−9.2199	−9.5256	10.8040	−1.6700	−1.6686	−8.6022
	(7.5125)	(12.2391)	(5.8246)	(27.8261)	(9.1016)	(5.3249)	(9.1589)
	[−1.9783]	[−1.6153]	[−2.2138]	[2.1705]	[−0.8853]	[−0.4466]	[−5.7188]
$Incquart3$	−20.9165*	−19.4829	−1.1955	−0.4923	0.6787	2.7497	10.1676
	(8.5874)	(12.9943)	(6.0164)	(31.1990)	(9.9819)	(5.6017)	(9.6030)
	[−4.0622]	[−3.4134]	[−0.2778]	[−0.0989]	[0.3598]	[0.7359]	[6.7596]
$Incquart4$	−17.7714	−27.2941	−2.8742	−5.6381	−2.4268	−4.4952	−2.3540
	(10.0803)	(16.5215)	(6.9935)	(38.8928)	(11.2007)	(6.7388)	(11.1886)
	[−3.4514]	[−4.7818]	[−0.6680]	[−1.1327]	[−1.2865]	[−1.2030]	[−1.5650]
$Spousewrk$	9.3093	3.7855	−4.3701	−16.9759	20.4004*	4.4706	−7.7691
	(6.9438)	(11.0633)	(4.9840)	(24.1511)	(7.9513)	(4.9081)	(7.5416)
	[1.8075]	[0.6631]	[−1.0159]	[−3.4112]	[10.8105]	[1.1962]	[−5.1657]
σ	96.6312	150.8365	79.7551	351.0168	159.7448	79.2661	151.9258
	(8.3253)	(5.9840)	(5.0325)	(8.8287)	(3.5385)	(3.5575)	(2.8422)
χ^2	134.86	606.99	158.49	782.49	153.12	160.71	382.75

Notes:
Robust standard errors in round brackets. Marginal impacts in square brackets. Other variables included are weekday anc quarter of the year indicators, and suburban/rural indicators.
* Significant at 5 per cent level; ** Significant at 1 per cent level.

302

included (model X), and then with the employment status variables omitted and the income quartile variable included (model Y). In model X, the coefficient estimates of the employment status variables were very close to those reported in Table 10.8 – same pattern and same significance levels. In model Y, however, the coefficient estimates of the income quartile variables were larger in absolute value and in most cases were statistically significant. These results tend to concur with Table 10.2 – higher-income individuals spend less time on well-being-detracting group A and B overlapping activities holding other things equal.

CONCLUDING REMARKS

This study focused on the little discussed but important dimension of time use, namely the performance of overlapping activities. Given the ubiquity of these activities, we proposed a method for classifying them on the basis of their effect on the individual's well-being. Next we explored the possible determinants of this notion of time intensity using 1992 Australian time-use data using multivariate estimation techniques to assess the effects of economic, social, and demographic factors on time intensity. Since few countries have collected time-use data consistently over time we were unable to examine trends in multitasking.

Our results, while not particularly startling, have important implications for quality-of-life issues. Our primary findings are as follows.

First, full-time workers spend less time on well-being-detracting overlapping activities and less time on well-being-enhancing overlapping activities, holding all else equal. This suggests that these workers may cope with 'time squeeze' by purchasing services (for example, child care) and labor-saving goods (for example, Chinese take-out) rather than through time intensity.

Second, individuals in the upper half of the income distribution spend less time on well-being-detracting overlapping activities (group A) than lower-income individuals, which provides further evidence that those who can afford to purchase services and labor-saving goods to cope with 'time squeeze' do so.

Third, women with children (married and unmarried) and, to a much lesser extent men with children, spend more time on well-being-detracting overlapping activities and less time on well-being-enhancing overlapping activities. These findings (and personal experience) suggests that gender norms and/or the presence of children increases time pressures which people cope with by the overlapping of activities. This overlapping of activities may increase stress levels and lower the quality of life for parents, especially working mothers. In addition, there could also be adverse consequences for the children.

Fourth, individuals with higher education spend more time on well-being-detracting overlapping activities than the less educated, other things equal. College-educated individuals may be under more time pressure than the less educated and cope by doing two things at the same time. It may be the fate of the well educated in industrialized countries to experience a time crunch and increased stress levels.

Unless time-use data and time intensity are given due recognition in policy formulations and evaluations, researchers and policy makers are likely to continue to ignore an important aspect of quality of life. Collecting data on overlapping activities allows for a more accurate measurement of time spent on valuable but uncompensated activities such as childcare, housework, and community improvements. These data also provide vital information about the quality of life that existing standard-of-living measurement (especially those based on market production of goods and services) do not convey.

Much needs to be done in order to understand the nature and factors that lead to time intensification. Further development of indicators and direct measurements of this important dimension of time use is required. It is hoped that the results presented in this chapter will provide a basis for developing a composite time intensity indicator. There is also a need for researchers to develop ways of incorporating this indicator and other observable dimensions of time use (for example, length of the working day or discretionary leisure time) into existing well-being or standard-of-living indices that can be used for assessing policy. Finally, we would stress the importance of a research program that explores more carefully the link between time intensity and observable aspects of a person's health and level of stress in addition to children's development, academic performance and health levels.

NOTES

1. The exception is Floro and Miles (2001).
2. The survey does not distinguish between the current main activity being retired or voluntarily inactive. We defined the retired as persons 55 years or older and who report being retired/voluntarily inactive since persons 55 years or older are eligible to receive pension benefits.
3. Completing secondary school is not a prerequisite for earning a trade certificate, consequently, some in this category have not completed secondary school.
4. Less than 1 per cent of the sample members do not report their educational attainment.
5. The time-use diary also allows the respondent to record a tertiary activity. However, 55 per cent of the respondents report engaging in tertiary activities for an average of 60 minutes per day. Five activities (watching TV, listening to music, conversation, playing with children and eating) account for about two-thirds of the time spent on tertiary activities. Tertiary activities are not considered in this study.

6. Our qualitative results and conclusions will be unaffected by how time spent multitasking is measured. Only our quantitative results will be rescaled.
7. The exception is unmarried men with children but this could be due to the extremely small cell size.
8. In the present case, the coefficient estimates from the tobit models are the marginal changes on the desired level of time spent on overlapping activities which can be negative (that is, $\partial E(T^*)/\partial x$). The marginal impact shows the impact of a variable change on the time spent (given the censoring) on overlapping activities (that is, $\partial E(T)/\partial x$) which is equal to the coefficient estimate times the probability T is positive.

REFERENCES

Atienza, Audie A., Patrick C. Henderson, Sara Wilcox and Abby C. King (2001), 'Gender differences in cardiovascular response to dementia caregiving', *The Gerontologist*, **41** (4), 490–98.

Australian Bureau of Statistics (1993), *Time Use Survey Australia 1992 User's Guide*, Canberra: Commonwealth Government Printer.

Baruch, G., L. Beiner and Rosalind Barnett (1987), 'Women and gender research on work and family stress', *American Psychologist*, **42** (2), 130–36.

Benton, Lauren (1989), 'Homework and industrial development: gender roles and restructuring in the Spanish shoe industry', *World Development*, **17** (2), 255–66.

Bittman, Michael, and George Matheson (1996), '"All else confusion": what time use surveys show about changes in gender equity', Social Policy Research Centre discussion paper series, no. 72, University of New South Wales.

Bittman, Michael, and Jocelyn Pixley (1997), *The Double Life of the Family: Myth, Hope and Experience*, Sydney: Allen Unwin.

Bittman, Michael, and Judy Wajcman (2000), 'The rush hour: the character of leisure time and gender equity', *Social Forces*, **79** (1), 165–89.

Douthitt, Robin A. (1994), '"Time to do chores?" Factoring home-production needs into measures of poverty', Institute for Research on Poverty discussion paper no. 1030-94, University of Wisconsin.

Ellison, Christopher G., Jason D. Boardman, David R. Williams and James S. Jackson (2001), 'Religious involvement, stress, and mental health: findings from the 1995 Detroit area study', *Social Forces*, **80** (1), 215–49.

Floro, Maria S. (1995), 'Economic restructuring, gender and the allocation of time', *World Development*, **23** (11), 1913–29.

Floro, Maria S., and Marjorie Miles (2001), 'Time use and overlapping activities: evidence from Australia', forthcoming in *Cambridge Journal of Economics*.

Folbre, Nancy (1997), 'A time (use survey) for every purpose: non-market work and the production of human capabilities', paper presented at the conference on 'Time Use, Non-Market Work and Family Well-Being', Washington, DC, 20–21 November, University of Massachusetts.

Folbre, Nancy (2001), *The Invisible Heart: Economics and Family Values*, New York: The New Press.

Goldschmidt-Clermont, Luisella, and Elisabetta Pagnossin-Aligisakis (1995), 'Measurements of unrecorded economic activities in fourteen countries', occasional paper no. 20, United Nations Development Programme, Human Development Report Office.

Hill, C. Russell, and Frank P. Stafford (1985), 'Parental care of children: time diary estimates of quality, predictability, and variety', in F. Thomas Juster and Frank P. Stafford (eds), *Time, Goods and Well-being*, Ann Arbor, MI: Institute for Social Research, pp. 415–37.

Hill, Martha S. (1985), 'Patterns of time use', in F. Thomas Juster and Frank P. Stafford (eds), *Time, Goods and Well-being*, Ann Arbor, MI: Institute for Social Research, pp. 133–76.

Hossain, H. (1988), 'Industralization and women workers in Bangladesh: from home-based work to the factories', in N. Heyzer (ed.), *Daughters in Industry*, Kuala Lumpur: Asia Pacific Development Center, pp. 51–79.

Ironmonger, Duncan (1994), 'The value of care and nurture provided by unpaid household work', *Family Matters*, *31*, 46–51.

Ironmonger, Duncan (1996), 'Counting outputs, capital inputs and caring labour: estimating gross household product', *Feminist Economics*, **2** (3), 37–64.

Juster, F. Thomas (1985), 'The validity and quality of time use estimates obtained from recall diaries', in F. Thomas Juster and Frank P. Stafford (eds), *Time, Goods and Well-being*, Ann Arbor, MI: Institute for Social Research, pp. 63–91.

Juster, F. Thomas, and Frank P. Stafford (1991), 'The allocation of time: empirical findings, behavioural models, and problems of measurement', *Journal of Economic Literature*, **29** (2), 471–522.

Lane, Paul M., Carol J. Kaufman and Jay D. Lindquist (1989), 'More than 24 hours a day', in *Marketing Theory and Practice*, presented at AMA Winter Educators' Conference, St. Petersburg, FL: American Marketing Association, pp. 123–30.

Lozano, Beverly (1989), *The Invisible Force: Transforming American Business with Outside and Home-Based Workers*, New York: Free Press.

Meyer, David E., and David E. Kieras (1997), 'A computational theory of executive cognitive processes and multiple-task performance: Part 2. Accounts of psychological refractory phenomena', *Psychological Review*, **104** (4), 749–91.

Redclift, N., and E. Mingione (eds), *Beyond Employment: Household, Gender and Subsistence*, Oxford: Basil Blackwell.

Robinson, John P. (1985), 'The validity and reliability of diaries versus alternative time use measures', in F. Thomas Juster and Frank P. Stafford (eds), *Time, Goods and Well-being*, Ann Arbor, MI: Institute for Social Research, pp. 33–62.

Robinson, John P. (1993), 'As we like it', *American Demographics*, February, 44–9.

Robinson, John P., and Geoffrey Godbey (1997), *Time for Life*, University Park, PA: Pennsylvania State University Press.

Rodahl, Kaare (1989), *The Physiology of Work*, London: Taylor & Francis.

Roldan, Martha (1985), 'Industrial outworking, struggles for the reproduction of working class families and gender subordination', in N. Redclift and E. Mingione (eds), *Beyond Employment: Household, Gender and Subsistence*, Oxford: Basil Blackwell, pp. 160–89.

Ruthruff, Eric, Harold E. Pashler and Alwin Klaassen (2001), 'Processing bottlenecks in dual-task performance: structural limitation or strategic postponement', *Psychonomic Bulletin and Review*, **8**, 73–80.

Schulz, Richard, and Scott R. Beach (1999), 'Caregiving as a risk factor for mortality: the caregiver health effects study', *Journal of the American Medical Association*, **282** (23) 2215–19.

Sichtermann, Barbara (1988), 'The conflict between housework and employment', in J. Jenson, E. Hagen and C. Reddy (eds), *Feminization of the Labor Force*, Cambridge: Polity Press, pp.276–87.

Strober, Myra H., and Charles B. Weinber (1977), 'Working wives and major family expenditures', *Journal of Consumer Research*, **4**, 141–7.

Strober, Myra H., and Charles B. Weinberg (1980), 'Strategies used by working and nonworking wives to reduce time pressures', *Journal of Consumer Research,* **6**, 338–48.

Szalai, Alexander (1972), *The Use of Time*, The Hague: Mouton.

Szebo, L., and E.A. Cebotarev (1990), 'Women's work patterns: a time allocation study of rural families in St. Lucia', *Canadian Journal of Development Studies*, **11** (2), 259–78.

Vickery, Claire (1977), 'The time-poor: a new look at poverty', *Journal of Human Resources*, **12** (1), 27–48.

Williams, Ross, and Sue Donath (1994), 'Simultaneous uses of time in household production', *Review of Income and Wealth*, **40** (4), 433–40.

Wolfe, Barbara, and Robert Haveman (1983), 'Time allocation, market work, and changes in female health', *American Economic Review*, **73** (2), 134–9.

Zick, Cathleen D., Jane McCullough and Ken R. Smith (1996), 'Trade-offs between purchased services and time in single-parent and two-parent families', *Journal of Consumer Affairs*, **30** (1), 1–23.

Appendix Table 10A.1   Definitions and means

Variable	Definition	Mean
Female	= 1 if female	0.5248
Married	= 1 if married or defacto married	0.7599
Children <15	= 1 if have children under 15 years	0.4335
Married female – no children	= 1 if married female with no young children	0.2047
Unmarried male – no children	= 1 if unmarried male with no young children	0.1037
Unmarried female – no children	= 1 if unmarried female with no young children	0.0874
Married male – children	= 1 if married male with young children	0.1903
Married female – children	= 1 if married female with young children	0.1942
Unmarried male – children	= 1 if unmarried male with young children	0.0105
Unmarried female – children	= 1 if unmarried female with young children	0.0384
Age	Age	3.9271
Age^2	Age squared	16.7612
Age^3	Age cubed	76.7845
Age^4	Age to the 4th	372.5102
Other Language	= 1 if English not spoken at home	0.1231
UI	= 1 if primary source of income is UI	0.0409
Fam Allow	= 1 if primary source of income is family allowance payments	0.0313
Sec School	= 1 if completed secondary school	0.1178
Trade	= 1 if has trade certificate	0.3831
Bachelor	= 1 if bachelors or higher	0.1217
Educ Missing	= 1 if education missing	0.0066
Part-time	= 1 if works part-time	0.1679
Unemployed	= 1 if unemployed	0.0719
NILF	= 1 if not in the labor force	0.2011
Weekday	= 1 if weekday	0.7411
Suburban	= 1 if lives in suburban area	0.3145
Rural	= 1 if lives in rural area	0.0822
Incquart2	= 1 if in 2nd total family income (equiv adjusted) quartile	0.2420
Incquart3	= 1 if in 3rd total family income (equiv adjusted) quartile	0.2528
Incquart4	= 1 if in 4th total family income (equiv adjusted) quartile	0.2376
Quarter 2	= 1 if 2nd quarter of the year	0.2205
Quarter 3	= 1 if 3rd quarter of the year	0.2266
Quarter 4	= 1 if 4th quarter of the year	0.2819
Spousewrk	= 1 if spouse works	0.5068
No. of observations		3615

Appendix Table 10A.2   Collapsing time-use activities into four categories

Work	Nonwork
Unpleasant	
• Work at main job, work for pay, unpaid work (01–30)	• Health care such as sick in bed (43)
• Job search (50)	• Communication and travel associated with personal care (47–48)
• Associated communication, associated travel (70–90)	• Helping sick or disabled adults, doing favors for friends (61, 62)
• Domestic activities (100–190), except gardening	• Civic responsibilities (65)
• Physical care of children, teaching or reprimanding children (20–23)	• Communication and travel associated with voluntary work and community participation (67–69)
• Communication and travel associated with child care (27–29)	
• Purchasing goods and services (30–38) except personal and window shopping	
Pleasant	
• Breaks at work (40)	• Personal care (40–46)
• Gardening (141–142)	• Educational activities (50–59)
• Personal and window shopping (314–315)	• Religious activities (64)
• Playing with children, passive minding of children (24–25)	• Other community participation (66)
• Voluntary community work (63)	• Social life and entertainment (70–78)
	• Active and passive leisure (80–99)

Note: Two- or three-digit numeric code in parentheses.

Appendix Table 10A.3   The 16 combinations of primary and secondary
                        activities

Primary activity	Secondary activity	Average time (minutes)	Number engaging in combination (unweighted)
Unpleasant work	*Unpleasant work*	8.28	661
Unpleasant work	Unpleasant nonwork	0.33	24
Unpleasant work	*Pleasant work*	26.56	844
Unpleasant work	*Pleasant nonwork*	122.13	2967
Unpleasant nonwork	Unpleasant work	0.30	25
Unpleasant nonwork	Unpleasant nonwork	0.05	8
Unpleasant nonwork	Pleasant work	0.64	70
Unpleasant nonwork	Pleasant nonwork	4.30	360
Pleasant work	Unpleasant work	1.36	164
Pleasant work	Unpleasant nonwork	0.11	4
Pleasant work	Pleasant work	3.26	236
Pleasant work	*Pleasant nonwork*	15.79	1188
Pleasant nonwork	*Unpleasant work*	10.78	933
Pleasant nonwork	Unpleasant nonwork	0.41	29
Pleasant nonwork	*Pleasant work*	76.27	1014
Pleasant nonwork	*Pleasant nonwork*	180.37	3305

Note: Data are weighted. The seven combinations in italics account for 98 per cent of the time spent multitasking.

11. Measuring worker rights and labor strength in the advanced economies

Robert Buchele and Jens Christiansen[*]

INTRODUCTION

Worker rights are important for two reasons. They are important in themselves because they shape our work lives – our job security, autonomy, and voice in the workplace. And they are important because they affect – or are believed to affect, for better or for worse – such macroeconomic outcomes as the unemployment rate, the rate of economic growth, and the distribution of income. Worker rights, as defined in this chapter, are at the very center of the debate over the causes of high unemployment in Europe and are the target of those who advocate the 'deregulation' of European labor markets (see OECD 1994b; Mishel and Schmitt 1995; and Buchele and Christiansen 1998).

In this chapter, we develop an index that measures the relative strength of worker rights in advanced capitalist economies. Our aim is to project a relatively large number of variables measuring different aspects of worker rights onto a single scale that will allow us to compare worker rights across countries and to analyze their impact on economic well-being and living standards in the advanced nations. The obvious cost of aggregating quantitative measures that reflect diverse labor market institutions and social policies into a single index of worker rights is that we lose the possibility of identifying links between specific institutions and policies and specific social and economic outcomes. But there is an important theoretical rationale for this endeavor, in addition to the practical uses of such an index. This rationale is that, 'Labor institutions and rules fit together in systematic ways that make the impact of any single labor policy or social program depend on the environment of other institutions and rules in which it operates, (Freeman 1994, p. 236). The aim of this chapter is to show how countries' diverse rules and institutions 'fit together' into a coherent worker rights regime, and how they affect particular measures of economic and social welfare.

In the following sections, first, we define worker rights and discuss a

311

number of measures that quantify important aspects of worker rights, second, we consider various approaches to mapping these diverse measures of worker rights onto a single scale, and third, we investigate the relationship between such an index of worker rights and several important measures of economic welfare, including income distribution and leisure, as well as the growth of per capita GDP, labor productivity, and real wages.

WORKER RIGHTS AND THEIR MEASUREMENT

We consider three distinct aspects of worker rights: employment protection, representational strength, and income security and social protection. Each of these is measured by two or three variables, which are described in Table 11.1.

Employment Protection

Our data include three measures of protection against job loss: the strictness of protection against dismissal of individual regular (that is, permanent) workers (*EPR*) and individual temporary workers (*EPT*), and the strictness of protection against collective dismissals (*EPC*). Employment security can be provided by collective bargaining agreements and common law (court decisions), legal statutes (legislation), and even (nonlegally binding) social norms. Our three measures of employment protection are drawn from the *OECD Employment Outlook* (OECD 1999, Ch. 2). That analysis is based, in turn, on indicators of employment protection developed by Grubb and Wells (1993) and expanded in the *OECD Jobs Study* (OECD 1994b, Ch. 6).

   Our measure of *EPR* is based on 12 indicators of strictness of employment protection for regular employees developed by the OECD (1999). They include procedural delays and inconveniences (for example, whether a third party such as a works council or government authority must be consulted), months of advanced notice and severance pay, length of the trial period during which new employees are unprotected by unfair dismissal legislation, and the costliness to employers of losing an unfair dismissal claim. (The last includes the level of compensation due to employees who are found to be unfairly dismissed, and whether they have the right to reinstatement even against the employer's wishes.) OECD analysts assigned to each of these indices a numerical 'strictness' score that ranges from 0 to 6 on a cardinal scale (meaning that if a country has a score of 4.0 on some measure, it is twice as strict on that measure as another country with a score of 2.0).

Table 11.1   Definitions and data sources: worker rights index

Variable name	Definition and data source
1. *EPR*	Strictness of Employment Protection legislation, Regular employment (mid-1990s): procedural requirements and delays, advance notice and severance pay requirements, difficulty of justifying individual dismissals. *Scale:* 0–6, with higher values indicating stricter laws. *Source: OECD Employment Outlook* (1999, Table 2.5).
2. *EPT*	Strictness of Employment Protection legislation, Temporary employment: fixed-term contracts and temporary work agencies (mid-1990s); limitations on types of work that are allowed under temporary employment and maximum time are person can be employed as a temporary employee. *Scale and source:* Same as *EPR*.
3. *EPC*	Strictness of Employment Protection against Collective dismissals (mid-1990s): the number of workers necessary for laws governing collective dismissals to apply, the delays, costs and difficulties involved in collective dismissals. *Scale:* 0–12. *Source:* Same as *EPR*. (The OECD indicates difficulty of collective dismissals *beyond* the difficulties associated with individual dismissals that is, net of *EPR*. We create a 'stand-alone' measure of the difficulty of collective dismissal by adding *EPR* to the OECD measure for protection against collective dismissals.)
4. *UDEN*	Union Density: percentage of workforce unionized (1994). *Source: OECD Employment Outlook* (1997, Table 3.3).
5. *CBCOV*	Collective Bargaining Coverage: per cent of workforce whose wages are set by collective bargaining (1994). *Source:* Same as *UDEN*.
6. *COORD*	Collective Bargaining Coordination: degree of coordination among unions, on one side, and among employers, on the other. *Scale:* 1–3, with higher values indicating greater coordination (1994). *Source:* Same as *UDEN*.
7. *UIRRA*	Unemployment Insurance Replacement Rate, percentage of before tax wages, Adjusted for duration of eligibility (1991). *Source:* Blöndal and Pearson (1995, Table 4).
8. *SOCTR*	Social Spending on Transfers to working-age population as a percentage of GDP (1992). *Source:* MacFarlan and Oxley (1996, Table 1).

Table 11.2   Worker rights data

Country	EPR	EPT	EPC	UDEN	CBCOV	COORD	UIRRA	SOCTR
Australia	1.0	0.9	3.6	35	80	1.50	27	5.4
Austria	2.6	1.8	5.9	42	98	3.00	31	6.7
Belgium	1.5	2.8	5.6	54	90	2.00	43	8.7
Canada	0.9	0.3	4.3	38	36	1.00	28	6.7
Denmark	1.6	0.9	4.7	76	69	2.25	52	11.9
Finland	2.1	1.9	4.5	81	95	2.25	39	12.7
France	2.3	3.6	4.4	9	95	2.00	37	7.0
Germany	2.8	2.3	5.9	29	92	3.00	27	6.0
Italy	2.8	3.8	6.9	39	82	2.50	3	3.7
Japan	2.7	2.1	4.2	24	21	3.00	9	1.2
Netherlands	3.1	1.2	5.9	26	81	2.00	51	12.7
New Zealand	1.7	0.4	2.1	30	31	1.00	26	8.4
Norway	2.4	2.8	5.2	58	74	2.50	39	9.9
Sweden	2.8	1.6	7.3	91	89	2.00	29	11.7
Switzerland	1.2	0.9	5.1	27	50	2.25	22	4.3
United Kingdom	0.8	0.3	3.7	34	47	1.00	18	8.1
United States	0.2	0.3	3.1	16	18	1.00	11	3.2

An overall measure of strictness of employment protection for regular employees was then calculated as a weighted average of these 12 indicators (as described in OECD 1999, Annex 2.B).[1] The overall *EPR* scores for the mid-1990s, shown in the first column of Table 11.2, range from 0.2 (least strict) for the United States to 3.1 (most strict) for the Netherlands. This measure was originally calculated for two time periods, which are described as the 'late 1980s' and 'late 1990s', although examination of the OECD's data sources suggests that the underlying data relate more closely to the middle of these decades. Finland, whose strictness score fell from 2.7 to 2.1, was the only country among those in our sample with any significant change in *EPR* between these periods.

Indicators of the strictness of employment protection for temporary employment and for the regulation of collective dismissals were constructed by a similar procedure. Restrictions on the use of temporary employment (*EPT*) are broken down by regulations governing fixed-term contracts and those governing the operation of temp work agencies. In both areas, there is an indicator of limitations on the types of jobs that employers are allowed to fill using fixed-term contracts or temp agency workers (for example, whether they are limited to jobs that are inherently temporary, such as, seasonal work). Other indicators of strictness of regulation of both fixed-term contracts and temporary work agencies are limits on the number of successive renewals and on the maximum (cumulated) duration of employment on fixed-term contracts or jobs arranged through temp work agencies. In all, the overall measure is based on six separate indicators.

In contrast to the stability of the regulation of regular employment, many countries in our sample significantly scaled back their regulation of temporary employment between the mid-1980s and mid-1990s. These include Belgium (4.6 to 2.8), Germany (3.8 to 2.3), the Netherlands (2.4 to 0.9), Norway (3.5 to 2.8), and Sweden (4.1 to 1.6).

Finally, protection against collective dismissals (*EPC*) was gauged according to four separate measures: (i) the size of the layoff required to trigger the application of collective dismissal regulation, the existence of (ii) notification requirements, (iii) additional delays, and (iv) other special costs, beyond those applicable to individual dismissal. The overall strictness of regulations of collective dismissals (on top of restrictions on individual dismissals) varies from 0.4 (in New Zealand) to 4.5 (in Sweden). Since this measure indicates restrictions on collective dismissals, *above and beyond* existing restrictions on individual dismissals, a country's value on this measure depends as much on how strictly it regulates individual dismissals as on how strictly it regulates collective dismissals. Thus, for example, the US value of 2.9 for this measure (only slightly below the sample mean) has more to do with the nearly complete absence of restrictions on individual dismissals (the assumption of 'employment at will') than it does with the strictness of regulations governing mass layoffs in the United States. Consequently, the OECD's 'net of *EPR*' measure may seriously misrepresent differences across countries in the strictness of regulation of collective dismissals. We deal with this by adding each country's score on *EPR* to its score for collective dismissals to obtain an augmented *EPC*. This variable ranges from 2.1 and 3.1 (for New Zealand and the United States, respectively) to 6.9 and 7.3 (for Italy and Sweden, respectively).[2]

Collective Bargaining and Representational Strength

Under collective bargaining, pay rates, benefits, rules governing staffing levels, the deployment of labor, and other workplace practices are negotiated, rather than unilaterally determined by employers. The more pervasive collective bargaining is, the more uniform and stable the terms of employment are, and the less short-run 'flexibility' management has in adjusting wages and employment levels.

While this aspect of union influence is viewed in a negative light by those who uphold a free-market ideal of employment relations (for example, Siebert 1997), we argue that there can be important positive effects. Union representation and collective bargaining promote long-term employment relations and enhance the job security of long-term employees. In so doing, they foster an expectation on the part of employees of continued employment and a fair share of productivity gains. In short, they encourage employees to work as though they have a stake in the long-run competitive success of their employer and thus to actively participate in the process of technological and organizational innovation.

Our first two measures of workers' representational strength are union density and collective bargaining coverage. As the ratio of rank and file members to the total labor force, union density ($UDEN$) is the most direct measure of workers' collective strength. In most of the countries in this study, however, collective bargaining coverage ($CBCOV$) exceeds – and sometimes far exceeds – union density, as regional or sectoral wage agreements negotiated between unions and employer associations are extended by mandate to other employers, whether or not their employees are unionized or they themselves are members of the employer association that negotiated the agreement.[3] $CBCOV$ is, therefore, a better measure of the influence of collective bargaining and thus the degree of uniformity across firms in wages and benefits.

The degree of coordination in collective bargaining ($COORD$) refers to the extent to which unions, on one side, and employers, on the other, coordinate their bargaining demands. Ratings in Table 11.2 show that Austria, Germany, and Japan have the highest degree of coordination in collective bargaining and the United States, the United Kingdom, Canada, and New Zealand have the lowest. It is possible to have coordination with decentralized bargaining, as occurs in 'pattern bargaining', where an agreement between a single major firm and an industrial union sets the pattern for all other negotiations in the industry. Generally, however, countries tend to have similar rankings on measures of coordination and centralization. The single major exception to this is Japan, where bargaining is decentralized (taking place between companies and company-based unions) but is nevertheless highly coordinated by national guidelines set in *shunto*, the trade unions' annual nation-wide spring wage offensive.

Income Security and Social Protection

Our last category of worker rights is measured by two variables: the duration-adjusted unemployment insurance replacement rate ($UIRRA$) and a more comprehensive measure of social transfers to the working-age population as a percentage of GDP ($SOCTR$). There are two basic principles governing eligibility for unemployment benefits in the countries of our sample (see Reissert and Schmid 1994; OECD 1994b, Ch. 8): (i) the insurance principle, in which eligibility depends on previous work experience and benefits are set in relation to previous earnings for a limited period, and (ii) the social welfare principle, in which eligibility is means tested and the emphasis is on guaranteeing a minimum level of income for a longer duration. Some countries – such as Germany and Austria – have developed schemes based on a combination of both principles, generally with more welfare-oriented unemployment assistance taking over when unemployment insurance benefits are exhausted.[4]

The *UIRRA* series reported in Table 11.2 is obtained from Blöndal and Pearson (1995). It is calculated as a simple average of replacement rates for beneficiaries in three different family circumstances (single, dependent spouse, working spouse), two earnings levels (average and two-thirds average earnings), and three durations of unemployment (the first, the second and third, and the fourth and fifth years of unemployment).[5] According to this measure Denmark has the most generous unemployment insurance system, being the only country replacing over 50 per cent of former earnings over the long run, and Italy the least generous, replacing only about 3 per cent of former earnings.[6]

Social transfers to the working-age population are our basic measure of the level of 'social protection' provided a country's workers and their dependents. While not a labor market institution *per se*, the level of social protection impacts employment relations because it governs the degree to which workers are dependent on their jobs – and thus on employers – for access to basic necessities (for example, health care, food, and shelter). It is therefore an important determinant of the relative power of labor and capital.

Our measure of social transfers (*SOCTR*) is taken from MacFarlan and Oxley (1996) and includes:

1. Social insurance against income loss due to unemployment, disability, sickness, maternity, occupational injury and disease. These benefits are usually linked to previous income and are not means tested.
2. Social assistance programs aimed at keeping people, whether working or not, from falling below the poverty line. These benefits are usually means tested and, where applicants are employable, require availability for work. They take the form either of cash payments or the subsidization of basic necessities, such as food, heat, and housing.
3. Child allowances, aimed particularly at aiding large families.

As reported in Table 11.2, social transfers are highest in Finland and the Netherlands (12.7 per cent of GDP) and lowest in Japan (1.2 per cent).[7]

CONSTRUCTING A WORKER RIGHTS INDEX

We have identified three distinct aspects of worker rights – employment protection, representational strength, and social protection – and eight distinct (but in many cases highly correlated) measures of the relative strength of these rights in the early to mid-1990s for our sample of 17 advanced capitalist countries. We now discuss our attempts to combine these eight measures into an index of worker rights that allows us to compare the relative strength of worker rights among these countries on a single scale. We consider two approaches to this problem and develop three alternative worker rights indices.

The first is simply to standardize each of the eight variables measuring different aspects of worker rights, add them together, and divide them by eight.[8] This approach rescales the measures so that a country's value on each one is given by how many standard deviations it is from the mean for all countries (which is zero, since it has been standardized). Each country's worker rights 'score' is then calculated as the mean of its values on these eight standardized variables. This worker rights index will have a mean of zero (since it itself is the mean of standardized variables). The values for each country on this index, named **WR1**, are shown in Table 11.4, below (column 1).[9]

The second approach uses factor analysis to combine our eight separate measures into a single index of worker rights.[10] The idea here is that there exists an (unobserved) underlying worker rights component or *factor* that unifies and gives coherence to a country's labor market institutions and income maintenance policies. This factor (or several factors) is presumably revealed by patterns of covariation among our (observed) worker rights measures. Factor analysis derives a factor, or linear combination of the original variables (our eight worker rights measures), that 'explains' the greatest possible amount of the variance in those variables.[11] Then a second factor is extracted that is orthogonal to the first and accounts for the greatest amount of remaining variance, and so on.

The first two factors obtained by this procedure are shown in Table 11.3 (initial factor loadings). These factor loadings indicate the correlation between the factor and its constituent variables. The square of the factor loadings shows the amount of variation each variable shares with that factor. Thus, EPR shares $0.811^2 = 0.658$ of its variance with the first factor, and the first and second factors account for $0.811^2 + 0.312^2 = 0.755$ of the variance in EPR. Thus, the communality of EPR with the first two factors is 75.5 per cent.[12] The first factor explains 48.1 per cent of the variance in the eight original variables and the first and second together account for 75 per cent of the variance in these data. More factors could be extracted to

Table 11.3   Factor analysis of worker rights measures

Variable	Initial factor loadings		Rotated factor loadings		Communality
	Factor 1	Factor 2	Factor 1	Factor 2	
EPR	0.811	−0.312	0.854	0.160	0.755
EPT	0.687	−0.521	0.858	−0.008	0.743
EPC	0.818	−0.211	0.807	0.249	0.713
UDEN	0.531	0.549	0.164	0.746	0.583
CBCOV	0.863	0.101	0.682	0.539	0.755
COORD	0.728	−0.492	0.878	−0.004	0.772
SOCTR	0.502	0.828	−0.001	0.968	0.937
UIRRA	0.489	0.709	0.004	0.861	0.743
Per cent of variance explained	48.1	26.9	42.3	32.8	
Cumulative per cent		75.0		75.0	

explain the remaining variation, but at this point, we run into diminishing returns.[13]

Thus far, we have derived two factors (linear combinations of the eight original variables), which account for 75 per cent of the variation in our worker rights measures. Factor analysis is most commonly used for precisely this purpose: to reduce a relatively large number of variables to a smaller set of (presumably) underlying components.[14] To interpret a factor – that is, to say what aspects of worker rights it represents – we consider which of the original worker rights measures are most highly correlated with it (that is, have high factor loadings). If we (admittedly arbitrarily) set the bar at a loading of two-thirds (0.667), then the first factor loads high on employment protections and collective bargaining coverage and coordination, and the second factor loads high on the social protection and income security measures.

Interpretation may be facilitated by rotating these factors in a way that emphasizes each factor's uniqueness in the sense that it is either highly correlated with a given variable or uncorrelated with it.[15] This procedure may clarify the interpretation of factors by reducing ambiguous instances, in which a variable has moderately high loadings on more than one factor. Rotation does appear to improve the resolution of factor loadings (see Table 11.3), except in the case of *CBCOV* which was strongly correlated with the first unrotated factor but is now moderately correlated with both factors. Examining the pattern of rotated factor loadings in the table, we

Table 11.4   Alternative worker rights indices

Country	WR1	WR2	WR3.1	WR3.2	WR3
Australia (AS)	−0.50	−0.71	−0.72	−0.17	−0.90
Austria (AU)	0.52	0.86	1.01	−0.004	1.01
Belgium (BE)	0.47	0.63	0.31	0.67	0.99
Canada (CA)	−0.73	−1.13	−1.28	−0.07	−1.36
Denmark (DE)	0.46	0.44	−0.44	1.55	1.12
Finland (FI)	0.68	0.84	0.10	1.42	1.53
France (FR)	0.23	0.41	0.67	−0.32	0.35
Germany (GE)	0.44	0.80	1.20	−0.43	0.77
Italy (IT)	0.32	0.73	1.64	−1.29	0.36
Japan (JA)	−0.44	−0.48	0.61	−1.91	−1.30
Netherlands (NE)	0.58	0.79	0.27	1.07	1.34
New Zealand (NZ)	−0.83	−1.31	−1.46	−0.12	−1.59
Norway (NO)	0.61	0.82	0.60	0.58	1.18
Sweden (SW)	0.86	1.22	0.65	1.26	1.92
Switzerland (SI)	−0.46	−0.60	−0.23	−0.77	−1.00
United Kingdom (UK)	−0.81	−1.23	−1.33	−0.16	−1.50
United States (US)	−1.42	−2.06	−1.62	−1.29	−2.92

interpret the first factor as a measure of the strength of employment protection and the influence of collective bargaining and the second factor as
measure of the strength of unions and the level of income maintenance and
social protection. We note that the first rotated factor no longer explains
the maximum possible amount of variance in the data, but the two rotated
factors together explain exactly the same amount of variance as the initial
(unrotated) factors do. The communality of each original measure with the
rotated factors is the same as its communality with the initial (unrotated)
factors and is over 70 per cent for every measure except *UDEN*.

The factor loadings shown in Table 11.3 can be used to calculate a factor
score for each country on a given factor. For example, the factor scores on
the first unrotated factor in Table 11.3 are shown under the name **WR2** in
Table 11.4. Countries with relatively high values on the worker rights measures that load highly on the first unrotated factor in Table 11.3 (for example,
EPR, *EPC*, and *CBCOV*) will be those with the highest scores on that factor,
that is, the highest values on **WR2**. Thus Sweden, which has high values on
these measures, has the highest score on **WR2** (1.22) and the United States,
which has especially low values on these measures, has the lowest score
(−2.06). This second candidate for a worker rights index, **WR2**, is a standardized variable with a mean of zero and a standard deviation of one.

The basic difference between these two approaches is that **WR1** weighs each of the eight worker rights measures equally in aggregating them into a single index, whereas the construction of **WR2** weighs them in relation to their factor loadings on the relevant factor (the first column in Table 11.3). This approach gives the greatest weight to those measures that cluster near this factor (for example, *EPR*, *EPC*, and *CBCOV*) and relatively little weight to those that do not (for example, *SOCTR* and *UIRRA*).[16]

Finally, our third proposed worker rights index is constructed by calculating the factor scores for each country on each of the two rotated factors shown in Table 11.3. In this case, countries with high values on the employment protection measures and on collective bargaining coordination will have high scores on the first (rotated) factor, and countries with high levels of social protection, income security, and (to a lesser extent) union density will have high scores on the second one. The factor scores associated with the two rotated factors in Table 11.3 are labeled **WR3.1** and **WR3.2** in Table 11.4. In order to combine these into a single index, we simply add them together. The result is shown in Table 11.4 under the variable name **WR3**.[17]

Our alternative approaches to constructing a worker rights index have yielded three candidates: **WR1**, **WR2**, and **WR3**. It is reassuring that these indices produce quite similar results, with high pairwise correlations (0.992 for **WR1** and **WR2**, 0.993 for **WR1** and **WR3**, and 0.973 for **WR2** and **WR3**) and very similar country rankings. As a purely empirical matter, the choice among these three indices would seem to be a toss-up. In the analysis that follows, we (somewhat arbitrarily) employ **WR3** as our index of worker rights.

Table 11.5 shows our 17 countries' positions on this scale, ranging from Sweden, at one extreme, to the United States, at the other. These two countries stand as prototypes of, respectively, strong and weak worker rights regimes. The remaining Scandinavian countries (Finland, Norway and Denmark) and the Netherlands stand somewhat below Sweden, while the United States stands well apart from even its closest 'neighbors' on this scale (New Zealand and the United Kingdom). The other sizable gap in the country rankings separates those with a positive worker rights score (all of the continental European countries, except Switzerland) from those with negative scores (all North American and Asian countries plus the United Kingdom and Switzerland).

WORKER RIGHTS AND SOCIOECONOMIC PERFORMANCE

There is a strong presumption among US economists in favor of free markets, minimal redistribution, and a highly circumscribed public sector.

Table 11.5   Country ranking on worker rights (WR3)

WR3	Country
— 2	Sweden (1.92)
	Finland (1.53)
	Netherlands (1.34)
	Norway (1.18)
	Denmark (1.12)
	Austria (1.01)
— 1	Belgium (0.99)
	Germany (0.77)
	Italy (0.36)
	France (0.35)
— 0	
	Australia (−0.90)
— −1	Switzerland (−1.00)
	Japan (−1.30)
	Canada (−1.36)
	United Kingdom (−1.50)
	New Zealand (−1.59)
— −2	
— −3	United States (−2.92)

The contemporary version of this worldview is the neoliberal model, which emphasizes financial and labor market deregulation, globalization of trade and investment, and privatization of public enterprises. Against this 'American' or 'free-market model' stands a 'social market model' of economic development, which is less willing to allow living standards to be determined by unconstrained market forces. In the words of French Prime Minister Lionel Jospin, 'Yes to the market economy, no to the market society' (Barber 2001, p. 1).

The question is, can we have one without the other? Of course, no society leaves the terms of employment and the distribution of income to be determined solely by market forces; even the United States has a Fair Labor Standards Act. Focusing on the labor market, the practical question is, how compatible (or incompatible) are European-style employment relations, wage-setting institutions, and social safety nets with the goal of long-run economic growth and improvements in living standards? We do not attempt a thorough analysis of this question here. However, we do offer a 'first look' at the relationship between worker rights (in which increasing rights imply the progressive substitution of rules for market forces) and some key measures of economic well-being and competitiveness: growth of per capita GDP, labor productivity, and real wages, income distribution, leisure, and integration in the world economy. More precise definitions and sources of these measures are provided in Table 11.6.

Economic Growth

We begin with a look at the relationship between worker rights and per capita GDP growth. Although Figure 11.1 offers no strong evidence of a positive relationship between these variables, it decisively rejects the rather widely held view that worker rights undermine economic growth.[18] We have argued elsewhere that the lack of a significant relationship between worker rights and per capita GDP growth is actually the net result of a *positive* relationship between worker rights and productivity growth (value added per hour) and a *negative* relationship between worker rights and employment growth (hours per capita) (Buchele and Christiansen 1999b).

Figure 11.2 provides evidence of a positive relationship between worker rights and productivity growth.[19] We argue that worker rights promote productivity growth by encouraging workers to contribute to innovations that raise productivity. Workers do so because strong worker rights increase the likelihood that workers have a secure stake in the long-run benefits of productivity growth (see Buchele and Christiansen 1999a). While worker rights do not eliminate the inherent conflicts in capitalist employment relations, they may encourage greater cooperation simply by highlighting the shared interests of employers and workers in raising productivity and by foreclosing 'low-road' options, for example, wage cutting and 'speedup' (see Buchele and Christiansen 2002).

Table 11.6 Definitions and data sources: measures of economic welfare

Definition	Data source
Average Annual Growth Rate of Real GDP per Capita (1990–99)	OECD *Economic Outlook*, June 2000, Table 1 (GDP); Maddison 2001, Tables A1-a and A3-a (population)
Average Annual Growth Rate of Real GDP per Hour (1990–99)	OECD *Economic Outlook*, June 2000, Tables 1 (GDP) and 20 (employment); OECD, *Employment Outlook*, June 2000, Table F; Maddison 2001, Table E-3
Average Annual Growth Rate of Real Compensation per Employee	Mishel et al. 2001, Table 7.5
Gini Index, Personal Income (early–mid-1990s)	World Bank, *World Development Report*, 1999/2000, Table 5 (pp. 238/9).
Minimum Mandated/Common Annual Vacation and Holiday Time in Weeks (1992). Set by law, in Italy, the UK, and the US, and augmented by collective bargaining agreements in many countries	OECD 1994, Part II, Table 6.12; Green 1997.
A.T. Kearney/Foreign Policy Magazine Index of Globalization (late 1990s). An index based on trade, capital flows, cross-border personal contact (for example travel, phone calls, and remittances), and internet access	A.T. Kearney, Global Business Policy Council (direct communcation, 4 May 2001); Kearney and Carnegie Endowment 2001.

Wage Growth, Income Distribution, and Leisure

Figure 11.3 indicates a positive relationship between worker rights and real wage growth. We argue that there is both a direct and an indirect causal link between these variables: worker rights raise real wage growth because they raise productivity growth (as shown in Figure 11.2) and because they enhance labor's bargaining power *vis-à-vis* employers (and thus labor's ability to claim its share of productivity gains).[20]

Figure 11.4 shows a strong negative relationship between worker rights and the Gini index of income distribution (in which a lower value indicates greater equality). This, again, should not surprise us, given the well-documented leveling influence of unions and collective bargaining on

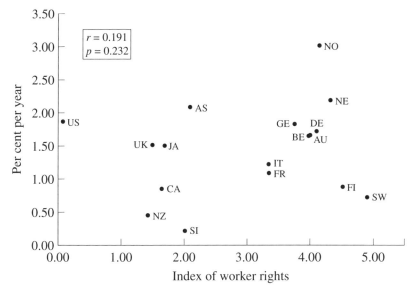

Figure 11.1   Average annual growth rate of real GDP per capita, 1990–1998

wages and the widespread use, at least in Europe, of income transfers to raise income floors (see Freeman and Katz 1994). Although we acknowledge that it is a 'value judgment' to say so, we believe that (at least in this range of Gini coefficients) socioeconomic welfare increases as income is more equally distributed. Greater equality reduces poverty and relative deprivation, and on a more instrumental level, there is persuasive evidence that, controlling for per capita income, countries with more equal income distributions have lower mortality rates and longer life expectancy (Wilkinson 1996; Glyn and Miliband 1994).

Leisure is another important aspect of quality of life, which is overlooked by such measures as per capita GDP. By 'leisure' we simply mean time off the job, either in the form of a shorter work week or fewer days of work per year, both of which have historically been goals of the labor movement everywhere (though less so in post-World War II US). Here we do not focus on hours per week, which are generally considerably higher in the United States and Japan, but on vacation time (see Green 1997). Figure 11.5 indicates a strong positive relationship between worker rights and weeks of vacation and holiday time per year, with workers in countries with

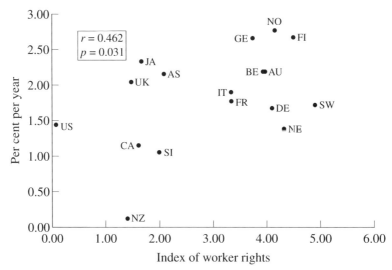

Note: For key, see Table 11.4.

Figure 11.2 Average annual rate of growth of real GDP per hour, 1990–1998

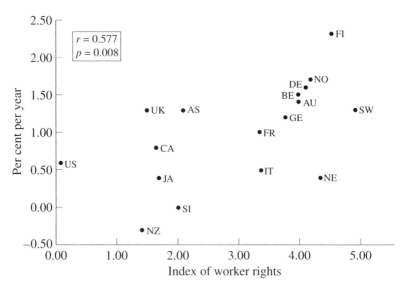

Note: For key, see Table 11.4

Figure 11.3 Average annual growth rate of real compensation per employee, business sector, 1989–1998

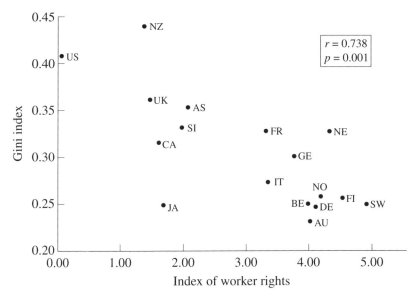

Note: For key, see Table 11.4

Figure 11.4   Gini index, personal income, early to mid-1990s

the strongest rights enjoying roughly three weeks more time off work each year than those in countries with the weakest rights.

International Competitiveness

We consider one final measure – an 'index of globalization' – not because it is a measure of economic well-being, but in response to the general presumption that worker rights are in conflict with globalization (in particular, with unrestricted free trade and capital mobility). Figure 11.6 suggests, to the contrary, that on average, countries with more worker rights score higher on this index.[21] This result is consistent with Rodrik's (1997) finding of a positive relationship between a country's 'openness' (exports plus imports as a percentage of GDP) and its spending on social protection (as a percentage of GDP). Rodrik argues that the most open economies have sought to reduce the social impact of openness on workers and to maintain a domestic consensus in favor of open markets through increased income transfers and social spending. Thus, 'the welfare state has been the flip side of the open economy' (Rodrik 1997, p. 28).

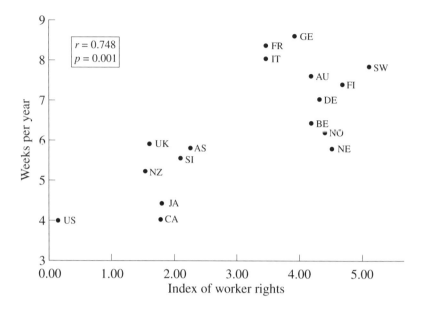

Note: For key, see Table 11.4.

Figure 11.5   Minimum mandated or common annual vacation and holiday time, 1992

CONCLUSION

We conclude that on a variety of welfare measures – including productivity growth, income distribution, and leisure – countries with stronger worker rights have better social and economic outcomes. Advocates of labor market deregulation believe that it will bring improved performance, especially in the area of employment growth, which we have not examined in this chapter (OECD 1994b). While there may be some truth to this, we argue that worker rights also promote beneficial, welfare-enhancing outcomes, and that there may well be more to lose than there is to gain by weakening them.

NOTES

*   We wish to thank Shreya Jain for invaluable assistance in preparing this chapter and participants at the Levy Institute conference and its organizer, Ed Wolff, for their thoughtful comments and suggestions.
1.   Weights were reduced where there were multiple indicators of the same underlying aspect

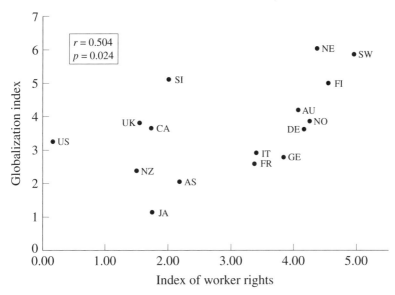

Note: For key, see Table 11.4.

Figure 11.6   A.T. Kearney/Foreign Policy index of globalization, late 1990s

  of employment protection and where one aspect was thought to be less important than another. For example, a week of advance notice was treated as the equivalent of 0.75 weeks of severance pay.
2. The OECD (1999) study, which is the source of our data on employment protection, does not provide data on protection against collective dismissals for the 1980s.
3. France provides the most dramatic example of collective bargaining coverage (95 per cent) exceeding union density (9 per cent). It may be the case that the automatic extension of union negotiated collective bargaining agreements to virtually all workers acts as a disincentive for non-union workers to unionize, since they already enjoy the primary benefit of union representation.
4. Many labor economists see the relatively long duration and generosity of European unemployment insurance schemes as the primary cause of relatively high European unemployment. Evidence that these may be, at least, the most statistically significant cause of unemployment (in a list of regressors including employment protection, union density, bargaining coverage, and coordination as well as replacement rates and duration of benefits) is found by Nickell (1997).
5. Blöndal and Pearson's summary measure of benefit entitlement unfortunately does not explicitly incorporate benefit *coverage*. The *OECD Jobs Study* (OECD 1994b, Table 8.4) reports coverage rates which show that countries with relatively generous benefit levels (for example, those of Northern Europe) have the highest coverage rates (generally over 90 per cent), while those with the lowest benefits (Italy, Japan, and the US) have the lowest coverage (roughly 20–35 per cent). Due to this positive correlation between our benefit series and the coverage data, it is unlikely that explicitly factoring coverage into our measure would appreciably change the relative position of these countries.
6. The very low adjusted replacement rate for Italy applies to the country's general unemployment insurance scheme, which covers only a small portion of the unemployed. This

commonly quoted rate for Italy excludes workers covered by the relatively more generous wage compensation fund (*Casa Integrazione Guardagni*), which guarantees a base-level income to redundant industrial workers who remain formally employed (Reissert and Schmid 1994). However, we were unable to find data on the coverage or replacement rates of the *CIG*.

7. We realize that there is likely to be more than the normal amount of measurement error associated with the worker rights data assembled in Table 11.2. This is true both because some of these measures (specifically the employment protection and bargaining coordination measures) involve the quantification of essentially qualitative data and because stated regulations do not always reflect actual practice. While it would always be beneficial to have better data, we are confident that we have the best available comparative data, and we believe that the large variety of interrelated measures provides a 'useful redundancy' that protects us from being thrown too far off course by random measurement error in using these data to create an overall index of worker rights.

8. Specifically, we standardize x_{ij}, the value of measure j in country i, obtaining $z_{ij} = (x_{ij} - \bar{x}_j)/\sigma_j$, and then compute country i's value on this index as $\mathbf{WR1}_i = 1/8\Sigma_{j=1}^8 z_{ij}$, $i = 1,2, ..., 17$. This approach was suggested to us (independently) by Brendan Burchell and Jim Stanford.

9. Note the ordinal nature of this index, indeed, of all the scales presented in Table 11.3. Thus, for example, if countries A, B, and C have scores of 1.0, 2.0 and 4.0 on the first worker rights index **WR1**, we can say that country C is 'twice as far' from country B as country B is from country A. But since the origin of the scale is entirely arbitrary – for example, their respective values could just as well be 101, 102, and 104 – we cannot say that worker rights in country C are 'twice as strong' as they are in country B or 'four times as strong' as they are in country A.

10. For a practical introduction to factor analysis, see Afifi and Clark (1990, Chs 14 and 15) or Tacq (1997, Ch. 9).

11. In this procedure, the original variables are first standardized to have a mean of zero and a variance of one, so the total variance in these data is eight. The extraction procedure defines a new variable (a linear combination of the original variables) that shares more variation with the original variables than any other linear combination of them does.

12. These factor loadings correspond to standardized regression coefficients with (for example) *EPR* as the dependent variable and the factors as the independent variables. The factor loadings are the simple correlations between *EPR* and each factor, and since the factors are orthogonal (uncorrelated), their squares are the percentage of the variance in *EPR* accounted for by each factor.

13. The next factor (not shown in Table 11.3) accounts for only 8.8 per cent of the variance in the data. Since this is less than the variance contributed by a single (standardized) variable (each of which contributes one-eighth, or 12.5 per cent of the total variance), the third factor is not 'pulling its own weight', and we retain only the first two factors.

14. Some readers may be concerned about our small sample size (17 countries) relative to the number of variables (eight) in the analysis. In response, we emphasize that we are using factor analysis here only for purposes of data reduction, that is to define one or two factors that underlie these measures. Since we are not using factor analysis for statistical inference or to test a priori hypotheses about the underlying structure of the data, we are not so concerned here about issues of sample size and degrees of freedom. In any case, these issues are no more relevant (or irrelevant) to our use of factor analysis for this purpose than they are to the previous 'mean of standardized measures' approach.

15. Geometrically, if the factors are thought of as axes in (say) three-dimensional space, rotation seeks to drive each axis through a separate data cluster so that each factor becomes identified with (and accounts for most of the variance in) a unique group of variables. The rotation procedure used here (called varimax) maintains the orthogonality (statistical independence) of the factors. 'Oblique' rotation (that does not preserve the orthogonality of the factors) is also an option but is not pursued here.

16. Note also that both approaches give greater weight to those aspects of worker rights on which we (happen) to have more data. Thus, there is less weight given to social protec-

tion/income security (which is measured by two variables) than to employment protection or to collective representation (which are each represented by three measures).

17. Of course, there is no special reason why worker rights need to be measured on a single scale. More than one factor score may be used to indicate a country's worker rights environment, for example, as independent variables in a regression analysis (see Buchele and Christiansen 1999a). We adopt the (admittedly ad hoc) procedure of adding them together in order to create a single index that can serve as the independent variable in the graphical analysis that follows.

18. In all figures, we have added a constant of three to our worker rights index (shifting the mean value of the index from zero to three) to simplify the visual presentation of the data.

19. While we argue on theoretical grounds for a causal relationship between rights and productivity growth (specifically that worker rights 'promote' productivity growth), we acknowledge that positive correlations – even statistically significant ones – in these cross-country data do not preclude the possibility of reverse causation, simultaneity, or spurious correlation. We have tried to strengthen the causal case by measuring worker rights at the beginning or middle of the period over which we have measured productivity growth. We acknowledge that if productivity growth fosters rights (for example, by reducing employer resistance) then any estimate of the net effect of worker rights on productivity growth is biased upwards. But as long as the causation runs both ways, this is no argument against a 'high-road' (strong worker rights/high labor productivity) industrial relations system.

20. Using a sample of 80 advanced and less-developed countries, and controlling for labor productivity, income level, and a 'democracy index' (whose effect was his main focus), Rodrik (1999) finds that neither union density nor ratification of the International Labour Organization's basic worker rights conventions have a significant effect on wages. Our finding of a significant positive effect of worker rights on wage growth applies, in a sense, to a subset of his countries all of which are economically advanced and (relatively) strong democracies.

21. This index measures trade, capital flows, personal contact across borders (for example cross-border travel, phone calls, and remittances), and internet access. It was developed jointly by A.T. Kearney and *Foreign Policy* (see Kearney, A.T. Inc 2001) and generously made available to us by Jay W. Scheuer of A.T. Kearney's Global Business Policy Council.

REFERENCES

Afifi, A.A., and V. Clark (1990), *Computer-Aided Multivariate Analysis* (2nd edn), New York: Van Nostrand Reinhold Co.

Barber, Lionel (2001), 'Europe seeks a third way to prosperity', *Financial Times*, 15 January, p. 1.

Blöndel, S., and M. Pearson (1995), 'Unemployment and other non-employment benefits', *Oxford Review of Economic Policy*, **11** (1), 136–69.

Buchele, R., and J. Christiansen (1998), 'Do employment and income security cause unemployment? A comparative study of the US and the E-4', *Cambridge Journal of Economics*, **22** (1), 117–36.

Buchele, R., and J. Christiansen (1999a), 'Labor relations and productivity growth in the advanced capitalist economies', *Review of Radical Political Economy*, **31** (1), 87–110.

Buchele, R., and J. Christiansen (1999b), 'Employment and productivity growth in Europe and North America: the impact of labor market institutions', *International Review of Applied Economics*, **13** (3), 313–32.

Buchele, R., and J. Christiansen (2002), 'Employment relations', in Malcolm Warner (ed.), *The International Encyclopedia of Business and Management* (2nd edn), London: International Thompson Publishing, pp. 1683–98.

Freeman, R.B. (1994), 'Lessons for the United States', in R.B. Freeman (ed.), *Working Under Different Rules*, New York: Russell Sage, pp. 223–39.

Freeman, R.B., and L.F. Katz (1994), 'Rising wage inequality: the United States vs. other advanced countries', in R.B. Freeman (ed.), *Working Under Different Rules*, New York: Russell Sage, pp. 29–62.

Glyn, A., and D. Miliband (eds) (1994), *Paying for Inequality: The Economic Cost of Social Injustice*, London and Concord, MA. IPPR/Rivers Oram Press.

Green, F. (1997), 'Union recognition and paid holiday entitlement', *British Journal of Industrial Relations*, **35** (2), June, 243–55.

Greenwood, Daphne (2001), 'Local indicators of quality of life: a preliminary look at the Pikes Peak region', working paper no. 6, Center for Colorado Policy Studies, accessed at http://web.uccs.edu/ccps.

Grubb, D., and W. Wells (1993), 'Employment regulation and patterns of work in EC countries', *OECD Economic Studies*, **21**, 7–58.

Kearney, A.T. Inc. and the Carnegie Endowment for International Peace (2001), 'Measuring globalization', *Foreign Policy*, January–February, 56–65.

MacFarlan, M., and H. Oxley (1996), 'Social transfers: spending patterns, institutional arrangements and policy responses', *OECD Economic Studies*, **2** (27), 146–93.

Maddison, Angus (2001), *The World Economy: A Millennial Perspective*, Paris: Organisation for Economic Co-operation and Development.

Mishel, L., J. Bernstein and J. Schmitt (2001), *The State of Working America 2000–2001*, Washington, DC: Economic Policy Institute.

Mishel, L., and J. Schmitt (1995), *Beware the U.S. Model*, Washington, DC: Economic Policy Institute.

Nickell, S. (1997), 'Unemployment and labor market rigidities: Europe versus North America', *Journal of Economic Perspectives*, **11** (3), Summer, 55–74.

OECD (1994a, 1997, 1999), *OECD Employment Outlook*, Paris: Organisation for Economic Co-operation and Development.

OECD (1994b), *The OECD Jobs Study: Evidence and Explanations*, Paris: Organisation for Economic Co-operation and Development.

OECD (2000), *OECD Economic Outlook*, vol. 67, June, Paris: Organisation for Economic Co-operation and Development.

Reissert, B., and G. Schmid (1994), 'Unemployment compensation and active labor market policy', in G. Schmid (ed.), *Labor Market Institutions in Europe*, Armonk, NY: M.E. Sharpe, pp. 83–119.

Rodrik, D. (1999), 'Democracies pay higher wages', *Quarterly Journal of Economics*, **64** (3), 707–38.

Rodrik, D. (1997), 'Sense and nonsense in the glozalization debate', *Foreign Policy*, Summer, 19–37.

Savageau, David, and Gregory Loftus (2000), *Places Rated Almanac: Your Guide to Finding the Best Places to Live in America*, 6th edn, New York: Macmillan.

Siebert, H. (1997), 'Labor market rigidities: at the root of unemployment in Europe', *Journal of Economic Perspectives*, **11** (3), Summer, 37–54.

Tacq, J. (1997), *Multivariate Analysis Techniques in Social Science Research*, New York: Sage.

Wilkinson, R. (1996), *Unhealthy Societies: The Afflictions of Inequality*, London and New York: Routledge.
World Bank (1999/2000), *World Development Report*, New York: Oxford University Press.

12. Measuring quality of life with local indicators

Daphne T. Greenwood

INTRODUCTION

Concern with the quality of life in the United States and other industrialized nations has led to a variety of local projects addressing this issue. Many community-based indicator projects have moved beyond traditional economic measures of well-being. The locally-based approach has both advantages and problems, as this chapter outlines. Three communities – Austin, Texas; Jacksonville, Florida; and Seattle, Washington – stand out from the many projects around the United States in developing indicators that incorporate economic, environmental and social factors as well as linkages among them.

This chapter reviews the results of the three projects, with more detail presented in the appendices. In addition, recommendations are made as to how local indicators could be more useful and more accurate measures of the quality of life. While some things can be learned from the changes in these local indicators, it is difficult to extrapolate from the results of only three communities to assess whether quality of life is improving as a whole in the United States. In this chapter, we suggest conclusions that can reasonably be drawn from the results presented here and from other studies comparing quality of life in various cities across the United States.

WHY QUANTIFY 'QUALITY OF LIFE'?

Sustained economic growth in the United States and other industrialized countries has led to renewed interest in quality of life as well as income levels. Economists once assumed that educational and health needs would be addressed as a byproduct of income growth, but cross-country comparisons show that their correlation to income levels is weaker than one would expect (Slottje 1991). Concerns about inequality, environmental degradation, the breakdown of the social structure of society, and investment in future gen-

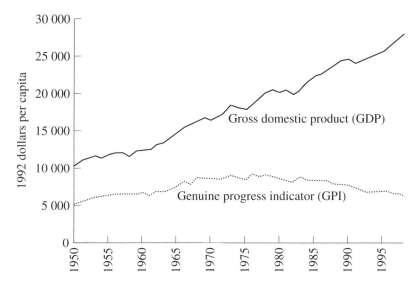

Source: Redefining Progress, Tyler Norris and Associates

Figure 12.1 Genuine progress indicator: an alternative measure of progress

erations and physical infrastructure have led to widespread dissatisfaction with growth in gross domestic product (GDP) as a unilateral goal.

At the national level, the Genuine Progress Index (GPI) subtracts some of the costs of growth from GDP while adding an estimated value for non-market activities like household and volunteer work (see Appendix 12A1). Developed in 1994, the GPI is directed at measuring more of what actually 'affects people's lives' in order to create better measures of economic well-being for policy use (Rowe and Anielski 1999). In Figure 12.1, the GDP portrays almost steady economic advance from the 1950s to the present, while the GPI rose until the mid-1970s and has fallen slightly ever since. Although the GDP indicates that the economy has been growing quite rapidly during most of the last few years, social and environmental costs now outweigh the benefits of growth in the GPI.

The Index of Social Health, developed at Fordham University in 1987, tracks annual changes in a variety of social indicators going back to 1970. Just as the GPI diverges from GDP growth in the mid-1970s, the Index of Social Health peaks at 75 of a possible 100 during the mid-1970s and then falls fairly steadily in the early 1980s. Values over the last 20 years have fluctuated somewhat between 38 and 45 but did not increase with economic growth (Miringoff and Miringoff 1999).

Communities around the nation are also grappling with ways to move beyond traditional economic measures to broader concepts termed 'quality of life', 'healthy communities', or 'sustainable development'. Much of what is subtracted from GDP in the GPI measure, such as the costs of crime, environmental damage, income inequality or child poverty, time spent in commuting, appears in the indicators communities choose to supplement traditional economic measures. Local indicators also reflect some of what the GPI adds to GDP, such as unpaid volunteer work, the value of public open space, the arts, and basic infrastructure maintenance.

Although theoretically distinct,[1] in practice the terms 'quality of life' and 'sustainability' tend to be used almost interchangeably in local projects. The Jacksonville quality-of-life indicators include information on a variety of human capital variables. Infant mortality and child poverty rates are both sustainability concepts in regard to the future workforce in addition to serving as current standard-of-living benchmarks. The Sustainable Seattle project collects information on volunteer hours in public schools, which is more a short-term quality-of-life measure than one of capital stock.

WHY COLLECT QUALITY OF LIFE INFORMATION AT THE LOCAL LEVEL?

Indicators as a Means to Encourage Local Action

While economic forces are largely national, or even global, many changes necessary to improve other aspects of quality of life – altered development patterns, better public schools, less racism, or community policing – require collective action at the local level. For this reason, it makes sense for communities to work toward a shared vision and priorities.

The use of broadly-based community indicators is often based on the premise that collecting new data will lead to addressing problems previously ignored. A leading guide for the development of community indicators says:

> By convening citizens to consider how to measure their overall well-being, the community as a whole is spurred to create new visions of the future, develop new working relationships across old boundaries, and define its assets, problems, and opportunities in new ways. (Norris et al. 1997, p. 1)

In the Jacksonville, Austin, and Seattle experiences, combinations of concerns about rapid population and land-use growth, along with inequality of economic opportunity, led to citizen-based initiatives with local government support. Passage of growth management legislation by the Nevada state legislature led to an indicators project for the greater Reno (Truckee Meadows) area, where growth patterns could be compared with target quality-of-life variables to assess needed policy changes at the city and county levels (Besleme et al. 1999). These are typical of the local concerns that spur a movement for indicators that go beyond traditional economic measures.[2]

The Importance of Place and Community in Quality-of-life Considerations

Many qualitative or noneconomic variables are best measured in connection with place or community rather than the individual. Examples include air and water quality, open space or parkland, outdoor recreation opportunities, or exposure to environmental hazards. Individuals are unlikely to be able to answer survey questions about these issues accurately. The high cost of measuring individual values of air quality or parkland access would also be unwarranted, since the same results often apply to large population groups within a geographic area.

A community-based measure is also appropriate for public safety. While individual surveys can measure whether or not the respondent was a victim of crime, the overall crime rate in an area is a better indicator of perceived safety. As crime rates increase, individuals will be less willing to walk alone after dark or answer the door for an unknown caller. They will spend more on security systems and other methods of private crime prevention in relation to the threat of crime, not just their own individual experience.

Sense of community is another important part of quality of life for most people. Surveys can ask individuals about their willingness to help neighbors or whether there are people they could ask for help. But community-wide measures of trust, helpfulness, or civic awareness are useful in establishing the level of 'social capital' (Putnam 1993, Dasgupta 1997). Measures of trust, neighborliness or membership in voluntary organizations reflect the social environment of the community of residence in much the same manner that air and water quality do for the natural environment.

Finally, the quality of education, although often the focus of national election debates, is also best measured at the local level. National or state averages include so much variability that they do not have much meaning for any individual. Survey data might be able to match individual educational experiences with other economic and demographic data, but at a very high cost. In any event, the social dimension of educational quality as it affects the community would be lost if only individual experiences were measured.

VARIABILITY OF LOCAL PREFERENCES

People with similar values often cluster, creating communities with varying sets of values and priorities (Blomquist et al. 1988). Within a metropolitan area, some communities seek to preserve single-family homes on large lots, while others welcome the density that will allow better rapid transit or cultural variety. Access to bike paths may be important to quality of life in Boulder, Colorado, while preserving access to hunting may be of higher value in Cheyenne, Wyoming. Defining quality-of-life variables at the local level accommodates the varying priorities of communities.

While almost everyone says they value education, quality schools are clearly a higher priority in some areas than others. The sorting of people into those who prefer low-tax, low-service environments and those who prefer high-tax, high-service ones leads to different levels of publicly provided amenities (Gyourko and Tracy 1991). Even when tax and service levels are high they may be concentrated on transportation systems or the preservation of outdoor recreation rather than schools, which reflects differing community priorities.

PROBLEMS WITH MEASURING QUALITY OF LIFE AT THE LOCAL LEVEL

Defining Quality of Life

Decisions about which indicators will be used to quantify quality of life are difficult, and vary by community. Each of the communities reviewed here used a lengthy process involving a broad spectrum of community groups in the decisions.[3] It is interesting to see the similarity of ideas in the Jacksonville, Seattle, and Austin projects, despite the fact that the last two define themselves as sustainability indicator projects rather than quality-of-life indicators.

- The Jacksonville project defines quality of life as 'a feeling of well-being, fulfillment, or satisfaction resulting from factors in the external environment' (Jacksonville Community Council, Inc. 2000, p. 1). While stressing the importance of interpersonal relationships to actual feelings about quality of life it concentrates on the external environment.
- The Seattle project focuses on sustainability although the term 'quality of life' is also used. It asks 'How do we protect our environment, meet everyone's basic needs, keep our economy dynamic, and

maintain a just society? How do we make difficult trade-offs and balanced judgments that take everyone's interests into account, including those of our children and grandchildren?' (Sustainable Seattle
1998).
- The Central Texas Indicators, based in Austin, also focuses on sustainability as the guiding principle while acknowledging the importance of quality of life. They state their goal as 'recognizing the
  interdependence of the environment, economic development, and
  social equity . . . with a decision-making climate that invests in what
  is good for today without compromising the future for our children,
  a climate that benefits each person and the common good'
  (Sustainability Indicators Project of Hayes, Travis and Williamson
  Counties 2000).

Quality of Life: Having, Loving, and Being

One way of understanding quality-of-life indicators is through Allardt's
(1993) model of 'having, loving and being'. 'Having' deals with the satisfaction of basic needs, while 'loving' includes all social relationships with other
people, including coworkers and the larger community. 'Being' encompasses
needs for personal growth and for harmony with nature. It includes the
degree of self-determination an individual has, as well as their opportunities
for political activities, meaningful work, enjoying nature, and leisure time.

Many quality-of-life measures simply extend the range of 'having'
beyond market goods and services. Air quality or access to open space are
consumed by individuals and affect health and well-being although we do
not pay for them in the private market. Access to cultural or recreational
activities are characteristics of a community, even if ability and willingness
to pay are characteristics of the individual consumer. Even measures of
neighborliness are to some degree measures of consumption possibilities –
proxies for our ability to have certain needs met beyond the circle of family
and friends but outside the market system. The more we can rely on neighbors, the less we need to rely on paid services for watering the garden when
out of town, paying for a drive to the store for a cup of sugar, or even enter-
ing a nursing home when elderly.

Measures of 'having' are necessary to supplement income and arrive at
a better measure of the standard of living. In Allardt's view, a true quality-
of-life measure must go further, incorporating measures of loving and
being, such as the well-being of others and political or social freedom.
Measures of 'social capital' (Putnam 1993; Sen 1993; Coleman 1988)
should be included in quality of life, along with measures for the natural
environment.

Many of Allardt's ideas are reflected in the measures used by Jacksonville, Austin, and Seattle. 'Having' includes measures like access to child care as well as air and water quality. 'Loving' includes measures like perceived racism, family violence and the divorce rate. 'Being' includes indicators of access to cultural resources, nature, and recreation as well as many equity and civic participation measures. Although the discussion of indicators for each project does not articulate choices using this language, the indicators chosen demonstrate community concerns in each of these areas.

Limited Focus or Time Duration of Indicator Projects

Most of the communities reporting indicator projects in Appendix 12A2 have produced very little data. Many of the projects have not moved beyond discussion of community values. Often, a focus on sustainability or quality of life actually reflects other community concerns such as a faltering economy or an influx of new population. The commitment to data collection fails to gain enough political or financial support or falters once the other concerns have been addressed. The Sustainable Seattle project, one of the models for many other groups in the US, is operational again after a hiatus of several years in which insufficient funding was available.

Where data has been collected it is often limited to one particular area of concern, such as health, environmental issues, economic factors, or children's well-being, without placing it in a larger context. Austin, Jacksonville, and Seattle are unusual in their linkage of the economic, the environmental, and the social and their acknowledgment of tradeoffs within and between these areas.

Loss of Distributional Information for Some Indicators

Another limitation of locally collected indicators is a reliance on mean values that fail to reflect the distribution of highly skewed indicators. While aggregation at some level is necessary to capture certain environmental and social components of well-being that are spatially related, for other measures the use of averages may not adequately reflect the community. Library circulation or book sales per capita reveals a dimension of the community, but may not reveal much about large subpopulations of the community. Similarly, there is often a substantial difference between the measurement of crime and educational variables in the more affluent suburbs and in the central core of the city.

Some criticize community indicators as having an inherently middle-class or suburban bias (Wish 1986). While this may be true for some of the popular rating guides,[4] the studies discussed here all include indicators designed to capture the distribution of well-being and opportunity across the population and others directed toward the degree of racial harmony or tension. By using a number of measures regarding income, for example (the ratio of median income to median housing price, the poverty rate, the hours necessary to meet basic needs) a fairly realistic picture of the community can be formed from the results.

Local Economic or Civic Agendas

Many local quality-of-life studies are based on a desire to attract capital or jobs (Rogerson 1999). Accurate measurement of quality of life can be complicated by civic or economic 'boosterism', local agendas for environmental improvement, growth limits, or other social causes. When driven by a desire to promote, measurements may be ruled out unless they give positive results. When driven by a desire to avoid growth or change, there may be an undue emphasis on indicators with negative results. It is not unusual for local chambers of commerce and economic development associations to lobby magazine editors and writers and other outside groups who develop ratings of cities and to want as much positive evidence as possible to cite in their lobbying efforts.

Cross-sectional and Time-series Comparisons between Communities

As we have seen, a particular strength of the community indicator movement is the ability to focus on issues of specific local concern. However, this local focus makes it difficult to compare different communities even when they address the same issues. For example, each of the three communities reviewed here (Austin, Jacksonville, and Seattle) was concerned about affordable housing. But their choice of indicator to measure the change in housing affordability was very different. Austin measured housing affordability with the percentage of households whose income qualifies them to purchase the median-priced home or rent the average two-bedroom apartment. Jacksonville set a goal of having the average single-family home cost no more than two-and-a-half times family income and tracked this over time. Seattle calculated affordability for median buyers and first-time buyers using mortgage rates and mortgage insurance as well as home prices, as well as rental data from a local consulting firm. Using this information, we can see the directional change in housing affordability for each community (see Table 12.8, which appears later in this chapter), but cannot use the results to compare housing affordability among the three cities.

Analysis across time is also limited by lack of record-keeping and by reliance on sporadic surveys or one-time academic studies. This makes it difficult to use statistical techniques to relate changes in one series to changes in another and to better understand the relationships between social, environmental and economic components of quality of life across cities. Not surprisingly, communities find that their most reliable data, with the longest history and the greatest comparability to other communities, is federally collected economic or demographic information. Second in availability and reliability is data collected by the Environmental Protection Agency as far back as the 1970s.

LOCAL INDICATOR PROJECTS

Three excellent examples of community indicator projects encompass economic, environmental, and social measures and address the linkages between them. Jacksonville and Seattle include data going back to the 1980s. Austin completed its first study in year 2000 and has at most three to five years of data per indicator. There is a great deal of similarity in the issues addressed by the communities, although unique concerns such as preserving wild salmon runs in Seattle and tracking the number of new patents granted in Austin are interesting local variations on the quality-of-life or sustainability themes.

Jacksonville (Duval County), Florida

One of the oldest and most comprehensive sets of quality-of-life indicators comes from Jacksonville, Florida (Jacksonville Community Council, Inc. 2000). In 1985, the Jacksonville Community Council, in partnership with city government and the Chamber of Commerce, convened over 100 volunteers to develop a model for measuring changes in the local quality of life.[5] It has been updated regularly through the year 2000. Telephone surveys were used for certain indicators reflecting public opinion or perception. Some of the survey numbers fluctuate in what appears to be a random pattern, suggesting major variability due to sampling error.[6]

The nine major elements of quality of life in Jacksonville were identified as:

- *Education*   Public K-12 and higher education, including adult education.
- *Economy*   Standard of living for individuals and economic health of community.

- *Natural Environment*   Quality of the ecosystem and visual aesthetics.
- *Social Environment*   Equality of opportunity, racial harmony, family life, human services, philanthropy, and volunteerism.
- *Culture and Recreation*   Supply and use.
- *Health*   Individual health and the system of health care.
- *Government/Politics*   Participation in public affairs, informed citizenry, leadership, and performance in local government.
- *Mobility*   Opportunities for and convenience of travel within Jacksonville and with other locations.
- *Public Safety*   Perception as well as incidence of crime and accidents, quality of law enforcement, fire protection, and rescue services.

Using changes in a selected key indicator between the late 1980s to the end of the 1990s showed advances in four areas of quality of life, declines in two, two areas for which the direction of change was unclear, and one (culture and recreation) that lacked enough consistent data to draw a conclusion about the direction of change. Although greater detail can be found in Appendix 12A3, the major advances in Jacksonville quality-of-life indicators include:

- the economy, with net employment growth increasing;
- the natural environment, with the number of good air quality days increasing substantially;
- government and politics, as rating of city leadership as good increased from 33 to 71 per cent over the decade; and
- public safety, with substantial declines in the index crime rate (violent and nonviolent).

There was no clear pattern in the Jacksonville indicators chosen to represent:

- social environment, represented by the percentage seeing racism as a serious problem which fell only slightly from 51 to 49 per cent; and
- mobility, as measured by the percentage of workers with less than 25 minutes of commuting time, which remained close to the target value in most years (58 per cent).

Declines in quality-of-life indicators in Jacksonville included:

- education, as high-school graduation rates fell from 72.6 per cent in 1982 to 58.7 per cent (with a high of 80 per cent in 1993); and
- health, as the infant mortality rate increased to 10.2 per 10 000.

Areas where relying on multiple indicators would have made a difference in Jacksonville

The use of one key indicator to measure progress in an entire sector misses some of the complexity of Seattle's reliance on multiple indicators to assess a directional change for each category. Within measures of the natural environment, Jacksonville water quality[7] showed an erratic pattern from year to year, with no clear trend based on a variety of standards, in contrast to the clear improvement in air quality measures which was used as the key environmental indicator in the report.

While both violent and nonviolent index crimes decreased, along with motor vehicle accidents per 1000, victim surveys in Jacksonville showed no clear trend over the period. This suggests that the decline in reported crime may have been due to a decline in trust of police or the judicial system.[8] Using all of the public safety data available gives a much more mixed picture than does the simple reported crime rate. For example, serious violations of the school codes of conduct increased and the number of people who report feeling safe walking alone at night in their neighborhood fluctuated between 43 and 62 per cent over the 15-year period.

Jacksonville health quality declined based on the infant mortality rate as the key indicator.[9] But other health indicators tracked show a mixed pattern. The percentage of people surveyed who have no health insurance was down to 8 per cent in 2000 (below the target of 9 per cent) relative to 11 per cent in 1991 and a high of 24 per cent in 1995. At the same time, the percentage of people rating the local health-care system as good to excellent also declined fairly steadily from 70 per cent in 1986 to 62 per cent in 2000. Clearer evidence of reduced alcohol and tobacco use is shown by a fairly steady decline in the percentage of youths using alcohol, from 63 per cent in 1989 to 51 per cent in 1999, and a sharp downward trend in sales of cigarettes among the general population.

Comparing Jacksonville to the nation as a whole

Improvements in reported crime, air quality, teen birth rates, the overall economy, and health insurance in Jacksonville mirror national trends. The concentration of poverty among children and the decline in mobility indicators are also widespread nationally. There are two areas in which Jacksonville improved while most of the nation did not: a lower housing cost to income ratio and increased confidence in local government officials.

It is difficult to know how much of the change in quality indicators in a particular area is due to policy initiatives or individual behavioral changes that differ from national trends. For instance, Florida was one of the top four states in the United States for immigration from other countries in the 1990s. An influx of poorly educated, lower-income immigrants may have increased child poverty and high-school dropout rates despite improvement in many parts of the United States in the late 1990s.

Seattle (King County), Washington

Beginning in 1991, a volunteer citizens' network in Seattle, supported by major corporate and foundation funding, selected 40 economic, environmental, and social indicators.[11] Their initial document expresses the hope that results would be used by citizens and policy makers to guide behavior changes in the direction of a more sustainable course focused on measures of 'long-term health and vitality – cultural, economic, environmental, and social'. Some indicators refer to the city of Seattle proper, while others look at King County and still others the entire state of Washington. The second and third reports, in 1995 and 1998, used many of the same indicators, with some additions, and modifications based on improvements or changes in the underlying data.

The Seattle indicators are grouped into five categories:

- Environment.
- Population and Resources.
- Economy.
- Youth and Education.
- Health and Community.

But environmental variables such as toxic releases and water consumption are categorized into 'Population and Resources', and some youth-related variables such as low birthweight for infants are part of 'Health and Community'. On the other hand, health-care expenditures per capita and emergency room use for nonemergency purposes are classified as part of 'Economy'. The varied categorization of identical or similar indicators is characteristic of locally-based community indicator projects.

Advances in Seattle quality-of-life indicators include:

- reductions in water use due to conservation and more efficient system operation;
- more good air quality days;
- reduced toxic releases per capita;
- decreasing proportions of minority youth involved in the juvenile justice system;
- above-average rates of community service and volunteer activities for youth;
- decreased energy use per dollar of personal income;

- increased public participation in the arts; and
- higher voter participation.

There were mixed results in for the following indicators:

- soil erosion;
- housing affordability, which stabilized recently but worsened in the last few decades;
- emergency room use for nonemergency purposes;
- the percentage of low birthweight infants, which has improved but is still far higher among minority populations than the white population;
- asthma hospitalizations for children, which have fluctuated over time;
- inability to raise the ratio of minority teachers closer to that of minority students;
- juvenile crime, which has stabilized but is still too high; and
- perceptions of local quality of life, which remain fairly evenly divided.

Declines in Seattle quality-of-life indicators came in:

- greater dependence on the automobile, as measured by per capita fuel consumption and vehicle miles traveled;
- generation of solid waste per capita, somewhat balanced by more recycling;
- greater use of renewable and nonrenewable energy;
- greater income inequality and higher child poverty rates;
- hours of work required to meet basic needs, which rose substantially in the early 1990s, then declined slightly in late 1990s;
- higher spending on health-care services per capita.[11]

The Seattle-area data, presented in greater detail in Appendix 12A4, show a mixed picture of quality-of-life change over time. Of 40 indicators, the 1998 report shows 11 moving Seattle toward sustainability, 11 that are neutral, and eight moving in a negative direction. There is insufficient data for any conclusive statement on 10 of the indicators. The 1998 results of 11 improvements were an advance over eight improvements in the 1995 report.

Most of the improvements and declines mirror data for the rest of the nation. Air quality improved, but water quality had a more mixed record. Toxic releases have fallen, but dependence on the automobile has increased.

Unemployment rates are down but inequality is up. Low birthweight and infant mortality continue to be much higher for minority populations and have shown little improvement. However, in the Seattle area they have been below national averages for quite a while. The above-average rates of youth community service and adult volunteering stand out from most of the nation, although the measurement of the indicator is not replicated by other projects.

Austin (Travis, Hays, and Williamson Counties), Texas

The newest of the comprehensive indicator projects reviewed here also focused on sustainability issues. *Central Texas Indicators 2000* (Sustainability Indicators Project of Hays, Travis and Williamson Counties 2000) includes some data from a tricounty area as well as some only for the city of Austin. It attempts to go back five years in data collection and contrast results to national averages or other comparable cities where possible. The project was headquartered in the city of Austin planning department, but received initial assistance from the University of Texas Graduate Program in Community and Regional Planning. Local print and electronic media and other local businesses contributed in-kind resources toward its completion.

Indicators were grouped into four areas:

- Community and Children.
- Workforce and Economy.
- Health and Environment.
- Land and Infrastructure.

'Health and Environment' includes the sorts of individual health variables and environmental measures one would expect, but there are surprises in other areas. Transportation indicators are in the 'Land and Infrastructure' category, for example. Education indicators are part of 'Community and Children', along with measures of cultural access, public safety, and racial equity.

Advances, based on the last few years, include performance in:

- the economy, as dependence on top employers decreased, more new businesses survived, the number of patents granted increased, and the unemployment rate (consistently lower than state and national rates) declined over the decade; and
- educational opportunity, as the number of subsidized childcare spots and the percentage of children of all races enrolled in public schools rated 'exemplary' grew.

Mixed results included the areas of:

- public safety, since the indexed crime rate fell over the decade while reports of family violence (something not collected in the other studies) increased during the last three years;
- Equity of opportunity as poverty rates declined over the decade from 16 to 13 per cent, but were still above the national average, and racial/ethnic influences on the approval of home loans or youth encounters with the law remained evident over the last several years; and
- health, with the percentage covered by health insurance close to national and above state averages, but showing no clear trend over four years, while self-reporting of health status and suicide rates were stable and similar to national rates.

Declines in quality-of-life measures included:

- housing affordability, with the percentage of homes priced affordably for a median-income family declining from 62 to 57 per cent over the decade; and
- environmental measures, since releases of toxic materials decreased, but air and water quality worsened and public open space acreage per resident declined over the past four years.

For greater detail, see Appendix 12A5.

Comparisons between Indicators in These Areas

Where federal collection or national guidelines exist for an indicator (air quality, crime rates, median income) there is fairly direct comparability for an indicator between geographic areas. However, where definitions and data are less standardized, the reader should look carefully at differences in the definitions, criteria, or collection processes as detailed further in each of the studies. In addition, although the data presented in the tables below for Austin and Jacksonville are generally for year 2000, the most recent Seattle data are from 1996 and 1997.

Table 12.1, shows several economic indicators often used to supplement traditional income and job growth measures. Table 12.2 includes typical environmental and land-use indicators, while Table 12.3 covers health and public safety indicators. Civic indicators are included in Table 12.4, cultural and educational indicators in Table 12.5, and transportation and mobility indicators in Table 12.6. Many indicators could easily be classified in two

Table 12.1   Sample supplementary economic indicators

Indicator	Austin	Jacksonville	Seattle
Child poverty or overall poverty rate	13.0		15.7
Per cent of children in families below basic need level or on school lunch program		46.5	33.0
Median home price/median income		2.25	
Per cent of households able to purchase median priced home	59.0		
Rental affordability[1]	59.0		
Per cent average rent above affordability for low-income households[2]			60.0
Rate of change of median income/rate of change in CPI	3.6		
Per cent of new businesses surviving 3+ years	75.6		
Per cent of total jobs in public sector	21.5		
Per cent of total jobs from top 10 private employers	11.1		16.0
Per cent of new jobs: top 10 industry sectors	37.0		

Notes:
1. Percentage of households for which average apartment rent would be less than 35 per cent of household income.
2. Affordability defined as no more than 30 per cent of income for households at 50 per cent or less of median income.

or three different categories, and in different cities and different projects they often are. Should vehicle accident rates be an indicator of public safety or of transportation? Different communities make different decisions about these categorizations as well as about the choice of key indicators.

Table 12.1, supplementary economic indicators, includes measures of the diversification of the employment base, the affordability of housing, and the degree to which income growth is spread throughout the community. If available, the overall poverty rate or child poverty rate can indicate how widely the benefits of job and income growth are spread throughout the community. Where recent poverty rates are not available, the percentage of K-12 pupils on free and reduced lunches provides an alternative measure of child poverty, since it is based on poverty-line criteria.

The percentage of jobs, or job growth from the largest employers or industrial sectors gives an indication of the stability of employment over the business cycle. Measures of the number of new businesses and their viability over time are important to communities such as Austin because they view the entrepreneurial sector as a vital source of income and jobs.

Table 12.2   Sample environmental and land-use quality indicators

Indicator	Austin	Jacksonville	Seattle
Toxic releases in pounds, annually	243 296		750 000
Solid waste generated per capita per day	8.6		8.1
Solid waste recycled per capita per day			4.0
Good air quality days		325	320
Days not meeting national ozone standards	20		
Open space or park acreage per 1000*	60.3	13.02	
Per cent living near urban open space			87
Newly platted for development acreage as per cent of total undeveloped land approved for conversion	1.06		
Water bodies meeting state standards (per cent)	45.5	59	
Daily per capita water consumption (gallons)	194	49.6	92.5
Per cent of land surface impervious to water			32
Gasoline consumption per capita, annual		607	530

Note: *The Austin figure is for a three-county area but includes only publicly owned parks, recreation areas, wildlife preserves, and hunting grounds.

Housing affordability measures compare both rents and home prices to wage and income levels. To be comprehensive, measures of housing afford-ability must address more than what is happening to the 'average' buyer and find ways to capture the experience of lower-middle-income buyers and low-income renters.

Table 12.2 includes a sample of environmental and land-use measures used by communities. Open space per capita, proximity to open space, and the percentage of undeveloped land newly platted for development are all measures relating to land use. There are enormous differences in measure-ment between areas, making these difficult to compare between commu-nities. Other measures such as per capita consumption of water or gasoline, or the number of good air quality days, are much more directly compar-able. Toxic release data is influenced by the amount and type of industry within a community. Many of these measures are more useful to a particu-lar community over time, as they track changes that occur and their effects on other aspects of quality of life.

Table 12.3 includes a variety of measures used to assess the quality of health and public safety in a community. Some communities use surveys to ask the population the quality of their health or their health care. Lung cancer death and suicide rates are more objective measures of more limited dimensions of health. Use of cigarettes and alcohol, especially among the

Table 12.3   *Sample health and public safety quality-of-life indicators*

Indicator	Austin	Jacksonville	Seattle
Per cent with no health insurance	20	8	
Emergency room use for nonemergencies			89.6
Per cent reporting good health status/health care	51	62	
Per cent of babies born at low birthweight			5.7
Infant mortality rate per 1000		10.2	
Per cent of youth (ages 12 to17) reporting alcohol use		51	
Packs of cigarettes sold per person		90	
Lung cancer deaths per 100000		61.2	
Suicides per 100000	10		
Per cent feeling safe walking at night		62	
Indexed crime rate per 100000	6373	6900	
Family violence/child abuse reports per 1000	10	13.5	

youth population can be leading indicators for future health problems. The infant mortality rate, or the discrepancy between races in mortality along with the percentage of babies born at low birthweight and the percentage of pregnant mothers receiving prenatal care in the first trimester indicate how broadly good health and health care are shared among the population. Measures indicating the share of the population with no health insurance or the percentage of emergency room applicants who appear for nonemergencies due to lack of other health-care options are important indicators.

Along with the indexed crime rate, more specific measures of child abuse or family violence, along with survey questions asking the percentage of people who feel safe walking alone in their neighborhood at night, can lead to a broader measure of public safety.

Civic participation measures, included in Table 12.4, generally include voting in local elections as well as some survey questions about quality of life, trust in government, confidence in elected officials, and so on. Communities also attempt to measure volunteer activities, the degree of neighborliness its members feel, and either access to or participation in cultural activities. They measure racial inequities or tensions in a variety of ways. Jacksonville asked survey questions of its citizens, while Austin and Seattle used racial disparities in juvenile courts as a measure of racial problems.

Educational quality may be measured by high-school graduation rates, performance on achievement tests, and a host of other variables. Increasing awareness of the importance of early childhood development has led many

Table 12.4 Sample civic quality-of-life indicators

Indicator	Austin	Jacksonville	Seattle
Per cent of registered voters voting in local elections[1]	19.3	22.8	22
Per cent reporting trust in city leaders/ government		71	
Per cent reporting very good quality of life			55
Per cent perceiving racism a local problem		49	
Racial disparities in juvenile courts[2]	1.8		3.3
Per cent volunteering time without pay	47	67	
Per cent who know or help neighbors	72		56

Notes
1. Austin data is a composite of local and school election turnouts, Seattle is for primary, and Jacksonville is for local elections.
2. For Austin, the likelihood of an African American youth being prosecuted in the criminal court is 1.8 times their population representation, while for whites it is 0.78 and for Hispanics 1.15. For Seattle, the likelihood of an African American youth being prosecuted in the juvenile court is 3.9 times greater than their population representation, while for whites, Asians and Hispanics the ratio is 1:1.

Table 12.5 Sample cultural and educational quality-of-life indicators

Indicator	Austin	Jacksonville	Seattle
High-school graduation rate		59	60
Per cent of students at or above grade level according to state test	74	18 math 9 reading	
Per cent of licensed childcare workers replaced annually	31		
Per cent attending artistic or cultural activities during past year	61	40	69
Library circulation per capita		4.9	10.2

communities to search for measures of childcare quality, such as turnover among childcare workers. (See Table 12.5.)

With traffic congestion a major issue in many cities and transportation costs a rapidly rising share of the consumer's budget, indicators about transportation quality are important. Some measure of commuting time, of availability of alternative transportation (biking, walking, and mass transit) and of airport access is used in most local indicators projects. (See Table 12.6.)

Table 12.6   Sample transportation quality-of-life indicators

Indicator	Austin	Jacksonville	Seattle
Per cent with commute time less than 25 minutes		70	
Average work community time (minutes)	21.4		
Vehicle miles per capita (daily)	27.6		25.9
Vehicle accidents per 1000	18.6	17.9	10.8
Per cent street miles with sidewalks			80
Street miles with striped bike lanes			16
Direct air flight destinations daily		59	

WHAT DO CHANGES IN LOCAL INDICATORS REVEAL ABOUT THE QUALITY OF LIFE?

Although each community is unique, it is not unusual for many local trends to track national patterns. When the unemployment rate or the percentage of individuals without health insurance falls nationally, they fall in most communities around the country. Even when worsening or improved performance is counter to the national, it is difficult to say whether this was caused by local actions or policy decisions or by forces outside the control of the community. Climate patterns influence air quality, immigration patterns influence student performance in schools, and state laws influence the definition of child abuse and domestic violence, and hence the increase or decrease. Indicators generally raise as many questions as they answer. Their value lies in stimulating debate within a community about the special factors and problems that cause better performance in some areas and weaker performance in others.

Indicator Choice as a Sign of Declining or Increasing Quality of Life

It is difficult enough to assess whether quality of life has increased in a particular city, but applying that knowledge to the question of national change is even more problematic. The popularity of quality-of-life indicators, whether for ranking cities or assessing change in individual cities across time is itself an indicator. Does their popularity demonstrate that higher incomes and widespread satisfaction of basic economic wants have generated increased demand for the amenities often called quality of life? Or is rising concern with quality a reflection of the increasing costs of growth accompanying affluence?

Table 12.7   Do the indicators chosen reflect costs of growth or increased affluence?

Quality-of-life indicator	Costs?	Affluence?	Austin	Jacksonville	Seattle
Vehicle accidents	*			*	
Family violence/child abuse		*	*		*
Equity in education		*	*		
Equity in leadership		*	*		
Participation in arts		*	*	*	*
Neighborliness	*		*		*
Quality of child care	*		*		
Air and water quality	*		*	*	*
Attractive landscape/bike trails	?	*			*
Preservation of open space or rural land	*		*		*
Time spent commuting	*		*	*	*
Poverty rate	*	*	*	*	*
Work hrs for basic needs	*				*
Infant mortality rate		*		*	*
Housing affordability	*	*			
Civic participation	?	?	*	*	*

Examining the indicators communities choose may help answer these critical questions and move us closer to evaluating whether quality of life is increasing, or not, in the United States and other industrialized nations. Table 12.7 contains some representative indicators, along with my assessment of whether they primarily reflect new priorities based on widespread affluence or whether they are based primarily on concern with the costs of increased GDP. Some indicators reflect both costs of growth and demand for superior goods or amenities.

The indicators chosen include measures of amenities, such as bike trails or participation in the arts. Others reflect concerns with environmental degradation, traffic congestion, and loss of open space or agricultural land. Still others, such as housing affordability or health insurance coverage, reflect concern with the fact that the fruits of income growth have not been distributed equally.

If inequality is a byproduct of growth in today's economy, these indicators could be considered in part a response to costs of growth. However, they may also be a product of affluence, as higher incomes raise the level of concern for those not sharing in prosperity. On balance, it is difficult to say whether the costs of growth or the increased demand for amenities predom-

Table 12.8   Economic indicators for local communities

Indicator	Austin	Jacksonville	Seattle
Unemployment rate	+	+	+
Diversity of employment base	+		+
Housing affordability	−	+	~
Poverty or child poverty rate	−	−	−
Health-care quality and access	~	~	~
Transportation access and cost	?	−	

Note: + = improvement; − = decline; ~ = mixed or unclear trends; ? = lack of adequate data.

Table 12.9   Environmental quality indicators for local communities

Indicator	Austin	Jacksonville	Seattle
Toxic releases	+		−
Solid waste per capita	−		−
Water quality	−	~	?
Open space/park acreage	−	?	
Good air quality days	−	+	+

Note: + = improvement; − = decline; ~ = mixed or unclear trends; ? = lack of adequate data.

inate in the inequality-based indicators or in the full set of indicators, even for the three cities studied here. Both forces have been important in creating a demand for local indicator projects as well as the choice of individual components of quality-of-life measures.

Comparisons between Areas

Selected categories are compared across the three local indicator projects reviewed in the tables above. Table 12.8 shows the kinds of economic indicators often used to supplement traditional income and job growth measures, Table 12.9, typical environmental indicators, and Table 12.10, social and community indicators. Since many measures, including housing affordability and educational quality are defined differently in the various studies, only directional change is indicated (see notes to tables).

Many of these local trends are consistent with what is happening across much of the nation. Even for trends that run counter to national ones, it

Table 12.10   Social quality-of-life indicators for local communities

Indicator	Austin	Jacksonville	Seattle
Child abuse or family violence	~	~	
Infant mortality/low birthweight		−	~
Racism/equity in justice	+	~	+
High-school dropouts		~	?
Civic participation/leadership		~	+
Volunteering/charitable giving	?	~	+
Index crime rate	+	+	+

Note: + = improvement; − = decline; ~ = mixed or unclear trends; ? = lack of adequate data.

is often not possible to say whether better or worse performance was caused by policy decisions in the local community or by largely uncontrollable forces. These are subjects for debate in the particular community.

Rapid population growth, particularly of lower-income immigrant populations, may drive down performance on a social or educational variable. Improved air quality may be partly due to temporary climatic factors. Rather than measuring all the components of quality of life, some would argue that we should simply observe migration patterns.

Economic Analysis of Quality-of-life Differentials

In contrast to direct attempts to measure quality-of-life variables not included in economic data, many economists advocate a revealed preference approach. Persistent differentials between income-earning opportunities and land and housing prices reflect preferences for unmeasured amenities in a particular locality. People will be willing to pay more – that is, to accept lower wages relative to housing costs – to live in desirable, or high quality-of-life areas.

Kahn (1995) used data from the 1980 and 1990 population and housing censuses to rank cities. Since individuals would have lowered their housing prices relative to their wages by moving to Houston or Chicago from Los Angeles or San Francisco, he assumes that the lack of equalization reflects unmeasured quality-of-life variables in the two California cities.[12] Although there is a great deal of logic in this approach, by the time this paper was published the great exodus from California to the Pacific Northwest and the Rocky Mountain states was several years old. A later analysis of census data between 1990 and 2000 may confirm that desirable areas can quickly become less desirable.

Clearly, the components and perceptions of quality of life are highly fluid. The relative quality of life (or at least beliefs about relative quality) can change rapidly. There are two very different conclusions we might draw from changes in migration patterns. They may indicate that people are fleeing areas with which they are dissatisfied because there is a decline in quality of life in the United States in general. On the other hand, this fairly rapid change in preferences could be another indicator of increased affluence and ability to make more choices.[13] Climate and geography are critical variables in the locational aspect of quality of life, according to popular ranking systems and econometric analysis (Berger et al. 1987). Neither is susceptible to change by economic growth, policy decisions, or individual behavior. Out-migration from older urban areas to the south and west is increasingly driven by quality-of-life variables rather than traditional economic concerns according to Graves (1979) and Power (1996), although some other studies continue to find a dominant role for economic variables (Greenwood and Hunt 1989; Gyourko and Tracy 1991).

The cycle of the Pursuit of Quality of Life

The increased popularity of sunbelt cities owes a great deal to the availability of air-conditioning technology and relatively cheap energy, while increased settlement in the arid west has been aided by the ability to transport food cheaply over long distances. Both of these are results of economic growth and the ability to make more choices regarding location, as well as the availability of relatively cheap energy sources.

It seems that cheap energy, along with a desire to escape some of the costs of growth, has led to a quest for the 'best places' to live. This, in turn, has increased population pressure on the environment, community, and economy in the 'desirable' areas. Some communities use quality-of-life ratings to attract new businesses or retirees but then have to deal with declines in particular elements of quality of life as a result of rapid growth. For example, so many people have come to Colorado seeking 'wide open spaces' that most of Colorado's urban communities have passed special sales taxes to finance the purchase of open space before it all disappears. An influx of people attracted to inexpensively priced housing has driven up housing prices to levels above the national average, and faster than local wages have risen. As a result, although conventional economic measures look good, there are increasing numbers of people who cannot afford basic housing in Colorado. This is not an unusual picture in the United States today.

The American tradition contains both the idea of moving in search of quality of life and of joining together to better conditions at home. The local indicator movement may be an attempt to emphasize the latter in response to pressures caused by the former, as well as a way to relate environmental and social concerns to where people live and work.

Understanding Linkages between Economic, Environmental, and Social Factors

At the national level, multidimensional measures of quality of life such as the Index of Social Health and the Genuine Progress Index have not captured the popular imagination in the way that economic indicators have. The print and electronic media give extensive coverage and analysis to movement in the Dow-Jones average, Federal Reserve interest rate changes and the likelihood of a recession (versus slow growth) this year. Predicting whether GDP growth will be slightly negative or slightly positive is almost an obsession with the press, despite the fact that the outcome is likely to have little effect on the long-run economy or the standard of living of large portions of the population.

In contrast, we know that child poverty is a serious and ongoing problem that will affect the ability of students to perform in school, in the future job market, and to contribute to our social security system. Despite this knowledge and a long track record of child poverty rates that are extremely high, there is not a flurry of public concern requiring that action be taken to turn this indicator around.

The level of interest in locally-based indicators with linkages between social, economic, and environmental variables stands in contrast to relative apathy at the national level. Pollution, inequality, and congestion appear to be of much more concern to the average person when they exist nearby than far away. While nationally-based decisions, such as vehicle fuel standards, national energy policies, or income and estate tax changes have major impacts on local outcomes, a great many critical decisions are made at the local level. People may be more interested because they feel they have more control over those decisions, private and public.

Local land use and zoning determine patterns of sprawl and traffic, and thereby influence levels of air quality and access to open space. Local school boards still have the major role in spending patterns, curriculum, and discipline policies in public education. The devolution of major components of welfare and housing programs to the city and county level increases the importance of local decision making. For these reasons, developing locally-based indicators and holding local officials accountable for how their policies affect key indicators can have substantial popular appeal.

RECOMMENDATIONS FOR LOCAL QUALITY-OF-LIFE INDICATORS

Choosing Variables for a Local Quality-of-life Index

The communities studied here used fairly similar criteria to select indicators. These criteria include clarity, availability, reliability, policy relevance, and reflection of community values. The process of determining community values is an arduous, but necessary one (Connor et al. 1999; Miringoff and Miringoff 1999). It is almost always true that some of the information people want is not already being collected and that funds must be raised to accomplish this.

A set of quality-of-life indicators that reflects the values communities across the nation choose would include:

1. Economic measures addressing distribution and long-term economic sustainability better than the indicators we use today.
2. Educational measures of achievement, access and quality for adults and children.
3. Child-centered measures of education, health, and public safety that reflect a recognition of children as the human resources of the future.
4. Civic participation and quality of governance measures beyond voting statistics to an informed citizenry, trust in government, and participation in public processes.
5. Access to and use of cultural and recreational opportunities by different age, economic and racial groups in the community.
6. Health-care system measures of quality, cost, and access, and measures of the health of individuals.
7. Measures of the quality and sustainability of the natural environment.
8. Measures of the social environment such as equality of opportunity, racial harmony, family life, human services, philanthropy, and volunteerism.
9. Measures of the quality of the 'built environment' such as historic preservation, compatibility of new construction with community or neighborhood character and values, appropriate tradeoffs between transportation needs and human or environmental values.
10. Mobility and transportation measures that focus on alternatives to the automobile and air travel while giving them an important role.
11. Public-safety measures, which include perception as well as incidence of crime, including domestic violence and child abuse, traffic and other accidents, and quality of fire protection, emergency, and rescue services.

Generally, four to six indicators are grouped into a category so that change in that category is not dependent on only one measure. None of the communities discussed here has chosen to weight values into an index, because the decision of how to weight different priorities is even more contentious than the decision about which indicators to use. However, the Seattle project was able to create a readily understandable format in which each indicator used was given an up or down arrow, as were each of the five groups (environment, population and resources, economy, youth and education, health and community) depending on the behavior of the indicators it contained. This made it possible to present a quick summary chart of performance on less than one page.

Improving the Quality of Local Indicator Data

Despite the popularity of local indicators, many projects around the country have not progressed to regular data collection and analysis. Even the three used as models here have major gaps in their usefulness. Greater standardization, mirroring that of nationally collected economic, demographic, or environmental data, would make comparisons between communities easier. It would also allow researchers to explore cross-sectional statistical relationships in a more rigorous way and facilitate tracking change over time. This would require a continued commitment to high-quality data collection. At present, two of the cities discussed here now have over 15 years of data in some areas. But other variables are not collected on a regular basis due to lack of funds or shifting priorities. All of these factors limit our ability to use local or regional indicators to say as much as we would like to about changes in quality of life across time.

If there were adequate data for statistical analysis, correlations between indicators could be established. This could save resources used tracking measures that have similar patterns. In addition, more indicators that truly lead measures of concern could be used. Although using leading indicators is a stated goal for most projects, the measures chosen are primarily outcome measures. For example, the high-school graduation or dropout rate is a typical community indicator. However, in order to influence either of these rates in a positive direction, indicators about young children (such as child poverty) and schools (such as reading achievement levels in 3rd grade) must be used to anticipate problems and make early intervention possible. If more data were available, statistical analysis could be used to improve their usefulness for policy purposes.

If the move toward locally-based quality-of-life and sustainability indicators continues, perhaps it will be the impetus needed to collect quality-of-life or sustainability indicators nationally. The availability, reliability and consistency of local economic and environmental data was far superior to many other kinds of data collected locally with no federal assistance or guidelines. Improving the quality, consistency and frequency of collection in other areas would enable communities to better track changes in the quality of life and thus to sustain them into the future.

NOTES

1. Quality of life measures are oriented toward current outcomes and specific community values, while sustainability refers to the preservation of capital stocks used to produce quality of life, now and in the future. To assess changes in the current standard of living one needs 'quality of life' indicators. In order to assess expected changes in the level or quality of capital stocks and the inherent linkages between them, sustainability indicators are needed.
2. For a different point of view on the connection between broadly based community indicators and specific action, see Cobb (2000).
3. See Miringoff and Miringoff (1999) or Connor et al. (1999) for more detail on the processes used and a useful discussion of some of the strengths and weaknesses of community based indicator projects.
4. See Appendix 12A6 for a brief discussion of these.
5. In 1991 a new task force of volunteers reviewed the indicators for clarity, validity, and reliability of data. It eliminated several, revised some, added some, set goals for year 2000 and identified key indicators.
6. Some of these survey numbers fluctuate in what appears to be a random pattern, suggesting major variability due to sampling error, although they are listed in the report as accurate within $+5$ or -5 at a 95 per cent confidence level.
7. As measured by the frequency of compliance in the St. Johns River and tributary streams with water standards for dissolved oxygen and fecal-coliform-bacteria.
8. This compares to a 1999 national survey conducted by the Pew Center for Civic Journalism which reported 80 per cent of respondents saying they would feel safe.
9. Infant mortality actually declined from 14.2 in 1985 to the target level of 8 in 1996, but rose again to 10.2 by 1999.
10. See Appendix 12A4.
11. This reflects an assumption that higher spending is primarily due to higher prices and/or wasteful spending rather than to improved quality or level of services. The alternative view is not discussed at all in the report.
12. To eliminate some of the effect of migation costs, he uses only renters in estimating wage and housing cost advantages of migration.
13. See also Appendix 12A6 for a discussion of popular rating systems and the changes they show over time.

REFERENCES

Allardt, Erik (1993), 'Having, loving, and being: an alternative to the Swedish model of welfare research', in Martha Nussbaum and Amartya Sen (eds), *The Quality of Life*, Oxford: Clarendon Press, pp. 88–94.
Becker, R., L. Denby, R. McGill and A.R. Wilks (1987), 'Analysis of data from the Places Rated Almanac', *American Statistician*, **41**, 169–86.

Berger, M., G. Blomquist and W. Waldner (1987), 'A revealed preference ranking of quality of life for metropolitan areas', *Social Science Quarterly*, **68**, 761–78.
Besleme, Kate, Elise Maser and Judith Silverstein (1999), *A Community Indicators Case Study: Addressing the Quality of Life in Two Communities*, San Francisco: Redefining Progress.
Blomquist, G., M. Berger and J. Hoehn (1998), 'New estimates of quality of life in urban areas', *American Economic Review*, March, 89–98.
Boyer, R., and D. Savageau (1981), *Places Rated Almanac: Your Guide to Finding the Best Places to Live in America*, Chicago: Rand McNally.
Cobb, Clifford (2000), *Measurement Tools and the Quality of Life*, San Francisco: Redefining Progress.
Cobb, Clifford, Ted Halstead and Jonathon Rowe (1995), *The Genuine Progress Indicator: Summary of Data and Methodology*, San Francisco: Redefining Progress.
Coleman, James (1988), 'Social capital in the creation of human capital', *American Journal of Sociology*, **94**, S95–S120.
Connor, Ross F., Sora Park Tanjasiri and Doug Easterling (1999), *Communities Tracking Their Quality of Life: An Overview of the Community Indicators Project of the Colorado Healthy Communities Initiative*, Denver: The Colorado Trust, accessed at: http://www.coloradotrust.org.
Dasgupta, Partha (1997), 'Trust as a commodity', in Frank Ackerman, David Kiron, Neva R. Goodwin, Jonathan M. Harris and Kevin Gallagher (eds), *Human Well-Being and Economic Goals*, Washington, DC: Island Press, pp.231–3.
Garoogian, Rhoda, Andrew Garoogian and Patrice Walsh Weingart (1998), *America's Top-Rated Cities*, 6th edn, Boca Raton, FL: Universal Reference Publications, accessed at: http://www.universalreference.com.
Graves, P.E. (1979), 'A life-cycle empirical analysis of migration and climate, by race', *Journal of Urban Economics*, **6**, 135–47.
Greenwood, M., and G. Hunt (1989), 'Jobs vs. amenities in the analysis of metropolitan migration', *Journal of Urban Economics*, **25**, 1–16.
Gyourko, Joseph, and Joseph Tracy (1991), 'The structure of local public finance and the quality of life', *Journal of Political Economy*, **99** (4), 774–806.
Jacksonville Community Council Inc. (2000), *Quality of Life in Jacksonville: Indicators for Progress*, Jacksonville, FL: Jacksonville Community Council, accessed at: http://web.jcci.org/quality of life/quality of life.pdf.
Kahn, Matthew E. (1995), 'A revealed preference approach to ranking city quality of life', *Journal of Urban Economics*, **38**, 221–35.
Luger, Michael (1996), 'Quality of life differences and urban and regional outcomes: a review', *Housing Policy Debate*, **7** (4), 749–71.
Miringoff, Marc L., and Marque-Luisa Miringoff (1999), *The Social Health of the Nation: How America is Really Doing*, New York: Oxford University Press.
Power, Thomas M. (1996), *Lost Landscapes and Failed Economies: The Search for a Value of Place*, Washington, DC: Island Press.
Putnam, Robert (1993) 'The prosperous community: social capital and public life', *The American Prospect*, Spring, 35–42.
Rogerson, Robert J. (1999), 'Quality of life and city competitiveness', *Urban Studies*, **36** (5–6), 969–85.
Rowe, Jonathon, and Mark Anielski (1999), *The Genuine Progress Index, 1998*, San Francisco: Redefining Progress, accessed at: http://www.rprogress.org.

Savageau, David, and Gregory Loftus (2000), *Places Rated Almanac: Your Guide to Finding the Best Places to Live in America*, 6th edn, New York: Macmillan.

Sen, Amartya (1993), 'Capability and well-being', in Martha Nussbaum and Amartya Sen (eds), *The Quality of Life*, Oxford: Clarendon Press, pp. 30–53.

Slottje, Daniel J. (1991), 'Measuring the quality of life across countries', *Review of Economics and Statistics*, **73** (4), 684–93.

Stover, M., and C. Leven (1992), 'Methodological issues in the determination of the quality of life in urban areas', *Urban Studies*, **29**, 737–54.

Sustainability Indicators Project of Hays, Travis and Williamson Counties (2000), *Central Texas Indicators, 2000*, Austin, TX: Sustainability Indicators Project Advisory Board, accessed at: http://www.cityofaustin.org.

Sustainable Seattle (1998), *Indicators of Sustainable Community*, Seattle, WA: Sustainable Seattle, accessed at: http://www.sustainableseattle.org.

Tyler Norris and Associates (1997), 'Redefining Progress and Sustainable Seattle', *The Community Indicators Handbook*, San Francisco: Redefining Progress.

Wish, Naomi Bailin (1986), 'Are we really measuring the quality of life?', *American Journal of Economics and Sociology*, **45** (1), January, 93–9.

APPENDIX 12A1   ADJUSTING GDP TO GPI: THE GENUINE PROGRESS INDEX

Base:
   Personal consumption (1992 dollars)
   Adjustment for income inequality using index number based on nor-
   malized Gini coefficient, using 1968 as base year

Additions include:

   Value of housework and parenting time
   Value of volunteer work
   Services of household capital
   Services of streets and highways
   Net capital investment

Subtractions include:

   Depletion of nonrenewable resources
   Long-term environmental damages, including ozone depletion
   Loss of wetlands, farmland, old growth forests
   Cost of water, air, and noise pollution
   Cost of household pollution abatement
   Cost of consumer durables
   Cost of commuting
   Loss of leisure time
   Cost of family breakdown
   Cost of auto accidents
   Medical costs from pollution and lifestyle-induced disease
   Cost of crime prevention and punishment
   Cost of underemployment
   Net foreign lending or borrowing

Source: Rowe and Anielski (1999), also Cobb et al. (1995).

APPENDIX 12A2   PARTIAL LIST OF COMMUNITY INDICATOR PROJECTS IN NORTH AMERICA

United States

Alaska: Juneau
Arizona: Phoenix, Sonora, Tucson
California: Pasadena, San Francisco, Santa Monica, San Jose, Silicon Valley
Colorado: Boulder, Healthy Mountain Communities Indicator Project
Connecticut: New Haven, Hartford
Florida: Gainesville, Tallahasee, Jacksonville
Georgia: Atlanta
Kansas: Manhattan
Massachusetts: Cape Cod, Boston, Cambridge
Maine: Statewide Economic Growth Council, statewide Sustainable Maine group
Mississippi: Jackson
Missouri: Kansas City, St. Louis
Montana: Flathead County, Missoula County
Nevada: Truckee Meadows (Reno/Sparks)
New Jersey: Sustainable State
New Mexico: Sustainable Albuquerque
Ohio: Cleveland
Oregon: Portland Benchmarks, Sustainable Sherwood
Pennsylvania: Delaware Valley
South Carolina: Greenville County, Spartanburg County
Tennessee: Chattanooga
Texas: Austin, Amarillo
Virginia: Russell County
Washington: Seattle, South Puget Sound
Wisconsin: State of Public Wisconsin, Wausau

Canada
Alberta: Edmonton
Ontario: Hamilton-Wentworth, Toronto

Source: Norris, Tyler, and Associates, et al. (1997).

APPENDIX 12A3   JACKSONVILLE (DUVAL COUNTY), FLORIDA QUALITY-OF-LIFE INDICATORS[1]

Cultural and Recreational Opportunities

On balance, these indicators seemed to have improved. The key indicators (which follow) had only been measured during the last few years:

- number of major events and performances open to the public (+)
- attendance per 1000 at major musical and sports performances (+)
- per capita financial support for key arts organizations (+)
- public park acreage per person (+)
- library circulation per capita (+)

Political/Governmental Aspects

These aspects of quality of life were measured by:

- a survey evaluating local leadership (+)
- the percentage of the adult population registered to vote (+)
- the percentage of registered voters actually voting (~)
- the percentage reporting 'keeping up with local government news'[2](~)
- the percentage of adults naming two current city councillors[3](~)

Economic Area

This also included, along with net employment growth:

- the child poverty rate rose from 36 per cent in 1984 to 46.5 per cent in 1999 (−)
- the ratio of housing costs to income, which fell to target level (+)
- the level of real monthly utilities costs also falling to target level (+)

---

1. Note: + indicates improvement, − a decline, ~ mixed or unclear trends, and ? lack of adequate data.
2. This ranged from 43 to 58 per cent throughout the decade, with no clear trends.
3. This fell from 43 per cent in 1986 to the mid-20 per cent range by the late 1990s, jumping to 37 per cent in year 2000.

Mobility Indicators

These included:

- increase in average commuting to work time ($-$)
- decline in bus ridership ($-$)
- increase in miles of bus service increased ($+$)
- accessibility to airline flights and destinations via air ($\sim$)

Social Environment

These indicators also include:

- child abuse and neglect, which declined somewhat from 1993 to 1999 ($\sim$)
- births to mothers under 18 also decreased fairly steadily as a percentage of total but remain above target level ($\sim$)
- data on volunteerism and charitable giving showed no clear trends ($\sim$)

Natural Environment

This section also included measures such as:

- gallons of motor fuel sold per person ($\sim$)
- water level in aquifer wells ($\sim$)
- compliance with water standards in major rivers ($\sim$)

Source: Jacksonville Community Council, Inc. (2000).

APPENDIX 12A4   SUSTAINABLE SEATTLE INDICATORS, 1998[1]

Environment

This category has seven subcategories, some of which are built from several indicators. These are:

- open space acreage near urban villages (?)
- the level of air quality (+)
- the percentage of drainage lands now impervious to surface water (?) soil erosion (~)
- pedestrian- and bicycle-friendly streets (?)
- ecological health: condition of a sample of local streams and loss of natural vegetative cover due to urban development (?)
- wild salmon runs (~, short term) (–, 15 year/long term)

Population and Resources

Other environmental variables are placed in the population and resources category, such as:

- solid waste generated and recycled (–)
- use of renewable and nonrenewable energy (–)
- direct toxic releases and sewage heavy metals (+)
- water consumption (+) 12 per cent less use since 1990

along with:

- population (~) less growth, still pressure on environmental systems
- local farm production (–)
- dependence on automobiles (–): vehicle miles traveled per capita fuel consumption per capita

Economy

In the category of economy, Sustainable Seattle lists:

- energy use per dollar of income (+)
- employment concentration (+) – more diversification
- unemployment rates (+)

1. Note: + indicates improvement, – a decline, ~ mixed or unclear trends, and ? lack of adequate data.

- distribution of personal income (−)
- children living in poverty (−)
- work required for basic needs (−)
- housing affordability (∼) – stabilizing in the short term, worse in the long term
- community reinvestment by banks (?)
- emergency room use for non-ER purposes (∼)
- health-care expenditures per capita (−)

Youth and Education

Under the youth and education category is information on:

- high-school graduation rates for all groups (?)
- ethnic diversity of teachers (∼)
- youth involvement in community service (?) – higher than national averages at almost 50 per cent
- juvenile crime (∼) – relatively stable
- volunteer involvement in schools (+)
- arts instruction (?)
- adult literacy (?)
- equity in justice (+) – proportion of minority youth in juvenile justice system falling

Health and Community

However, other youth-related variables appear under the health and community category:

- low birthweight infants (∼)
- asthma hospitalizations for children (∼)

along with adult-oriented variables such as:

- voter participation (+)
- gardening (+)
- perception of 'quality of life' (∼)

and those that include both adults and children:

- library and community center use (∼)
- public participation in the arts (+)
- neighborliness (?)

Historical Pattern of Quality-of-life Indicators in Seattle

Data go back to the early 1980s or earlier for air quality, water consumption, vegetative cover lost to urban development, stream turbidity, miles of marked bicycle lanes, solid waste generation, and energy use.

Since the early 1980s, the concentration of employment by industry or major employers has been collected by local groups, who have also compiled a series of 'work required for basic needs' using the countywide average wage and the cost of a basic market basket of goods and services. This rose from 83 hours per month in 1982 to a high of 93 in 1993 and 1994 and had fallen to 89 in 1998.

Housing affordability data also extend back to the early 1980s, using a few different series on home prices, mortgage costs, and average rental rates. They have been improving for low-income renters and median home-buyers, with some worsening in the late 1980s and early 1990s.

But some data, like those on local stream quality, are from a one-time study that may or may not be repeated. One-time surveys have asked students about their involvement in community service, adults about their literacy, and tested several local streams for their turbidity.

Although the project has been collecting data since 1991, public open space and land surfaces impervious to water were first mapped in 1995. Inappropriate use of the emergency room, an indicator of lack of health insurance, was first collected in 1993. Cumulative high-school completion rates by cohort and ethnicity have been tracked by the Seattle public school system since 1994, while volunteer hours per school have been tracked only periodically in the last decade.

As in the rest of the country, data on child well-being have not been as favorable as on many other variables. The percentage of babies with a low birthweight rose in the late 1980s and early 1990s for Native American and African American deliveries, but have been falling since then. It was lower during that period for Asian infants than it had been in the early 1980s. However, the percentage has consistently been lower in the Seattle area than nationally over the last few decades. Childhood asthma hospitalizations were significantly higher in the 1990s than in the 1980s, with a downturn in 1998.

There is little evidence of change in the areas of civic participation or satisfaction with the quality of life in the Seattle data over a 10-year period. Voter registration rates and participation rates were only slightly higher in the late 1990s than in the 1980s. Roughly the same percentage of people told surveyors that the quality of life in Seattle was getting worse as thought it was getting better between 1995 and 1998 (22 per cent) while the majority said it was about the same.

Source: Sustainable Seattle (1998).

APPENDIX 12A5   AUSTIN, TEXAS (TRAVIS, HAYS AND WILLIAMSON COUNTIES) INDICATORS

Community/Children

1. Community safety – indexed crime rate
2. Safety in the home – family violence incidents
3. Adult literacy – national survey data
4. Student academic performance – performance on state test
5. School quality – state rating system
6. Equity in education – race/ethnic disparities among top-rated schools
7. Equity in law enforcement – race/ethnic disparities in justice system
8. Equity in access to capital – race/ethnic disparities in loan rejections
9. Equity in leadership positions – race/ethnic/gender disparities in civic and business leadership
10. Participation in the arts – percentage attending two or more activities
11. Philanthropy and volunteerism – incidence of volunteering/giving
12. Neighborliness – percentage comfortable asking a neighbor for help/favor
13. Quality of childcare – turnover rate of childcare workers
14. Access to childcare – number of subsidized childcare spaces
15. Civic engagement – voting in local elections by registered voters

Workforce/Economy

16. Government effectiveness – cost of local government/median household income
17. Cost of living – percentage increase in median household income/percentage increase in CPI
18. Housing affordability – percentage able to buy median-priced home or rent median-priced rental unit
19. Household income – poverty rate
20. Labor availability – net change in labor force/net change in employment
21. Job training availability – number of training slots in high-demand occupations relative to identified new job openings
22. Exporting industries growth – net new jobs in 'exporting' industries
23. Job opportunities – unemployment rate
24. Diversity of industries – percentage of total job growth from top 10 private industry sectors
25. Diversity of employers – percentage of total job growth by top 10 private employers

26.   Entrepreneurship – percentage of new businesses surviving third year
27.   Technological innovation – patents issued to institutions and individuals

Health/Environment

28.   Individuals' physical health – percentage reporting good/excellent health
29.   Individuals' mental health – suicide rate
30.   Health insurance coverage – percentage adults with health insurance
31.   Air quality – days failing to meet national ozone standards
32.   Hazardous materials – pounds of toxic release (Environmental Protection Agency)
33.   Water quality – percentage of monitored water bodies meeting state standards
34.   Energy use – per capita consumption of nonrenewable energy[1]
35.   Solid waste – solid waste sent to local landfills, per capita[2]
36.   Water availability – per capita water consumption

Our Land/Our Infrastructure

37.   Attractiveness of the landscape – percentage seeing improvement in natural and built environments in recent years
38.   Rural land in the region – percentage of farm/ranch/other undeveloped land approved for conversion to residential and commercial use
39.   Public open spaces – acres of public land per 1000 residents
40.   Density of new development – population per developed acre
41.   Vehicle miles traveled – daily vehicle miles traveled per capita
42.   Time spent commuting – average commuting time

Source: Sustainability Indicators Project of Hays, Travis and Williamson Counties (2000).

1. Does not include energy used in products imported into the area.
2. Does include landfill waste from other regions.

APPENDIX 12A6   POPULAR RATING SYSTEMS FOR CITIES

The first local 'quality-of-life' measures appeared in the 1980s as ratings of various communities. Popular rating systems, some by magazines such as *Money* or *Sierra*, show enormous variety in rating cities as desirable places to live (Boyer and Savageau 1981).[1] Becker et al. (1987) point out a number of problems with an early version such as use of statewide averages for property taxes, omission of apartment rentals from housing costs, and arbitrariness of the 'climate' variable. They also examine the sensitivity of ranking to changes in the weighting system. The weighting of climate and other geographic variables, economic opportunity, housing costs, taxes, educational quality, and other cultural and recreational aspects make an enormous difference in how cities are rated on quality of life (Stover and Leven 1992). More recent ranking systems address some of the issues raised here.

The 2000 version of the Places Rated Almanac (Savageau and Loftus 2000) lists Salt Lake City as the most desirable with Seattle coming in 3rd, Houston 34th and San Francisco 20th. New York City fell from 26th to 62nd, consistent with the findings of decline in econometric studies cited earlier. Chicago and Houston stayed almost exactly the same while Los Angeles rose slightly and San Francisco fell slightly. These rankings are inconsistent with the earlier findings cited indicating that people were willing to pay a financial premium to locate in Los Angeles or San Francisco from Houston and Chicago (Kahn 1995). The discrepancy may be due to the fact that his study was based on changes in census data between 1980 and 1990 as discussed earlier.

In the ratings game, Seattle moved from 5th in 1981 to 2nd at the time of writing, while Jacksonville fell from 60th to 83rd and Austin rose from 107th to 45th. The relative move for Seattle was very small, but for Austin it was substantial. We could conclude from this move that (a) quality of life improved substantially in Austin (b) quality of life worsened elsewhere or simply that (c) perceptions and information changed over the period.

America's Top-Rated Cities (Garoogian et al. 1998) rates cities only on specific criteria and uses a questionnaire of preferences and priorities to establish a 'personal' rating. It cites Austin as 44th on *Money*'s list, 29th by the *Ladies Home Journal*'s rating, and 44th by the Children's Environmental Index, all for 1997. Jacksonville was ranked 9th by *Money*

1. These ratings are generally based on index numbers developed by equal weighting of a series of available measures, economic and noneconomic. As Becker et al. demonstrate, slight variations in weights can cause enormous variations in results.

and given high marks for home affordability and racial diversity. It ranked 141st on the *Ladies Home Journal* list, and 121st on the Children's Environmental Index, again for 1997.

While these are all recent assessments, rather than providing time-series data, they certainly support the hypothesis that communities with many highly positive characteristics tend to worry enough about preserving those or improving areas where they are lacking to support measurement through broad-based indicators. The local indicator projects reviewed in this chapter were from cities with high or advancing quality-of-life ratings in the rating systems cited above.

Index

401(k) plans 17, 21, 215
absolute
    consumption 84
    poverty 34
accounting services 91
accumulation 133–7
adjusted disposable income 157–8
adolescence
    growth during 259–60
    indicators for 345–6, 347, 369
affluence, effect on quality of life
        concerns 353–4
after-tax
    average wage 132
    money income 54
Africans, stature 260
age and multitasking 290–91, 297
aggregation formula 93, 97
    evaluating CPI bias through 110–12
AIDS 90
air conditioning 65–7, 72, 102
air quality 136, 339, 346, 350
alcohol
    health implications 271, 344, 350–51
    spending on 69–70
alimony 156
Allardt's (1993) model 339–40
amenities, demand for 354–6
America's Top-Rated Cities 373
American Housing Survey (AHS) 60,
        61, 67
Amherst, stature of students 268
'antebellum puzzle' 266
anthropometric data to measure
        standard of living
    evolution of the field 258
    methods and sources 259–63
    research and policy needs 271–2
    stature of native-born Americans
        263–71
anti-smoking campaigns 90
antibiotics 268

apartments 60
apprenticeship programs 4
Asia
    children's well-being 370
    see also Bangladesh; Japan; Taiwan
assault 65, 72
asset literature, United States 214–20
assets, direct transfers of 220, 226–7
attire
    fashion changes 94–5
    quality bias of 106
    standards of 89
Austin (Travis, Hays and Williamson
        Counties), Texas 347–8, 373
    comparisons with other areas
        348–53
    quality of life indicators 336–7,
        338–41, 371–2
Australia
    cash/non-cash benefits 161, 162,
        177
    children's real incomes 174
    equality 167
    female participation in workforce
        276, 277
    life chances of children 171
    real incomes 163, 169
    welfare reforms 276
Australian Time Use Survey (1992)
        (TUS) 276, 280–82
Austria
    collective bargaining 316
    equality 166
    families with children 157
    unemployment benefits 317
average
    consumption flows 130–33
    hourly real wages 126–7
averages, use of 340

Baker, Dean xxv
Bangladesh, women workers 278